The Shield of Nationality

When Governments Break Contracts with Foreign Firms

There is extraordinary variation in how governments treat multinational corporations in emerging economies; in fact, governments around the world have nationalized or eaten away at the value of foreign-owned property in violation of international treaties. This even occurs in poor countries, where governments are expected to, at a minimum, respect the contracts they make with foreign firms, lest foreign capital flee. In *The Shield of Nationality*, Rachel L. Wellhausen introduces foreign-firm nationality as a key determinant of firms' responses to government breach of contract. Firms of the same nationality are likely to see a compatriot's broken contract as a forewarning of their own problems, leading them to fight or to take flight. In contrast, firms of other nationalities are likely to meet the broken contract with apparent indifference. Evidence includes quantitative analysis and case studies that draw on field research in Ukraine, Moldova, and Romania.

Rachel L. Wellhausen is an assistant professor of government and holds courtesy appointments at the McCombs School of Business and the Center for Russian, Eastern European, and Eurasian Studies at the University of Texas at Austin. She is co-editor of *Production in the Innovation Economy* (2014), an interdisciplinary volume emerging from the multi-year MIT project on the links between innovation and manufacturing in the United States and abroad. Wellhausen has published in the *Journal of Conflict Resolution, Business and Politics,* and *Systems and Synthetic Biology.* She has also worked in the political risk industry.

The Shield of Nationality

When Governments Break Contracts with Foreign Firms

RACHEL L. WELLHAUSEN

University of Texas, Austin

CAMBRIDGE
UNIVERSITY PRESS

CAMBRIDGE
UNIVERSITY PRESS

32 Avenue of the Americas, New York NY 10013-2473, USA

Cambridge University Press is part of the University of Cambridge.

It furthers the University's mission by disseminating knowledge in the pursuit of education, learning and research at the highest international levels of excellence.

www.cambridge.org
Information on this title: www.cambridge.org/9781107443167

First published 2015
First paperback edition 2016

A catalogue record for this publication is available from the British Library

Library of Congress Cataloguing in Publication data
Wellhausen, Rachel L.
The shield of nationality : when governments break contracts with foreign firms / Rachel Wellhausen.
    pages   cm
Includes bibliographical references and index.
ISBN 978-1-107-08276-2 (hardback)
1. Public contracts – Developing countries.   2. Business enterprises, Foreign – Government policy – Developing countries.   3. International business enterprises – Developing countries.   4. Investments, Foreign – Developing countries.   5. Developing countries – Commercial treaties.   6. Developing countries – Commercial policy.   I. Title.
HD4420.8.W45   2015
346.02´3–dc23   2014027989

ISBN 978-1-107-08276-2 Hardback
ISBN 978-1-107-44316-7 Paperback

To my parents

Still, though the one I sing,
(One, yet of contradictions made,) I dedicate to Nationality,
I leave in him Revolt, (O latent right of insurrection! O quenchless,
indispensable fire!)

Walt Whitman, 1871

Contents

List of Figures and Tables	*page* viii	
Preface	xi	
1.	Nationality and Leverage in a Globalized World	1
2.	When Governments Break Contracts	15
3.	National Diversity and Contract Sanctity	36
4.	Explaining Breach Around the World: Quantitative Tests	61
5.	Foreign Firms and Their Diplomats in Ukraine	112
6.	Moldovan Deterrence Versus Romanian Gold	156
7.	Investor-Government Relations in History	194
8.	When National Diversity Erodes Property Rights	220
Case Studies: Methodology	235	
References	243	
Index	255	

Figures and Tables

FIGURES

2.1	International Investment Agreements	*page* 28
2.2	Count of Public International Investment Arbitrations and Countries Sued	30
2.3	Distribution of Public International Investment Arbitrations Worldwide	31
4.1	FDI National Diversity, African Countries	63
4.2	FDI National Diversity, South and Central American Countries	64
4.3	FDI National Diversity, Middle East and North African Countries	65
4.4	FDI National Diversity, Emerging European Countries	66
4.5	FDI National Diversity, Emerging Asian Countries	67
4.6	FDI National Diversity, Advanced Industrial Countries	68
4.7	FDI Industry Diversity, Available Countries	70
4.8	FDI National Diversity and FDI Stock per GDP	71
4.9	FDI National Diversity and FDI Stock in Emerging Economies	73
4.10	Trends, FDI National Diversity in Emerging Economies	74
4.11	Components of *Contract Risks* by World Region	77
4.12	Marginal Effect of FDI National Diversity Interacted with Types of BITs	84
4.13	Marginal Effect of FDI National Diversity on the Likelihood of Arrears If Reporting Firm Is Foreign-Owned by Industry	94
A4.1	Effects of Share of FDI Stocks on Probability of a Public International Investment Arbitration Filing	105
5.1	FDI National Diversity in Ukraine as Compared to Russia	114
5.2	FDI Nationality Distribution in Ukraine (2003)	116
5.3	FDI Nationality Distribution in Ukraine (2008)	119

5.4	FDI Stock in Ukraine by Industry	120
6.1	FDI Inflows and FDI as a Percent of GDP in Moldova	160
6.2	FDI National Diversity in Moldova and Romania	162
6.3	FDI Inflows and FDI as a Percent of GDP in Romania	164
6.4	FDI Stock in Romania by Industry	166
7.1	Emerging Economies that Nationalized Foreign Property	196
7.2	Annual Count of Emerging Economies Breaking Contracts with Foreign Firms	200
7.3	Total World FDI Outflows and Traditionally Large FDI Home Countries' Shares	209
7.4	Countries Reporting Outward FDI to the IMF	210

TABLES

2.1	Public International Investment Arbitrations by Industry	32
4.1	FDI National Diversity and Contract Risk Measures	79
4.2	FDI National Diversity, BITs, and Contract Risks	82
4.3	Examples of Revenue-Raising Expropriations Leading to Public International Investment Arbitrations (IAs)	87
4.4	Examples of Non-Revenue-Raising Expropriations Leading to Public International Investment Arbitrations (IAs)	89
4.5	Count of Public International Investment Arbitrations (IAs) in Sample by Type	89
4.6	FDI National Diversity and International Investment Arbitration (IA) Types	90
4.7	Effects of FDI National Diversity on Foreign Firms, Firm-Level Surveys	93
4.8	Effects of Co-National and Other IAs on Directed Dyad FDI Flows	99
A4.1	Effects of FDI Share Size on International Investment Arbitration (IA) Filing	104
A4.2	Countries Analyzed in Tables 4.1 and 4.2	105
A4.3	Summary Statistics, Tables 4.1 and 4.2	106
A4.4	Correlations (Selected), Tables 4.1 and 4.2	107
A4.5	Countries Analyzed in Table 4.6	108
A4.6	Summary Statistics, Table 4.6	108
A4.7	Correlations, Table 4.6	109
A4.8	Countries Analyzed in Table 4.7	109
A4.9	Summary Statistics, Table 4.7	110
A4.10	Home Countries Analyzed in Table 4.8	110
A4.11	Summary Statistics, Table 4.8	111
5.1	Summary, Major Contract Disputes in Ukraine	122
6.1	Summary, Major Contract Disputes in Moldova and Romania	165

6.2   Moldova: Largest Multinational Affiliates by Nationality and
         Industry (1999)   167
6.3   Moldova: Foreign Capital's Share by Industry (2008)   168
7.1   Regimes that Nationalized Property in Banking, Natural
         Resources, Services, and Manufacturing   198
7.2   Outward FDI from Selected Emerging Economies   208
7.3   Count, Multinational Banks by Home Region   211
7.4   EU-27 Outward and Inward Investment Stocks   212
A7.1   Summary, Attempted Multilateral Agreements on the Treatment
         and Regulation of FDI   214
M.1   Key Characteristics of Ukraine, Moldova, and Romania
         (Average 2000–2008)   236
M.2   Interview Subjects   239

Preface

Governments balance domestic priorities with all that is to be gained from economic integration. Finding that governments sometimes have room to tip the scales toward the domestic, despite the demands of international capital, motivates me. My first goal in this book is to establish that one finger on the scale is nationality – a testament to the notion that ours is really an international political economy. But the normative implications of the tipping of the scales are ambiguous. My second goal is that this book spurs readers to reflect on that ambiguity.

Once, a respondent at a multinational subsidiary gifted me a box of his firm's chocolates after our interview. As my luggage was already stuffed, I tried to re-gift the chocolates to my kind taxi driver. He said thanks but no, and showed his toothless smile. I pressed them on him anyway, telling him to give them to his children. Delving too deeply into the sentimental, perhaps, I felt in that moment the tension between what multinationals can contribute, who the hoped-for beneficiaries are, who might benefit in the end, and (with political science on the brain) how governing institutions might mold these outcomes.

I cannot express enough thanks to the many executives, government officials, and others who agreed to give up their time to be interviewed as part of this research. As promised, I hold their identities in the strictest confidence (see Case Studies: Methodology for details). The hours I have spent in offices – and taxis – around the world have been some of the most important of my career. As conflict simmers in a region I hold dear, I hope that the contributions of these people, the people behind economic integration, can have pacifying effects.

To the reader with a legal eye, I acknowledge that my use of the term "breach of contract" conflates a number of different issues, ranging from abrogation of written contracts to violations of treaty commitments, from expropriations that remain international legal disputes to those that have been adjudicated (see Chapter 2). I do this because I understand the presence of breach of contract from the investor's point of view rather than from a legalistic one. I do not intend sympathy toward the investor (or the state) with this approach. A companion analysis of what this book's findings mean for the legalities of investor–state dispute settlement is in order.

I am lucky to have many benefactors to thank for research support. This research was assisted by an award from the Eurasia Program of the Social Science Research Council with funds provided by the State Department under the Program for Research and Training on Eastern Europe and the Independent States of the Former Soviet Union (Title VIII). Additional support was provided by the Harvard Center for European Studies, the MIT Center for International Studies, the Kyiv School of Economics, the Danyliw Research Center at the Chair of Ukrainian Studies at the University of Ottawa, the MIT Production in the Innovation Economy Project, and the Niehaus Center for Globalization and Governance at the Woodrow Wilson School at Princeton University. I thank the University of Texas at Austin College of Liberal Arts and the Department of Government, as well as the McCombs School of Business and the Center for Russian, East European, and Eurasian Studies. Portions of Chapter 4 draw from "Investor–State Disputes: When Can Governments Break Contracts?" (2015, *Journal of Conflict Resolution* 59[2]).

My sincerest thanks go to Nathan Jensen, Layna Mosley, Mark Copelovitch, and Andrew Kerner for their close readings of the manuscript and their insightful commentary. I also thank my colleagues at the University of Texas at Austin, including Terrence Chapman, Michael Findley, Patrick MacDonald, and Scott Wolford. For their immense help on parts of the manuscript and research, I thank Anar Ahmadov, Torben Behmer, Andreas Fuchs, Leslie Johns, and Tsveta Petrova. At workshops and conferences along the way, I was grateful to receive feedback from Jim Alt, Phil Arena, Cynthia Buckley, David Carter, Stephen Chadouin, Pey-Yi Chu, Christina Davis, Evgeny Finkel, Jordan Gans-Morse, Benjamin Graham, Farid Guliyev, Jens Hainmueller, Kathryn Hendley, Yasheng Huang, Juliet Johnson, Noel Johnston, Robert Keohane, Richard Locke, Yonatan Lupu, Helen Milner, James Morrison, Erica Owen, William Pomeranz, Ken Shepsle, Beth Simmons, Erin Snider, Edward Steinfeld, Jennifer Tobin, Teppei Yamamoto, and many others, including many anonymous reviewers. Cambridge University Press has been very supportive throughout the publication process, and I thank Robert Dreesen and Elizabeth Janetschek in particular.

I could not have completed this project without the encouragement of my colleagues and friends in graduate school at MIT. Special thanks go to Akshay Mangla, Hanna Breetz, Laura Chirot, Nathan Cisneros, Erica Dobbs, Francisco 'Paco' Flores, Phil Haun, Anita Kafka, Joseph Kannegaard, Gabrielle Kruks-Wisner, Joyce Lawrence, Gautam Mukunda, Timea Pal, Hiram Samel, Kathleen Searle, Gustavo Setrini, Joshua Shifrinson, and Paul Staniland. The support of Greg Distelhorst and Jonas Nahm has meant more than I can say.

Suzanne Berger is one of the most creative, inquisitive, compassionate mentors I have ever had. I cannot thank her enough for teaching me how to wrangle large projects, how to interview executives, how to save myself from getting lost in the weeds. Kenneth Oye refreshed my curiosity about the world. Nothing I write here can convey my thanks to David Andrew Singer for his guidance. I would not be where I am if not for him.

I thank my dear brother, Kurt, and his growing family. I thank my intrepid sister, Emily. And my parents – I thank them for contributing so much to my life. My mom's generosity is overwhelming. The hours I spend learning from my dad are nowhere near enough. This book is dedicated to them.

I

Nationality and Leverage in a Globalized World

In May 2009, the slot machine hall at a Russian-owned casino in the Ukrainian city of Dnepropetrovsk caught fire. Nine people died. Ukraine immediately ordered the closure of the country's 100,000 gambling establishments. The Estonian firm Olympic Entertainment Group, owner of twenty-four casinos in Ukraine, sent its 655 employees home without pay.[1]

But just one day after the official shutdown, it appeared that "almost half" of Ukraine's casinos were back in operation.[2] Even the Russian firm that owned the charred casino opened its other branches. Observers speculated that political fights over the distribution of lucrative gaming licenses – which Russian and Ukrainian firms tended to win – were now being played out through selective law enforcement.[3]

The Estonian firm Olympic was in a bind: it could not legally reopen, but Ukraine's selective enforcement of the gambling ban privileged Russian and domestic firms at its expense. The Ukrainian government was breaking its legal commitments to provide Estonian firms fair treatment as codified in the Ukraine–Estonia Bilateral Investment Treaty. Olympic waited twenty-seven days before choosing to liquidate its assets, claiming that the Ukrainian state caused them approximately US$28 million in lost profits and damages.[4]

In an era of economic globalization, conventional wisdom would have it that a government like Ukraine's would seek to encourage investment from a firm like Estonia's Olympic. Ukraine, like other emerging economies around the

---

[1] Marson, James, "All Bets are Off: Russian and Ukraine Ban Gambling," *Time*: 2 July 2009.
[2] "Estonia's Olympic Hoping to Reopen Ukrainian Casinos," *Baltic Business Daily*: 18 May 2009.
[3] Brettell, Ashley, "Olympic Cashes in Ukraine Chips," *The Baltic Times*: 15 July 2009.
[4] Whatever settlement might have occurred between Olympic and the Ukrainian state is not public. However, a law firm did fail to persuade Olympic to sue the Ukrainian state, which it could have done per the terms of the Ukraine–Estonia treaty. Interview, law firm, Ukraine, 2009.

world, wants foreign direct investment (FDI).[5] FDI brings capital to capital-scarce locales and has the potential to bring tax revenue, employment, and spillovers to the domestic economy as well. The protection of private property rights, and certainly of foreign firms' property rights, is widely claimed to be the foundation for access to FDI.[6] Indeed, the Ukrainian government's broken commitment to Estonia's Olympic caused the firm to flee. Most costly to a government like Ukraine's, however, is the notion that such broken commitments send signals that deter not just a specific aggrieved firm but FDI in general. To violate commitments to protect foreign firms' property rights – in effect, to violate "contracts" made with foreign firms – is thought to scare off new firms and drive a wide swath of existing firms away.

But despite such predictions, the Ukrainian government's decision to violate its contract with Olympic is anything but extraordinary. Examples of government breach of contract with foreign firms abound.[7] Sometimes, as in the Ukrainian casino case, governments unlawfully privilege some foreign firms over others. The Greek firm OTE was promised a time-delimited monopoly when it bought the national Armenian telecommunications firm in 1998. However, the Armenian government forced renegotiation of that contract in 2004, and it facilitated the entry of a Lebanese-owned competitor in a non-transparent process. In 2012, a British mining firm sued Indonesia for allowing another firm to operate in its concession. Sometimes, governments discriminate against foreign firms in favor of domestic actors. In Uzbekistan, the Korean firm Daewoo invested in a textile firm in the mid-1990s, but the Uzbek government nationalized Daewoo's share after the firm achieved a leading position in the Uzbek cotton industry. Venezuela nationalized fourteen foreign firms in 2005 alone. By 2010, Kazakhstan fully nationalized the assets of the private Moldovan oil and gas firm Ascom after the Moldovan president sent Kazakhstan's president a letter urging just that (Chapter 6). Sometimes, foreign firms face straightforward discrimination. An American firm sued Oman in 2011 over the cancellation of its rights to a limestone quarry. A Turkish agro-industrial investor sued Turkmenistan in 2013, after the United Nations High

---

[5] As FDI flows into even the poorest countries, I prefer to extend the moniker "emerging" very widely. Thus, "emerging economy" in this book refers to what other sources might call "middle-income," "low-income," and "less developed" countries. The presumption is that emerging economies tend to face capital scarcity and to be capital-importers. They also have relatively weak domestic judicial institutions, implying that foreign firms look for other informal or formal means to ensure contract enforcement.

[6] E.g., De Soto 2000; Williamson 2000; Shleifer and Vishny 2002; Acemoglu and Robinson 2006; Rodrik 1997; Alfaro, Kalemli-Ozcan et al. 2008; Coase 1960.

[7] Foreign firms' views on an adverse government action are expected to be the trigger for costly actions toward the host government. Therefore, although blame in contract disputes is hotly contested, this book takes foreign firms' complaints as evidence of what I will call "government breach of contract." Government breach of contract refers to all events that foreign investors see as expropriatory, whether or not they are legally adjudicated as such. Chapter 2.

Commissioner for Refugees found that local criminal proceedings against the firm's president had violated his right to a fair trial.[8]

In fact, foreign firms have, at one time or other, accused the overwhelming majority of emerging-economy governments of violating the contracts they make to protect foreign firms' property rights. Governments around the world have sometimes nationalized, expropriated, or unlawfully eaten away at the value of foreign-owned property in a wide variety of industries. From 1990 to 2013, governments in some 110 countries nationalized at least 150 investments and were publicly sued by foreign investors well over 550 times in industries as varied as oil and gas, utilities, banking, services, transportation, manufacturing, media, and more.[9] These international legal actions represent only a slice of what one multinational executive calls pervasive instances of "everyday breach of contract" by governments in emerging economies.[10]

Nevertheless, many implicit and explicit contracts between foreign firms and host governments remain intact. Indeed, some 82,000 multinational corporations with over 800,000 foreign affiliates engage in FDI contracts with governments today, and the accumulated FDI stock in emerging economies reached US$6.6 trillion in 2010.[11] Host governments regularly respect contracts with foreign firms even when disputes arise.[12] Ukraine has backed off public threats to devalue the property of an American retailer. Bulgaria decided against nationalizing a major steel mill. Bolivia and South Africa maintain their commitments to some Bilateral Investment Treaties (BITs) even after withdrawing from others. Yet governments do not always prioritize the property rights of foreign firms, despite the expectation that foreign firms exert strong, steady pressure on them to do so.

In this book, it is assumed that foreign firms want their property rights to be respected, and they resist violations in ways costly to the host government in order to secure their property rights. Variation comes, however, in what foreign firms do or do not do to pressure a host government to respect its contracts. All foreign firms do not exert steady pressure on host governments to respect all contracts. Breach of a given firm's contract does not lead current and potential foreign investors to react en masse in ways costly to the government.

---

[8] *Omar Faruk Bozbey v. Turkmenistan, CCPR/C/100/D/1530/2006.*

[9] Hajzler 2012, Minor 1994. Author's records. United Nations Conference on Trade and Development (UNCTAD) Database of Treaty-based Investor-State Dispute Settlement Cases (pending and concluded). Accessed February 2014.

[10] Interview, foreign firm in financial services sector, Moldova, 2009.

[11] UNCTAD. Emerging economy FDI includes FDI into "developing countries" and "transition countries." It accounts for 35 percent of the world FDI stock as of 2010. In this book, the following are interchangeable: foreign firm, foreign investor, and multinational corporation. Some sources refer to this type of firm as a "transnational corporation." All of these terms refer to a firm with at least one affiliate in a foreign country.

[12] "Host" refers to the country in which a foreign firm invests. "Home" refers to the country from which a foreign firm originates.

As we will see, foreign firms do not behave as a unified bloc even when observing contract breach in their own sector. To explain the varying pressures host governments face from foreign actors to maintain contact sanctity, I turn to a new explanation: firm nationality.

THE SHIELD OF NATIONALITY

Economic globalization is embedded in nation-states at both ends of the investment transaction. On one end, national governments sometimes break contracts with foreign firms. But nationality is equally important at the other end of the transaction: foreign firms' national origins shape the risk that host governments will break contracts.

Foreign firms of the same nationality, or "co-national firms," face common determinants of contract sanctity. These common determinants are the result of a set of institutional, political, and cultural factors. In particular, investor nationality is integrated into international investment law, as instruments like BITs make firms' access to legal remedies conditional on their national origins. Bilateral politics has always spilled over into foreign investment, when host governments change relations with a particular nationality of investor due to matters of war and peace or when responding to the more mundane tensions and cycles of diplomacy. Firms of certain nationalities share historical and linguistic ties with particular host countries that shape their vulnerabilities with the host government, for better or worse. In operational terms, co-national firms often share methods of financing and means of contracting that differentiate their interactions with host governments from those of other firms. All of these factors influence the status of co-national firms' contracts with host governments.

Of course, co-national firms vary: they sometimes seek markets and sometimes seek resources; they include both giant corporations and small enterprises; and they invest in a variety of sectors. But despite these differences, firms of the same nationality share many sources of contract risks. Shared risks make a co-national's relations with the host government relevant to the future of a firm's own contract: all else equal, threats to one firm are likely to spill over to co-national firms. Co-national firms share in a collective good of contract sanctity.

Because they share this collective good, firms have incentives to act in ways costly to host governments when a co-national's contract sanctity is threatened. Co-nationals can impose costs on a government in two ways. First, new information on threats to contract sanctity can lead firms of the same nationality to change their investment behavior. Current investors can draw down FDI by stopping reinvestment, incrementally withdrawing capital, changing from direct investment into trade or sub-contracting relationships, or totally exiting the host country. Potential investors into the host country can divert capital away from the host country to friendlier climes with better track records for respecting contracts. The threat of foregone FDI from one national group can be great enough to pressure a capital-poor host government to honor contracts.

The second form of costly action co-nationals can take in response to breach draws on the unique resources that national groups of firms have at their disposal. Home country diplomats can provide co-nationals with privileged leverage against host government officials. Diplomats can raise the stakes of breach through issue linkage. When potential trade sanctions, the loss of bilateral aid, or other diplomatic penalties compound the costs of lost capital, host governments can feel squeezed to respect a national group's contracts. Additionally, home governments have aided their investors by signing treaties that ensure their firms have access to international law. These treaties, of which BITs are the most common, allow firms from the home country to sue host governments – often without resorting to local courts in the host country and without the explicit approval of the home government. In this way, co-national firms can use home-country institutions to aid in the enforcement of their property rights without a diplomat in the room. Finally, co-national firms often overcome barriers to collective action by organizing formal or informal national investor associations. Such groups can help co-national firms lobby home governments for support as well as lobby host governments directly.

All told, co-national firms have considerable power to stop government breach of contract: they can credibly threaten to divert capital; they can benefit from issue linkage and bilateral relations between the home and host countries; they can access lobbyists in the form of nationality-tied investor associations and diplomatic missions; and, often, co-national firms can exercise legal rights reserved to them by their nationality.

Put differently, co-national firms in a given host country benefit from a kind of common shield that helps preserve their contract sanctity. Nationality is a focal point for information about changes to the sanctity of a firm's contracts with the host government, because shared risks make the effectiveness of one firm's defenses against breach relevant to every other co-national firm's defenses. Nationality also provides resources that firms can use to battle back against host government threats to contract sanctity. Diplomats and national investor groups can protect against and deflect threats, giving co-national actors reason to stand side by side. Depending on the particular bilateral relations between the home and host country, a shield might be stronger or weaker.[13] Regardless, if the shield is penetrated, the contract sanctity of not one but all co-national firms is at stake.[14] But when a contract is broken with a firm of one nationality, other nationalities' shields are likely to remain intact. To support a firm of a different nationality in its contract dispute would mean emerging from behind one's

---

[13] Does the size of the shield matter? Quantitative and qualitative evidence goes to show that host governments can and do break contracts with both the biggest and smallest of national investor groups. Chapters 4, 5, and 6.

[14] As a pertinent contrast, firms in the same industry do not share a shield regarding contract sanctity. "Co-industrial" firms can sometimes come together to lobby over broad policies affecting the industry as a whole, but when it comes to contracts, one firm's loss can be its competitor's gain. Chapter 3.

shield. Certainly, all firms tend to prefer to stay out of the spotlight and maintain the status quo (or better) in their interactions with a host government. But co-national firms and their diplomats are more likely to be pushed to act in costly ways following breach, because a given breach puts co-nationals' contract sanctity at stake, too. These, in brief review, are the ideas that will be explored in the book.

DO MULTINATIONAL CORPORATIONS EVEN HAVE NATIONALITIES?

The idea that nationality creates a shield for co-national firms is built on the premise that multinational corporations have a nationality in the first place. This contention is controversial, as the claim that multinational corporations have no nationality is a common one. Already in the late 1990s, scholars wrote of "outdated notions of home country" in a "borderless world."[15] The "coming irrelevance of corporate nationality" meant that "economic gain can be pursued independently of sovereignty."[16] In 2008, *The Economist*'s special report on the "stateless multinational" predicted that "truly global" firms would be the next phase in the evolution of the multinational corporation.[17] Multinational corporations' marketing departments have taken advantage of the idea that national borders are irrelevant: HSBC is "the world's local bank," IBM provides "solutions for a small planet." Other firms have shed their nationality-tied names: British Petroleum is BP, and Royal Dutch Shell commonly drops the first two words. For member states of the European Union, many think (or hope) that the nationalities behind commerce now go unnoticed. Most-favored-nation (MFN) clauses are widespread in international treaties, giving some multinational corporations the same treatment whatever their particular home country negotiated. In an interview, the local director at a multinational affiliate in Ukraine told me: "We are technically British, people think we're American, and I'm Australian . . . but what does it matter anyway?"[18]

Multinational corporations' detractors, too, often characterize them as entities outside of the bounds of national governments. Anti-globalization advocates point to the popularity of firm registrations in tax havens to demonstrate the slipperiness of nationality. When multinational corporations register their operations outside of the country that common sense would say is their "true" home, they free themselves from the "true" home's legal restrictions. This wrinkle in home-country registration, the argument goes, makes firms

---

[15] Stopford 1998, Ohmae 1999.
[16] Kobrin 2001, Evans 1997.
[17] "In praise of the stateless multinational," *The Economist*, 18 September 2008. Days later, as the financial crisis set in, multinational corporations began to pay close attention to their home countries – the source of bailout funds.
[18] Interview, British firm in manufacturing, Ukraine, 2011.

supra-national actors for whom national origin is but an accident. Much like the Seattle protesters at the 1999 World Trade Organization (WTO) meeting, the Occupy Wall Street movement laments that in a world where multinational corporations are autonomous and unaccountable, "no true democracy is attainable."[19] In this view, corporations can make emerging-economy governments adopt policies that corporations prefer, like weak environmental, labor, and regulatory standards. That power has to do with economics and has little to do with home country governments; external pressure on domestic policy comes via Wal-Mart rather than diplomatic channels. Many scholars argue that host countries' reliance on foreign capital gives governments little to no space to resist the dictates of international economic actors.[20] Again, the assumption is that multinational corporations exert power on their own, undirected by home country governments.

Recent scholarship has added considerable nuance to this picture. Mosley and Locke find that corporations sometimes have power to shape labor rights in emerging economies, but they identify conditions under which corporate decisions can strengthen rather than weaken labor rights.[21] Nevertheless, the notion that multinationals can exert their influence without the backing or approval of home country governments is the same. Another literature identifies the circumstances under which multinationals are not policymakers, identifying persistent variation in national policy in issue areas as varied as trade, intellectual property, environment, and finance.[22] But again, this research agenda begins from the premise that multinational corporations are powerful, independent forces in the global economy. In this vein, many scholars choose to call firms investing abroad "transnational" corporations, emphasizing that their origins are not key to their definition.[23]

In stark contrast to these views portraying multinational corporations as trans- or meta-national, this book shows how powerful a foreign firm's nationality remains. Part of the power of nationality is in its ability to help foreign firms focus on information relevant to the status of their contracts with host governments. In an information-saturated world, prioritizing co-national firms' experiences allows firms to efficiently economize on search costs, ever more important as more and more firms enter into more and more relationships with host governments. The other source of nationality's power is in home governments' continued ability to project power on their firms' behalf. As long ago as the turn of the twentieth century, emerging economy host governments tried with the Calvo Doctrine to forbid home governments from interfering on

---

[19] "Declaration of the Occupation of New York City," Occupy Wall Street Movement (nycga.net).
[20] Cardoso and Faletto 1979, Evans 1979, Van Harten 2005. This view is associated with the *dependencia* school.
[21] Mosley 2011, Locke 2012. See also Mosley and Uno 2007.
[22] Kono 2006, Oye and Wellhausen 2009, Vogel 1997, Singer 2007, Mosley 2011, Drezner 2001.
[23] Hirst and Thompson 1999.

behalf of their nationals' firms abroad. Although host governments tried to codify it many times, the Calvo Doctrine never made it into law (Chapter 7). Home governments still can and do use tools available to them to fight their nationals' contract disputes. Even in an era when many think multinational corporations are their own international actors, we will see that home governments remain relevant and powerful.

Whether or not nationality matters to foreign firms in all times and places is an open question. But in the extreme moment of a threat to a firm's contract sanctity, nationality is a source of information for firms and a means of accessing the power of home governments. Co-nationals share a shield protecting contract sanctity. When breach occurs, foreign firms do not form a united front, nor is it every firm for itself. Co-national action rises to the fore and – sometimes – can be sufficient to deter government breach of contract.

"ROOM TO MOVE"

Given variation in the risks to contract sanctity across different national investor groups, a counterintuitive result emerges at the level of the economy as a whole: greater national diversity among a host country's foreign firms opens permissive space for a host government to break contracts. This permissive space is the result of a simple dynamic among the nationalities of foreign firms in a host country. When a government is host to a greater diversity of national investor groups, any one group's decision to divert FDI has relatively less influence on the host government's current and future access to capital. Additionally, home country diplomats are less likely to have leverage over the treatment of their firms when those firms' continued presence matters less to the host government's capital access.[24] Diplomats are unlikely to expend political capital on a broken contract they have a low likelihood of repairing. When the proportion of co-national actors taking costly actions toward the host government in response to a given breach shrinks too far, breach and FDI can co-exist. This co-existence generates permissive space that is best characterized in Layna Mosley's terms – as "room to move."[25]

Such room to move, on something as extreme as foreign firms' property rights, shows that governments continue to have real flexibility even under conditions of economic globalization. Wider integration with more national groups of foreign firms gives host governments the power to prioritize other interests over foreign firms' property rights. A major scholar of economic globalization, Dani Rodrik, argues otherwise. In his "globalization paradox," Rodrik writes that governments cannot simultaneously prioritize foreign

---

[24] Access to FDI is not only about capital, but also about the taxes, technology, employment, and spillovers that may accompany it. However, I will use "capital access" as a shorthand in this book.

[25] Mosley 2000, 2003, 2005.

economic actors' preferences, pursue democracy, and exercise national deter-mination.[26] At best, governments can choose two out of three. If emerging-economy governments choose deep economic integration, the "paradox" hits hardest: governments must give up democracy or sovereignty. In Rodrik's estimation, deep integration with a great variety of foreign investors must correlate with weaker democracy and curtailed sovereignty, as acting against foreign property would cut a country off from the international economy. In a direct challenge to this logic, I identify space in which governments retain access to some (though not all) sources of FDI while exercising sovereignty through breach of contract with foreign firms. Whether host governments choose to use their "room to move" on foreign firms' property rights to engage in democratic practices is, however, up to them.

WHY GOVERNMENTS BREAK CONTRACTS

This book is about the permissive space that host governments have to break contracts with certain nationalities without incurring penalties from other nationalities. Lurking behind this is the following question: why do governments break contracts with foreign firms? As with all contracts, uncertainty mars the explicit contracts governments enter into with foreign firms as well as governments' implicit commitments to respect and protect foreign firms' prop-erty rights. Add to this initial uncertainty the inevitable changes to circumstances that come with time, and a government may decide that it would be better if a given contract were called off. Incentives to renege on commitments are not unique to governments, of course. Whether we speak of state-level privatizations or individual consumers' cell phone contracts, the temptations to breach are relatively constant and universal – and this book takes them as such.

We can, however, get a handle on the kinds of motivations host governments have in breaking contracts. Governments, and the individuals and bureaucracies of which they are made, face incentives to breach in order to derive benefits from positions of authority as well as to remain in power. Governments can use breach to privilege one nationality of foreign investor over another, to create unfair domestic market players, or to change the status of certain investments. Breaking contracts in these ways can help governments to achieve a plethora of goals. Empirically, these goals tend to fall into four categories: enhancing revenue; responding to the particular circumstances of an asset or sector; target-ing firms in order to enact foreign policy; and catering to domestic interests.

Foreign firms are some of the wealthiest actors in emerging economies, and their ready access to parent-firm resources can make them attractive targets with which governments can break tax rate commitments, as we will see in Chapter 5 on foreign firms' experiences in Ukraine. Governments can also enhance revenue by stopping payment on contracts; countries like Togo and Bolivia have done

[26] Rodrik 2011.

this with energy and water concessions. Asset- or sector-specific breach can enhance revenue but tends to be framed in terms of issues of fairness between foreign and domestic actors. Oil-rich nations, for example, have forced contract renegotiations in the sector in order to capture unexpected profits. At other times, asset-specific breach is about re-regulation after a contract is in place, in what is known as "regulatory taking." For example, countries including Tanzania and Mexico have broken water and sewage service contracts, citing failures in service quality. As we will see in Chapter 6, Romania effectively revoked the permits of a Canadian mining firm on environmental grounds.

Another category of breach is more explicitly bilaterally motivated, as governments can use breach to enact foreign policy. Such motives likely stood behind the Ukrainian government's refusal to pay the gas prices contracted with Russia's Gazprom in disputes that have spanned the 2000s. One may also imagine foreign policy motivations behind the preferences (sometimes) given to Russians over Estonians in Ukraine. Finally, a variety of motivations fall into the category of breach that seeks to satisfy domestic interests. Public opinion can indeed favor breach. For example, support in Eastern Europe for extracting additional value from privatized firms is widespread, and many of these firms have foreign ownership.[27] Breach can be important in pursuit of votes: in the late 2000s, Slovakian political parties ran on the platform of breaking energy contracts with German and Italian providers.

Government actors may break contracts for corrupt reasons; certainly, this is an accusation foreign investors often level at governments. Then again, what might appear as another sort of motivation, corrupt or otherwise, may be simply the government's attempt to get out of a commitment that seems unwise ex post. Cases of government breach of contract, which appear throughout this book, tend to be backed by multiple and fluid motivations that are aimed at achieving one or more of these goals. The important takeaway is that these categories of motivations are incredibly broad. Understanding government motivations for breaking contracts is a rich area of research to which a variety of literatures in international and comparative political economy can speak. In this book, however, I tackle the question: given so many incentives to breach, how can we know whether the government in fact has the space to breach? The diversity of FDI nationalities helps to determine whether governments face low enough costs to breach in the ways they desire. I find that "room to move" on foreign firms' property rights exists, and this room is intimately tied to firm nationality.

BREACH IN ARGENTINA

Foreign firms in Argentina provide an example of co-national coordination and apparent cross-national indifference. Argentina has become infamous for breaking contracts with foreign investors thanks to its 2001–2002 default

[27] Wellhausen 2010; Denisova et al. 2009, 2012.

and surrounding financial crisis. The shock of the default and currency devalua-
tion led the Argentinian government to stop paying its bills.[28] By 2012,
Argentina was years overdue in paying legal awards of US$300 million to two
American firms.[29] President Obama linked the issue to international trade and
suspended American trade benefits for Argentina in retaliation. The Argentinian
president complained, "not even one of our lemons can enter their market."[30]
But other home governments and other national groups of investors in
Argentina did not publicly back American actions.

Months later in 2012, the Argentinian government nationalized a Spanish-
owned firm that was the dominant energy firm in Argentina. In retaliation,
Spain linked breach to trade and stopped importing Argentinian biodiesel,
which had earned Argentinian exporters approximately US$1 billion in
2011.[31] But neither the United States nor Spain publicly linked their national
firms' expropriations to the other. Moreover, Spain promised that the European
Union would undertake "very clear interventions" on Spain's behalf, but the EU
issued only a non-binding resolution.[32] An anonymous EU official summed up
the EU's inaction: "This is a matter of investment and expropriation which is
dealt with by the bilateral treaty."[33] In fact, just months after nationalizing the
Spanish investment, Argentina and the nationalized energy firm held a roadshow
searching for strategic investors from the UK and elsewhere.[34] Argentina
has faced bilateral rather than broader diplomatic punishments for its broken
contracts, even when it appeared logical for US and Spanish interests, not to
mention European interests, to coordinate more broadly.[35]

The long-term impact of Argentina's actions remains unclear.[36] Commentators
have warned the Argentinian government with an ominous refrain: expropriating

---

[28] For excellent discussion of just how much was at stake in the crisis, see Tomz (2007) and
Blustein (2005).

[29] The overdue payments were from awards in international investment arbitrations (IAs). "Azurix
calls for action against recalcitrant Argentina," *Global Arbitration Review*, 29 September 2010.

[30] "We Can't Even Manage to Send a Lemon to the US, CFK," *Buenos Aries Herald*, 26 March
2012. Reprinted at bilaterals.org.

[31] Minder, Raphael, "Spain Stings Argentina over Oil Company Nationalization," *The New York
Times*: 20 April 2012. "Biodiesel Trade to be Affected by Argentine Oil Company Takeover,"
Bridges Trade BioRes, Vol. 12(8), 25 April 2012. Reprinted by the International Centre for Trade
and Sustainable Development (ictsd.org).

[32] Spain called for international organizations like the World Bank, IMF, and WTO to push
Argentina "to return [to] the path of international rule of law," but those organizations did not
take public action. Quoted in "Biodiesel."

[33] Quoted in "Biodiesel."

[34] Trotman, Andrew, "Argentina seeks UK funds for expropriated oil group YPF," *The Telegraph*
14 September 2012.

[35] EU countries – as well as Latin American countries and the United States – have taken joint action
against Argentinian tariffs. This is a different, shared issue, in contrast to contract sanctity, which
is a nationality-specific issue.

[36] In 2014, the Spanish firm Repsol accepted US$5 billion in Argentinian government bonds to
compensate for the nationalization. This was less than half of the amount they demanded in

foreign assets risks "cutting a country off from the main flows of credit, invest-ment, and commerce."[37] The nationality shield theory, however, accounts for the permissive circumstances in which Argentina has taken strong action against foreign firms. As one of the most attractive South American markets (despite its macroeconomic troubles), Argentina has been host to a great variety of FDI nationalities throughout much of the 2000s and into the 2010s. With a great diversity of investors, Argentina has been able to trade off one nationality's contract sanctity for continued investment from others. Thus, Argentina has been able to breach some contracts while still maintaining (albeit not maximizing) capital access.

PLAN OF THE BOOK

In Chapter 2, I define and explain the phenomenon of government breach of contract, discussing what it is to break a contract, why governments might want to break contracts, and the variety of ways in which contracts are broken. With this necessary background, the remainder of the book focuses on the constraints under which governments are able to act on incentives to breach.

Chapter 3 lays out the nationality shield theory and considers its observable implications. Economic globalization generates pressure for emerging-economy host governments to protect foreign firms' property rights, but foreign firms do not act as a monolithic bloc to enforce their property rights. Capital does not uniformly exit the host country following a government breach of contract, nor do foreign firms uniformly protest breach. When foreign firms have different national origins, one firm's broken contract is less likely to motivate the other to exit or protest. As FDI is spread over more national groups, the host government has increasing space to breach contracts and sacrifice FDI from one national group without threatening its broader access to current or future FDI. An environment of higher FDI national diversity makes foreign firms less effective at enforcing their own contracts and, as a result, increases the likelihood of government breach of contract in the economy as a whole. Host governments gain the space and autonomy to act against foreign firms' interests. The counter-intuitive implication is that the presence of a greater variety of investor nation-alities in the host economy undermines, rather than reinforces, foreign firm property rights.

In Chapter 4, I conduct quantitative tests of the effect of FDI national diversity on the likelihood of government breach of contract. First, I show that a novel measure of FDI national diversity is positively associated with both investor perceptions about breach and the incidence of breach, using national-level data. I then provide evidence from firm surveys that firms in countries with

cash in international investment arbitration. For analysis of the politics of expropriation compensation, see Johnston (2013).

[37] Lampreia, Luiz, "Argentina the Outcast," *Project Syndicate: A World of Ideas*: 4 May 2012. Lampreia was formerly Brazil's Minister for Foreign Relations (1995–2001).

more FDI national diversity report a greater incidence of breach of contract, as measured by government non-payment. Finally, I use dyadic FDI and operationalize breach as the instances in which foreign firms have, as a last resort, committed resources to publicly sue governments. I find that annual FDI flows in a directed dyad decrease significantly when co-nationals have sued in the previous several years, but, as hypothesized, firms do not significantly change their investment behavior when a firm of another nationality sues. I also extend the analyses to explore the effects of different kinds of BITs on breach; how FDI national diversity relates to government motivations for breach; the effects of FDI national diversity on firms in different industries; and how the size of a nationality's investment in a host country conditions relationships.

Chapters 5 and 6 use case studies to trace the role and effectiveness of diplomacy as well as collective action in deterring breach under different levels of FDI national diversity. Qualitative evidence is supported by 161 interviews conducted between 2009 and 2013 with local heads of foreign firms, government officials, foreign investor associations, legal professionals, and multilateral organizations in Ukraine, Moldova, and Romania as well as Azerbaijan, Russia, the United States, and Germany.[38] Case studies are drawn from Ukraine, Moldova, and Romania, which are useful settings in which to test the nationality shield theory. These countries do not have the market size or natural resource endowment that may give some host governments special leverage over foreign firms.[39] They vary in levels of economic development, providing an opportunity to demonstrate that breach of contract is not only a phenomenon in relatively poorer or richer countries. And, their shared geography and history help to constrain the set of foreign direct investors either currently investing or interested in investing in the region (*Case Studies: Methodology*).

Over-time variation in the nationality diversity of the investor community in Ukraine provides leverage in Chapter 5 to explain both the presence and absence of firm and diplomatic efforts that successfully deterred breach. In Chapter 6, I compare the experience of foreign firms and diplomats in Moldova and Romania, two countries that have similar levels of dependence on FDI. Moldova is the poorest country in Europe with complex ties to Russia and its Soviet past; Romania has joined the European Union. Nevertheless, low FDI national diversity in Moldova contributes to effective co-national lobbying and the low incidence of breach there, while high FDI national diversity in Romania coexists with less successful lobbying by co-national actors and numerous examples of high-profile contract breach.

---

[38] Interviews on cases in Ukraine, Moldova, and Romania were also conducted in Germany and the United States. All interviewees were promised confidentiality. The nationality, industry, and host country of foreign firms have been provided wherever possible to do so without violating confidentiality. See Case Studies: Methodology for more information on the interview strategy.

[39] Rudra and Jensen 2011.

In Chapter 7, I situate modern government breach of contract in historical context. Since the early twentieth century, various international institutions have tried and failed to codify foreign-firm rights and host-government responsibilities with respect to FDI in emerging economies. After repeated failures at multilateral treaties, it has fallen to BITs to codify investment protection. Ironically, while providing some protection to property rights, these treaties have increased the visibility of variegated forms of breach of contract around the emerging world. I trace the backstory of the book's theory by demonstrating growth over time in the key form of foreign-firm variation under consideration: nationality.

In the final chapter, I consider what the nationality shield theory and evidence mean for our expectations about the link between economic integration and rule of law. The book's explanation as to why host governments sometimes breach contracts with foreign firms exposes a substantial flaw in what has been accepted as a basic effect of economic globalization. We should not always expect FDI to be doing the work of increasing government respect for rule of law with regard to foreign direct investors themselves. In fact, deeper global integration, via exposure to a greater national diversity of foreign firms, can even undermine government commitments to contract sanctity and rule of law.

2

When Governments Break Contracts

Foreign direct investors build new factories, enter into ventures with domestic firms, buy "brownfield" property, and own office space in host countries. Direct investors operating in the host government's jurisdiction rely on the basic contract that the state will not interfere with their tangible physical property, intellectual property, or money-as-property. Host-government contracts with foreign firms take a variety of forms. Governments are the direct counterparty on privatizations; they license foreign firms to run infrastructure and natural resource concessions; they enter into joint ventures with foreign firms; and they commit to regulatory standards and tax rates in the terms of investment agreements. Moreover, once governments allow foreign firms to enter the domestic economy, they make a myriad of more or less formal commitments to ensure foreign firms' ability to operate. I label this suite of explicit and implicit commitments to protect foreign firms' property rights "contracts" between host governments and foreign firms.

Why do governments sometimes break contracts and sometimes honor them? The benefits of foreign direct investment (FDI) are great enough that governments around the world compete to attract and grow FDI. But, as for any counterparty to an agreement, breach of contract by the government has been and continues to be a means for actors to capitalize on changed circumstances despite pre-existing commitments. This chapter discusses why governments seek out FDI and goes on to outline why governments might benefit from breaking contracts with foreign firms once invested. I then present data on the many ways in which governments break contracts – everything from nationalization through "creeping" expropriation, regulatory taking, violations of international treaty commitments, and more. Given government motives to breach and evidence that governments do at times breach contracts (at least from a foreign investor's point of view), I set the stage for a firm-level explanation that accounts for the space governments have to sometimes break contracts with foreign firms.

FOREIGN DIRECT INVESTMENT

Firms undertaking foreign direct investment (FDI) have long been thought to have aces in their pockets when it comes to ensuring protection of their property rights: host governments want the development contributions typical of FDI, especially as compared to other international capital flows. The International Monetary Fund officially defines FDI as a "lasting interest" of 10 percent or more in a foreign enterprise, which "implies the existence of a long-term relationship between the direct investor and the direct investment enterprise, and a significant degree of influence by the investor on the management of the enterprise."[1] Foreign direct investors thus typically have long time horizons, taking management positions in their investments. In this way, foreign firms not only provide capital to host economies but can also transmit management know-how and technology. Transmission mechanisms may be formal, such as licensing agreements; joint ventures with local partners, whether state-owned or private; or collaborations between foreign and local workers employed within the multinational and its local affiliate.[2] By introducing both codified and tacit knowledge into the host economy, these relationships can facilitate local learning. Other transmission mechanisms are more informal. For example, development officials hope that multinational corporations enhance domestic productivity as their methods and standards spill over to local suppliers, to domestic firms consuming the multinational's product or engaging in downstream activities, and to other domestic firms in the same industry.

Foreign direct investors typically intend their capital to be used in one or more of several ways: to serve the domestic markets of the foreign countries in which they invest, to use foreign countries as export platforms, to take advantage of labor and capital inputs available there, or to exploit natural resources found in particular geographies in the world.[3] Foreign firms with any of these motivations can make positive contributions to local development. For example, firms that use operations as export platforms can increase a host country's export volume, likely beyond what domestic firms would have done in their absence. Firms that exploit natural resources often do so with levels of efficiency otherwise unavailable domestically. Sometimes foreign firms' contributions add up to increases in local standards of living or a host economy's overall economic growth.[4] Not to be forgotten, foreign firms are key sources of tax revenue, as they are often among the richest players in an emerging economy.

---

[1] "Definition of Foreign Direct Investment (FDI) Terms." 2004. IMF Committee on Balance of Payments Statistics and OECD Workshop on International Investment Statistics, Direct Investment Technical Expert Group. Issue Paper 20. Prepared by Art Ridgeway, Statistics Canada.

[2] Blomström and Kokko 1995.

[3] Dunning 1980.

[4] E.g., Farrell et al. 2004.

Host governments have found the potential benefits of FDI good enough to fight for. President Atatürk of Turkey expressed respect for foreign firms already in 1923, saying, "Do not suppose that we envy foreign capital. No, our country is extensive. We require great effort and great capital. Therefore, we are always prepared to provide the necessary security to foreign capital on the condition that its profits be regulated by law."[5] Since the 1980s, the easing of cross-border regulations and concerted investment attraction activities in nearly every country in the world show that these sentiments are alive and well. China treats foreign firms with kid gloves because the country's own political economy would be dysfunctional in their absence.[6] The Czech Republic promptly paid a US$350 million settlement to a foreign firm "in order to safeguard the nation's reputation abroad," according to the foreign minister.[7] Nearly all countries in the world (and many regions) have Investment Promotion Agencies (IPAs) tasked with enticing FDI, a cornerstone of many countries' development strategies. At the same time, the rise of the Internet, advances in logistics, lower oil prices, deverticalization, the break-up of supply chains, and other advances in technology and business organization have encouraged firms to seek new sources of revenue via foreign affiliates. This combination of interest from potential host countries and the growth of potential investors has led to rapid increases in FDI. By the 2000s, FDI accounted for some two-thirds of world foreign investment flows. In 2011, the accumulated stock of FDI in the world surpassed US$20 trillion. This value is nearly four times the US$5 trillion in world FDI in 2000 and twenty-nine times the US$700 million in 1980. Some 82,000 multinational corporations, with over 800,000 affiliates, undertake FDI. Foreign affiliates employ some 69 million workers, responsible for US$7 trillion in value added.[8] FDI in emerging economies is a growing part of this picture. In 2011, accumulated FDI stock in emerging economies reached US$7.3 trillion, or 36 percent of world FDI stock.[9]

For their part, foreign investors offer a set of carrots and sticks that many believe can help establish informal property-rights enforcement. At its best, FDI provides jobs, technology, export growth, tax revenue, and other contributions to development in capital-scarce emerging economies. Now, the consistency with which FDI provides these hoped-for developmental goodies is up for debate.[10] But to expropriate foreign firms would be to severely undercut the probability of getting such benefits. Why invest when the security of investments and the returns from investments are in doubt?

[5] Robinson 1963: 106. Quoted in Lipson 1985: 72.
[6] Huang 2003.
[7] Kerner 2009: 78.
[8] UNCTAD World Investment Report: Toward a New Generation of Investment Policies (2012): xi.
[9] UNCTADStat, accessed May 2013. Emerging economy FDI includes FDI into "developing countries" and "transition countries."
[10] See Moran et al. (2005) for excellent and nuanced analyses of the developmental effects of FDI.

WHY GOVERNMENTS BREAK CONTRACTS

Access to and the accumulation of FDI has been important to emerging economies and their governments' development strategies. But, like any counterparty,
breach of contract has been and continues to be a means for actors to capitalize
on changed circumstances despite pre-existing commitments. Host governments
and their constituent parts are interested in remaining in office and otherwise
deriving benefits from their positions of authority. In the pursuit of those
interests, government actors might find themselves facing short-term motivations that outweigh broader long-term interests in capital access.[11] What do such
short-term motivations look like? The basic conceit of this book is that the
temptations to breach are many. With so many reasons to break contracts, I
focus on explaining the conditions under which governments find permissive
space to do so. Yet given all the benefits that FDI can confer on a host economy,
it is worth spelling out the sorts of temptations that can tip the scales toward
breach. Based on analysis of the kinds of motivations governments offer (or are
accused of) in legal communiqués, as well as conversations with the heads of
multinational subsidiaries and government officials in Eastern Europe, I offer
four broad motivations for government breach of contract with foreign firms:
enhancing revenue; responding to the particular circumstances of an asset or
sector; achieving foreign policy goals; and catering to domestic interests.[12] While
corruption certainly has a role to play, these kinds of motivations for breach
suggest that unlawfully violating contracts with foreign firms may sometimes
have normatively ambiguous or even positive implications.[13]

First, some governments have used breach of contract with foreign firms as a
means to supplement budgets in hard times. Foreign firms are often the wealthiest firms in an emerging economy, with parent company resources on which to
draw. Breach in the form of withholding payments can provide a third budgeting
option apart from cutting spending or raising taxes from domestic actors. This
kind of breach has been particularly visible in times of financial crisis, when
governments face dual incentives. On one hand, upholding commitments to
foreign firms may help a government to maintain access to long-term capital

---

[11] Along these lines, Albertus and Menaldo (2012) find that large-scale expropriation helped Latin
American dictators survive in power. Their analysis includes expropriations of domestic and
foreign-owned assets.

[12] In Kindleberger's words, arguments against FDI rise from the "peasant, the populist, the mercan-
tilist, or the nationalist which each of us harbors in his breast." Kindleberger, Charles, 1969. *Six
Lectures on Direct Investment*, New Haven, CT: Yale University Press, 145. Quoted in Kobrin
1987: 610.

[13] I use the term "unlawful" rather than "illegal" to characterize government breach of contract, as
breach may or may not clearly violate a written set of domestic or international laws. However,
from the point of view of the foreign firm, government actions that reduce the value of foreign-
owned property outside the scope of an original contract and/or in a discriminatory way are
unlawful.

or even short-term multilateral capital. In a case discussed in Chapter 5, Ukraine had for some time withheld repayment of Value Added Tax (VAT) to multinational exporters, allowing the government to effectively increase tax rates on some foreign firms and, in the process, remain solvent. But when the worldwide financial crisis hit Ukraine in the late 2000s, the IMF pressured Ukraine to repay VAT as a condition for accessing IMF support. On the other hand, breach may be at least domestically justified as a necessary step to deal with potential financial disaster. Argentina infamously withheld and canceled payments to many foreign firms in the midst of its 2001–2002 default and surrounding financial crisis. Indeed, Argentina has argued that its economic crisis constituted a valid justification for breach, as the government would have faced deeper and broader deficits and crises had it honored its contracts. What is more, breach allowed the government a way to deal with mass protests, hunger, and hardship among the Argentinian population. Financial crisis led Cyprus, too, in 2013 to choose to freeze and expropriate bank deposits, an action that mainly affected investors from Greece and Russia, even as it imposed hardship on the domestic population. Quickly thereafter, the Cypriot government faced protests and threats of litigation from Greek and Russian firms, claiming these expropriations disproportionately and thus unlawfully discriminated against them.

Outside of times of crisis, governments have also violated contracts with foreign firms and benefited from increased revenues or the avoidance of liabilities. The government in Togo had by 2006 accrued years of payment arrears to a French-owned electricity concession, effectively trading its commitment to pay for electricity for the freedom to spend those dedicated government funds elsewhere.[14] A firm from the United Arab Emirates has protested that after the Mubarak government fell in Egypt, it was asked to pay the new Egyptian government in kind and in cash to offset the shortfall against a revised assessment of their land value.[15] Governments have also declined to pay even small amounts, for example, when Russia refused to settle a debt for some US$300,000 in equipment that an Italian firm supplied to a previously Soviet trading enterprise.[16] Foreign firms are not constituents of the host government and they are relatively rich, especially in emerging economies. The temptations to raise money at their expense are real, in or out of crisis.

Perhaps the most popularly recognized set of motivations for government breach of contract are sector-specific. Often, sectoral expropriations come along with economic nationalist ideologies. Beliefs about the sovereign right of a host country to profit from its natural resources, articulated by less developed countries in the United Nations in the 1970s and still present today, have spurred dissatisfaction with the fairness of foreign contracts (Chapter 7). Such ideologies have

---

[14] As reported in *Togo Electricite v. Republic of Togo (ICSID CONC/05/1)*.
[15] As reported in *Hussain Sajwani, Damac Park Avenue for Real Estate Development S.A.E., and Damac Gamsha Bay for Development S.A.E. v. Arab Republic of Egypt (ICSID ARB/11/16)*.
[16] As reported in *Cesare Galabini SpA v. Russian Federation (UNCITRAL 2009)*.

often made investments in natural resources ready targets. Since 1990, governments in Venezuela, Ecuador, Kazakhstan, the Democratic Republic of Congo,
Mongolia, Mali, Ghana, Burkina Faso, and elsewhere have forced renegotiation
of contracts or have expropriated foreign-owned assets in resource industries.
Professed motivations include dissatisfaction with foreign management when
commodity prices are down.[17] In times of commodity price booms, governments
may face particular pressure to redistribute new wealth. As a result, more publicly
accountable democratic governments may in fact be more likely to expropriate
than autocratic governments under those same conditions.[18] Certainly major
expropriations in oil and natural gas, infrastructure, and the like provide fodder
for the ideological and material interests of some government actors.

Motivations for breach can also be asset-specific, beyond sector-based motivations. Often, such breaches of contract manifest themselves as a government
simply getting out of what it sees as a bad deal. In Lithuania, for example, Vilnus
issued a tender for a new parking system and awarded the contract to a
Norwegian firm. After much back and forth over double-decker parking garages
and credit-card-reading parking meters, Vilnus broke the contract and subsequently faced litigation from the Norwegian firm.[19] The terms of a particular
agreement over a particular set of assets thus provided motivation for government breach of contract, without a clear ideological or redistributive overlay.

Government breach of contract may also have less banal motivations, such as
when breach is a means to achieve foreign policy goals. The bilateral determinants of contract risks, described in detail in Chapter 3, can directly inspire
government targets for breach. For example, host governments can use breach of
contract as a means of conducting diplomacy through issue linkage. Oye calls
this kind of issue linkage "bracketing" – when diplomats threaten that inaction
on one issue, in this case government breach of contract with foreign firm(s) of
that nationality, will trigger punishments in another issue area.[20] For example,
in the 1980s, a textile quota reduction by the United Kingdom spurred Indonesia
to impose an "embargo" on a British firm that had been given a contract to
construct a large chemical plant.[21] Certainly, in times of conflict a belligerent's
property is expropriated; Georgia, for example, took over Russian-owned property and largely forbade the entry of new Russian investors during the 2000s.
Incidentally, conflict can inadvertently cause a breach of contract: in Sri Lanka,
the government is thought to have used expropriation to target opposition
supporters, but a Hilton hotel and other Western-owned assets numbered
among those expropriated.

---

[17] Guriev et al. 2011.
[18] Duncan 2006. See also Guriev et al. 2011. Greater compliance in autocracies also follows the
finding in Reinhardt (2000) that, contrary to previous literature, democracies participate in more
trade disputes in the GATT/WTO and resolve them less cooperatively.
[19] As reported in *ParkeringsCompagniet AS v. Republic of Lithuania (ICSID ARB/05/8)*.
[20] Oye 1992; Lohmann 1997, Davis 2004.
[21] Stopford et al. 1991.

Foreign policy interests can overlap with asset-specific interests when a particular nationality's ownership threatens national security. Chapter 5 relates the case of a Norwegian firm with which the Ukrainian government was eager to keep its contract so as to prevent an effective Russian takeover of the telecommunications industry. In Lithuania in 2006, the government prevented a Russian state-owned enterprise from recovering an oil refinery that had been owned by the dismembered oil firm Yukos. The Russian state had authorized the recovery as compensation for Yukos's unpaid Russian back taxes. The Lithuanian government declared that Russian ownership of the oil refinery – the biggest in the Baltic region and one of Lithuania's major assets – would be contrary to Lithuania's security interests. Lithuania quickly sold the refinery to a Polish firm. From the Russian firm's and the Russian government's points of view, rightful Russian assets were expropriated. From Lithuania's point of view, however, the breach of contract supported the country's foreign policy interests by growing the presence of Polish investors at the expense of Russian investors. The assertion of power over Russia buoyed domestic support for the Lithuanian government, and it was viewed positively by the European Union.[22]

Breach of contract can satisfy domestic interests in a variety of ways. For convenience, this book often refers to a "host government" as a singular entity. Of course, host governments are not unitary actors, and internal politics contributes to decision-making around contract sanctity. The benefits from breach may be unevenly distributed across political parties, bureaucracies, or other parts of the host government. Different actors in the host government may also be more or less sensitive to the costs of foregone capital and any diplomatic pressure exercised on a targeted firm's behalf. As demonstrated by the case studies in Chapters 5 and 6, the divisions created by these asymmetries can help or hurt co-national foreign firms and their advocates in their efforts to deter breach.

In general, FDI can produce social tensions that result in significant industrial conflicts.[23] For example, Fails finds that when the executive is highly constrained, income inequality increases the risk of expropriation, thanks to its redistributive possibilities.[24] In general, government actors can take advantage of social tensions to gain domestic approval at foreign firms' expense. In the "water war" in Bolivia in 2005, Evo Morales (later to become president) capitalized on local and national protests when he revoked the American firm Bechtel's contract in the town of Cochabamba. The contract was revoked because Bechtel increased rates on water and sewage services and suspended

---

[22] For a retelling of the story, see Kramer, Andrew, "Lithuanians are given a taste of how Russia plays the oil game," *New York Times*, 28 October 2006.

[23] Robertson and Teitelbaum 2011. Though, as Ancelovici argues, economic explanations do not provide full accounts of the "magnitude, form of the constituency, and ideology of the opposition to globalization." Ancelovici 2002: 428.

[24] Fails 2012.

services to customers in arrears.[25] Energy pricing is another issue area in which governments often clash with foreign firms over levels of redistribution. In Slovakia, for example, the party in power threatened in 2006 to expropriate an Italian electricity producer, accusing it of overcharging its Slovakian customers. In 2008, the Slovakian government threatened the German and French owners of the national natural gas monopoly with renationalization if they increased prices. Invoking breach reinforced the government's credentials with the domestic population on the much-reviled issue of energy price increases, even as it angered international observers.[26] In the end, the Slovakian government gained foreign firms' cooperation over energy price controls and got re-elected – without following through on expropriation threats.

Winners and losers from privatizations have not always emerged from fair processes, and Frye points out that property rights are politicized when the public views them as illegitimate. This leads to demands for the state to step in and reallocate.[27] The view that privatization, including corrupt or non-transparent privatization, has been privileged over other social and nationalistic goals is one point of dissatisfaction that democratic institutions allow into national discourse. In Ukraine after the 2004 Orange Revolution, one party in the coalition government used notions of inequality to advocate the nationalization and reprivatization of unspecified privatized assets; this threatened the property of foreign (and domestic) firms across the country. The reprivatization campaign was supported by an overwhelming majority of Ukrainian citizens, buoying the party leader's standing at least for a time (Chapter 5). As of 2006, in Bosnia and Herzegovina 8 percent of 1100 large-scale privatization contracts were terminated.[28] By 2009, 1600 Romanian privatizations were abrogated, including 350 with foreign owners.[29] *Ataka*, the Bulgarian nationalist party whose platform includes the position that "privatization contracts are subject to revision," won 9 percent in the 2005 legislative elections and 12 percent in the 2009 European Parliament elections, making even bigger gains in 2013. *Jobbik*, a similar party in Hungary, pledged in their 2010 Manifesto to "initiate legislation designed to protect state assets, which will result in those seeking to disown the nation of its property punishments of up to life imprisonment." Support for *Jobbik*, in various kinds of elections, has grown from 2.2 percent in 2006 to 16.7 percent in 2010.[30] The presence of such party platforms undoubtedly raises the salience and probability of privatization revision,

[25] Forero, Juan, "Who Will Bring Water to the Bolivian Poor?" *New York Times*, 15 December 2005.
[26] Malov and Ucen 2009.
[27] Frye 2006; Denisova et al. 2009, 2012.
[28] Personal communication with Enes Ganić, Director of the Agency for Privatization in the Federation BiH (9 October 2006).
[29] Interview, Romanian market analyst, Romania, 2009.
[30] Elections for Hungarian Parliament in 2006 and 2010.

although much of the debate concerns redistributing the benefits of privatization rather than returning to a state-owned society.[31]

Another means of satisfying domestic interests through breach is "regulatory taking," when a government's extra-contractual devaluing of foreign property accomplishes what amounts to a targeted and not economy-wide regulatory change. Breach can allow governments to re-regulate after having committed to regulatory standards under conditions of uncertainty or asymmetric information, when domestic demand for regulation was lower, or when regulatory norms were otherwise different. For example, in a controversial lawsuit brought under the Chapter 11 investor protection portion of the North American Free Trade Agreement (NAFTA), an American firm argued that changed Mexican regulations on hazardous waste disposal unlawfully prevented the American firm from operating.[32] In this case, arguments about the Mexican government's right to regulate were dismissed and the American firm won the suit. Some observers are disappointed in legal decisions like this one that label regulatory taking as illegitimate government breach of contract.[33] For example, re-regulation through breach can align with governments' commitments to international organizations. In Uruguay, the tobacco firm Philip Morris has filed suit under BIT protections in response to legislation enacting some of the world's most stringent tobacco packaging and branding laws. Philip Morris argues that the "plain packaging" legislation devalues their intellectual property in favor of lesser-recognized local brands.[34] The World Health Organization, for its part, supports Uruguay.[35] The Australian government, too, has since enacted parallel laws and is facing analogous suits from Philip Morris Hong Kong. Chapter 6 presents a case in Romania in which local and international environmental groups laud the government's effective expropriation of a Canadian-owned gold mine, an action that has received the unofficial approval of the European Union, too. In situations of regulatory taking, governments sometimes get the backing of international actors when at the same time satisfying domestic demands for improved health, safety, and other regulatory standards.

Of course, corruption is a key means by which government officials can use breach to benefit from their authority – satisfying a very particular set of domestic interests. Indeed, accusations of government corruption often figure prominently in foreign investors' arguments at international legal proceedings around breach. One might posit that broad-scale nationalization, involving investors of many nationalities, threatens a country's capital access to the

---

[31] Wellhausen 2010; Denisova et al. 2009, 2012.
[32] *Metalclad Corporation v. United Mexican States (ARB[AF]/91/1)*. Brought in 1997; award rendered in 2000.
[33] See, for example, the non-governmental organization the Network for Justice in Global Investment.
[34] *Philip Morris Brand v. Oriental Republic of Uruguay (ICSID ARB/10/7)*. Brought in 2010.
[35] See, for example: Wilson, Duff, "Cigarette Giants in Global Fight on Tighter Rules," *New York Times*, 13 November 2010.

point where corruption and executive rent-seeking must play a motivating role. Hugo Chavez's government in Venezuela was the most headline-grabbing example. Detractors of Chavez's expropriation campaigns throughout the 2000s and into the 2010s saw his actions as an abuse of power. Nevertheless, even the extreme actions of the Chavez government likely had multiple motivations beyond corruption. Indeed, these motivations fall into the categories outlined here: the Chavez government nationalized some of the most lucrative assets in the country; it initially targeted high-profile natural resource firms; it used expropriations of American assets as a platform for anti-US rhetoric; and it used nationalistic rhetoric about protecting and prioritizing Venezuelans.

Understanding the depth, breadth, and effects of particular motivations for breach is a rich area for future research. Some conclusions can be drawn from the points made here, however. One is that both small and large investors can face breach of contract. For example, a government may target the largest investors to raise revenues or target the smallest share to achieve corrupt motives with less disruption. Or, motives for breach may be orthogonal to the size of the investor. Neither must host government motives correlate with the size of FDI stock in an emerging-economy host country. More FDI in aggregate does not in itself suggest that all motives for breach will be washed away or, alternatively, become more prominent. Rather, what we can conclude from this plethora of motives is that host governments need not be capital-seeking above all else. When given the opportunity, host governments have reason to exercise their sovereign power over foreign firms in favor of other goals.

A final point is necessary about what is a common refrain in investor-host-government disputes: it was the other side's fault. If a foreign firm does not adhere to the terms of its contract, the host government responds in kind. Of course, fault is rarely, if ever, a clear-cut issue. Regardless, the legitimacy of a contract breach is not under consideration here. The label of "government breach of contract" in this book is based on foreign firms' understanding of government actions that unlawfully affect the value of their property. When a government allows an event understood to be a breach to occur, the implication is that the government stands behind its action or is playing a high-stakes game of chicken with the foreign firm. In either case, the government's actions generate doubt around contract sanctity that contributes to an inhospitable investment environment. Whatever the ultimate legality of any particular breach, the costs of other current and potential investors responding adversely to breach can, under the right conditions, deter host governments from undertaking what foreign firms see as breach of contract.

HOW GOVERNMENTS BREAK CONTRACTS

Today, the opportunity costs of foregoing foreign capital altogether have become too high for all but the most isolationist regimes. Accordingly, in the period since 1990, breach has only rarely been about a rejection of foreign ownership per se. However, just as governments make a variety of commitments to non-interference with foreign firms' property rights, they have developed a repertoire of ways to (sometimes) appropriate benefits from FDI. The set of relevant government actions ranges from the full transfer of ownership from a foreign firm to the state, to breach that unlawfully reduces foreign firms' ability to benefit from their investments even when ownership status is left unchanged.[36] Often, how governments break contracts follows from the why.

Nationalization, or "the forced divestment of the equity ownership of a foreign direct investor,"[37] is the most widely recognized form of government breach of contract. Nationalization is the full or near-full expropriation of foreign assets that moves ownership and control from a foreign private entity to the host government. Lipson argues that the term "nationalization," which emerged after World War I, reveals a kind of expropriation that is "rooted in broad conceptions of the social character of property rights."[38] Nationalization can come about when armed soldiers storm a foreign installation and wrest control in the name of domestic interests. More broadly, however, we can think of nationalization as a phenomenon wherein foreign firms are coerced into selling their property to the government at a small (or non-existent) fraction of the property's market price.[39] Incremental or partial nationalization is another type of breach, in which host governments strike a sort of balance, allowing host governments to achieve some benefits of national ownership while retaining some access to the expertise offered by foreign firms. Often these nationalizations go just far enough to give the host government a majority stake in the investment. In this book's parlance, forced change in ownership makes nationalization a breach of contract whether or not compensation is paid. Predictably, it is rare (or non-existent) that foreign firms and host governments are equally pleased with the amount of compensation when it is provided.[40]

From 1990 to 2009, some 41 emerging economies have nationalized approximately 150 foreign-owned firms.[41] The Democratic Republic of Congo nationalized railways and gold mines; Egypt nationalized some hotels; Kazakhstan nationalized investments in aluminum, iron, coal, oil, and telecommunications; Lesotho nationalized diamond mines; Venezuela nationalized assets as diverse as corn processing, ketchup manufacturing, and cement manufacturing. Nationalization of foreign-owned farmland has been an issue in Paraguay, Zimbabwe, Brazil, Namibia, South Africa, and elsewhere. At least a handful of states have nationalized property each year. Thus, governments around the

---

[36] Kobrin 1980, 1984.
[37] Kobrin 1980: 65.
[38] Lipson 1985: 120.
[39] Tomz and Wright 2010.
[40] Of course, nationalizations adjudicated behind closed doors may be agreeable to both parties.
[41] Hajzler 2012.

developing world sometimes break contracts with foreign investors even to the extent of transferring ownership to the state.

Nationalization is not the only way governments can violate foreign firms' contract sanctity, however. One window into the variety of ways governments break contracts with foreign firms is the political risk insurance (PRI) industry, which has grown to provide foreign firms one means of managing the risk of breach of contract.[42] From 2008 to 2012, at least US$168 million was paid in PRI expropriation claims.[43] Lloyd's of London, the insurance market responsible for much privately provided PRI, offers coverage for confiscation risks, expropriation of tangible assets, (written) contract frustration, and more.[44] The World Bank Group chartered a PRI affiliate, the Multilateral Investment Guarantee Agency (MIGA), in 1988. Like other providers, MIGA sells coverage against government actions "that may reduce or eliminate ownership of, control over, or rights to the insured investment."[45] Subsidized PRI comes from national organizations, such as the US Overseas Private Investment Corporation (OPIC) founded in 1971. OPIC's Expropriation/Improper Government Interference policies cover "abrogation, repudiation, and/or impairment of contract, including forced renegotiation; imposing of confiscatory taxes; confiscation of funds and/or tangible assets; and outright nationalization." OPIC also specifies coverage for "creeping expropriation that results from a series of actions that, in sum, deny your rights to a project."[46] Kobrin defines "creeping expropriation" as the "deprivation of the benefits of ownership" rather than change in ownership per se.[47] Put differently, the host government acquires value from or takes value away from a foreign-owned investment rather than acquiring an equity stake. Governments can force renegotiations of written contracts; block repatriation of capital; discriminate against a foreign firm in favor of another (domestic or foreign) market player; target changes in tax and regulatory regimes toward particular foreign assets; revoke licenses; stop payment to foreign firms performing services for the host government; and more.[48] The cases discussed through this book demonstrate the wide variety of creative ways governments have carried out contract breach with foreign firms.

---

[42] As is true of insurance in general, payouts from political risk insurance rarely make a foreign firm whole. In particular, the investor is often only compensated for the value of the assets without taking into account future cash flow.

[43] Data from the Berne Union. Countries with the most publicly known PRI exposure at the end of 2012 included Russia, China, Kazakhstan, Turkey, India, and Brazil. This is excluding private claims, especially those made through Lloyd's of London, a major PRI provider.

[44] Bolt, Tom, "Market Bulletin: Lloyd's Risk Code Scheme," Ref. Y4399, *Lloyd's*, 25 May 2010.

[45] MIGA website. http://www.miga.org/investmentguarantees/. Baker 1999.

[46] OPIC website. http://www.opic.gov/insurance/coverage-types/expropriation.

[47] Kobrin 1980: 68.

[48] Kobrin 1982, Lipson 1985, Jakobsen 2006. Kobrin identifies four kinds of adverse state action: expropriation without due process in local law, "extra-legal forced transfer of ownership," forced sales, and forced contract renegotiation. Kobrin 1980: 68.

My use of the terms "government breach of contract" and "contract risk" excludes instances of political violence, civil unrest, terrorism, and war. These excluded categories pose real risks for foreign firms investing in emerging economies and can result in broken contracts. However, this book focuses on the conditions under which governments break contracts in a way that is not a by-product of a larger violent crisis.[49] Rather, breach occurs when government actions have the effect of discriminating against foreign firms' property in favor of domestic property, or against one foreign firm in favor of another; when direct commitments to particular foreign firms are broken; or when the government takes action that devalues a foreign firm's property without regard to the general principle of non-interference with private property that is part of the concept of rule of law. In these situations, government policy changes are not merely "unfriendly" to foreign firms but rather violate particular commitments the state has made to allow foreign firms to operate. Such instances, when sovereignty trumps foreign firms' property rights, constitute a real puzzle, given the expectation that economic globalization pushes governments to prioritize this most basic of foreign firms' interests.

BILATERAL INVESTMENT TREATIES (BITS) AND BREACH

For years there were no formal, international legal protections of foreign investors' property rights in host countries, despite concerted efforts by traditional capital-sending and capital-receiving countries to develop a multilateral investment protection regime (Chapter 7). But a substitute form of international legal protection, Bilateral Investment Treaties (BITs), has spread across dyads to create a web of treaty protections for foreign firms' rights abroad. Germany and Pakistan signed the first BIT in 1959, but only 386 treaties were signed by 1989, mostly initiated by Western European countries. The United States started pursuing BITs only in the 1980s, at which time it gave up its long-time focus on Friendship, Commerce, and Navigation Treaties. US buy-in helped to legitimate BITs as "the policy tool of choice" for all countries.[50] With emerging economies looking to private foreign firms for external capital after the 1980s debt crisis, conditions were right for BITs to take off. BITs became the popular device through which host governments could commit to foreign firms in order to encourage FDI, and the credibility of BITs was enhanced by the deterrence of FDI that was expected to result from BIT violations. Moreover, as a state's neighbors signed BITs, the state faced greater incentives to likewise incur "sovereignty costs" in order to remain a competitive destination for foreign

---

[49] Actions covered by the theory include instances in which the original breach may have been inadvertent, but the government later commits to that adverse action – as signified by, for example, allowing an international legal action to go forward.

[50] Jandhyala et al. 2011.

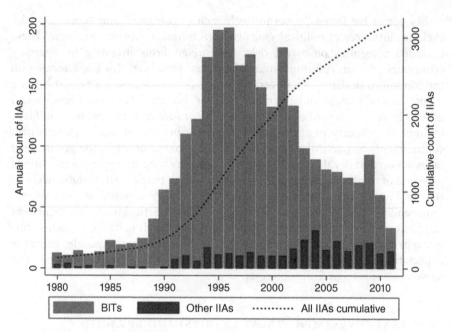

FIGURE 2.1 **International Investment Agreements (IIAs) (1980–2011)** Through the end of 2011, UNCTAD counted 318 non-BIT instruments that included investment protections, as compared to 2731 BITs.
Source: UNCTAD.

investment.[51] Additionally, in the late 2000s, South-South BITs, or BITs signed between capital importers, were a growing phenomenon. By 2011, over 3,000 BITs, as well as Preferential Trade Agreements (PTAs) that include investment protection chapters, had been signed (see Figure 2.1).[52]

BITs are inter-state treaties while, at the same time, they act as "meta-contracts" confirming host governments' commitments to non-interference with foreign firms' property rights. BITs vary in important ways but, in general, they codify many of the implicit commitments host governments make to foreign firms' contract sanctity (Chapter 3). BITs generally provide foreign investors the guarantee of national treatment as well as most favored nation (MFN) treatment, so that foreign investors from all home countries with BITs and MFN clauses receive treatment identical to the best treatment offered to any nationality of investors. Non-discrimination is generally required

---

[51] Elkins et al. 2006. For example, in Chile, prominent politicians used rhetoric about FDI competition to "sell" the ICSID convention and the country's first BITs in the early 1990s. Montt 2007: 21.

[52] Included in this network as of 2009 are 77 PTAs that explicitly cover investment. 56 have a services chapter, 49 have an investment chapter, and 7 replace a BIT with a new investment chapter. Hicks and Johnson 2012, Salacuse 2010.

"post-establishment," or after foreign investments have been made in the host economy.[53] BITs limit restrictions on exchange controls, ensuring that foreign firms can repatriate capital. Requirements for prompt, adequate, and effective compensation for expropriated investments are also standard. The vast majority of BITs contain few if any legal obligations of foreign investors toward host governments.

The most vital and unique component of BITs is the procedural right to sue host governments directly in international investment arbitrations (IAs).[54] In this way, BITs get around "espousal," avoiding the mechanism "whereby an injured national's country assumes the national's claim as its own and presents the claim against the country that has injured the national."[55] While firms with trade grievances must get their home governments to bring their claims before the WTO, BITs allow firms themselves to take action against sovereign governments. In fact, home governments may not know when or how their investors are using a BIT.[56]

Moreover, firms can often file IAs without first exhausting local courts.[57] Alongside avoiding "espousal," legal observers see this as one of the strongest protections that many (though not all) BITs afford. From the capital-sending government's point of view, allowing firms to avoid domestic courts gives those firms the opportunity to avoid potential bias and/or corruption in host-country legal systems. Indeed, legal observers were surprised when, in one of the biggest host government–foreign firm conflicts of the early 2000s, Chevron agreed to go to Ecuadorian courts instead of exercising its right to go to international arbitration. In 2011, an Ecuadorian court found Chevron liable for US$8.6 billion in environmental damages, which a later Ecuadorian court increased to $18 billion when Chevron did not make a public apology. The US Supreme Court refused to hear an appeal blocking the judgment.[58] Whether Chevron would have fared better in IA is, of course, impossible to say. Even if Chevron had been found liable in IA, there is no formal appeals process and cases cannot be annulled as a result of reinterpretation of facts.[59] However, the inclusion of

---

[53] This allows host governments to discriminate against foreign firms "pre-establishment," or prior to their entry. All states apply pre-establishment measures, such as restrictions on the industries in which foreigners can acquire assets. Vandevelde 1998. The United States and Japan are known to press for "pre-establishment" protections in BITs as well as the traditional post-establishment protections.

[54] Throughout the book, I focus on public international investment arbitration, which is part of a larger category of investor-state dispute settlement (ISDS) techniques, including alternative dispute resolution (ADR) through private mediation.

[55] Sauvant and Sachs 2009: 5.

[56] State-to-state arbitration on behalf of foreign investment is also possible under some investment treaties but has been rarely used.

[57] Franck 2007, Yackee and Webb 2008, Blake 2013.

[58] "Chevron Corp on Tuesday lost a US Supreme Court bid to block an $18.2 billion judgment against it in Ecuador in a case over pollution in the Amazon jungle," *Reuters*, 9 October 2012.

[59] The United States has made reference to an appeals process, should one emerge, in BITs in the early 2010s. Sauvant 2008.

direct-to-international-arbitration clauses in many BITs implies that many home countries believe that their firms are likely to fare better outside of host-country legal systems.[60]

BITs and public IAs have had the effect of codifying and publicizing a variety of government breaches of contract like never before. As Simmons puts it, BITs have brought to light the phenomenon that "if you build (sign) it, they will come (litigate)."[61] Public IAs are the manifestation of that ugly reality of litigation. As BITs have spread, so too have more foreign firms filed IAs against host governments. Most BITs allow firms the ability to keep IAs private, so the observable public trends should be taken as only a slice of the population of IAs. Still, the number of public IAs has increased rapidly throughout the 2000s (see Figure 2.2). The most public venue for IAs is the

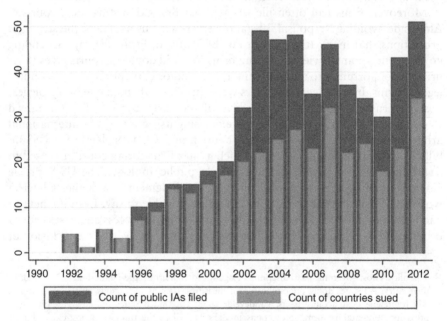

FIGURE 2.2 **Count of Public International Investment Arbitrations (IAs) and Countries Sued (1990–2012)** In this period, at least 110 countries have been sued in at least 541 public IAs.

Sources: Data on publicly disclosed IAs is assembled from author's records, in addition to the United Nations Conference on Trade and Development (UNCTAD) Database of Treaty-based Investor-State Dispute Settlement Cases. International Arrangements Section, Division on Investment, Technology, and Enterprise Development. Accessed March 2013.

[60] See Chapter 5 for a discussion of interactions between domestic and international legal systems in the context of contract breach in Ukraine.

[61] Simmons 2014: 30.

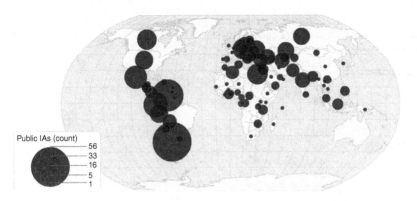

FIGURE 2.3 Distribution of Public International Investment Arbitrations (IAs) Worldwide (1990–2012)
Sources: See Figure 2.2. Map from chartsbin.com.

International Center for the Settlement of Investment Disputes, a World Bank entity that provides rules for arbitration as well as public three-person tribunals.[62] Other public IAs tend to be brought under a set of rules developed by the United Nations Commission on International Trade Law (UNCITRAL) and heard at a variety of venues, including the International Chamber of Commerce, the Permanent Court of Arbitration, the London Court of International Arbitration, the Stockholm Chamber of Commerce, and others. Parties also engage in ad hoc arbitration under UNCITRAL rules, the terms of domestic investment protection laws, or contract-specific clauses. IAs brought on an ad hoc basis or in these kinds of venues tend to allow parties to keep their IAs private. Nevertheless, some IAs that have taken place in these kinds of circumstances have been made public.

Figure 2.3 indicates the spread of public IAs around the world. Some 110 countries have been public respondents in IAs from 1990 to 2012. Of 541 public IAs in this period, forty-two (8 percent) have been brought against or occurred between developed countries – mostly between the United States and Canada under the terms of NAFTA Chapter 11. Many suits have been brought against Latin American states, with Argentina having faced fifty-six public IAs, many of which can be traced to its 2002 default and concomitant government non-payment of many of its direct obligations to foreign investors. Venezuela has faced a significant number of suits, resulting in its case from a greater number of underlying events. The countries of Central and Eastern Europe, too, have faced a high number of public IAs. This is puzzling, as the 1990s and 2000s have been the key transition years in which these post-communist countries set about making their international reputations as credible market economies. East Asian

---

[62] The existence of and parties to an ICSID IA are made public although the content of the case can be kept somewhat private.

TABLE 2.1 *Public International Investment Arbitrations (IAs) by Industry (1990–2012)*

Industry	Count	Pct
Energy	98	18%
Utilities	78	14%
Manufacturing	74	14%
Services	69	13%
Construction	49	9%
Mining	45	8%
Finance	42	8%
Communications	34	6%
Agriculture	22	4%
Trade	15	3%
Unknown	15	3%
Total	*541*	

Source: See Figure 2.2.

countries have in the early 2010s begun to face a handful of public IAs, although levels are still lower than in other parts of the world.

Public IAs typically deal with aspects of "creeping" expropriation: forced contract renegotiations, regulatory infringements, discriminatory policy changes, and other undue interference with foreign firms' operations. Some have to do with government breach of contract with what were once state-owned, now privatized, assets. BITs and the public IAs they engender have thus helped to make public more instances of broken contracts in ways beyond the transfer of ownership to the state.

Table 2.1 classifies public IAs by the sector of the claimant, demonstrating that they have a wide variety of origins. As might be gleaned from the popular press, a large portion of the 541 public IAs brought worldwide from 1990 to 2011 have been brought by firms in the energy sector, particularly in oil and gas. A significant proportion has also occurred in utilities, with many dealing with electricity transmission grids or water and sewage concessions. There have also been numerous public IAs in services and manufacturing, despite the fact that these industries are often thought of as the most difficult to expropriate, because investments are relatively easy to move.[63] Service sector IAs have concerned industries like tourism, gambling, and the management of airports and ports, while manufacturing IAs have dealt with everything from pharmaceuticals to textiles, tobacco processing, and cement production. Other cases are spread across a variety of sectors: construction, mining, finance, communications, agriculture, and trade. Thus, while there is certainly an idiosyncratic

[63] E.g. Vernon 1971.

selection process behind whether a particular firm's broken contract makes it all the way to a public IA, firms across a variety of sectors have nevertheless taken advantage of the institution of investment arbitration.

In the case of a public IA, several conditions hold: foreign investors have access to a BIT or another mechanism through which the host government has committed to international investment arbitration; foreign investors commit resources to a costly and imperfect means of getting restitution; host governments commit to their actions enough to refuse to settle and to allow an accusation of contract breach to go public; and parties are willing to make the dispute visible to other current and potential foreign investors. Indeed, a dispute must wind its way through many steps before becoming a public IA: the government threatens breach, breach occurs, the foreign firm threatens to sue, and a suit occurs. As a result of this selection process, not every instance of breach or nationalization results in a public IA. Moreover, many disputes make it into national newspapers but not the international legal system. Still more broken contracts may be common knowledge to interested investors but may not make it into business media.[64] Still others are kept private by firms. Therefore, public IAs should be thought of as the tip of the iceberg of government breach of contract, while the size and shape of the iceberg is unknown. Nevertheless, the rise of BITs and public IAs allows us to see the spread and depth of the phenomenon of government breach of contract with foreign investors as never before.

A BIT OF DETERRENCE?

If BITs now encode foreign firms' contracts, and carry penalties for breaking them, why have they not conclusively stopped the incidence of government breach of contract? The coexistence of breach and BITs highlights the limits of international law as a source of explanation for variation in government breach of contract with foreign firms. Abbott and Snidal argue that the presence or absence of normative covenants created by "soft law" can be decisive in explaining whether or not, say, a treaty commitment is upheld.[65] Indeed, like any entity that makes contracts, a host government only cares to maintain a credible commitment to foreign firm contracts if it benefits from making that commitment. As such, a BIT is "founded on a grand bargain: a *promise* of protection of capital in return for the *prospect* of more capital in the future."[66] To the extent that the second half of this bargain (and the normative covenant that stands behind it) does not hold, there is less reason to expect BITs to conclusively stop host governments from breaching contracts with foreign firms.[67] In fact, the

---

[64] Such disputes are the focus of Chapters 5 and 6 on Ukraine, Moldova, and Romania.
[65] Abbott and Snidal 2003.
[66] Salacuse and Sullivan 2005: 5 [emphasis in original].
[67] This also presumes that the knock-on costs BIT violations might have in other issue areas are sufficiently low.

evidence on whether BITs successfully attract increased foreign investment is mixed at best: some find little or no evidence of increased FDI,[68] while others find only conditional evidence that BITs increase FDI.[69] Indeed, if governments are signing BITs in large part because everyone else is, there may be little reason to expect them to be effective.

The relative invisibility of BIT benefits to scholars, let alone policymakers, has led several host governments to question their commitments.[70] The United States had an "awakening of sorts" that being sued might be more trouble than it is worth; in 2001 the United States, Canada, and Mexico agreed on limits to arbitrator discretion under NAFTA's Chapter 11, which had been equivalent to standard BIT protections.[71] Indonesia, Pakistan, South Africa, Bolivia, Ecuador, Nicaragua, India, and Venezuela have been publicly skeptical of BITs; since 2008, Bolivia, Ecuador, Venezuela, and Indonesia have withdrawn from some (though not all) investment treaties.[72] As of 2014, Brazil has not ratified any BITs, though it has engaged in some BIT negotiations. And in the early 2010s it emerged that Argentina had not paid any of its outstanding IA awards, and the government went on to effectively declare that it would not pay. Argentina has struggled to remain "judgment-proof," which means keeping assets at home rather than overseas where award winners can claim them in lieu of other compensation.[73] By 2013, however, some investors began accepting Argentinian government bonds as substitutes for their full outstanding awards (a risky move given that the government's solvency was again in question).

Thus, while BITs remain the de facto basis of the international investment protection regime, there is pushback by signatories, not to mention advocacy groups, against the constraints that BITs place on host government behavior. What is more, even when BITs are in place, host governments undertake actions that violate them – "off-equilibrium" behavior that the existence of a BIT is thought to deter. The presence and persistence of government breach of contract – as embodied, for example, by public IAs – suggests that there is more permissive space for even capital-seeking governments to act contrary to foreign firms' interests than we might have otherwise thought.

---

[68] Hallward-Dreimeier 2003, Tobin and Rose-Ackerman 2004, Yackee and Webb 2008, Poulsen and Aisbett 2013, Aisbett 2009.

[69] Salacuse and Sullivan 2005, Neumayer and Spess 2005, Kerner 2009.

[70] Young and Tavares 2004.

[71] Free Trade Commission (NAFTA), Notes of Interpretation of Certain Chapter 11 Provisions, 30 July 2001.

[72] Van Harten 2010: 2–5.

[73] Enforcement lawyers chart the asset flows of these countries and look for opportunities to make claims. The docking of an Argentinian naval vessel in Ghana in 2012 provided one such opportunity to take over Argentinian assets, although ultimately ownership of the vessel remained with the Argentinian government. Argentina successfully argued before the International Tribunal for the Law of the Sea that warships have immunity from civil claims when they dock at foreign ports.

WHEN GOVERNMENTS BREAK CONTRACTS

Governments around the world are tempted to and sometimes follow through with government breach of contract. This is despite the fact that FDI, in aggregate, is thought to confer development benefits through the transfer of technology and management know-how, not to mention long-term capital, employment, and tax revenues for host countries. But short-term gains can be as tempting for governments as they are for any party to a contract. Governments can use breach of contract to raise revenues at foreign firms' expense, act on sector- and asset-specific motivations, carry out foreign policy, and satisfy domestic interests, whether via corruption or otherwise. Governments may simply want to get out of bad deals. The spread of BITs and the rise of public IA have made it easier for us to see evidence of the many ways in which governments act out these motivations, not only through nationalization but also through a variety of policies that have the effect of unlawfully devaluing foreign property. Given that so many motivations to breach exist, that governments breach in so many ways, and that breach continues despite the institutionalization of international law that makes breach events visible and codified like never before, the question arises: what are the conditions under which governments have the permissive space to break contracts with foreign firms?

3

National Diversity and Contract Sanctity

Many observers believe that economic globalization has a destructive impact on the nation-state. In this view, the effects of the integration of global markets are especially constraining for capital-poor countries that need foreign investment for employment and development. Governments in these countries face pressure to align their policies and institutions with foreign firms' interests in order to gain investors' trust and remain competitive destinations for mobile capital. Some scholars see the conflict between host-government autonomy and foreign firms as a stark and intractable problem that creates a major tension between democracy and economic integration.[1] Others have identified issue areas where domestic policymakers still exercise some autonomy, such as labor and environmental regulation.[2] These domains are often seen, however, as exceptions in a world in which the overall pressures of the market work to advance investor interests. Whatever variation there may be in investor interests over policy, the idea that investors' interests converge on the protection of private property rights is virtually unquestioned.

From a foreign firm's point of view, rule of law in a destination country reduces to the host government's commitment to allow the foreign firm to operate once invested. Without the protection of its property, a foreign firm has little reason to believe investment is in its best interests. In investment transactions, the protection of private property can show up in a number of guises. Host governments are the counterparty on privatizations; they license foreign firms to run infrastructure and natural resource concessions; they commit to regulatory standards in the terms of investment agreements; and they have signed some 3,000 BITs and other instruments that protect foreign firms under the force of international law. In hopes of enabling productive foreign

[1] Rodrik 2011, 1997; Berger 2000; Kobrin 2001; Strange 1996.
[2] E.g., Mosley 2011, Murphy 2004, Vogel 1997.

36

investment, host governments commit to upholding property rights protections by entering formal and informal contracts with foreign firms. Without a commitment to contract sanctity by the host government, the expectation has been that foreign firms will divert their investments and flee.

But the fact is that, at some time or other, the overwhelming majority of emerging-economy governments has violated contracts made with foreign firms. Host governments sometimes forcibly transfer ownership of foreign property through nationalization and expropriation, and they also devalue foreign holdings through forced contract negotiations, discriminatory policy changes, and other undue interference with foreign firms' operations. Nevertheless, emerging-economy governments, keen to access foreign capital, do not always break contracts, even when disputes arise. Even as FDI has flowed into emerging economies worldwide, when, why, and how such host governments respect the prior contracts they have entered into with foreign firms varies across countries and over time.

The crux of my explanation for variation in foreign firms' contract sanctity is that the prospect of capital flight does not universally shield foreign firms from adverse government action. Not all foreign firms respond in ways costly to the host government when the host government breaks contracts with them. Instead, capital flight following breach is most likely to occur along national lines, and public protest over breach is limited to co-national actors of the targeted firms. Contrary to the conventional wisdom, nationality and nation-states are embedded in economic globalization at both the home and host ends of the investment transaction. National governments sometimes renege on commitments to foreign firms, and foreign firms' national origins shape the risk that host governments will renege.

Nationality affects firms' contract sanctity via numerous pathways. Nationality is structurally important to a foreign firm's property rights, as it is a cornerstone of the modern, bilateral institutions that codify foreign investor rights. Bilateral politics, whether acrimonious or friendly, spill over into investor decision-making. Home-country business traditions shape the kinds of contracts firms enter into with host governments. These factors make firms of the same nationality, or "co-national firms," more likely to share a collective sense of risks to their contract sanctity. When the host government breaks a contract, firms of the same nationality are the most likely to respond with actions that are costly to the host government. These costly actions include FDI exit and diversion as well as protest exercised together with home-country diplomats. In contrast, non-co-national actors are less likely to share a collective sense of contract sanctity. When firms do not share this collective good, they are unlikely to draw down or divert investments or engage in protest around breach. Shared nationality is a powerful shield against breach, but nationality shields stop at national borders. Thus, the expectation that aggregate investor behavior will enforce foreign firms' contracts is flawed, because investor willingness and ability to act punitively toward a host government depends on nationality.

When we consider "nationality shields" against breach at the level of the economy as a whole, we see that firm nationality has a surprising effect on contract sanctity. Greater national diversity among a host country's foreign firms makes it easier for a host government to breach contracts. With more diverse FDI present in the host economy, governments can more easily recoup the loss of capital brought about by breach of contract with any one national group, because governments can turn to other groups for current and future capital access. Higher FDI national diversity leaves more opportunities for host governments to exploit other nationalities' indifference when penetrating one nationality's shield.[3] Thus, the set of foreign firms present in a host economy shapes the risks any given firm faces and the opportunities host governments have to capitalize on low costs to breach.

Ultimately, if we take hosting a more diverse set of foreign firm nationalities as an indicator of the degree of integration of the host country into the global economy, an important implication emerges: economic integration need not move together with increased respect for foreign firms' property rights. Instead, economic integration with more nationally diverse firms reinforces the host government's national autonomy, including the autonomy to act contrary to rule of law.

In this chapter, I first describe research focusing on state-level characteristics as explanations for breach. Finding these wanting, I move to the level of the firm to explore why and how national origin matters to foreign firms' contract sanctity abroad and to firms' access to resources with which to protest breach. Next, I explain how foreign firms' willingness and ability to deter breach depends on the diversity of investor nationalities present in an economy. I then address another form of firm-level heterogeneity – by industry – and describe how industry effects may exist alongside an independent role for national ties. I conclude by previewing the quantitative and qualitative research strategies used to test the nationality shield theory, as employed in the second part of the book. Common national identity can be a source of power for foreign firms in their relations with host governments, but increasing FDI national diversity generates opportunities for host governments to reconsider their commitments to foreign firms' property rights.

STATE-LEVEL EXPLANATIONS

The quickest off-the-shelf explanation for the incidence of government breach of contract predicts that governments in countries with weaker rule of law, with weak domestic institutions and arbitrary government behavior toward domestic actors, should breach more with foreign actors. However, breach of contract is

---

[3] Certainly, executives at non-co-national firms can be sympathetic to the plight of other foreign firms. But from the host government's point of view, the absence of protest by non-co-national firms is observationally equivalent to indifference. Chapter 8.

spread across the world. Some 110 countries at both high and low levels on rule-of-law indicators have been respondents in litigation brought by foreign firms over property rights violations. Rule-of-law measures are insufficient to explain variation, at least when not conditioned on other factors.

Much work in political science looks at whether some governments are by nature more opportunistic than others and thus more likely to violate foreign firms' property rights. In particular, scholars debate the ability of different regime types to make more or less credible commitments to refrain from breach of contract. O'Neal first argued that foreign direct investors are drawn to authoritarian regimes, because, whatever the risks those governments might present, rates of return are higher there than in countries with democratic regimes.[4] Jensen has done much to discredit this notion, finding ample evidence that FDI moves together with democracy.[5] For example, Jensen finds that US multinationals have smaller operations in countries that are more autocratic.[6] The debate has since turned to what exactly it is about democracy that might be attractive or not to foreign investors. Li and Resnick contend that it is not democracy as a whole but democracies' ability to more credibly commit to contract sanctity that attracts FDI. In their analysis, elements of rule of law attract FDI, but the policy uncertainty associated with democratic institutions actually deters FDI.[7] Jensen and Young find that multinational corporations investing in democratic regimes enjoy lower premiums on expropriation insurance, but, consistent with Li and Resnick, this is particularly true in countries with highly constrained executives in which policy uncertainty is less of an issue.[8] Humphreys and Bates also find that more political competition and more checks on the executive predict policies that are less extractive in African countries.[9] And in an analysis of nationalization events from 1960 to 1990, Li shows that democracies with lower executive turnover were less likely to expropriate than other democracies, while democracies as a whole are less likely to expropriate than autocracies.[10] Taken together, this literature suggests that democracies with higher policy stability are significantly more likely to maintain contract sanctity with foreign firms and thus attract FDI in part because of those credible commitments.

The parties responding to those credible commitments, however, remain unspecified. When it comes to explaining variation in contract sanctity, state-level explanations fall short because they have little to say about the relationship

---

[4] O'Neal 1994.

[5] Jensen 2003, 2006.

[6] Jensen 2008.

[7] Li and Resnick 2003.

[8] Jensen and Young 2008.

[9] Humphreys and Bates 2005.

[10] Li 2009. Li complicates the story somewhat: he finds some evidence that longer leader tenure in autocracies decreases the incidence of nationalization, providing new support for the idea that policy stability can attract investment even if it comes within an autocratic regime.

between threatened firms, the host government, and other firms. What are the implications of a given broken contract for other foreign firms? On one hand, Jensen and Johnston imply that a broken contract increases risks that all foreign firms will be subject to opportunism by the host government, for breach has generated more resources for the government that could now offset costs of future breaches.[11] On the other hand, we might posit that a given foreign firm's broken contract only signals increased risks to subsets of other investors. To discern whether the signal sent by a breach of contract is indeed universal, we need a fuller theory of foreign firms' understanding of their contract sanctity. I contend that nationality is a key axis of variation in the value of signals sent by breach. Foreign firms' national origins generate variation in their ability and willingness to act in ways costly to the host government following a breach of contract with a firm of a given nationality.

NATIONAL ORIGIN AND CONTRACT SANCTITY

Foreign firms observing a host government's breach of contract with another firm face this question: are we next, or can we safely ignore that firm's broken contract? Firms do not form a single identical estimate of risks to contract sanctity in a host country, and they need not interpret or draw the same conclusion from information provided by another's broken contract. Only those firms that see the host government's actions as threatening to their own contracts are likely to react negatively. More indifferent firms, on the other hand, are unlikely to change their investment plans or their behavior toward the host government in response to a given breach of contract.

I explain variation in the constraints firms place on host governments by focusing on which firms are most likely to react negatively to a given broken contract. To do this, I turn to an under-explored firm characteristic: nationality. Nationality differentiates the contract risks faced by foreign firms, which makes firms more likely to respond negatively to government breach of contract with a co-national than they would otherwise. In what follows, I describe how the shield of nationality is constituted: various aspects of nationality come together to make nationality a focal point, and nationality provides a variety of resources that form a defense against breach. Nationality acts through legal, diplomatic, business, and domestic political mechanisms to generate a collective sense of contract sanctity among co-nationals and to give co-nationals the ability to defend that collective good.

The modern structure of foreign firm property rights embeds investor national origins in contract sanctity. BITs and related instruments encode and protect foreign firm property rights, replacing failed efforts at a multilateral investment protection regime (Chapter 7). Since the 1990s, BITs have come close to saturating advanced–emerging economy dyads and are

---

[11] Jensen and Johnston 2011.

spreading to emerging–emerging economy dyads. BITs enable public international investment arbitrations (IAs), or international lawsuits that make the offending government and the offense public. One has to know who has been expropriated in order to punish the government for expropriation; BITs and IAs help with this advertisement. But the consequence of the network of bilateral commitments is that national origin determines the international legal rights to which a firm has access.[12] BITs and "public IAs" advertise investment protections and breach of contract by nationality.

The protections afforded to particular national groups of investors under BITs vary with both home- and host-country characteristics at the time of BIT negotiations. For example, thanks to differences in home- and host-government bargaining power, BITs vary on whether disputes must be settled at the World Bank's International Center for the Settlement of Investment Disputes (ICSID), the most public setting for IAs.[13] French BITs tend to give priority to ICSID, while German BITs allow cases to be heard at all international arbitration tribunals; British BITs fall somewhere in between.[14] BITs also vary in the extent of host-government obligations to foreign investors and the circumstances under which host governments agree to IAs.[15] Legal scholars characterize Norwegian BITs as being more sensitive to host-country environmental policies, giving host governments more latitude to prioritize the environment over Norwegian investor interests. France, for its part, insists on an exception for cultural activities in its BITs that necessarily works in both directions. Dutch BITs offer foreign investors very high levels of protection, so much so that accessing these BITs may be one factor behind some firms' incorporation in the Netherlands to acquire Dutch nationality.[16] Additionally, "fair and equitable treatment" (FET) standards have become one of the most important parts of BITs in litigation, but the breadth of interpretations of FETs differs by BIT.[17] As a result of such specificities in each home country's set of bilateral treaties, claims made under the particular BIT to which a firm has access sends more relevant signals of contract sanctity

[12] Limited multilateral and regional treaties with chapters on investment protection exist, but as of 2011, only the Energy Charter Treaty, the North American Free Trade Agreement (NAFTA), and several Latin American regional trade and investment agreements have been cited in public IAs. The vast majority of public IAs have been facilitated by BITs.

[13] Allee and Peinhardt 2011.

[14] Dolzer, Rudolf, "BITs Around the World: Different Substantive and Procedural Approaches" (presentation, *50 Years of Bilateral Investment Treaties Conference*, December 2009, Frankfurt, Germany). Dolzer and Stevens 1995.

[15] Blake 2013.

[16] Dolzer, Rudolf, "BITs Around the World: Different Substantive and Procedural Approaches" (presentation, *50 Years of Bilateral Investment Treaties Conference*, December 2009, Frankfurt, Germany).

[17] Interview, US official, Washington, D.C., 2013. Tudor (2008) counts seven categories of drafting formulations of FETs in an analysis of 365 BITs.

than claims made under other BITs.[18] Further, should firms of different nationalities face a common threat of breach – say, by industry – legal action over that breach is likely to be divided along national lines. Finally, for firms without access to a BIT, and thus without guaranteed international legal recourse, the operations of BITs are even more remote to contract sanctity. Structurally, investor national origins do much to determine investors' property rights protections under international law.

Domestic law in home countries can also set apart the risks a particular national group of investors faces in a host country. The US Foreign Corrupt Practices Act of 1977 (FCPA) provides credibility to the claim that American firms cannot pay bribes, something executives (American and otherwise) with experience in many countries readily acknowledge makes a difference on the ground. For decades, the FCPA had no equivalent in other advanced industrial countries. Finally, advanced industrial countries' laws on foreign corrupt practices converged with the 1997 OECD Convention on Combating Bribery of Foreign Public Officials in International Business. However, variation continues in OECD home countries' commitments to enforcing their anti-bribery laws, which allows different nationalities different latitude in forming deals with host governments.[19] The United Kingdom Bribery Act of 2010 goes farther than the OECD Convention or the American FCPA: it prevents British firms from paying government officials to expedite bureaucratic processes. Due to enforcement and legislative differences, then, American and British firms continue to face particular constraints when contracting with host governments. Variation in constraints on bribery generates variation in the kinds of contracts being entered into by different nationalities. Correspondingly, firms of different nationalities have different expectations about the legitimacy and thus expected sanctity of each other's contracts.

Foreign-firm nationality has long carried with it the burden or blessing of bilateral politics. Firm decision-making is influenced by bilateral political factors – and one firm's investment decisions are unlikely to be influenced by a different nationality's bilateral politics. Bilateral trade treaties tie some home and host countries closer together economically than others. Military and diplomatic relations, cultural ties, and the role of a particular home country in the host country's domestic politics generate uneven levels of attention to a national group of investors, on the part of both home- and host-country officials.[20] Variation in government attention to or the prominence of particular

---

[18] This evidence of variation by home country goes against some scholars' arguments that BITs are effectively interchangeable (Elkins et al. 2006, Kerner 2009) or that signals diffuse widely (Büthe and Milner 2009). The presence of "most favored nation" (MFN) clauses in BITs does make them more interchangeable. However, MFN interpretations have varied considerably across public IAs.

[19] Kaczmarek and Newman (2011) find that US actors continue to take the lead in anti-bribery enforcement.

[20] Hirst and Thompson 1995. For example, Romanian diplomats are said to have good access to officials in Beijing – particularly when it comes to commercial relations – thanks to historical and

national groups translates into varying contract risks. For example, bilateral FDI flowing from advanced to emerging economies decreases in the presence of a bilateral military conflict, as well as in the presence of bilateral economic sanctions.[21] On the other hand, bilateral FDI increases in the presence of a military alliance.[22] Emerging economies with a US troop presence receive more US-origin FDI but not more aggregate FDI.[23] While these examples concern matters of war and peace, further evidence suggests that firms take even incremental changes in bilateral relations into account when making investment decisions. For example, Desbordes finds that American firms increase their required return on investment when diplomatic tensions heighten with developing countries.[24]

When home governments themselves act as foreign investors via state-owned firms, the link between national origin and contract sanctity is even clearer. State-owned firms have incentives to sacrifice profit-maximization in exchange for meeting foreign policy goals, which can make them more likely than private foreign firms to invest in the riskiest emerging economies.[25] When a home government has higher levels of ownership or involvement in the affairs of its nationality's firms investing abroad, host governments are primed to tie the treatment of those firms to bilateral political relations. Home governments' investments in the form of Sovereign Wealth Funds (SWFs) could act as an economic stick wielded to protect contract sanctity: home governments could credibly commit to divert SWF investments in response to contract breach. In sum, so long as a host country's political and diplomatic relationships vary across home countries, bilateral politics can generate variation in foreign firm contract sanctity by national origin.

High politics continues to be a factor in host governments' treatment of particular national groups of foreign firms.[26] From the 1950s to the 1970s, emerging-economy governments frequently broke contracts with ex-colonial foreign investors (Chapter 7). Tanzania openly targeted British-owned banking, real estate, agriculture, and manufacturing for nationalization, just as Algeria targeted French FDI in the oil and gas sector.[27] Today, investment coming from China is highly politicized in Taiwan and a major point of contention between

cultural ties. Meunier, Sophie (presentation, Princeton Workshop on Outward Chinese Foreign Direct Investment, November 2012, Princeton, NJ).

[21] Biglaiser and Lektzian 2011, Li and Vashchilko 2010. Lee and Mitchell (2012) find that bilateral FDI has no effect on states' decisions to start interstate conflicts, but higher bilateral flows reduce the probability of violent escalation.

[22] Li and Vashchilko 2010.

[23] Biglaiser and DeRouen 2006.

[24] Desbordes 2010. Davis and Meunier (2011) find that changed relations between advanced industrial countries do not have a significant impact on bilateral FDI flows.

[25] Knutsen et al. 2011.

[26] Certainly, the idea that firms of particular nationalities can be made vulnerable by high politics is not new: the onset of World War II led to the expropriation of German assets in Allied countries.

[27] Akinsanya 1981.

the island's two major political parties; on the other hand, US investors into Taiwan are welcomed heartily and receive informal if not formal preferential treatment.[28] Tendencies to discriminate against particular ethnic groups can also be translated into governmental relations with foreign firms. In Moldova, for example, Turkish investors have found it beneficial to play down their national origins, lest they be targeted for breach in forms like extra-contractual "tax payments."[29]

In the shadow of high politics, change in one nationality's contract sanctity provides little information to investors of other national origins. For example, foreign firms operating in post-communist Europe understand that Russian-origin firms have different relationships with host governments in this region that Russia calls the "near abroad" rather than simply "foreign."[30] Because politics in Eastern Europe is often tied up with host governments' interactions with Russia, political turnover in Eastern European host countries can result in increased or decreased contract risks for Russian-origin firms. These dynamics behind Russian contract sanctity differ from those faced by firms of other national origins invested in the region.

A firm's national origins can also give a host-country government and polity expectations about the contributions the firm's investments will make to local development. FDI provides capital to capital-seeking emerging economies, but it is set apart from other capital flows by the possibility that it will provide technology transfer, spillovers to the domestic economy, managerial and operational know-how, and other direct contributions to the local economy. These gains, however, have often proven elusive. Comprehensive surveys of literature on the effects of FDI provide inconsistent evidence that FDI leads to economic growth.[31] If all FDI is not created equal, host governments and polities have incentives to privilege some firms and types of investments over others. Firms from wealthy Western home countries can carry "national brands" that make host governments expect more reliable knock-on benefits from their FDI than, say, from the FDI of investors from the global South. For example, Ukrainian officials were concerned that "selling an aluminum plant to Russians is not development," preferring instead to sell it to a firm from a European Union member state.[32] Multilateral organizations like the World Bank and European Union have spread the best practice of trying to attract FDI from certain home countries in hopes of gaining broader growth-promoting resources; generally, the targets for investment promotion are Western (although

---

[28] Meetings with Taiwanese economic development officials and US actors (13), Taiwan, August 2013.
[29] Interview, Turkish firm, Moldova, 2009. Turkish investors do receive good treatment in Gagauzia, a sub-region in Moldova where the local population has Turkish roots. Chapter 6.
[30] In Russian: *лижнее зарубежье*.
[31] E.g., Moran et al. 2005.
[32] Interview, domestic think tank, Ukraine, 2011.

desire for Chinese-origin FDI is growing, particularly in the global South).[33] However, high expectations can lead host governments to break contracts with Western firms if investments do not result in the expected benefits. This dynamic sat behind the cancellation of US and Spanish firms' water and sewage contracts in Argentina and broadly in Asia in the early 2000s, when improvements in service quality (and higher prices) did not match host-government expectations.[34] Local beliefs about the contributions a nationality's FDI will make to domestic development make nationality relevant to the government's mutable expectations of firms and, thus, to firms' contract sanctity.

Bilateral ethnic, linguistic, and cultural ties also differentiate the willingness and ability of host governments to breach contracts with certain groups of investors rather than others. Cultural similarities between home and host countries can reduce transaction costs between foreign firms and the host government, allowing investors to rely less on codified contracts with the host government and more on shared norms and tacit knowledge.[35] Common language and colonial history are standard, positively signed controls in studies of the determinants of FDI, and scholars have found that FDI flows are higher when countries have similar levels of corruption[36] and when countries have similarly egalitarian cultures.[37] Similarly, diaspora ties and cross-border social networks make it easier for firms to operate under informal and incomplete contracts, which changes the nature of diaspora firms' contracts with the host government as compared to firms with arms-length relations.[38] Because tacit and arms-length contracts rely on such different institutions for their maintenance and the resolution of conflicts, the sanctity of one type is necessarily different than the sanctity of the other. Put differently, broken arms-length contracts do not signal the same risks to investor groups that have different sorts of historical and cultural bargains underpinning their government relations.[39] For example, Makino and Tsang attribute the varying treatment firms from France, China, and Hong Kong have faced in Vietnam to variation in formal and informal historical ties.[40] When bilateral ties shape the kinds of contracts firms enter into with the host government, it follows that different national groups face uneven risks to contract sanctity.

Co-national firms can benefit from dense networks of ties built up at home, through commercial interactions, lobbying efforts, shared hometowns, and simply the experience of having operated in the home country. Firms with

[33] Loewendahl 2001. Interview, European Union consultant for Investment Promotion Agencies, Moldova, 2009.

[34] Post 2009.

[35] Williamson 1979.

[36] Wu 2006, DeBacker et al. 2012.

[37] Siegel et al. 2011, 2013.

[38] Bandelj 2008, Leblang 2010.

[39] Hirst and Thompson 1995.

[40] Makino and Tsang 2011.

the same national origin operate in similar ways abroad, embodying the formal and informal institutional constraints of their country of origin.[41] They are more likely to use the same kind of financing for their operations, whether because they use formal institutions provided by their home government, or because they are predisposed to use certain ownership structures by virtue of home country experiences.[42] Commonalities among co-national firms make them efficient sources of local knowledge for each other, able to communicate among themselves in culturally understandable ways.[43] In other words, co-national ties can help firms to overcome what Stephen Hymer termed the "liability of foreignness."[44] Indeed, scholars argue that the greater the separation between home- and host-country cultural norms as well as regulatory institutions, the more difficult it is for a nation's foreign investors to gain legitimacy with the host-country polity and government.[45] Knowledge provided by co-nationals is particularly relevant for firms from national groups that have "a high degree of outsidership" in the host economy, because these firms find it more difficult to establish reliable, trust-based relationships with local actors.[46] Co-national firms can benefit from a "legitimacy spillover" if, for example, early entrants of the same national origin have already had time to cultivate strong government relations.[47]

Because of these many sources of commonality in contract dynamics, national origin becomes shorthand for shared risks to contract sanctity. Investors see co-national firms' broken contracts, worry that they are next, fear for the sanctity of their investment, and therefore are more likely to decide to draw down an existing investment or divert planned investments in response.

Investors of different nationalities, in contrast, are less likely to see a firm's broken contract and fear for the sanctity of their investments. The signal that contract breach sends to non-co-national firms is highly diluted. A non-co-national firm does not share the same bilateral legal institutions. A non-co-national firm's contract sanctity is unlikely to be negatively impacted by the dynamics of the targeted firm's home–host relationship. A non-co-national firm is less likely to have acquired financing in the same way, or written similar contracts, or relied on the same cultural networks as the targeted firm. In short, the targeted firm's broken contract is less likely to provide useful information on the sanctity of the non-co-national firm's contract. Thus, when the targeted firm's contract is broken, rational non-co-national firms are unlikely to expect their own contract risks to change greatly. As such, they are unlikely to update their behavior in ways costly to the host government. From the host

---

[41] North 1990, Holburn and Zelner 2010, Doremus et al. 1999.
[42] Doremus et al. 1999, Li et al. 2011.
[43] Tan and Meyer 2011.
[44] Hymer 1976.
[45] Kostova and Zaheer 1999.
[46] Tan and Meyer 2011, Wells and Ahmad 2007.
[47] Ibid.

government's point of view, non-co-national firms' reactions are observationally equivalent to indifference. That indifference is what can, in sufficient concentration, enable breach.

NATIONAL ORIGIN AS A RESOURCE

Foreign firms entering emerging economies take measures to protect their investments from political risks, including the risk of government breach of contract. When new risks arise, however, firms have incentives to augment their existing strategies with additional "recuperation mechanisms" in order to recover previous levels of contract sanctity.[48] FDI exit or diversion is the recuperation mechanism that exerts direct pressure on host governments' access to foreign capital. However, from the foreign firm's point of view, exit can be an expensive option of last resort. Firms choosing to exit or divert capital in response to changed risks leave behind sunk capital and incur transition costs.

What is more, the loss of capital may not effectively deter future government breach of contract. Just as there are a multitude of reasons to invest in a host country, there are a multitude of reasons for investors to exit that country. In interviews, executives themselves can be wary of directly attributing investment drawdown to breach, because so many factors are at play in investment decisions. Deterrence might be played out not through investment drawdown but rather when firms change their mode of entry – for example, when firms choose to make further investments in arms-length transactions like subcontracting.[49] Without a consistent and direct tie between breach and exit, host governments may not interpret changes in aggregate FDI statistics as a reflection of their decision to encroach on some contracts. When exit results in relative but not absolute losses of FDI, incumbent governments may continue to benefit from increasing aggregate levels of FDI. As many emerging economies have experienced a secular increase in FDI in the last decades, relative but not absolute FDI decline is pervasive. The complex counterfactual reasoning of what might have been in the absence of government breach makes for a difficult opposition slogan. For these reasons, co-national exit alone may not deter a government from breaking contracts with a national group of investors, because it may not sufficiently affect a host government's ability to remain in and benefit from its position of authority.

However, exercised alongside or in lieu of exit, protest can be a cheap and effective option for foreign firms to recoup contract sanctity. As Hirschman expressed it, protest or "voice" occurs when actors articulate their interests in order to get an organization, or in this case a government, to return to its previous performance. The exercise of protest requires an interested group of

---

[48] Hirschman 1970.
[49] Henisz and Williamson 1999, Mosley 2011.

actors that has the capacity to lobby through direct or collective action.[50] Exercising protest requires some dedication, as it can be risky. But co-national actors – both diplomats and firms themselves – share resources to overcome obstacles to effective organization and the incentives to protest against breach.

Diplomacy

Co-national firms have unique access to their home governments. Even prior to breach, home governments make forward-looking commitments to their firms' property rights abroad by signing BITs and other investment agreements with host governments. But, should a contract dispute arise, home governments can and do respond in real time, usually before legal proceedings.[51] The existence of a formal BIT can make it easier for a foreign firm to recruit its home government's assistance.[52] "Gunboats" no longer come to the rescue of foreign firms facing broken contracts, if they ever did.[53] But home-country diplomats link firms' contract sanctity to other issues in the bilateral relationship, such that the future costs of lost capital are compounded by the costs of declining bilateral relations and threats to particular issue areas. We can think of this kind of issue linkage as "bracketing": diplomats make threats that inaction on one issue will trigger punishments in another issue area.[54] Governments have often linked other economic issues to the circumstances of particular firms, by threatening bilateral trade relations or foreign aid distribution in retaliation for breach of contract. Security issues can also play a role in a home government's fight against breach, just as they can in a host government's motivations to breach. In general, support from commercial attachés, ambassadors, and home-country politicians gives foreign firms access to their home government's clout with host-government decision-makers. By lengthening the shadow of the future, a home government can elicit cooperation from a host government and increase the credibility of the host's commitments to contract sanctity.[55] In the words of a respondent at an investor-relevant United Nations agency, embassies "make a foreign investment relationship visible, so it is known that something will be a problem."[56]

---

[50] Hirschman 1970.

[51] The ICSID convention suspends the right of diplomatic protection during the arbitral process (Article 27) but "resurrects that right" if and when state has "failed to abide by and comply with" an award as obligated to do under the convention (Article 53). Bishop 2009: 6.

[52] Interviews (2), former US government officials, Washington, D.C., 2009. Büthe and Milner 2009.

[53] Tomz 2007, Lipson 1985, Wells and Ahmad 2007. But see Mitchener and Weidenmier 2010.

[54] Oye 1992; Lohmann 1997, Davis 2004.

[55] Diplomacy can extend to the enforcement stage after an IA award is made. Under some BITs, the home government could initiate arbitration if the host government refuses to comply with the award, or the home government could bring a claim before the International Court of Justice. Bishop 2009, 14.

[56] Interview, United Nations agency, Moldova, 2009.

The empirical record shows that co-national actors regularly draw on home-country officials and institutions to respond to threats to contract sanctity. Even at the turn of the twentieth century, US politicians came out in support of US firms facing disputes abroad. In his first "annual message" in 1909, William Howard Taft talked about putting pressure on Chile when "diplomatic intervention became necessary to the protection of the interests" of a particular US firm.[57] Since then, the United States has legislated issue linkages between the status of foreign firms abroad and other aspects of the bilateral relationship, pre-emptively creating tools for diplomatic leverage. The "Hickenlooper Amendment" to the Foreign Assistance Act of 1962, for example, required the US government to suspend foreign aid to countries that expropriate US property without just compensation. The Amendment came about in response to mass Cuban expropriation of US property and fears that similar actions could take place again. However, formal sanctions were applied only once in Ceylon (Sri Lanka) and the Amendment was repealed in 1972.[58] American firms, in fact, felt that the diplomatic threat was too strong and pushed for a softer – though by no means absent – US government hand in contract disputes.

Indeed, built-in threats to deter breach are still present in the American diplomat's toolkit. For example, in 1994 the "Helms Amendment" prohibited US foreign aid or US approval of international financial institution financing to countries that have expropriated property in which US citizens hold at least 50 percent ownership. The United States invoked this Amendment and delayed a US$175 million Inter-American Development Bank loan to Costa Rica until Costa Rica consented in 1995 to an IA with a US firm.[59] The 2000 African Growth and Opportunity Act and the 1991 Andean Trade Preference Act also allow the government to withhold benefits from countries facing outstanding American expropriation claims.[60] And, to be eligible for the Generalized System of Preference (GSP), an important source of benefits for US trading partners, a host country has to be free of expropriation claims from American firms. This is the linkage that led the United States in 2012 to withdraw GSP benefits in retaliation for Argentina's non-payment of two US firms' IA awards, which themselves dated back to breach of contract during Argentina's 2002 default (Chapter 1).

---

[57] "Many years ago diplomatic intervention became necessary to the protection of the interests in the American claim of Alsop and Company against the Government of Chile. The Government of Chile had frequently admitted obligation in the case and had promised this Government to settle ... Now, happily, as the result of the recent diplomatic negotiations, the Governments of the United States and of Chile ... have agreed by a protocol to submit the controversy to definitive settlement by His Britannic Majesty, Edward VII." Taft, "First Annual Message," 7 December 1909. Described in Veeser 2002.

[58] For a discussion of diplomatic positions taken by US embassies at the time, see Behrman et al. 1975: 84–89.

[59] Helms Amendment: 22 USC sec. 2378 a. (30 April 1994). As reported in *Compañia del Desarrollo de Santa Elena S.A. v. Republic of Costa Rica (ICSID ARB/96/1)*.

[60] Wells 2005: 442.

In 2012, the role of home-government involvement in one nationality's investments abroad became quite explicit. President Putin of Russia issued a decree that certain Russian multinationals must get approval from the Kremlin before complying with foreign investigations and court or administrative orders in host countries. Whether they are public or private firms, "strategic" Russian multinationals in oil and gas, telecommunications, media, finance, and other major industries will not be given permission to comply by the Russian government if "compliance would be deemed detrimental to Russian economic interests."[61] Certainly, this decree is of questionable legality and enforceability. Yet whether the Kremlin exercises this authority or not, the sentiment behind the decree sets the legal risks surrounding contracts with Russian multinationals apart from the risks surrounding contracts with other firms. It also suggests that the Russian home government is more than willing to come to the aid of its nationals' firms abroad, both pre-emptively and in the course of a dispute.[62]

Home governments have an important role to play in deterring contract breach, but diplomats are not always willing or able to come to their nationals' aid in contract disputes. From the home government's point of view, pursuing a national's dispute could use up political capital better spent on other aspects of the bilateral relationship. Or, points of leverage like issue linkages may not be readily apparent. If there is already a BIT in place, home governments have made a prior effort on behalf of their firms abroad and might be less willing to engage in real-time support once a BIT violation arises. On the other hand, BITs can facilitate a home government's formal diplomatic representation (démarche) on behalf of its firm in a host country. Some firms carry enough influence in their home countries to get reliable access to diplomatic resources, whether formal or informal. And home governments that push for better treatment in response to threats to their nationals' contract sanctity today can save resources that would otherwise have been spent on other, future disputes. Any one firm's problem, however, need not constitute a diplomatic priority.

Because diplomatic pressure in a given contract dispute is not certain, co-national firms' ability to come together and lobby their home government for support is an important determinant of diplomatic involvement. Firms of the same nationality can benefit from previous shared interactions with the home country government to successfully access diplomats. But even the largest of a home country's firms in an emerging economy increases its leverage over a home government when it builds a coalition of co-national firms, as a coalition keeps a firm's dispute from being dismissed as the problem of only one.[63] Formal

---

[61] Greene, Sam, "A Rare Moment of Policy Transparency in Russia: Why the Government Just Ordered Companies Not to Obey Laws," *The Monkey Cage*, 13 September 2012. Russian Presidential decree: "Указ о мерах по защите интересов России при осуществлении российскими юридическими лицами внешнеэкономической деятельности," issued 11 September 2012.

[62] See Chapters 5 and 6 for examples.

[63] Olson 1965.

and informal co-national investor associations, which are common around the world, allow co-national firms a platform from which to advocate for diplomatic intervention to restore their collective contract sanctity. What is more, co-national firms can and do use such organizations to come together and lobby host governments directly.

Co-National Protest

Diplomatic efforts regularly take place alongside collective action by co-national firms. Foreign firms are often highly visible players in emerging economies, which, combined with lobbying experience from their home countries, can make them influential in emerging economies' sometimes underdeveloped lobbying environments.[64] Groups of co-national firms have often already overcome collective action problems in forming formal or informal nationality-based investor organizations that can facilitate protest. Pre-existing formal and informal ties between co-national firms help to increase the effectiveness of their commitment to mutual support. Thus, even before protest takes place, co-nationality can send a signal to the host government that, should a contract be broken, these co-national firms are likely to take costly action in response. Should a government attempt a contract breach, co-national firms have the incentives and resources to organize what can be effective campaigns. In 2009, for example, Chinese policymakers took an American light manufacturing firm's products off the market and left competing local products untouched. This would have effectively kept the firm from operating in China. After advocacy from American diplomats and lobbying via American investor associations, the decision was reversed.[65]

One can think of the dynamic between co-national firms in terms of military alliances. Like the presence of an alliance, nationality increases the probability that each firm will intervene on another firm's behalf.[66] The shared good of contract sanctity among co-nationals gives the "alliance" teeth and incentivizes co-nationals to act collectively in response to each other's broken contracts. In the words of an Argentinian official, "Foreign investor associations like the American Chamber of Commerce fight, but they fight their own fights."[67]

Yet just as diplomats do not always lobby for their nationals, firms do not always engage in co-national collective action. Firms incur costs when taking a public stand, such as tarnishing their reputation with the government, local suppliers, or the domestic population. To offset the potential costs of protest, co-national firms must have an expectation that their efforts will be successful.

[64] Desbordes and Vauday 2007.
[65] Interview, US firm, Washington, D.C., 2010. The future chair of the Shanghai American Chamber of Commerce understood the importance of co-national lobbying when he said the organization must "make our voice heard in the halls of government ... [and] improve business conditions *for members*." Emphasis added. Jensen et al. 2012: 116.
[66] Morrow 2000, Fearon 1997.
[67] Interview, Germany, 2009.

Consistent with the argument throughout this book, diplomatic and co-national protest is likely to provide a strong shield against breach when FDI national diversity is low, but protests are quieter and the shield is weakened when FDI national diversity is high. This prediction helps to account for cross-national variation in, for instance, the mission and strength of US investor institutions. As we see in Chapters 5 and 6, the American Chambers of Commerce in more homogenous Moldova and Ukraine have fought directly for members' contract sanctity while, in contrast, the American Chamber of Commerce in diverse Romania has focused more on networking activities.[68] I take the correlation of such variation with FDI national diversity as an additional piece of evidence for the nationality shield theory.

"TRUE" MULTINATIONALS AND TAX HAVENS

Before considering the effects of national diversity at the level of the economy as a whole, I stop here to consider: if nationality matters for multinational firms, what about firms that have roots in multiple home countries? Mergers and acquisitions leave some multinationals with more than one set of national ties, and sometimes firms invest in third countries via second country subsidiaries. The steel giant ArcelorMittal, for example, has British, French, and Luxembourgian ownership, and it invested in Ukraine via its well-established subsidiary in Germany (Chapter 5). Such multinationals are often seen as the world's most powerful holders of leverage over host governments.

Firms also take advantage of the secrecy and lax regulations of tax havens, sometimes known as offshore financial centers, when engaging in FDI. Those most commonly agreed to be tax havens include household names – the Bahamas, Bermuda, and the Cayman Islands – although Palan et al. identify ninety-one jurisdictions labeled tax havens by different governmental and non-governmental bodies.[69] These include Malta and Cyprus as well as the Netherlands, Switzerland, and in some cases, the United Kingdom and the United States. Tax havens are more likely to be "pass-through" countries for FDI, though certainly not all FDI passes through, as some tax havens are also major destination countries for FDI. To make matters more complicated, a subset of capital taking advantage of tax havens comes from "host" countries themselves. That is, Chinese capital flows through Hong Kong and some of it back to China and, as we see in Chapters 5 and 6, Eastern European firms sometimes use Cyprus as a location through which to "round-trip" capital.

One might question whether firms investing via subsidiaries, in tax havens or otherwise, pick up characteristics of the pass-through nationality. I contend that, far from existing outside of national boundaries, "true" multinationals and tax

---

[68] American Chambers of Commerce determine their mission and activities very much on a local basis, especially those outside of Western Europe. Interview, Washington, D.C., 2012.

[69] Palan et al. 2010. Chapter 7.

haven investors are made vulnerable to contract risks associated with more than one bilateral relationship. By choosing to involve an intermediate country in a firm's aggregated nationality, a firm exposes itself to vulnerabilities or preferences afforded investors from that intermediate country in the ultimate destination country.

Firms investing via the same intermediate home country share many similar determinants of contract sanctity, just as firms from the same traditional home country do. Domestic laws in the intermediate country shape the kinds of contracts firms can enter into with ultimate host countries in ways unrelated to those faced by traditional foreign investors. For example, preferential Double Taxation Treaties (DTTs) can give these investors tax privileges and simultaneously potential contract vulnerabilities if the host polity sees those deals as too lucrative ex post. Moreover, intermediate homes that require low levels of disclosure or due diligence may allow firms more flexibility in contracting with host governments. This, too, translates into different contract vulnerabilities should flexible relationships turn sour. Taking institutions into account, the legal rights available to intermediate home firms are a product of both their ultimate home and of their intermediate home. For example, there is legal precedent that firms invested in intermediate homes have access to that country's BIT if the intermediate home investment is robust enough.[70] As a result of such factors, firms investing via a given intermediate home are likely to be interested in the fate of contracts made by similarly invested firms, just as they are likely to be interested in the fate of contracts made with firms of their ultimate home nationality. In Chapter 5, for example, we see that Russian firms investing in Ukraine via Cyprus-incorporated entities look to each other and to the Russian government when evaluating their political risks.

Whether or not firms with intermediate firms can access multiple (or any) sources of diplomacy is not ex ante clear, but what is clear is that the diplomatic access afforded to one intermediate home firm is more likely to resemble that afforded to other firms with claims on the same combination of countries. Firms with claims on more than one home country can have access to multiple sets of diplomats that advocate around contract breach: ArcelorMittal in Ukraine benefitted from advocacy by France, the United Kingdom, Germany, and Luxembourg (Chapter 5). However, firms' access to diplomats is not unconditional. For example, the ability to access both intermediate and ultimate home-country diplomats may be undermined if the decision to invest via second countries has negative political connotations at home. Diplomats from the Bahamas and the Cayman Islands have proved unwilling to advocate on behalf

---

[70] The 2004 jurisdiction decision in *Tokios Tokeles v. Ukraine (ICSID ARB/02/18)* provides the (non-binding) precedent for this access. To be heard at ICSID, a complainant must be a national of an ICSID country and not a national of the host country. ILA German Branch/Working Group, *The Determination of the Nationality of Investors Under Investment Treaties – A Preliminary Report*, December 2009.

of particular firms' broken contracts in FDI destination countries, though these governments' commitments to maintaining secrecy provisions may de facto aid firms in fighting breach.

In short, the nationality shield theory and evidence in this book go to show that firms with multiple national identities do not become meta-national.[71] Rather, a "true" multinational firm is most likely to receive signals about and advocacy for its own contract sanctity from (only) those multiple national groups to which it belongs.

FDI NATIONAL DIVERSITY

Firms' perceptions of risks to their contract sanctity vary with national origin, and this variation shapes firms' willingness to exit in response to breach of contract as well as their ability to wield protest to deter breach. When considered at the level of the host economy as a whole, we see that foreign firms' reactions to breach with any given firm are not uniformly costly to the host government. Rather, costliness is conditioned on the nationality of the targeted firm and the nationalities of other firms. Although firms of the targeted nationality exit or generate diplomatic costs for the host government, other foreign firms' investment plans and interactions with the host government are likely unchanged. Non-co-nationals' behavior is thus likely to be observationally equivalent to indifference to a given breach. As a more nationally diverse set of firms presents alternative sources of current and future FDI to the host country, any one nationality's costly response is less likely to constrain the host country's overall access to foreign capital.

The nationality diversity of the investor community in a host country takes into account two factors: the number of national investor groups present in the host country and the distribution of existing FDI stock across national groups.[72] The absolute number of national groups matters particularly for the host country's future access to FDI. Even if a given national group invests a small amount of FDI today, the fact that firms of that nationality have already entered makes that national group a more reliable source of capital tomorrow than another, as-yet-unrepresented nationality. As the sales adage goes, it is easier to grow a client than to get a client.

The second component of FDI national diversity is the distribution of accumulated FDI stock across nationalities. Suppose a country hosts two nationalities of foreign firms. When each group accounts for half of the country's FDI, the host government has an alternate, ready source of FDI that can help

---

[71] Undercounting these hybrid groups in conventional FDI data makes it harder to demonstrate the theorized, positive effect of FDI national diversity on breach. Chapter 4.

[72] In quantitative analysis, I use: FDI national diversity = $1/(s_{1t}^2 + s_{2t}^2 + s_{3t}^2 + \ldots + s_{nt}^2)$ where s_n is nationality n's share of the annual FDI stock from OECD countries to country i in year t. This is an inverse Herfindahl-Hirschman Index. Chapter 4.

compensate for lost capital were it to breach with either group. But when one nationality represents a very large share of FDI stock, breach of contract with that group would threaten the country's main source of FDI, effectively reducing the probability of its breach as well as breach in the economy overall. Because risks to contract sanctity are overwhelmingly bilateral, breach with the second, smaller national group would not be a substitute for breach with the large group; breach with it would also be costly in reducing the diversity of capital available to the host economy. In fact, the likelihood of breach would be inversely related to size if breach with smaller national groups is less likely to bring about the kind of benefits host governments desire from breach.[73] Many variables determine the size or thickness of any particular nationality shield, and the level of FDI national diversity does not in itself suggest which firms or contracts may be targeted for breach. Rather, the expectation is the more even the distribution of FDI across national groups, the higher the likelihood that the government can act on its incentives to breach where it would like to, somewhere in the economy as a whole.[74]

CONSIDERING INDUSTRY EXPLANATIONS

Often, industry springs to mind when we think about variation among firms. How do arguments about the effects of co-nationality align with expectations about industry and contract risks? Literature beginning with Vernon points to the importance of industry in determining which firms might be more likely targets for expropriation. Vernon's "obsolescing bargain" logic posits that foreign firms hold the upper hand in negotiations before entering a host country, but after investors incur sunk costs, the host government is tempted to violate its contractual commitments.[75] Governments can take over productive investments from firms that cannot easily move (all of) their assets elsewhere. Vernon put it poetically: "Almost from the moment that the signatures have dried on the document, powerful forces go to work that quickly render the agreements obsolete in the eyes of the government."[76] The more sunk costs a firm incurs, the less mobile the firm, the less credible the firm's exit options, and thus the less credible the government's contractual commitment.[77]

Observers usually turn to industry to identify which firms are those unlucky, immobile ones.[78] Expropriation is often associated with oil installations, gold

---

[73] As explored in Chapters 2 and 4, we see empirically that both large and small investors have been targets of government breach of contract.

[74] Indeed, if every nationality has only a single firm investing at the same amount, extreme national diversity will leave firms no co-nationals to fight breach through collective action.

[75] Vernon 1971.

[76] Ibid.: 47. Despite the obsolescing bargain, successful investors are enticed to remain in the country "by the sinking of commitments and by the sweet smell of success" (53).

[77] Moran 1973.

[78] Wolf 2004, Henisz 2002.

mines, electricity transmission grids – assets with owners that are hamstrung by their industries' sizes, shapes, and capital intensity. Frieden determines that site-specific investments, which are easily seized and for which rents are concentrated, are subject to extensive initial sunk costs.[79] The particular vulnerability of site-specific investments helps to explain cases like the changing relations between Namibia and the diamond giant De Beers,[80] the early 1970s copper firm nationalizations in Zambia and Zaire,[81] oil and gas nationalizations,[82] and even the struggles of relatively immobile manufacturing firms in India.[83]

Scholars have extended the obsolescing bargain framework in various ways, using it to model trends in expected future returns for foreign firms over time;[84] to account for the bargaining between home countries, host countries, and multilateral institutions that sometimes precedes private FDI;[85] to explain the role non-governmental organizations (NGOs) can play in international investment;[86] or to justify new contractual clauses that attempt to take account of the dynamics of investor–host government relations.[87] Throughout these applications and extensions, however, the backbone of the argument remains that immobile firms have more vulnerable contracts than other, mobile firms.

However, industry and asset mobility fail to fully explain the permissive space governments have to sometimes break contracts for five main reasons. First, firms' investments are in fact not so readily segregated into mobile and immobile groups along industry lines. More and more contemporary foreign firms across many industries find themselves stuck in the locations they choose. Some firms are tied to particular host countries through social networks, as in diaspora investment.[88] Bandelj argues that executives draw on social networks and cultural understandings to undertake foreign investments.[89] If one accepts that entry into a historic homeland is a firm's primary motivation in investing abroad, these firms, too, are relatively immobile and subject to the obsolescing bargain. For firms using host countries as export platforms in a world of deverticalized production, a change of location entails a reorganization of supply chains. And for FDI seeking local market entry, significant assets are sunk into retail and distribution networks, not to mention that a change in

---

[79] Frieden 1994.
[80] Kempton and Preez 1997.
[81] Shafer 1983.
[82] Hajzler 2012.
[83] Vachani 1995.
[84] Thomas and Worrall 1994.
[85] Ramamurti 2001.
[86] Nebus and Rufin 2009.
[87] For example, Land (2009) discusses the use of dynamic contractual clauses like progressive taxation that allows for a "fair" reallocation of assets over time given changing circumstances.
[88] Leblang 2010, Graham 2014.
[89] Bandelj 2008.

location would entail a major change in firm strategy. Sometimes, local market entry is about capturing remaining market share in the world. For example, Western European banks have been expanding into Eastern Europe, and their investments have not necessarily been chosen for immediate efficiency but, rather, because executives increasingly feel that they have "nowhere else left to go."[90] Accordingly, even investors in banking – a quintessentially mobile industry – are rendered less mobile and more vulnerable to contract risks. Given that so many firms' threats of exit are compromised across and within industries, a focus on industry alone makes it difficult to understand why breach does not always occur.

Second, even investors in classically vulnerable industries can cancel planned projects or stop reinvestment in a host country. An oil firm's threat to stop new exploration or a mining firm's threat to stop operations is credible, because capital not yet deployed is still mobile. Thus, the bargaining power of such firms is not fated to wholly obsolesce as firms retain leverage traditionally associated with mobile investors.[91] And the spread of risk management strategies – from bodyguards, to diversification across geographies, to political risk insurance, to book-sized contracts – lead firms in traditionally immobile industries to feel they can sufficiently account for contract risks upon entry into a host country. Now, firms certainly have interests in updating their expectations of government breach of contract once disputes occur in a host economy. Indeed, this logic underlies both the conventional wisdom and this book's twist on the costly responses host governments face when engaging in breach of contract. But innovation in risk management has allowed traditionally immobile investors to mitigate at least some of the vulnerabilities that the obsolescing bargain suggests.

Third, consider how a given firm might react following a breach of contract somewhere in its industry. Following a breach, co-industrial firms may find new investment opportunities: a competitor's broken contract could be a boon for their local business prospects. Because firms in the same industry might perceive both risks and opportunities following a co-industrial's broken contract, it is unclear ex ante that a co-industrial firm would react to a given breach by diverting or drawing down its own capital. Indeed, there is reason to believe co-industrial firms might even increase investments in response. After Argentina nationalized the Spanish oil and gas firm Repsol in 2012, for example, firms from the United States, China, and Norway expanded investments in the sector. Further, countervailing competitive pressures suggest that co-industrial firms are unlikely to take a stand on behalf of a competitor. The benefits to any formal or informal industry organization of "staying out of it" are likely to outweigh the

---

[90] Lanine and Vander Vennett 2007. Interviews (4), foreign banks, Ukraine, Romania, and Moldova, 2009.

[91] Likosky 2009.

benefits of spending political capital on one firm's problem.[92] In contrast, because co-national organizations are made up of non-competitors (at least in part), they are not by necessity strained by the same countervailing pressures.[93]

The fourth and fifth reasons industry is insufficient to explain breach are empirical. As is shown throughout this book, contracts continue to be broken both inside and outside of traditionally immobile, obsolescing bargain industries. And, since motivations behind government breach of contract have been about raising revenue, specific assets, foreign policy, domestic audiences, corruption, and more (Chapter 2), it is not obvious that breach of contract with a firm in an immobile industry is the best way to achieve any of these various goals.

These arguments aside, breach of contract can sometimes be in response to sector-specific motivations. In such cases, industry would be a focal point for investors' perceived contract risks. Can an "industry shield theory" thus explain variation in sector-wide breach? For "co-industrial" firms to benefit from a shared shield, they would have to react in ways costly to the host government following a breach in the sector. Costly reactions could take two forms: the differential drawdown of capital by firms in the same industry and co-industrial protest against breach. If an industry as a whole is a target of breach, however, the government has effectively decided that the drawdown of FDI within that industry is a goal rather than a cost. Thus, a "shield of industry" would have to be born of common protest that could impose enough costs on a host government to make it change its behavior. Put bluntly, it is unlikely that protest by exactly the population of firms the government is targeting would make the government change its mind.

In fact, the nationality shield theory implies that responses to breach will still operate along co-national cleavages even when cross-national action seems more logical. By implication, we should see co-national protest even when a whole sector is targeted. Why? Co-national firms enjoy diplomats and nationality-tied investor organizations that can be willing and able to align against contract breach. As one example of co-nationality trumping co-industry, a Western European manufacturer in Ukraine drew on embassy support as well as groups of co-national foreign firms to stop legislation that would discriminate against its international trademarks. While the legislation was industry-specific, diplomats and co-national organizations advocated against the legislation, fearing for the integrity of their nationals' marketing campaigns in Ukraine more generally. The CEO of the targeted firm complained that industry-based lobbying (by firms of

---

[92] Industry organizations would be more likely to spend their political capital on common issues, like lobbying over industry-wide tax rates and regulatory obligations.

[93] Of course, co-national firms might also be co-industrial firms. It is an empirical question as to whether such firms are willing to coalesce in support of their compatriot. The analyses in this book provide evidence to establish that nationalities do not have a one-to-one correspondence with industries in host countries.

various nationalities) was, in contrast, weak and ineffective.[94] As we will see again in Chapters 5 and 6, industry need not provide the resources that nationality can.

Industry can provide a focal point for investors, but it does not come along with the ex ante expectation that co-industrial actors will pull down investment and engage in protest in ways that are costly for a host government. FDI industries (or their diversity) are not a sufficient determinant of the space governments have to break contracts. By controlling for possible industry effects throughout the empirical sections of the book, I find that nationality is a crucial – though heretofore overlooked – factor.

SHIELD OF NATIONALITY

Many studies of contracting relationships explain variation in compliance under "renegotiation-proof" contracts, effectively defining away the conflicts addressed here. Indeed, from this point of view, government breach of contract with foreign firms is off-equilibrium path behavior. Work that explains off-equilibrium behavior has on the whole been applied to contracts between private actors.[95] However, the concept of private–public contracts between foreign and domestic actors raises a unique issue: one party to the contract has the sovereign ability to act outside of a contract and above the rule of law, whatever the contracted terms. Put differently, states have the ability to breach even the elusive "perfect" contract with a foreign firm in a way that private actors contracting under commercial law do not.[96] This book can be seen as advancing understanding of the behavior of sovereigns in contracting with private parties. When are governments constrained to honor contracts that are not renegotiation-proof, and when should we expect off-equilibrium behavior in investor–host government relations?[97] To answer these questions, this book looks at the effects of third-party pressure – from other firms, investor organizations, and diplomats – on a government's respect for any given contract.

Under economic globalization, the expectation has been that third-party foreign firms in large part generate informal property rights enforcement, because FDI diversion follows from contract breach. Consistent with this claim, co-national actors can and do exert power over a host government that considers breaking a contract with a given foreign firm. But third parties of other national origins are unlikely to act in ways costly to a host government following breach with a non-co-national. By starting from the behavior of firms and

---

[94] Interview, Ukraine, 2011.
[95] Williamson 1979, Ahlquist and Prakash 2009. For an example at the inter-state level, see Pelc (2010) for an explanation of why efficient breach is underprovided at the WTO.
[96] Economics scholars have modeled the conditions under which breach of private contracts is efficient. E.g., Simpson and Wickelgren 2007, Stremitzer 2010.
[97] For models of contracts that allow for equilibria in which expropriation occurs with a positive but stochastic probability, see Eaton and Gersovitz 1984, Cole and English 1991.

aggregating to the level of the economy as a whole, we see that the informal enforcement of FDI contracts with host governments relies disproportionately on co-national action. Even firms of the same industry need not band together to impose costs on host governments following breach of contract with co-industrial firms.

Foreign firms of the same national origins share risks and resources that make their response to co-national breach punitive, particularly so when FDI national diversity is low and their actions have a greater influence on the host government's access to capital. Indeed, when an increasingly diverse set of foreign firms is present in a host country, the government gains more permissive space to breach contracts with one national group without threatening the contract sanctity of other groups. Put plainly, the greater the national diversity in a host country's population of foreign firms, the higher the likelihood of government breach of contract.

Taking exposure to more bilateral FDI relationships as an indicator of economic integration, the nationality shield theory challenges the conventional wisdom that the development of private property rights protections moves together with economic globalization. Far from having faded from relevance in a world of economic globalization, bilateral relations play a major role in shaping foreign firm and diplomatic interests in responding to breach.

In fact, as the world continues to integrate economically, the signaling power of nationality when it comes to contract sanctity should continue to increase. Foreign direct investors use information to maximize expected returns, but they are constrained by the costs of collecting and acting on information.[98] With more investment opportunities comes more information, and market participants have no choice but to economize more on information processing.[99] Already, firms have a plethora of incentives to look toward the status of co-nationals' contracts to understand their own contract sanctity. As more and more opportunities open up in emerging economies, economizing on information will only reinforce these incentives to look to co-nationals. Today and in the future, national diversity can be a liability to firms and an opportunity for host governments to exercise autonomy even in a globalized world.

[98] Mosley 2000, 2003.
[99] Calvo and Mendoza 2000.

4

Explaining Breach Around the World: Quantitative Tests

Is there a systematic relationship between foreign investor nationality and government breach of contract around the world? This chapter uses country- and firm-level data to conduct quantitative tests of the effect of FDI national diversity on the likelihood of breach of contract. I also use dyadic data to test a key mechanism underlying this relationship: breach with a firm of a given nationality is expected to affect co-national firms' investment behavior but not other firms' investment behavior. This chapter proceeds in four parts. First, I develop a novel measure of FDI national diversity and explore its variation across countries and over time. I also address the measure's relationship to FDI diversity by industry, a type of firm heterogeneity more traditionally addressed in the political economy literature.

Second, I use this new measure to test the hypothesis that higher FDI national diversity increases the likelihood of government breach of contract in the economy as a whole. To get at breach of contract, I rely on investors' perceived contract risks as well as the incidence and type of public international investment arbitrations (IAs), which are lawsuits brought by foreign firms against host governments. I also distinguish between the types of events that cause public IAs, generating insights about the relationship between government motivations for breach and FDI national diversity. Results are consistent across multiple approaches: a greater diversity of firms' national origins is associated with more expected and actual broken contracts.

Third, I analyze firms' responses to World Bank Enterprise Surveys to demonstrate that foreign firms report more breach of contract in countries with high FDI national diversity. In particular, foreign firms report more breach of contract as measured by an egregious form of breach: government non-payment. This evidence at the level of the firm supports the previous findings at the level of the economy. Firms themselves report different outcomes in environments in which a diversity of foreign investment provides alternative sources of capital to capital-seeking governments.

Fourth, I test directly the effect of one firm's broken contract on other firms' investment decisions. Breach of contract with a firm's co-national is expected to generate a focal point and signal for co-nationals that their risks of breach have increased, which should result in differential FDI drawdown. Using dyadic FDI flows from OECD countries to emerging economies, I show that this differential drawdown takes place: flows decrease following a co-national firm's broken contract, while other broken contracts have no significant effect on bilateral flows. I operationalize breach as the incidence of public IAs. These public lawsuits make instances of government breach of contract more visible to investors of all nationalities than ever before (Chapters 2, 7). If co-national firms are the ones that respond negatively to a given public IA, we have more evidence that nationality shapes investors' risk expectations and, accordingly, their investment behavior.

From the host government's point of view, the results in this chapter provide strong evidence that governments have more permissive space to breach contracts when FDI nationalities are especially diverse. One reason is that firms are more likely to predicate their investment decisions on co-national firms' broken contracts. Investor nationality is a key correlate of capital flight in response to adverse government behavior.

FDI NATIONAL DIVERSITY

To calculate *FDI national diversity*, I use a Herfindahl-Hirschman Index (HHI), originally an indicator of industrial fragmentation. For ease of interpretation, I use an inverse HHI:

$$Inverse\ HHI_{it} = 1/(s_{1t}^2 + s_{2t}^2 + s_{3t}^2 + \ldots + s_{nt}^2),\ j=1,\ldots,n \qquad (1)$$

where s_{jt} is nationality j's share of the annual FDI stock in country i in year t. In this formulation, each OECD nationality's FDI representation is the share of its FDI stock out of the total FDI stock reported by OECD countries in a given country-year.[1] In other words, the measure takes into account both the number of national investor groups present in the host country and the distribution of FDI stock across national groups.

Data for 1990 to 2011 is available for up to thirty-two OECD countries' investment shares in host countries. Values on FDI national diversity can be interpreted as the effective number of OECD nationalities represented in the host country, with high values implying that FDI is more evenly spread over more national groups. The variable ranges from a value of 1 to 11.1 (Turkey in 2010, Netherlands in 2005), with a mean of 2.4 effective nationalities per country-year. Figures 4.1 through 4.5 report average levels of FDI national diversity in recipient countries, by region. Countries that we might expect to have diverse foreign investors indeed rank high on the measure: South Africa, Brazil, Egypt,

---

[1] Other FDI stock is excluded from the denominator.

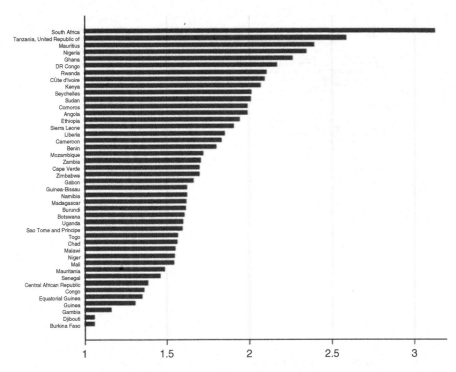

FIGURE 4.1 **FDI National Diversity, African Countries (Average 1990–2011)** *FDI National Diversity* is an inverse Herfindahl-Hirschman Index using FDI stock data. It measures the effective number of OECD investor nationalities present in the host economy.
Source: OECD FDI positions. Author's calculations.

Turkey, and India have the greatest average effective OECD nationalities present over this time period. In general, emerging European countries have relatively high averages (Figure 4.4). This is consistent with gravity model expectations that the many European OECD countries would look to invest in their "backyard." Indeed, the distance between a host country's most populated city and London is correlated -0.42 with FDI national diversity.[2]

Emerging Asia also includes several countries with high averages, like Singapore, South Korea, and Hong Kong (Figure 4.5). With these values in mind, we might expect FDI national diversity to be generally correlated with the national income of host countries. Indeed, FDI national diversity is correlated 0.40 with (logged) GDP per capita, which is somewhat high but far from a perfect relationship.

---

[2] Distance data from Mayer and Zignago (2011). Unfortunately, as distance does not vary over time, geography gives little leverage to test what are primarily over-time predictions generated by the nationality shield theory.

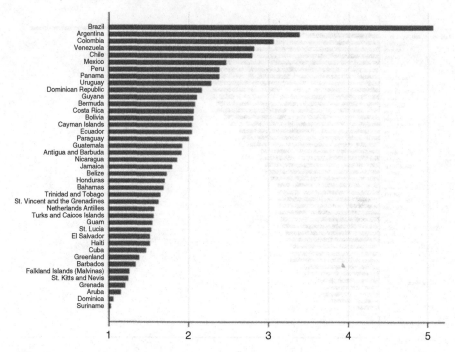

FIGURE 4.2 FDI National Diversity, South and Central American Countries (Average 1990–2011)
Source: See Figure 4.1.

Figure 4.6 focuses on average FDI national diversity in OECD advanced industrial countries for comparison to emerging economies. While not the focus of the book, these countries are included in analyses where possible. We see that rich and globally integrated economies like that of the United States, Germany, and the Netherlands rank as the most diverse in this group, and their averages of well over five effective OECD nationalities are generally above those in emerging economies, although there are numerous exceptions.

Data Issues

In the OECD data used here, FDI country of origin is based on the residence of an economic entity, as reported by OECD country national statistical offices. This means that firms are generally tied to what is understood to be their home country rather than sites of mere legal incorporation.[3] Even if some amount of

[3] "The residence of an economic entity is determined on the basis of the economic territory with which it has the strongest connection determined by its predominant center of economic interest." Glossary of Foreign Direct Investment Terms and Definitions, *OECD Benchmark Definition of*

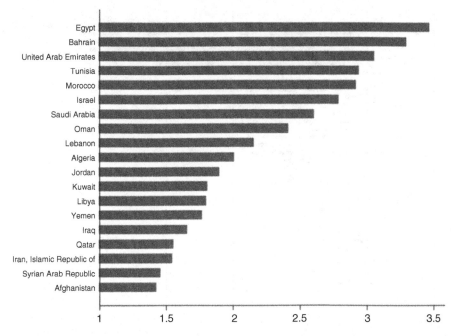

FIGURE 4.3   FDI National Diversity, Middle East and North African Countries (Average 1990–2011)
Source: See Figure 4.1.

FDI is attributed to what one might consider "intermediate home" countries or tax havens, the nationality shield theory remains relevant. Firms share interests in the contract sanctity of co-national firms, even when those nationalities are more legally derived than, say, ethnically derived. For example, the set of investors using an intermediate home country must deal with the negative publicity such a decision can generate; those investors also share access to resources like an intermediate home–host Bilateral Investment Treaty (BIT). Far from being "meta-national," such firms are made vulnerable to risks associated with more than one bilateral relationship, and they can call on diplomatic and co-national resources from more than one home country. This logic applies not only to firms with nationalities that might carry nefarious connotations but also to those multinationals with multiple countries of national origin as a result of mergers and acquisitions and the growth of international subsidiaries (Chapter 3).

"Round-tripped" firms are a particular subset of firms with two nationalities. Round-tripping occurs when host-country citizens incorporate firms outside of the host country and then reinvest funds back to the host country. By gaining

Foreign Direct Investment (Fourth Edition). Statistical units are assumed to have the same ability to identify "true" residence.

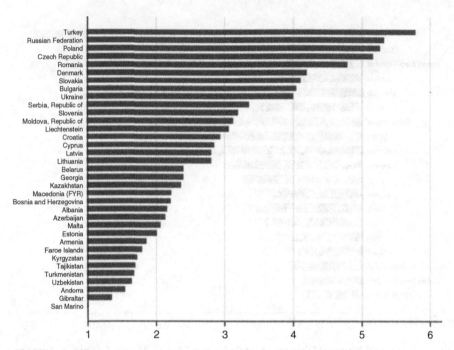

FIGURE 4.4 FDI National Diversity, Emerging European Countries (Average 1990–2011)
Source: See Figure 4.1.

foreign residency, round-tripped firms can access political risk management strategies otherwise restricted to foreign investors, such as the ability to sue governments under BITs.[4] Round-tripping thus makes them a kind of foreign firm and rightly included in data on FDI for our purposes. An ideal measure would account for the "national group" of foreign/domestic hybrids but, unfortunately, dedicated scholars are unable to provide good cross-national estimates of round-tripping, especially as the phenomenon overlaps with FDI coming from diaspora investors.[5] Regardless, by attributing firms with multiple homes to only one country's FDI, I underestimate the true spread of FDI across national groups. Moreover, if intermediate home co-national ties are either weak or non-existent, using this OECD data is more challenging for the theory: attributing FDI to intermediate countries would insert nationalities into the mix that do not have the interests or resources to behave as predicted. Thus, the data limitations exert a downward bias on the hypothesized positive effect of FDI national diversity on breach.

[4] Whether a round-tripped firm is "foreign enough" is often a point of contention in public IAs; the record is mixed on the ability of round-tripped firms to pass jurisdiction hurdles in their public IAs under BITs (See Chapter 5).
[5] On diaspora investors, see Leblang (2010) and Graham (2014).

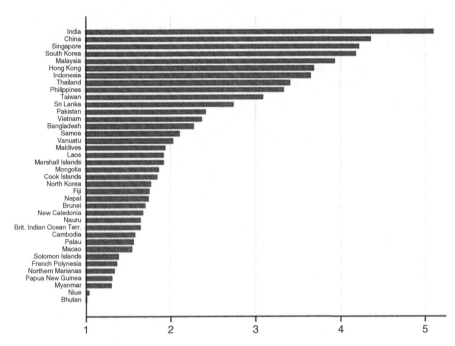

FIGURE 4.5 **FDI National Diversity, Emerging Asian Countries (Average 1990–2011)**
Source: See Figure 4.1.

Another concern is that OECD data does not capture the growing segment of South–South FDI in the world. In 2011, outward FDI from developing and transition economies amounted to 27 percent of world outward FDI flows (US$257 billion), up from 11 percent in 2001 (US$86 billion).[6] The worldwide trend is toward more FDI coming from more home countries from around the world (Chapter 7). Nonetheless, omitting FDI originating from other, non-OECD home countries in the measure again leads me to underestimate FDI national diversity.[7] This is true based on the plausible assumption that a small number of South investors do not account for such a large proportion of host-country FDI stock as to overwhelm the distribution of OECD investors. Some empirical confirmation of this notion is available. The correlation between this chapter's OECD-based measure and a world-based measure of FDI national diversity, available for 2009, is positive and large at 0.64.[8]

---

[6] Profit repatriation and intra-firm trade by multinational corporation subsidiaries from developed countries account for some of these outflows.

[7] The denominator of the HHI excludes non-OECD-origin FDI stock.

[8] This measure is calculated with data from the IMF "Coordinated Direct Investment Survey" on FDI country of origin for all countries in the world, which began in 2009.

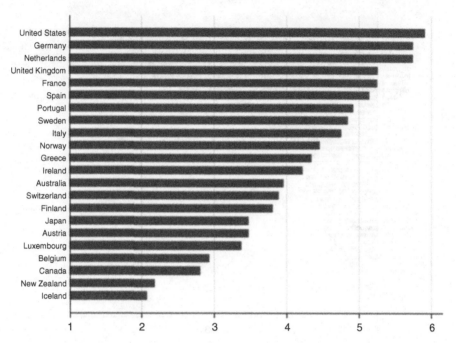

FIGURE 4.6 FDI National Diversity, Advanced Industrial Countries (Average 1990–2011)
Source: See Figure 4.1.

The OECD collects both home countries' reporting of FDI outward stock
and host countries' reporting of FDI inward stock. While these data should in
theory be identical, in practice differences in reporting standards can make
them vary. I choose to use data on FDI inward stock based on host-country
reporting, as this is the data source that best represents what a government
understands to be the levels of FDI that it hosts.[9] In constructing the FDI
national diversity measure, negative FDI stock is changed to zero, because
this is the appropriate lower bound for measuring the presence of a national
investor group in an economy.

One shortcoming of the OECD data is the presence of missing values. The
problem is that it is unknown whether a missing value indicates no stock in a
given home-host-year or the presence of unreported negative or positive
stock.[10] This issue has sometimes been addressed inappropriately in the literature: replacing the missing values with zeroes is inaccurate given uncertainty

---

[9] Fuentes and Saravia (2010) make this choice as well.
[10] Because FDI stock can be negative, zero, or positive, the problem is one of missing rather than
truncated data.

over their meaning, whether that replacement is done in the entire dataset or only in particular country pairs. Thus, in these analyses I follow Fuentes and Saravia in leaving values as missing.[11]

FDI National Diversity and Industry

Is FDI national diversity measuring what it is intended to measure? One might wonder whether FDI national diversity is really capturing nationality or rather some other aspect of FDI that might correlate with nationality. It may be that countries with particular industries, like natural resources, are more likely to have particular levels of FDI national diversity. In the analyses throughout the book, I control for this concern by including appropriate covariates as well as using case studies from the same industry in which breach outcomes vary.

A second concern is that FDI national diversity may be picking up FDI industry diversity. Qualitative evidence in Chapters 5 and 6 provides confidence that firms from, say, the United States or France do not flock to only one industry in the host countries under consideration; industry and nationality are not interchangeable. Cross-national quantitative evidence would provide a useful confirmation that industry diversity exists alongside nationality diversity in countries' FDI. Unfortunately, robust and reliable data on FDI by nationality and industry is not available.[12] I get at the issue using data from Eurostat, which reports FDI by European country-industry, although with limited destination country coverage. I generate FDI industry diversity using the same inverse Herfindahl-Hirschman approach described above. In this case, up to six industries from one nationality are included in the measure: agriculture, oil and gas, manufacturing, mining, real estate, and services. I calculate FDI industry diversity for up to twenty-four home countries investing into up to thirty-nine host countries, for each year from 2000 to 2009.[13] The correlation between FDI industry diversity and FDI national diversity is very low (0.04). Thus, this data on European country-industry-year investments provides some cross-national confidence that there is not a one-to-one correlation between industry and nationality of investor.

Figure 4.7 reports average FDI industry diversity, with industry diversity in host countries worldwide, offshore financial centers, and the OECD included for reference. All available host countries report average FDI industry

---

[11] Fuentes and Saravia 2010.

[12] The United States reports this data for a small number of emerging economies, as do Japan and the United Kingdom. However, time periods and reported host countries are (as yet) inconsistent, limiting the ability to perform statistical analyses.

[13] Unfortunately, missing data is a problem: out of 9,360 potential observations, only 3,047 are available.

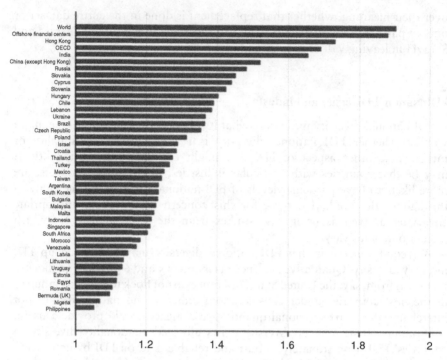

FIGURE 4.7 **FDI Industry Diversity, Available Countries (Average 2000–2009)** *FDI Industry Diversity* is an inverse Herfindahl-Hirschman Index using FDI stock data for six industry categories. It measures the effective number of industries in which firms from twenty-four available advanced industrialized home countries invest. For example, firms from the twenty-four available home countries invest in an average of 1.9 industries around the world.
Sources: Eurostat. Author's calculations.

diversity greater than 1. In fact, resource-rich countries like Russia and countries known for finance (services) like Hong Kong are among the most diverse, with Hong Kong surpassing the OECD average. What is more, offshore financial centers receive FDI from a diversity of industries. This helps to address the concern that FDI channeled through tax havens comes predominately from one industry.

Do massive foreign projects distort FDI national diversity, making it only another way of looking at the saturation of FDI stock in a host economy? Figure 4.8 plots country-year observations for FDI national diversity against FDI stock per GDP. There is a clear lack of a relationship between FDI national diversity and the saturation of FDI stock in the host economy. We can thus have confidence that FDI national diversity is not merely capturing relative quantities of foreign investment.

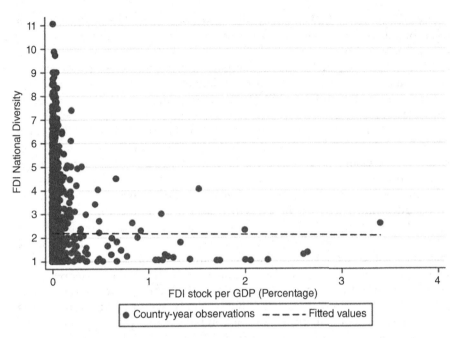

FIGURE 4.8 **FDI National Diversity and FDI Stock per GDP** This figure excludes advanced industrial countries. It also excludes outliers over 4 percent of FDI stock per GDP, which further obscure any relationship.
Source: OECD, World Bank World Development Indicators.

Change in FDI National Diversity

FDI national diversity varies over time as FDI from different national groups enters or exits the economy, for any of the many reasons that foreign firms choose to invest where they do. Rich literatures in political science, business, and economics have explored the correlates of FDI, including regime type, policy stability, membership in international organizations, and partisanship;[14] management strategies, risk tolerance, business networks abroad, and intra-firm considerations;[15] macroeconomic health, market size, resource endowment, and geographic distance. Those nationalities with firms in booming industries are likely to grow to represent bigger shares of a host country's FDI. Nationalities with firms that can exploit a host country's natural resources are also likely to grow their share of total FDI, as are nationalities with more market-seeking firms.[16] Further, no one investor has total leverage over the current and

---

[14] E.g., Jensen 2003, 2006; Li and Resnick 2003, Henisz 2002, Busse and Hefeker 2007, Büthe and Milner 2008, Pinto and Pinto 2008, Pinto 2013.
[15] E.g., Dunning 1980.
[16] Katzenstein 1985.

future distribution of FDI across national investor groups. The entry or exit of a large foreign firm may influence FDI national diversity, but its decision need not be representative of the investment decisions made by firms from other home countries. In short, FDI national diversity can change considerably with a change in circumstances unrelated to nationality per se. This is because one cannot reasonably expect the kinds of firms responding to the many different correlates of FDI to be evenly distributed across national groups.

On the whole, economies operating in an era of liberalized capital flows host whatever FDI national diversity emerges as a result of the many causes of FDI. Levels of and change in FDI national diversity are thus to some extent exogenous of the actions of host governments. That said, a host government does have some levers over the trajectory of its FDI national diversity. For example, a host government can use investment measures to stop certain investments "pre-establishment," or before the investment has been made. Most BITs allow a host government some latitude to discriminate against foreign firms before they enter the country.[17] Governments around the world, including those in OECD countries, readily exercise such measures in particular industries, such as defense or infrastructure. The exercise of investment measures against particular nationalities is less clear but certainly also present: even Canada has been accused of denying a US$6 billion bid for a natural gas firm because the bidder was the Malaysian state energy firm.[18] In times of conflict, a host government may impose economic sanctions on investors of certain nationalities. On the other hand, host governments sometimes try to spur the entry of foreign firms from particular national origins. Pandya argues that democratization trends around the world since the 1970s caused a "dramatic reversal" from what were once FDI restrictions into, now, FDI enticements.[19] Today, nearly every country in the world has an Investment Promotion Agency (IPA), which often targets investment from particular home countries. However, the record of success in nationality-targeting efforts around the world has been spotty at best.[20]

For an impression of general trends in FDI national diversity, Figure 4.9 plots average diversity against accumulated FDI stock, from 1990 to 2011. Average FDI stock in developing and transition economies took off in the mid-2000s, with a significant drop due to the Great Recession but something of a rebound already in 2011. Average FDI national diversity, too, has climbed over this period but not as dramatically as average FDI stock. We see some dips in FDI

---

[17] In the 1990s, the United States pushed for the inclusion of "pre-establishment" prohibitions in its model BIT. Pre-establishment measures include restrictions on the types of assets that can be acquired by foreigners; conditions on the structure of ownership; and environmental, employment, input, or export requirements (UNCTAD 1996 World Investment Report).

[18] "Door wide shut," *The Economist*, 27 October–2 November 2012: 40.

[19] Pandya 2014.

[20] Interview, European Union consultant for IPAs, 2009.

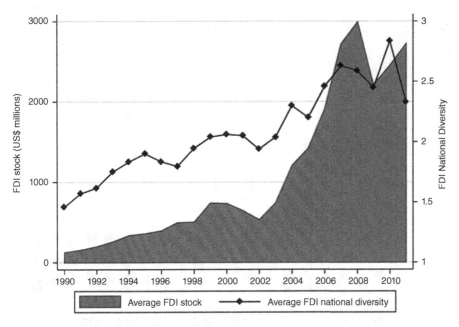

FIGURE 4.9 **FDI National Diversity and FDI Stock in Emerging Economies (Average 1990–2011)** FDI stock and FDI national diversity have generally been increasing in the developing world, although their trajectories are not highly correlated.
Sources: OECD FDI positions abroad. Author's calculations. World Bank World Development Indicators.

national diversity around 1997, 2002, 2008, and 2011, which roughly correspond to major crisis events in emerging as well as developed markets. Figure 4.10 presents FDI national diversity differently. The bars show average levels across emerging economies, the interquartile range is marked in gray, and labeled points fall outside two standard deviations of the mean. Country-years have clustered relatively consistently in the range of 1 to 3 effective OECD nationalities in this 21-year period, although the spreads of country-year values of FDI national diversity have increased.

One possible concern for the theory would be that the nationality diversity of the investor community had a direct influence on a foreign firm's decision to invest. Put differently, do FDI inflows today respond to previous levels of FDI national diversity? If investors did respond to previous diversity, then a more nationally diverse investor community would deter new entry and reinvestment: firms would be wary of entering an environment that would enable the government to break contracts. However, this logic in fact generates a prediction opposite to that made by the nationality shield theory. If foreign firms were indeed deterred from entering countries with highly nationally diverse investor communities, the result would be that national investor groups would exit or

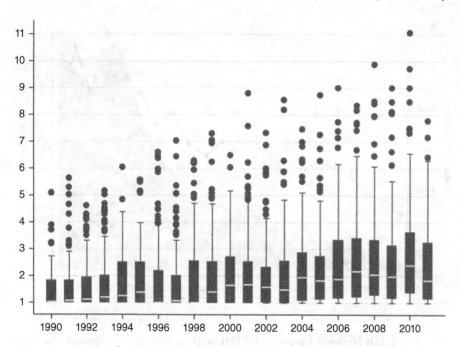

FIGURE 4.10 **Trends, FDI National Diversity in Emerging Economies (1990–2011)**
Mean FDI national diversity in the developing world has risen only moderately since
1990.
Sources: OECD FDI positions abroad. Author's calculations.

shrink. Thus, FDI national diversity would decrease as remaining groups
became more concentrated (or, in the case of equal exit across all national
investor groups, FDI national diversity would remain constant). The implication
would be that higher expectations of contract risks would be associated with a
lower (or constant) FDI national diversity – exactly opposite of the hypothesis
offered here.

Moreover, what we know about how firms make investment decisions suggests that it is implausible that the diversity of firm nationalities in a host country
per se plays a role in FDI entry. First, it is true that, according to nationality
shield theory, firms would be better off predicating their original and ongoing
investment decisions on today's FDI national diversity and on the trajectory of
that mix.[21] However, firms do not reasonably have the capacity to estimate
future trends in FDI national diversity. Accurate predictions would require
iterated estimates of all current and entering firms' investment decisions, aggregated by national group, and then combined into an economy-wide measure. In

---

[21] They would also be better off investing in locations where the possibility of co-national collective
action around contract breach is high (Chapter 8).

the absence of such a comprehensive, forward-looking measure at the time of investment, firms have incentives to pay attention to the dynamics of their nationality's relative position among the host country's FDI and how attitudes toward their nationality might be changing – to concentrate on the status of their shield. The qualitative case studies provide evidence of this behavior: Russian firms pay attention to their status in Ukraine as their relative power ebbs and flows (Chapter 5), and US actors give in to contract breach when they perceive that the Romanian government has more outside options for FDI (Chapter 6).

Further, foreign firms are profit seeking, and investment diversion due to potential contract risks can have prohibitively high opportunity costs. Firms invest abroad because they seek things like new markets, new and more competitive inputs, and new access to resources. Empirically, we see that such drivers of investment lead at least some foreign firms to enter and reinvest in risky countries around the world. Indeed, foreign firms have developed a range of risk mitigation tools to employ at the time of investment, ranging from political risk insurance to bodyguards. Firms can pick different modes of entry as another means of managing risk, choosing for example to engage in joint ventures with domestic or foreign firms as opposed to investing alone.[22] Firms use such tools to compensate for expected risks to contract sanctity, until the tipping point at which the costs of such strategies are not offset by the perceived success of an investment.[23] Thus, foreign firms do find ways to enter risky emerging economies. The issue at stake in this book is how firms adjust when contract risks are realized.

MONADIC TESTS: MORE DIVERSITY, MORE BREACH

In the first set of empirical tests of the nationality shield theory, I explore whether higher levels of FDI national diversity are associated with an increased likelihood of government breach of contract somewhere in the economy as a whole.[24] An appropriate dependent variable must be derived from the risks facing any foreign firm and not just foreign firms of a particular nationality. However, an aggregate annual measure of government breach of contract in each country in the world is difficult to come by. One must acknowledge that only selected contract breaches are elevated beyond interested investors' knowledge to the public record, and that selection mechanism is rather opaque. Chapters 5 and 6 use in-depth qualitative work to get at the incidence and absence of breach in three countries over time, the details of which rely in large part on interviews

---

[22] Henisz 2002.

[23] Investor contract risk-management strategies can create moral hazard for host governments if investors' precautions mitigate the direct loss of capital that might otherwise follow breach. However, the constraints of globalization are predicated on the actions of not the targeted firm, but of other firms. It is variation in the behavior of firms other than that with the broken contract that underlies the nationality shield theory.

[24] Wellhausen (2015) provides similar evidence using a more limited panel data set.

with local actors. As a result of the difficulty in assembling comprehensive quantitative data on contract breach, I use investor expectations of contract risks as well as multiple measures of the number and types of public IAs foreign firms have filed against host governments as proxies. While each proxy has its own limitations, in total they provide strong evidence to demonstrate that FDI national diversity has the predicted positive relationship with a host government's space to break contracts.

Investor Expectations of Breach

Aggregate investor expectations are an appropriate substitute for a well-formed direct measure of breach, as expectations are plausibly grounded in experience with or knowledge about the incidence of contract breach. I generate this dependent variable from the Political Risk Services International Country Risk Guide (ICRG), a set of indices used by both private and institutional clients to measure "potential risks to international business operations."[25] The ICRG data are based on expert analysis of the overall foreign investment environment (without regard to nationality) and informed by investor surveys. These data are a public analog to the kinds of indices produced by private firms in the political risk consulting industry and in-house political risk groups in some of the world's largest multinational corporations. The data are also commonly used as explanatory and dependent variables in the scholarly literature.[26] One useful aspect of these data is that they cover advanced and emerging economies. Thus, in this section I am able to test the nationality shield theory on a sample that includes countries in which breach is ex ante unlikely and FDI national diversity is likely high – stacking the deck against the hypothesized relationship between diversity and breach. All variables are transformed so that higher values indicate more risks.

The first dependent variable, *Risks to investments*, includes expectations about risks to contract viability, profit repatriation, and timely payments. Each of these factors is a core component of what this book identifies as a government breach of contract. Importantly, the variable is defined in such a way as to capture government breach in particular, as opposed to problems in the commercial sphere or in the domestic enforcement of commercial law. The second dependent variable I consider is *Corruption* with relevance to FDI, which includes investor expectations about the willingness of government actors to carry out financial breach including demands for excess payments, exchange controls, and similar. It also includes expectations that host-country actors use political power to deal unfairly with foreign investors through

---

[25] "A Business Guide to Political Risk for International Decisions: Part II. International Country Risk Guide," *Political Risk Services*, 27.

[26] For example, Allee and Peinhardt 2011, Jakobsen and de Soysa 2006, Li and Resnick 2003.

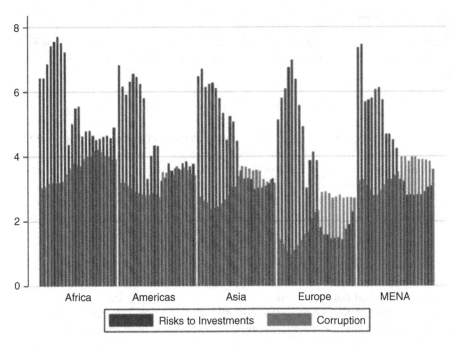

FIGURE 4.11 Components of *Contract Risks* by World Region (1990–2011)
Source: International Country Risk Guide (ICRG) Risk Ratings, Political Risk
Services.

actions like nepotism and job reservations. Figure 11 plots these variables by
region over time. *Risks to investments* were generally higher in the early 1990s
in each region and decreasing over time, with the exception of Sub-Saharan
Africa. *Corruption*, in contrast, was on average increasing over this period.[27]

The nationality shield theory posits a relationship between FDI national
diversity and government breach of contract, which may or may not be undertaken in the context of corruption. Thus, neither of these dependent variables
alone captures the broader concept of government breach of contract. Following
Humphreys and Bates, I sum *Risks to investments* and *Corruption* to capture a
government's "tendency to adopt distributive policies and to make opportunistic
use of public power."[28] From a firm's point of view, government opportunism is
a useful way to think about a government's propensity to breach contracts. I call
this summed variable *Contract risks*.

---

[27] The correlation between these two measures is 0.18.
[28] Humphreys and Bates 2005, 412.

Modeling Strategy

The basic multivariate regression framework used to estimate the effects of FDI national diversity on different measures of breach of contract is specified in Equation (1).

$$DV_{it} = \beta_0 + \beta_1(FDI\ national\ diversity)_{i,t-1} + \beta_2 X_{i,t-1} + \gamma + \tau_t + \varepsilon_{it} \qquad (1)$$

The coefficient of interest is β_1, which measures the effect of country i's *FDI national diversity* in period $t-1$ on breach of contract in period t. Following the nationality shield theory, β_1 is hypothesized to be positive. $X_{i,t-1}$ contains a set of lagged time-varying controls. The next two terms are region dummies and year dummies. Standard errors are robust and clustered by country. The panel covers 1990 to 2011. All independent variables are lagged one year. Because each dependent variable is an index with top- and bottom-censored values, I employ Tobit estimators.

All models include *BITs, running total* and *FDI stock (logged)* to approximate the quantity of contracts the host government has made with foreign firms.[29] The ideal control for the effect of the obsolescing bargain logic on a government's propensity to breach would account for the FDI position in immobile industries by country-year. In the absence of robust international data, I use *Natural resource rents per GDP*, assuming that FDI in natural resources – as the most quintessential immobile industry – moves together with total rents.[30] *GDP per capita (logged)* captures development levels as well as variation in infrastructure investment, also prone to the obsolescing bargain.[31] *GDP growth* accounts for the argument that economic downturn may make the short-term domestic benefits of breach more attractive to host governments. It also accounts for the contrary argument that governments have incentives to act opportunistically when times are good and fairness in distribution becomes a more salient issue.[32] I capture variation in the political and institutional correlates of FDI using *Political constraints*. This index from Henisz accounts for arguments about the effects of institutions and policy stability on property rights violations and FDI.[33] To account for arguments that partisanship may affect the propensity of a government to break contracts, I control for *Chief executive orientation*.[34] I use three measures to control for whether external economic constraints might affect a government's willingness or ability to break contracts. First, participation in an *IMF program* may put the government under heightened international scrutiny, and, as we see in

---

[29] Data from UNCTAD, World Bank World Development Indicators.
[30] Data from World Trade Organization.
[31] Frieden 1994.
[32] Guriev et al. 2011.
[33] Henisz 2002. Results are robust to substituting democracy measures from Polity IV.
[34] Pinto and Pinto 2008, Pinto 2013. Data from World Bank Database of Political Institutions.

Chapter 5, countries have been required to stop certain contract breaches as terms of IMF commitments. On the other hand, an *IMF program* or a precipitating *Sovereign debt crisis* or *Currency crisis* may encourage a government to break contracts simply as a means of raising revenue (or avoiding outlays), much like Argentina argues it was forced to do in 2001 and 2002 (Chapter 1). See Appendix Tables A4.2 for countries included in the sample, A4.3 for summary statistics, and A4.4 for the correlation matrix.[35]

Results

Table 4.1 reports results. In Model (1), we see that FDI national diversity has a positive and significant relationship with risks to investments. In Model (2), FDI national diversity has a positive but insignificant relationship with FDI-related corruption. When including both measures and more precisely capturing the

TABLE 4.1 *FDI National Diversity and Contract Risk Measures (1990–2011)*

	Model (1)	Model (2)	Model (3)
Dependent variable	Risks to Investments	Corruption	Contract Risks
Scale	0 to 12	0 to 6	0 to 18
FDI national diversity	0.092**	0.002	0.098**
	(0.039)	(0.024)	(0.046)
BITs, running total	−0.019***	0.003	−0.013*
	(0.007)	(0.004)	(0.008)
FDI stock (logged)	0.028	0.012	0.040
	(0.046)	(0.037)	(0.046)
Natural resource rents per GDP	0.014***	0.005*	0.019***
	(0.005)	(0.003)	(0.005)
GDP per capita (logged)	−0.667***	−0.617***	−1.237***
	(0.158)	(0.104)	(0.166)
GDP growth	−0.028	0.011	−0.021
	(0.018)	(0.010)	(0.023)
Political constraints	−0.288	−0.109	−0.353
	(0.465)	(0.400)	(0.582)
Chief executive orientation: Right^	0.171	−0.127	0.025
	(0.287)	(0.251)	(0.397)
Chief executive orientation: Left	0.089	−0.454**	−0.328
	(0.299)	(0.226)	(0.392)
IMF program	0.642**	0.098	0.688**
	(0.263)	(0.202)	(0.311)

(continued)

---

[35] The inter-item correlations are not high enough to generate concern.

TABLE 4.1 (*continued*)

	Model (1)	Model (2)	Model (3)
Dependent variable	Risks to Investments	Corruption	Contract Risks
Scale	0 to 12	0 to 6	0 to 18
Sovereign debt crisis	0.733	−0.416*	0.374
	(0.729)	(0.215)	(0.830)
Currency crisis	−0.038	0.019	0.004
	(0.175)	(0.116)	(0.218)
Capital account openness	−0.043	−0.095*	−0.110
	(0.072)	(0.051)	(0.082)
Region dummies	Yes	Yes	Yes
Year dummies	Yes	Yes	Yes
Constant	8.677***	9.136***	17.251***
	(1.372)	(0.940)	(1.603)
Observations	1403	1403	1403
Number of countries	97	97	97
Pseudo R^2	0.25	0.26	0.23

Tobit regression (range as specified) with all independent variables lagged one year.
^Excluded category: Chief executive orientation: Center
Robust S.E.s clustered by country, *** $p < 0.01$, ** $p < 0.05$, *$p < 0.1$

concept of government breach of contract in Model (3), the effect of FDI national diversity is positive and significant. Increasing FDI national diversity from the 25th to the 75th percentile (or an increase of 2.8 effective OECD nationalities) results in an increase of 0.27 on the contract risks index.[36]

Results on other covariates are generally signed as expected. Investors are more likely to expect higher risks in countries with more natural resource rents, although GDP per capita is negatively associated with contract risks. In Models (1) and (3), BITs are significantly associated with lower expected contract risks. Interestingly, IMF programs are associated with more contract risks, suggesting that IMF participation signals more potential problems than solutions for direct investors. In Model (2), investors are less likely to report high levels of FDI-related corruption in countries with left-oriented governments, countries that have experienced a sovereign debt crisis, and more open economies. That these variables are not significant in the other specifications reinforces the theoretical notion that FDI-related corruption is not itself a full measure of investors' perceived contract risks.

One concern with these analyses might be reverse causality: if FDI national diversity has a direct effect on investors' perceived contract risks, this could mean that investors incorporate FDI national diversity into their decisions,

[36] This change is equivalent to about 15 percent of one standard deviation of the *Contract Risks* index.

resulting in a reverse effect on perceived contract risks. This concern is implausible. Individual investors have little access to the information on the content and distribution of investment decisions necessary to make useful estimates of future FDI national diversity (Chapter 3). Investors' ability to update beliefs based on FDI national diversity expectations is thus constrained. Moreover, firms invest abroad for a variety of reasons, captured in quantitative analyses by the list of control variables necessary to explain FDI outcomes. Breach may not trump these other incentives for investment, especially when considering a range of breach including incremental takings. Indeed, some investors consider partial breaches the cost of access to politically risky environments.[37] Thus, it is not inconsistent to see investment alongside breach. Most importantly, a causal story in which FDI national diversity influences investor decision-making would in fact have the opposite effect to that found here. Foreign investors would be more likely to pull out of locations with high FDI national diversity, thus lowering the mix in places with a high likelihood of government breach of contract (unless all national groups exit at an equal rate, in which case the mix would remain constant). Consistent with these arguments, FDI national diversity does not have a significant effect on dyadic FDI flows (see Table 4.8).

Contract Risks and Types of BITs

The count of BITs in Table 4.1 helps to control for the population of contracts between the government and foreign firms. There is, however, interesting variation in the texts of BITs that might shape the effect of FDI national diversity on the likelihood of breach. If BITs are very restrictive, host governments likely intended the treaties to signal their strong commitment to foreign firms' property rights.[38] In an environment of high FDI national diversity, we might expect strong BITs to mitigate breach if they make governments more reluctant to breach than otherwise. On the other hand, governments might simply run afoul of their commitments in very restrictive BITs more often, whether inadvertently or on purpose, suggesting that strict BITs should be associated with more contract breach. By this logic, if high FDI national diversity is present, a positive association between strong BITs and breach could be augmented. It is thus an empirical question: do more restrictive BITs mitigate or augment the effects of FDI national diversity?

　　The texts of BITs are rather consistent but not identical, especially when it comes to national treatment provisions. National treatment provisions are based on the principle that a host government must "make no negative differentiation between foreign and national investors when enacting and applying its rules and regulations."[39] In a sample of 342 randomly chosen BITs, Blake

---

[37] E.g., Interviews (4), US and Western European executives at multinational subsidiaries in Russia and Azerbaijan, 2013. See also Chapters 5 and 6.

[38] Allee and Peinhart 2010.

[39] Dolzer and Schreuer 2012: 178, qtd in Blake 2013.

finds that about half have national treatment provisions (hereafter NT BITs).[40] However, a number of these treaties also have national treatment "carveouts," or categories that can be carved out of national treatment obligations such that the host government retains the policy space to treat foreign firms differently than domestic firms on those dimensions. Blake identifies carveouts in six areas – taxation, security and public order, public health, environment, economic sectors, and miscellaneous. Using his data on *BITs, NT BITs, and NT carveouts,* I test whether the characteristics of a BIT intermediate in the relationship between FDI national diversity and perceived contract risks.[41]

Table 4.2 reports estimations that take these potential conditional relationships into account. The dependent variable in each estimation is the index of *Contract risks* used in Model (3). We see in all Models that FDI national

TABLE 4.2 *FDI National Diversity, BITs, and Contract Risks^ (1990–2011)*

	Model (4)	Model (5)	Model (6)
FDI national diversity	0.195***	0.179*	0.129*
	(0.070)	(0.092)	(0.068)
BITs	0.007		
	(0.015)		
FDI national diversity * BITs	−0.004*		
	(0.002)		
NT BITs		0.215*	
		(0.115)	
FDI national diversity * NT BITs		−0.046*	
		(0.026)	
NT carveouts			0.126*
			(0.067)
FDI national diversity * NT carveouts			−0.029**
			(0.012)
FDI stock (logged)	0.015	0.004	0.018
	(0.048)	(0.048)	(0.048)
Natural resource rents per GDP	0.021***	0.026***	0.025***
	(0.005)	(0.005)	(0.005)
GDP per capita (logged)	−1.219***	−1.158***	−1.179***
	(0.169)	(0.172)	(0.172)

(continued)

[40] Blake 2013.
[41] In the sample of 342 BITs, the count of total BITs is correlated with FDI national diversity at 0.5. BITs with national treatment provisions (NT BITs) are correlated only at 0.4 and the count of BIT NT carveouts only at 0.2. Another measure of types of BITs is the presence of and strength of clauses allowing foreign firms to bring public international IAs at the World Bank's ICSID. Allee and Peinhardt 2010. ICSID clauses are correlated with FDI national diversity only at −0.07 and thus are of less interest in analyzing the robustness of results in Table 4.1. Including ICSID clauses as another marker of BIT diversity has no effects in regression analyses.

TABLE 4.2 (*continued*)

	Model (4)	Model (5)	Model (6)
GDP growth	−0.021	−0.035	−0.034
	(0.023)	(0.026)	(0.027)
Political constraints	−0.378	−0.094	−0.097
	(0.578)	(0.596)	(0.592)
Chief executive orientation: Right^^	0.049	−0.043	−0.099
	(0.392)	(0.387)	(0.389)
Chief executive orientation: Left	−0.333	−0.559	−0.589
	(0.386)	(0.376)	(0.382)
IMF program	0.645**	0.558*	0.538*
	(0.311)	(0.308)	(0.310)
Sovereign debt crisis	0.384	−0.069	−0.105
	(0.781)	(0.589)	(0.571)
Currency crisis	0.010	0.159	0.184
	(0.212)	(0.244)	(0.233)
Capital account openness	−0.114	−0.111	−0.115
	(0.082)	(0.089)	(0.094)
Region dummies	Yes	Yes	Yes
Year dummies	Yes	Yes	Yes
Constant	16.838***	15.734***	16.230***
	(1.687)	(1.607)	(1.620)
Observations	1411	1075	1075
Number of countries	97	92	92
Pseudo R^2	0.23	0.21	0.21

Tobit regression (range 0–18) with all independent variables lagged one year.
^Dependent variable: Contract risks (scale 0–18), as in Model (3).
^^Excluded category: Chief executive orientation: Center
Robust S.E.s clustered by country, *** $p < 0.01$, ** $p < 0.05$, *$p < 0.1$

diversity remains a positive and significant predictor of investors' perceived contract risks. Model (4) interacts FDI national diversity with the total count of BITs, finding a small but significant negative conditional relationship: in environments of high FDI national diversity, more BITs are associated with lower perceived contract risks. Model (5) further probes this relationship. Stronger BITs, in the form of NT BITs, have a significant and positive association with perceived contract risks. The interaction effect remains negative: in environments of high FDI national diversity, higher numbers of strong BITs are associated with lower perceived contract risks. Model (6) replaces the BIT measure with the count of NT carveouts in a country's BITs, which can be thought of as a measure of weak BITs. As in Model (5), the direct effect is positive. Yet again, the interaction effect remains negative. Thus, there is a consistent finding that in environments of higher FDI national diversity, more BITs confer a sense of contract sanctity.

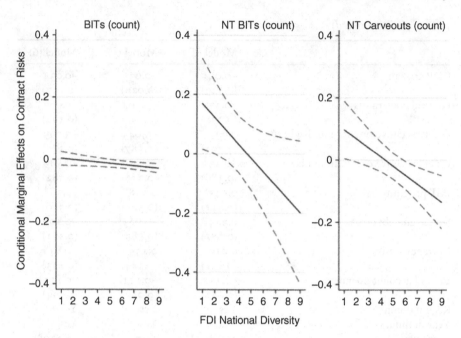

FIGURE 4.12 **Marginal Effect of FDI National Diversity Interacted with Types of BITs**
Based on Table 4.2.

When examined in context of the data, however, the effects of these interaction terms are not very meaningful. The mean level of FDI national diversity in the sample is 3.1 effective OECD nationalities, and one standard deviation above the mean is 4.9 effective nationalities. As shown in Figure 4.12, none of the interactions have a significant effect at that level. The conditional relationships for BITs and NT carveouts are negative only at higher levels, while the conditional relationship is not negative for NT BITs within the context of 99 percent of the sample (1 to 8.8).[42] Thus, while BITs may mitigate the effects of FDI national diversity at very high levels, for the vast majority of country-years the conditional relationships are not relevant. Hands-tying through BITs, weak or otherwise, does not appear to be a realistic means for countries to mitigate the direct effects of FDI national diversity.[43]

---

[42] The interaction is relevant for one outlier, the Netherlands in 2005 (11.1). As mentioned above, the ICRG data cover advanced economies in addition to emerging economies. The absence of a meaningful interaction in emerging economies is notable.

[43] As a further robustness check, positive associations in Table 4.1 between FDI national diversity and contract risks are robust to considerations of which home country accounts for the largest share of FDI national diversity. There are no significant direct effects of the United States, Germany, or other OECD countries' status as the largest investor in a host country, nor are there significant interaction effects with FDI national diversity.

Contract Risks and Public International Investment Arbitrations (IAs)

The next set of tests considers the effect of FDI national diversity on breach using a measure of the actual incidence of breach: public IA filings. IAs are lawsuits that foreign investors with the proper national credentials file against a host government under the appropriate international treaty, generally a BIT. I have coded public IAs for forty possible emerging economies from 1995 to 2011. Thirty-five of these countries faced public IAs in the period. This subsample of countries was chosen because their governments are readily able to borrow on international markets.[44] That such countries are engaging in government breach of contract is notable. One example of a public IA included in the dataset is from 2007, when an Austrian firm sued Ukraine for reneging on contracts concerning the construction of a hotel. The Austrian firm was ultimately awarded US$5.2 million in 2010.

The data-generating process behind public IAs is noisy, making public IAs an imperfect measure of breach of contract. Nevertheless, a positive association between FDI national diversity and the filing of public IAs in following years is an important test for the nationality shield theory. Public IAs capture a subsample of breaches that are so important to the firms involved that they risk much in choosing to file and to file publicly. The incident provoking a public IA – that is, the original broken contract – usually leads to out-of-court negotiations. If these prove unsuccessful, a foreign firm may choose to file an IA. At this point, fault over breach of contract has not yet been legally assigned. Nevertheless, filing alone is a sufficient indicator that the foreign firm involved perceives a breach of contract. Filing a public IA is a costly action for a firm: a foreign firm spends resources to bring a lawsuit, resolution often takes years, restitution if it comes is often incomplete, and the investor forgoes its goodwill with the government, casting doubt on the ability of that firm to successfully invest in the host country again.[45] Uncertainty around the outcome of a public IA underscores the notion that arbitration is a costly option of last resort.

The analyses here include cases brought at the most public of IA venues, the World Bank's International Center for the Settlement of Investment Disputes (ICSID). I have also collected public cases brought in other venues, typically under arbitration rules provided by UNCITRAL.[46] ICSID makes the litigants in all its cases publicly available as a matter of policy, whereas UNCITRAL rules and other venues allow parties to keep both the existence of a case and its

---

[44] That is, JP Morgan EMBI+ sovereign bond data and/or sovereign debt Credit Default Swap (CDS) data are available for these countries.

[45] Franck 2009.

[46] UNCITRAL cases are brought in ad hoc arbitration or in tribunals around the world, such as the International Chamber of Commerce, the Stockholm Chamber of Commerce, and the London Court of International Arbitration.

details private.[47] This state of affairs means that the true number of IAs is unknown. The censoring of private data is an issue for the current analysis; however, undercounting IAs should generally be associated with underestimating effects.

As described in Chapter 2, I collapse government motives for breach of contract into four rough categories: enhancing revenue, responding to the circumstances of a particular asset or sector, foreign policy goals, and catering to domestic interests. The analyses here help us to explore the link between the first two motives and FDI national diversity.[48] Is FDI national diversity more likely to motivate breach that did or did not raise revenue, or breach in certain types of industries?[49]

Government breach of contract and the resulting IA is coded as "revenue" when the underlying action either generated revenue for the national host government or reduced the host government's liabilities.[50] Revenue-generating actions include demanding taxes in excess of contracted amounts, forcing the sale of new equity stakes to the government, or the government otherwise acquiring property without due compensation. Revenue expropriations also take place when the government's action allows it to avoid liabilities, say, by unilaterally canceling a contract or by breaking contracted investment incentives intended to transfer funds to a foreign firm. These effects often have long-term implications. Offending governments avoid future payments by getting out of contracts, benefit from additional ongoing revenue by demanding extra-contractual taxes, gain access to profits by acquiring stakes in foreign-managed firms, and otherwise expropriate in ways that affect government balance sheets not just today but into the future. Table 4.3 describes four revenue IAs from the data set: excess taxes demanded in Ecuador; the denial of a subsidy in the Czech Republic; extra-contractual fees in Lebanon; and the withdrawal of tax breaks in Panama.

The amounts at stake in revenue IAs are large. In fifty-eight revenue IAs for which claims data is available, claimants demanded a total of US$944 billion or an average of US$16.3 billion per case (plus accrued interest and legal costs in almost all cases). These figures exclude Argentina, a country from which

---

[47] There is some hope of increasing the publicity of UNCITRAL rules-based IAs; rules on transparency became effective 1 April 2014. Petersen, Luke, "UN Working Group Finalizes UNCITRAL Transparency Rules, but They Won't Apply Automatically to Stockpiles of Existing Investment Treaties," *IA Reporter*, 14 February 2013.

[48] Cases in Chapters 5 and 6 focus first on foreign-policy and domestic-interest motives as well as revenue and asset-specific motives.

[49] For data collected by UNCTAD, see http://iiadbcases.unctad.org/. Other sources include Oxford Investment Claims Database, Investment Treaty Arbitration, IA Reporter, Global Arbitration Review, UNCTAD's IA Issues, and secondary journalism.

[50] In order to categorize IAs by type, I augmented the database of IAs with details concerning the content of the case and characteristics of the investor involved. These details are first culled from court documents. Where unavailable, searches of local press and international business press provide information.

TABLE 4.3 *Examples of Revenue-Raising Expropriations Leading to Public International Investment Arbitrations (IAs)*

Host	Year	Home	Investor's Claims	Case
Ecuador	2008	Spain	Hydrocarbons "Law 42" elevated taxes on windfall profits to 50 percent and then to 99 percent.	*Repsol YPF Ecuador, S.A. and others v. Republic of Ecuador and Empresa Estatal Petróleos del Ecuador (PetroEcuador) (ICSID ARB/08/10)*^
Czech Republic	2004	Netherlands	Beginning in 2000, Czech Republic sugar regulatory regime did not apply EU subsidy for sugar beet production to the investor's produce.	*Eastern Sugar B.V. v. Czech Republic (SCC 088/2004)*
Lebanon	2007	Italy	Highway contract signed in 1997. Investor faced changed customs duties, increased government fees, increased diesel prices over what was contracted.	*Toto Costruzioni Generali S.p.A. v. Republic of Lebanon (ICSID ARB/07/12)*
Panama	2006	USA	Signed contract to build and operate diesel-powered generation plant. Firm never received promised tax breaks or bonds and, as a result, effectively went bankrupt.	*Nations Energy, Inc. and others v. Republic of Panama (ICSID ARB/06/19)*

^ This is one of several public IAs resulting from Ecuador's "Law 42."

journalistic evidence suggests investors have demanded billions upon billions, particularly since its 2002 default triggered dozens of revenue IAs.[51] Claimants of course have an interest in inflating their award demands. Nevertheless, these sums suggest that revenue IA earnings or reductions in

---

[51] Cho and Dubash (2003) count that compensation claims against Argentina for gas and utilities non-payment top US$17 billion. Blake 2013.

government liabilities do have substantial effects on government balance sheets and thus are an important set of contract breach indicators to understand.[52]

The long-term nature of revenue IAs' effects stands in contrast to traditional notions of what expropriation accomplishes. Expropriation through mass nationalization is about the government reaping lump sum rewards alongside long-term liabilities as the new managers of firms. The broader definition of expropriation employed in this book, however, captures actions that affect government coffers not just today but into the future. It is unlikely that these kinds of expropriation are new phenomena. Instead, the absence of a dense network of BITs facilitating public IAs in the past made such expropriations difficult to observe.[53]

However, not all government breach of contract is about revenue generation. "Non-revenue IAs" generally arise when the government changes policies in such a way that devalues a foreign firm's property, a phenomenon associated with "regulatory taking." In the course of changing policy, the government does not directly gain revenues or avoid liabilities. Updating health and safety regulations or changing licensing procedures in ways that discriminate against foreign firms can generate a non-revenue IA. Table 4.4, for example, lists a non-revenue IA wherein a Spanish firm claimed discrimination when Chile denied it a fishing license. A non-revenue IA can also arise when the government changes its mind on a contract or set of policies, as when Vilnus, Lithuania pulled out of a contract that was backed by the Lithuanian central government, or when Slovakia re-regulated its insurance markets. Some non-revenue IAs emerge from what are perhaps strange scenarios in which foreign property was inadvertently involved with government action. For example, Canadian investors faulted the Costa Rican government for infringing on their property rights when the local police took down a Ponzi scheme.

In addition to considering the revenue-raising status of public IAs, I also code public IAs by industry. I use the industry of the project in which the investor filing a public IA was engaged, which means that industry could vary from the industry traditionally associated with the parent firm. Public IAs are filed by firms from a wide variety of immobile and mobile industries. Immobile industries include agriculture, energy, infrastructure, mining, real estate, and telecommunications. Mobile industries include finance, manufacturing, services, and trade. Expropriation, especially when broadly defined, is not just a phenomenon in natural resources and infrastructure industries (Chapter 2). Table 4.5 summarizes each type of IA in the sample analyzed here.

---

[52] For non-revenue IAs, claimants ask for awards comparable to revenue IAs, but of course these revenues never showed up on government balance sheets.

[53] Indeed, scholars did not put together a definition of "creeping expropriation" until Kobrin (1982) (Chapter 7).

TABLE 4.4 *Examples of Non-Revenue-Raising Expropriations Leading to Public International Investment Arbitrations (IAs)*

Host	Year	Home	Investor's Claims	Case
Chile	2004	Spain	Fisheries firm claimed discrimination in being denied a fishing license for certain offshore waters.	*Sociedad Anónima Eduardo Vieira v. Republic of Chile (ICSID ARB/04/7)*
Lithuania	2005	Norway	Vilnus issued a tender for parking system and eventually canceled the contract.	*Parkerings-Compagniet AS v. Republic of Lithuania (ICSID ARB/05/8)*
Slovak Republic	2008	Netherlands	Legislative reforms to the insurance market prevented the claimant from distributing profits to its shareholders.	*HICEE v. Slovak Republic (UNCITRAL)*
Costa Rica	2007	Canada	Individuals invested in a Ponzi scheme filed against the government once the scheme was taken down by the police, saying their loss was caused by the government.	*Alasdair Ross Anderson and others v. Republic of Costa Rica (ARB [AF]/07/3)*

TABLE 4.5 *Count of Public International Investment Arbitrations (IAs) in Sample by Type (1995–2011)*

Type	Count
IAs (total)	142
Revenue IAs	100
Non-revenue IAs	42
Immobile industry IAs	75
Mobile Industry IAs	65

Thirty-five out of a possible forty countries in the sample faced public IAs.
Note: Industry is not public in two IAs.

Modeling Strategy and Results

I test whether FDI national diversity is a correlate of the count of public IAs altogether and/or IAs of various types, using time series–cross sectional negative binomial regressions (1995–2011).[54] Models include lagged FDI national diversity, region dummies, and a dummy for the 1990s. To further account for over-time effects, I include the lagged dependent variable as a predictor of future public IA filings. See Appendix Tables A4.5 for countries included in the sample, A4.6 for summary statistics, and A4.7 for the correlation matrix.

Table 4.6 shows the results. Rather than reporting coefficients, the table reports incidence-rate ratios (IRRs), which are exponentiated coefficients. IRRs greater than one indicate that an increase in the covariate increases the likelihood of the outcome, while IRRs less than one indicate a decrease in the likelihood of the outcome. In Model (7), we see that a one-unit increase in FDI national diversity has a significant effect on the likelihood of a public IA filing against the host country, increasing the rate of the incident of filing 1.104

TABLE 4.6 *FDI National Diversity and International Investment Arbitration (IA) Types (1995–2011)*[^]

	Model (7)	Model (8)	Model (9)	Model (10)	Model (11)
Dependent variable[^^]	IAs	Revenue IAs	Non-revenue IAs	Immobile industry IAs	Mobile industry IAs
Lagged dependent variable	1.179	1.365**	0.163*	1.337	1.170
	(0.125)	(0.166)	(0.165)	(0.256)	(0.220)
FDI national diversity	1.104*	1.037	1.279**	1.154*	1.068
	(0.067)	(0.073)	(0.128)	(0.091)	(0.089)
Region dummies	Yes	Yes	Yes	Yes	Yes
1990s dummy	Yes	Yes	Yes	Yes	Yes
Observations	778	778	778	778	778
Number of countries	40	40	40	40	40

Time series–cross sectional negative binomial regression with lagged dependent and independent variable.
[^]The table reports Incident Rate Ratios (IRRs), or exponentiated coefficients.
[^^]All dependent variables are count variables.
*** $p < 0.01$, ** $p < 0.05$, * $p < 0.1$

[54] Distributions of public IAs have long tails, making them appropriate for negative binomial regressions. There is a trade-off between doing time series–cross sectional regressions and zero-inflated regressions on cross-sectional data. I choose the former, as it is important to model over-time variation in the data.

times. Models (8) and (9) divide the sample into revenue-generating and non-revenue IAs. The IRR on FDI national diversity is more than one for each, although it is significant only for non-revenue IAs. In this sample, a one-unit increase in FDI national diversity increases the likelihood of a non-revenue IA filing 1.278 times. These results imply that increases in FDI national diversity are associated with increases in underlying non-revenue breach events (assuming a positive relationship between the number of events and the number of IAs actually filed). In contrast, there is not a significant relationship between FDI national diversity and the likelihood that a revenue IA is filed. These non-results should be taken with caution, as much of the process behind the filing of an IA is not modeled here. Nevertheless, the analysis suggests that we should take seriously the idea that governments break contracts for reasons other than raising revenues.

In Models (10) and (11), the sample of public IAs is separated by the asset mobility status of the industry of the filing firm. The IRRs for FDI national diversity are greater than one in both models, although significant only in Model (10) for immobile industries. A one-unit increase in FDI national diversity suggests that a firm from an immobile industry is 1.15 times more likely to bring a public IA. Immobile industry investments, as relatively vulnerable targets, might be differentially susceptible to increased risks of breach in environments of high FDI national diversity (again, assuming a positive relationship between the number of events and the number of IAs actually filed).

These results generate additional pieces of evidence to support the nationality shield theory. They also give some insight into government motives for breach. In environments of high FDI national diversity, breach need not be about revenue-generation, nor are firms in mobile industries necessarily targeted. Rather, non-revenue motives may play a bigger role as FDI national diversity increases, as well as opportunistic motives to take advantage of an asset's immobility.

FIRM-LEVEL TESTS: MORE DIVERSITY, MORE GOVERNMENT ARREARS

The analyses above are conducted at the level of the country, although the nationality shield theory is built from firm-level predictions. The case studies in Chapters 5 and 6 provide one means of exploring the mechanisms behind and implications of the theory at the level of the firm. Here, a set of Enterprise Surveys conducted in 2003 and 2004 by the World Bank and its International Finance Corporation allow us to make some analogous quantitative insights at the firm level.[55] In these surveys, researchers interviewed top executives at a

---

[55] Quantitative analyses in this section expand on those in Wellhausen (2015).

variety of types of firms, including those with both foreign and domestic ownership. One question is particularly relevant: "What percent of your sales to government agencies or state-owned enterprises involve overdue payments?" This question captures an important aspect of government breach of contract: government arrears are a relatively common, clear form of breach in developing and transition countries. Non-payment stands behind many public IAs, including the dozens of public IAs Argentina faced as a result of its 2002 default.

I consider whether a firm reports the presence or absence of arrears.[56] Data on FDI national diversity and reports of government arrears are available for 6,102 firms operating in 21 emerging economies. Of these, 17 percent of 781 respondents at foreign-owned firms reported a positive level of overdue payments (17 percent of domestic firms also reported overdue payments). It is important to note that these figures are downward biased, as firms facing sufficient overdue payments are likely to differentially fail and fall out of the population of firms available to be surveyed. I use a logit analysis to test the association between FDI national diversity and the likelihood that a foreign firm reports government arrears. Equation (2) specifies the model.

$$\Pr(Arrears=1)_{ij} = \beta_0 + \beta_1(Foreign*Diversity)_{ij} + \beta_2(Foreign)_i$$
$$+ \beta_3(Diversity)_j + \beta_4 X_i + \gamma + \varepsilon_{ij} \tag{2}$$

The coefficient β_1 is the coefficient of interest. The nationality shield theory suggests an interaction effect: FDI national diversity should have a significant and positive effect on the presence of arrears when firms are foreign. The next two terms account for direct effects of *Foreign* and *FDI national diversity*. I control for firm-level characteristics and include region dummies. Robust standard errors are clustered by country.

Importantly, the World Bank Enterprise surveys allow tests of the effects of FDI national diversity while directly accounting for a relationship between industry and government arrears. Firms report whether they are in *Construction, Services, Manufacturing,* or *Agroindustry,* which I use as the excluded category. Additionally, it is crucial to account for firm selection into the population of firms that could possibly be interviewed. If government non-payment caused a firm to fail, those firms would non-systematically drop out of the population from which this sample was drawn and bias estimates in unpredictable ways. Thus, I control for whether a firm reports being an *Exporter,* which can allow firms access to foreign exchange that may help them to survive despite government arrears. See Appendix Table A4.8 for summary statistics and A4.9 for the countries in the sample.

---

[56] The distribution of reported levels of arrears is highly skewed. As the nationality shield theory predicts the presence and not the amount of arrears, the appropriate analytical approach is to collapse the data into a binary format.

Results

Table 4.7 presents results. Model (12) is the reduced form model without the interaction of interest. In Model (13), we see that the direct effect of a firm's status as foreign is to increase the likelihood of reported arrears. The interaction effect between *Foreign* and *FDI national diversity* is positive (Model 14). While the coefficient on the interaction is not significant, this does not imply the absence of substantive effects. Figure 4.13 plots the interaction effect, disaggregated across construction, services, and manufacturing. In all three plots in Figure 4.13, we see the hypothesized positive effect, which is significant at levels of FDI national diversity of about 2 or 2.5 and above. Once there are roughly two effective OECD nationalities present in the host country, foreign firms across these industries are significantly more likely to report arrears. Further, the size of the effect increases with FDI national diversity. In an environment of four effective OECD nationalities, foreign firms in construction and services are more than 6 percent likelier to report government

TABLE 4.7 *Effects of FDI National Diversity on Foreign Firms, Firm-Level Surveys (2003–2004)*
Dependent variable: Does the firm report that sales to government agencies or state-owned enterprises involve overdue payments? Yes=1, No=0

	Model (12)	Model (13)	Model (14)
FDI national diversity	−0.182*	−0.181*	−0.192**
	(0.098)	(0.097)	(0.097)
Foreign		0.322*	0.030
		(0.165)	(0.249)
Foreign * FDI national diversity			0.128
			(0.082)
Manufacturing^	−0.085	−0.075	−0.085
	(0.358)	(0.354)	(0.354)
Services	0.164	0.159	0.155
	(0.600)	(0.598)	(0.597)
Construction	0.604	0.594	0.594
	(0.555)	(0.556)	(0.554)
Exporter	−0.248	−0.303	−0.308
	(0.207)	(0.225)	(0.225)
Region dummies	Yes	Yes	Yes
Constant	−1.108**	−1.132**	−1.100**
	(0.560)	(0.554)	(0.555)
Observations	6102	6102	6102
Countries	21	21	21

Logit analysis.
^Omitted Category: Agroindustry
Robust S.E.s clustered by country, $*p < 0.1$ $**p < 0.05$ $***p < 0.01$

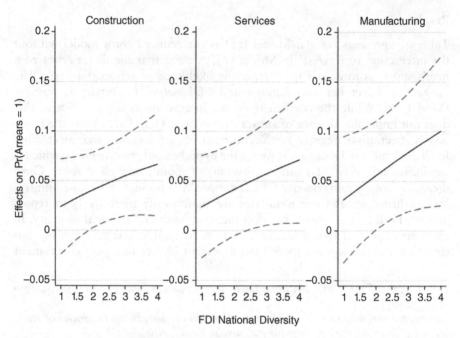

FIGURE 4.13 Marginal Effect of FDI National Diversity on the Likelihood of Arrears If Reporting Firm Is Foreign-Owned by Industry Based on Table 4.7.

arrears than are their domestic counterparts, and manufacturing firms are approximately 10 percent more likely to report arrears.

This analysis provides evidence that FDI national diversity has a positive relationship with breach, especially at higher levels.[57] That positive association is with foreign firms and, what is more, it is not isolated to any particular sector. Underlying these associations are expectations that the loss of capital from any particular nationality is less constraining on a host government as FDI national diversity increases. To substantiate the presence of this mechanism, we must find evidence that it is not all capital, but rather co-national capital that is more likely to exit a country following breach. To do this, dyadic analysis is appropriate.

---

[57] Further, the effect of FDI national diversity survives a placebo test, wherein the dependent variable is changed to firm responses to the following question: "Are government interpretations of regulations predictable?" FDI national diversity should not have an effect on foreign-firm responses to this question, as this question captures generalities about the investment environment and not firms' particular experiences with breach of contract. Indeed, *FDI national diversity* and its interaction with *Foreign* have no significant substantive effects.

DYADIC TESTS: DIFFERENTIAL FDI DRAWDOWN FOLLOWING BREACH

This book argues that the associations between FDI national diversity and risks of government breach of contract uncovered in the previous analyses result from two major forces: co-national firms' changing their investment decisions in response to co-national breach, and co-national firms' coalescing with each other and their diplomats to protest co-national breach. Lower levels of FDI national diversity are expected to capture an environment in which these mechanisms are more likely to grab the government's attention, influence its pocketbook, and successfully deter breach. Higher levels of FDI national diversity undermine the effectiveness of these co-national strategies to fight breach. In this section, I test the hypothesis that firms are more likely to draw down or divert investments following breach with co-national firms, while investors of other nationalities are unlikely to change their investments in response.[58] As a result of independent investment decisions made inside each firm, co-national firms' actions are expected to aggregate to become costly for capital-seeking governments following breach. Firms of other nationalities, however, are not expected to impose significant costs on governments in terms of lost capital following government breach of contract with a given firm.

Public International Investment Arbitrations (IAs) as Signals

To capture the instance of breach of contract, I turn again to the filing of public IAs. Public IAs filed by firms of one nationality serve as an important signal to other firms of that nationality that contract breach has occurred and that nationality's defenses were incapable of deterring the breach's escalation to the point of international litigation. A filing advertises that a foreign firm publicly accuses the host government of breach of contract, and it is that accusation that the theory here expects to be a trigger for costly actions. Certainly, firms and their lawyers have strategies about choosing to file a public IA. But if there is any moment at which other foreign firms would take notice and react in costly ways following a host government breach of contract, this is it. In a public IA filing, foreign firms make their claims in the context of codified, international law, and the host government is committed enough to its contrary position to let the suit go forward in public, rather than settle out of court.[59] This is a signal of the host government's resolve and attachment to a position contrary to that of a foreign firm's understanding of its property rights.[60]

---

[58] Chapters 5 and 6 provide tests of the operation of co-national protest. The exercise of protest lends itself better to qualitative analysis, since diplomatic and co-national investor association efforts are subject to measurement issues, especially in a cross-national setting.

[59] Elkins et al. 2006, Bebchuk 1984.

[60] In the event that co-national firms were sympathetic to the host government's position and do not take negative signals from a public IA filing, the effects of interest would be attenuated.

The filing and not the result of the IA is expected to send a signal of risks to contract sanctity. Foreign investors do not always win public IAs. Of the public IAs included here that have reached an outcome, many have been thrown out on jurisdictional grounds or other legalities, while in some cases arbitrators rule in favor of the host government.[61] However, a foreign firm's loss at IA does not mean that the foreign firm does not believe the breach took place. In support of this rationale, Allee and Peinhardt find that host countries that have been sued in public IAs – regardless of outcome – receive fewer future FDI inflows.[62] The hypothesis tested here goes a step further: FDI flows in a directed dyad should be lower following a co-national public IA, whereas public IAs filed by investors of other nationalities should have no effect on FDI flows in a directed dyad.

Importantly, we can assume that much if not all of the direct effect of an expropriation on FDI flows is accounted for before a public IA comes into play. Based on both qualitative research and secondary literature, it is clear that filing an IA is a strategy of last resort for a firm. The vast majority of public IAs are in response to events that occur at least a year in the past, and, in the interim, firms report engaging in negotiations with the host government over restitution.[63] Additionally, during the period before a public IA filing, the firm with the broken contract usually reports drastic drawdown of its (remaining) investment.[64] Indeed, filing a public IA is likely detrimental to the firm's future ability to invest in that host country. In Ukraine, for example, government politicians and bureaucrats interviewed for this study openly expressed animosity toward those firms that had sued the state.[65] Of course, when breach takes the form of total expropriation, the breach itself causes the firm to exit the host country.

Dyadic FDI

The focus here is on FDI flows from advanced industrial countries to emerging economies. The concept to be explained is variation in net FDI flows in the directed dyad, as I expect both current and potential co-national investors to reconsider investments following evidence of nationality-tied risks to contract sanctity. I use data for the time period 1998–2008 from the OECD, which collects statistics on dyadic FDI flows and stocks between its member states and a select group of non-OECD countries.[66] The analysis includes flows into

---

[61] Franck (2009) finds that development status does not significantly correlate with outcomes, nor does the nationality of the presiding arbitrator. There are no appeals in international IA; annulments are based on facts of law and not the content of cases. Van Harten 2005.

[62] Allee and Peinhardt 2011.

[63] Many BITs require a six-month or more mandatory cooling off period before a public IA can be filed.

[64] Allee and Peinhardt 2011.

[65] Interviews (4), government officials, Ukraine, 2009 and 2011.

[66] The OECD also has data on a select group of sending countries classified here as emerging economies; these are included in the analysis. Examining this limited time period helps to avoid the problem that public IAs were a rare event in earlier years.

106 host countries around the emerging world.[67] Appendix Table A4.10 lists the sending countries included in the analysis and the nineteen countries whose firms account for public IA filings in the dataset. For these analyses, I follow the literature in adding a constant value to the dyadic FDI flows large enough to shift negative values to positive values; this allows me to log-transform the data without losing observations that indicate net FDI divestment.[68]

Modeling Strategy

I choose a within-dyad, over-time identification strategy. Equation (3) specifies the estimation model:

$$(Net\ FDI\ inflow)_{i,j,t} = \beta_0 + \delta_1 IA_{i,j,t-1} + \delta_2 (Other\ IA)_{j,t-1} + \beta_1 X_{j,t-1} + \beta_2 X_{i,t-1}$$
$$+ \beta_3 X_{i,j,t-1} + \gamma_{i,j} + \tau_t + \varepsilon_{i,j,t} \tag{3}$$

The dependent variable is logged net FDI flows from OECD country i to emerging economy host country j in year t. The fourth, fifth, and sixth terms of Equation (3) are lagged time-varying host, home, and dyad controls; $\gamma_{i,j}$ and τ_t are dyad- and year-fixed effects.[69] Standard errors are robust and clustered by dyad. The panel covers 1998 to 2008.

The first independent variable of interest, $IA_{i,j,t-1}$, is a dummy of public IA(s) filed by firms from home country i against host country j in year $t-1$.[70] The expectation is that firms from home country i are disproportionately responsible for FDI diversion in response to their own IA(s); thus, the sign on δ_1 is hypothesized to be negative. The second independent variable of interest, $Other\ IA_{j,t-1}$, is a dummy of public IA(s) brought by nationals of other home countries against host country j in year $t-1$. IA(s) brought by firms that are not co-nationals are not expected to differentially affect FDI inflows in the directed dyad; thus, δ_2 is hypothesized to be insignificant. Models include dummies indicating IA(s) filed in the previous year, the previous two years, and the previous three years.[71]

---

[67] The data excludes observations where developed countries have been sued in IAs, which mainly occur between the United States and Canada under Chapter 11 investment protections written into the North American Free Trade Agreement (NAFTA). The theory implies that the fall-out from these broken contracts is largely a bilateral affair with few risks suggested to foreign firms of other nationalities. Firms of other nationalities should therefore remain uninvolved in these disputes and their possible resolution. Indeed, one does not see other firms coming out in favor of either Canadian or US interests in these cases. In particular, Mexican firms do not provide explicit support for firms of other nationalities, although Mexican firms do presumably have interests in the operation and scope of NAFTA provisions.

[68] Li and Vashchilko 2010.

[69] Results are robust to a difference-in-difference specification. Results are also robust to including a lagged dependent variable, which is ill-advised given the fixed-effects approach.

[70] Co-nationality is assigned based on the BIT under which an IA is registered. When IAs are brought under a multilateral instrument, the country of residency of the claimant is used as the claimant's nationality.

[71] Results are robust to the use of the count of IAs rather than dummies.

I account for several time-varying characteristics of the directed dyad, the host country, and the home country. The first key control is the presence of a BIT, in force, in the dyad.[72] A dummy variable for a *Dyadic BIT in force* is coded annually, based on records kept by UNCTAD. Second, I control for *Dyadic trade (logged)*, which scholars have long found to be associated with FDI flows.[73]

For the host country, the first important control is for *Host country political constraints*, which accounts for a correlation between both regime type and policy stability on firm decision-making.[74] Next, I control for *Host contract risks* in the host country. It is important to account for perceptions about risks to property rights that firms have likely already factored into their investment decisions. Public IAs are expected to send signals about additional information, whether generally confirming or contradicting previous expectations, that allows firms to update their prior beliefs. As in Table 4.1 Model (3), this variable follows the literature and is generated by summing two variables in the Political Risk Services International Country Risk Guide (ICRG): risks to investments and FDI-related corruption.[75] Following standard analyses of FDI flows, I also control for the host country's attractiveness as an investment destination with *Host GDP per capita (logged)*, *Host GDP growth*, *Host population (logged)*, and *Host capital account openness*.[76] Macroeconomic trends in the home country likely have an effect on the willingness of firms of a given nationality to invest abroad. I therefore control for *Home GDP per capita (logged)* and *Home GDP growth*. All independent variables are lagged one year.[77] The model includes fixed effects for dyad *ij*, to account for cultural and other time-invariant ties between home and host countries. It also includes year dummies. See Appendix Table A4.11 for summary statistics.

Results

Table 4.8 reports the regression results. Model (15) presents the basic specification without the IA variables of interest. In Models (16), (17), and (18), we see that co-national IAs in previous years have a consistent and significant negative correlation with future co-national net FDI inflows. Holding other variables at their means, change from zero IA(s) to the incidence of IA(s) in each model is approximately equal to a marginal decrease in dyadic FDI of US$1–2 million. The mean in the estimation sample is US$63.71 million

---

[72] If the parties have signed but not ratified a BIT, firms do not yet have the facility to public IAs under that BIT.

[73] Trade data are from the IMF Direction of Trade Statistics and the Correlates of War Project Trade Data Set (Barbieri et al. 2009).

[74] This measure is polconiii from Henisz (2002). Results are robust to replacing this measure with Polity IV data.

[75] "A Business Guide to Political Risk for International Decisions: Part II. International Country Risk Guide," *Political Risk Services*, 27. Results are robust to using only risks to investments (dependent variable in Model 1).

[76] *KAopen* is from Chinn and Ito (2006).

[77] Questions of endogeneity are mitigated, as it is previous FDI stocks (and not future FDI flows) that would contribute to the incidence of IAs, which are often the result of years-long disputes.

TABLE 4.8 *Effects of Co-National and Other IAs on Directed Dyad FDI Flows^* *(1998–2008)*

	Model (15)	Model (16)	Model (17)	Model (18)
Co-national IA (last year)		−0.001*		
		(0.001)		
Other IA (last year)		−0.000		
		(0.000)		
Co-national IA (last 2 years)			−0.001***	
			(0.001)	
Other IA (last 2 years)			0.000	
			(0.000)	
Co-national IA (last 3 years)				−0.002**
				(0.001)
Other IA (last 3 years)				0.000
				(0.000)
Dyadic BIT in force	−0.001	−0.001	−0.001	−0.001
	(0.001)	(0.001)	(0.001)	(0.001)
FDI national diversity	−0.000	−0.000	−0.000	−0.000
	(0.000)	(0.000)	(0.000)	(0.000)
Dyadic trade (logged)	−0.000	−0.000	−0.000	−0.000
	(0.000)	(0.000)	(0.000)	(0.000)
Host political constraints	0.000	0.000	0.000	0.000
	(0.000)	(0.000)	(0.000)	(0.000)
Host contract risks	0.000	0.000	0.000	0.000
	(0.000)	(0.000)	(0.000)	(0.000)
Host GDP per capita (logged)	0.003***	0.003***	0.002***	0.002***
	(0.001)	(0.001)	(0.001)	(0.001)
Host GDP growth	0.000	0.000	0.000	0.000
	(0.000)	(0.000)	(0.000)	(0.000)
Host population (logged)	−0.006	−0.007	−0.008	−0.008
	(0.006)	(0.006)	(0.007)	(0.007)
Host capital account openness	0.000	0.000	0.000	0.000
	(0.000)	(0.000)	(0.000)	(0.000)
Home GDP per capita (logged)	−0.003***	−0.003***	−0.003***	−0.003***
	(0.001)	(0.001)	(0.001)	(0.001)
Home GDP growth	0.000	0.000	−0.000	0.000
	(0.000)	(0.000)	(0.000)	(0.000)
Dyad fixed effects	Yes	Yes	Yes	Yes
Year dummies	Yes	Yes	Yes	Yes
Constant	12.073***	12.074***	12.099***	12.099***
	(0.098)	(0.098)	(0.111)	(0.110)
Observations	15860	15860	14788	14720
Home-host dyads	2684	2684	2682	2479
R^2 (within)	0.011	0.011	0.013	0.013

Time series-cross sectional OLS analysis with all independent variables lagged one year.
^ Dependent variable is the log of net FDI flows (US$ billions) from OECD country *i* to emerging economy *j*. The underlying distribution is shifted so observations of negative net flows are retained (see text).
Robust S.E.s clustered by dyad, *** $p < 0.01$, ** $p < 0.05$, *$p < 0.1$

per dyad-year, meaning that there is about a 2 percent annual decrease in average bilateral FDI flows due to a co-national IA. This loss, which accrues for years into the future, can generate real constraints over time in a foreign-capital-reliant economy. In contrast, filings of IA(s) by firms of other nationalities do not have a significant relationship with dyadic FDI in any of the specifications, as predicted. In all models, the coefficients for co-national and other IA(s) are significantly different (with 95–99 percent confidence) and their covariance is 0, as implied by the theory.

The directionality of control variables provides support for the overall model specification.[78] *Host GDP per capita* is associated with higher dyadic FDI flows. All else equal, *Home GDP per capita* is associated with lower dyadic flows, consistent with the notion that high GDP per capita is correlated with investment opportunities at home. Results are robust to multiple imputation to account for missingness in the control variables *Dyadic trade (logged)*, *Host GDP per capita (logged)*, and *Host growth*.[79] Results are also robust to using a running total of BITs in force in the host country, as Kerner as well as Büthe and Milner find that BITs have an effect on aggregate FDI, regardless of with whom they are signed.[80] Due to data constraints, including the incidence of *Preferential Trade Treatments (PTAs)* and dyadic *Militarized Inter-state Disputes (MIDS)* as additional possible dyadic correlates of dyadic FDI markedly reduces sample sizes. *PTAs* are a significant predictor of dyadic FDI flows at 90–95 percent confidence levels, in line with expectations from a rich literature on PTA effects.[81] Dyadic *MIDS* are not significant. The signs on the coefficients of interest for co-national IAs are negative as expected, though the variable loses statistical significance at conventional levels in some specifications. The *Other IA* variables are, as before, insignificant.

Interpreting Dyadic Results

The dyadic results in Table 4.8 capture a specific chain of events. First, a breach of contract occurs with a given firm. That firm begins pulling down its investment or, indeed, loses its investment as a result of the breach. This should result in lower FDI from the home to the host prior to the filing of a public IA. At the point at which a public IA is filed, often a year or more after the original breach, other firms in the host economy as well as potential investors receive a signal. Indeed, the use of lags in the above analyses go to confirm that signaling effects persist long after the original targeted firm has dealt with its broken contract.

---

[78] Note that the low "within" R^2 measures and the small coefficient estimates are to be expected when predicting a dependent variable as notoriously choppy as FDI flows.

[79] Honaker, King, and Blackwell 2013 ("Amelia II: A Program for Missing Data").

[80] The BIT coefficient remains positive but insignificant. Kerner 2009, Büthe and Milner 2009. Results are also robust to replacing the incidence of a dyadic BIT with the BIT's duration in force (capped at 11 years).

[81] Büthe and Milner 2008, 2014; Goldstein et al. 2007; Ghosn et al. 2004.

I contend that the signal sent by a public IA filing likely communicates increased risks to contract sanctity for co-nationals of the firm that has resorted to filing a public IA. As a result, current as well as potential co-national investors are likely to update their investment plans, in particular by stopping reinvestment, pulling out investments, or diverting planned investments. In contrast, the signal sent by another nationality's public IA is unlikely to provide information to non-co-nationals on their contract sanctity. Thus, non-co-nationals are unlikely to change their investment plans in response.

Take FDI from Germany into Thailand. In 1990, Thailand contracted with a German firm to build a major new toll road. Though the firm faced a series of setbacks, German diplomatic interventions helped it and its shareholders to survive the 1997 Asian financial crisis and multiple turnovers of the Thai government. Troubles began again in 1998, however, when Thailand signed a contract with a Hong Kong firm to build a virtually identical toll road. The German firm's patience ended when the Thai government refused to allocate land for exit ramp number four or to allow for toll adjustments as spelled out in the contract. Ultimately, the German firm sold its shares and sued Thailand in 2005.[82] The analyses here suggest that decreased FDI flows after 2005 reflect, at least in part, other German firms' decisions to divert capital in response to the public IA. Indeed, the conflict was still prominent years later in 2011 when, as reported in *Der Spiegel*, the Thai prime minister worried that events surrounding the breach "should not be allowed to hurt bilateral ties."[83]

These dyadic analyses of co-national FDI flows provide key evidence in support of the nationality shield theory. Setting diplomatic issues aside, these results demonstrate that co-national firms themselves respond differently to information on co-national firms' contracts. Nationality matters to firm decision-making. Chapters 5 and 6 take up diplomatic issues, using qualitative evidence to put co-national collective action on the left-hand side of the equation and FDI national diversity on the right.

Finally, does the size of a particular nationality's share of FDI influence their dyadic relationship? The Appendix to Chapter 4 uses public IA filings to find suggestive evidence that nationalities with both very small and very large shares of FDI enjoy better contract sanctity. Future research would do well to explore how other characteristics of national groups influence the likelihood of government breach of contract either cross-sectionally or in specific country contexts.

---

[82] The German firm won an award of some EUR30 million (US$40 million) in 2009. Narrative as reported in the resulting arbitration award. *In the Matter of an Arbitration in Geneva, Switzerland and Under the Treaty between the Federal Republic of Germany and the Kingdom of Thailand made on 24 June 2002 Concerning the Encouragement and Reciprocal Treatment of Investments and under the UNCITRAL Arbitration Rules 1976, between Walter Bau AG (In Liquidation) Claimant and the Kingdom of Thailand Respondent. Award, 1 July 2009.*

[83] Wassermann, Andreas, "Thailand Pledges to Settle Dispute Over Prince's Jet," *Der Spiegel*, 3 August 2011.

CO-NATIONAL PUNISHMENT

Though conventional wisdom would have it otherwise, foreign firms' responses to government breach of contract with foreign firms vary. As shown in the dyadic analyses here, when foreign investors are of different nationalities, one firm's broken contract is unlikely to have a significant effect on the investment decisions made by firms of other nationalities. When firms are of the same nationality, on the other hand, the incidence of a public IA decreases dyadic FDI flows for years into the future.

The monadic analyses in this chapter support the prediction that governments gain space to break contracts when FDI nationalities are more diverse. Whether measured by expectations about contract sanctity or legalized instances of breach, the analyses here show that greater FDI national diversity corresponds with more breach. Further, while robustly controlling for industry, firm-level surveys provide evidence that foreign firms in highly diverse environments face more breach of a particular form – government non-payment – than their domestic counterparts. The upshot is that investors of all nationalities benefit from low FDI national diversity, when FDI diversion carries greater weight, but investors of all nationalities can lose out when FDI national diversity increases.

What do these findings mean for our expectations of host government behavior? Host governments have the space to break contracts with a given nationality when they retain access to capital flows from a greater diversity of other FDI nationalities. Strategic host governments can trade off among national investor groups to accomplish other goals via breach, even as they remain open to (some) foreign capital. Firms themselves facilitate these trade-offs, because their behavior following a non-co-national breach is likely to be observationally equivalent to indifference. The next chapters demonstrate how home-government behavior, too, facilitates these trade-offs for host governments. Host governments incur the loss of co-national capital and potential diplomatic costs when breaching with one nationality, but are likely to retain at least status quo relations with other investor nationalities. When the space to breach exists, it is unsurprising that host governments take advantage of it.

CHAPTER 4: APPENDIX

SIZE OF FDI NATIONALITY SHARES

This book does not argue that any single nationality consistently enjoys more or less contract sanctity. A particular nationality's contract sanctity can vary over time and across countries. Rather, a firm's choice to act in ways costly to a host government is conditioned by the status of its co-nationals' contracts, and this can result in permissive space for governments to break contracts. However, one might hypothesize that a nationality that dominates a host country's FDI national diversity faces systematically better treatment than others. On the other hand, one could imagine that a well-represented nationality may be the most likely target, if a government is seeking to expropriate to enhance its revenues, for example. If the latter logic holds, nationalities with smaller shares may be able to fly under the host government's radar. Despite conflicting expectations, is there nevertheless an empirical trend in which nationalities with bigger or smaller shares of FDI face more breach?

To address this question, I analyze the relationship between a nationality's share of FDI in a given host country and whether a firm of that nationality files a public IA in the subsequent year. The dependent variable here is binary, suggesting a time series–cross sectional logit analysis, as specified in Equation (3).

$$\Pr(\textit{Public IA by j in i}=1)_{i,j,t} = \beta_0 + \beta_1(\textit{Share size})_{i,j,t-1} + \beta_2 X_{i,t-1}$$
$$+ \gamma + \tau + \tau^2 + \tau^3 + \varepsilon_{i,j,t} \qquad (\text{A1})$$

I operationalize *Share size* in three ways. First, I include a dummy for whether the home country accounts for the smallest FDI flow in the dyad-year. Second, I include a dummy if the home country accounts for the largest FDI flow in the dyad-year. Third, I include the raw size of share (from 0 to 1) and its squared term, to explore any potential nonlinearities in the data. I control for several factors that could influence a firm's decision to bring litigation. I include *FDI national diversity*, as the broader FDI environment could potentially affect a firm's litigation strategy. I control for whether a dyad has a *BIT in force*, as BITs are most often the instrument that give firms the ability to file a public IA.[84] I also control for *Total FDI inflows (logged)* into the host country. To account for political influences on the likelihood of public IA filing, I control for *Political constraints*.[85] Last, I control for host-country *GDP per capita (logged)* and *GDP growth*. All covariates are lagged one year. The models include region dummies and linear, squared, and cubic time trends.[86]

Results

Results are presented in Table A4.1. As expected, the presence of a BIT in force is a strong predictor of public IAs, as is the host country's relative poverty. While Model (A1) suggests no significant relationship between the smallest national groups and the propensity to file IAs, Model (A2) suggests that the largest national groups are more likely to file IAs when compared to groups of any other size. When a nationality represents the largest share, the predicted probability of its filing a public IA is 0.003, which is 36 percent larger than when a nationality does not account for the largest share.[87] However, Model (A3) suggests that the total relationship between FDI share and the likelihood of public IA filing is curvilinear: both the most and least represented nationalities tend to file fewer IAs than those in the middle of the distribution of FDI nationalities. Figure A4.1 plots the relationship at different levels of FDI share, with the likelihood of an IA filing peaking at a share size of around 0.6 to 0.7,

---

[84] Results are robust to including the duration in force of the dyadic BIT (capped at 11 years).

[85] Henisz 2002.

[86] Carter and Signorino 2010.

[87] Predicted probability calculations assume random effects are equal to 0. The most common home countries representing the largest share are the United States, Germany, and the Netherlands.

TABLE A4.1 *Effects of FDI Share Size on International Investment Arbitration (IA) Filing*^

	Model (A1)	Model (A2)	Model (A3)
Smallest share of FDI stock	-0.047		
	(0.392)		
Largest share of FDI stock		1.104***	
		(0.278)	
Share of j in i FDI stock			8.214***
			(1.391)
Squared share of j in i FDI stock			-6.472***
			(1.627)
FDI national diversity	0.016	0.033	0.029
	(0.070)	(0.070)	(0.070)
BIT in force	2.416***	2.324***	2.191***
	(0.318)	(0.315)	(0.308)
Total FDI inflows (logged)	0.096	0.125	0.343
	(0.680)	(0.671)	(0.653)
Political constraints	-0.700	-0.743	-0.587
	(0.601)	(0.598)	(0.586)
GDP per capita (logged)	-0.304**	-0.280**	-0.362***
	(0.141)	(0.138)	(0.135)
GDP growth	-0.004	-0.007	-0.003
	(0.025)	(0.025)	(0.026)
Region dummies	Yes	Yes	Yes
Time trends (t, t^2, t^3)	Yes	Yes	Yes
Constant	-9.907	-10.426	-12.356*
	(7.330)	(7.230)	(7.079)
Panel variance (log)	1.070***	0.972***	0.763***
	(0.216)	(0.220)	(0.233)
Observations	17066	17066	17066
Home–host pairs	2868	2868	2868

Time series-cross sectional logit analysis with all independent variables lagged one year (except BIT in force).
^Dependent variable is the incidence of a public IA filing by j in i.
*** $p < 0.01$, ** $p < 0.05$, * $p < 0.1$

although nationalities with shares in the 0.9 to 1 range still file more IAs than those in the 0 to 0.1 range. What might explain this relationship? It could be that middle-of-the-pack nationalities are subject to risks otherwise specific to larger nationalities, as well as risks otherwise specific to smaller nationalities. For example, middle-of-the-pack nationalities may be more susceptible to revenue-raising motives than smaller nationality groups, while they might also be less prominent in the host country than those at the top of the range, dampening potential diplomatic fallout around breach. It could also be that middle-of-the-pack nationalities are simply more litigious when they do face breach. Future research on the systematic effects of share size would be useful.

In sum, while the analyses in Table A4.1 cannot speak to the number of underlying events that could potentially spark IAs, they do raise doubts that large groups have strong protections against breach, or that governments linearly target national groups based on size. Indeed, as we will see in Chapters 5 and 6, governments in a variety of countries have targeted firms representing national groups of various sizes, for various reasons not obviously related to their size.

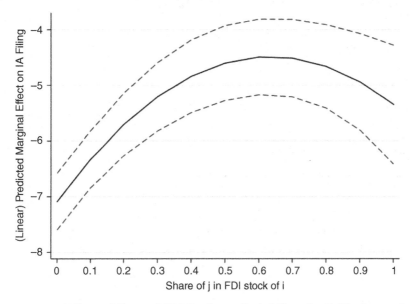

FIGURE A4.1 **Effects of Share of FDI Stocks on Probability of a Public International Investment Arbitration Filing** Based on Table A4.1.

TABLE A4.2. *Countries Analyzed in Tables 4.1 and 4.2*

Albania	Ghana	Norway
Algeria	Greece	Pakistan
Angola	Guatemala	Panama
Argentina	Guinea Bissau	Papua New Guinea
Australia	Guyana	Paraguay
Austria	Honduras	Peru
Bahamas	Hungary	Philippines
Bangladesh	Iceland	Poland
Belgium	India	Portugal
Bolivia	Ireland	Republic of Congo
Botswana	Israel	Romania
Brazil	Italy	Russia
Bulgaria	Jamaica	Senegal

(continued)

Burkina Faso	Japan	Sierra Leone
Canada	Kazakhstan	Slovak Republic
Chile	Latvia	Slovenia
China	Lebanon	South Africa
Colombia	Libya	South Korea
Costa Rica	Lithuania	Spain
Croatia	Madagascar	Sri Lanka
Cyprus	Malawi	Suriname
Czech Republic	Mali	Sweden
Democratic Republic of Congo	Malta	Tanzania
Denmark	Mexico	Thailand
Dominican Republic	Moldova	Trinidad and Tobago
Ecuador	Mozambique	Tunisia
El Salvador	Namibia	Turkey
Estonia	Netherlands	Ukraine
Ethiopia	New Zealand	United Kingdom
Finland	Nicaragua	United States
France	Niger	Uruguay
Germany	Nigeria	Venezuela
		Zimbabwe

TABLE A4.3 *Summary Statistics, Tables 4.1 and 4.2*

Variable	Observations	Mean	Standard Deviation	Minimum	Maximum
Contract risks	1411	3.725	2.395	0	11
FDI national diversity	1365	3.149	1.842	1	11.072
BITs	1411	20.529	22.343	0	122
NT BITs	1012	2.188	2.279	0	11
BIT NT carveouts	1012	1.922	3.460	0	21
GDP per capita (logged)	1411	8.391	1.488	4.415	10.643
FDI stock (logged)	1411	6.417	3.053	−3.058	12.954
Natural resource rents per GDP	1411	6.625	15.223	0	218.886
GDP growth	1411	3.584	3.881	−28.100	38.201
IMF program (dummy)	1411	0.486	0.500	0	1
Sovereign debt crisis	1411	0.021	0.142	0	1
Currency crisis	1338	0.114	0.317	0	1
Capital account openness	1411	0.711	1.581	−1.864	2.439
Political constraints	1411	0.378	0.170	0	0.720
Chief executive orientation: Right	1374	0.427	0.495	0	1
Chief executive orientation: Left	1374	0.463	0.499	0	1
Chief executive orientation: Center	1374	0.110	0.313	0	1

TABLE A4.4 Correlations (Selected), Tables 4.1 and 4.2

	Risks to investment	FDI-related corruption	Contract risks	FDI national diversity	GDP per capita (logged)	FDI stock (logged)	Natural resource rents per GDP	GDP growth	Capital account openness	Political constraints	BITs (total)	NT BITs
Risks to investment	1											
FDI-related corruption	0.066	1										
Contract risks	0.872	0.546	1									
FDI national diversity	-0.212	-0.260	-0.305	1								
GDP per capita (logged)	-0.384	-0.651	-0.641	0.407	1							
FDI stock (logged)	-0.344	-0.349	-0.460	0.616	0.621	1						
Natural resource rents per GDP	0.182	0.227	0.264	-0.193	-0.307	-0.124	1					
GDP growth	0.023	0.225	0.129	-0.087	-0.228	-0.106	0.137	1				
Capital account openness	-0.364	-0.390	-0.497	0.252	0.620	0.397	-0.269	-0.173	1			
Political constraints	-0.130	-0.254	-0.234	0.229	0.389	0.294	-0.227	-0.162	0.259	1		
BITs (total)	-0.459	-0.069	-0.419	0.530	0.302	0.540	-0.165	-0.040	0.286	0.077	1	
NT BITs	-0.046	-0.110	-0.092	0.406	0.210	0.370	-0.159	0.022	0.076	0.053	0.564	1
BIT NT carveouts	-0.026	-0.084	-0.063	0.191	0.105	0.222	-0.099	-0.022	0.128	0.004	0.355	0.574

TABLE A4.5 *Countries Analyzed in*
Table 4.6

Argentina	Kazakhstan
Belize	Lebanon
Brazil	Lithuania
Bulgaria	Malaysia
Chile	Mexico
China	Nigeria
Colombia	Pakistan
Croatia	Panama
Dominican Republic	Peru
Ecuador	Philippines
Egypt	Poland
El Salvador	Russia
Gabon	South Africa
Georgia	Sri Lanka
Ghana	Turkey
Hungary	Ukraine
Indonesia	Uruguay
Iraq	Venezuela
Ivory Coast	Vietnam
Jamaica	Yugoslavia

TABLE A4.6 *Summary Statistics, Table 4.6*

Variable	Observations	Mean	Standard Deviation	Minimum	Maximum
IA count	778	0.183	0.479	0	3
Revenue IA count	778	0.129	0.401	0	3
Non-revenue IA count	778	0.054	0.253	0	2
Immobile industry IA count	778	0.096	0.328	0	2
Mobile industry IA count	778	0.084	0.324	0	3
FDI national diversity	778	2.966	1.744	1	11.050

TABLE A4.7 *Correlations, Table 4.6*

	IA count	Revenue IA count	Non-revenue IA count	Immobile industry IA count	Mobile industry IA count
IA count	1				
Revenue IA count	0.850	1			
Non-revenue IA count	0.547	0.023	1		
Immobile industry IA count	0.732	0.552	0.512	1	
Mobile industry IA count	0.716	0.680	0.276	0.060	1
FDI national diversity	0.185	0.134	0.138	0.125	0.147

TABLE A4.8 *Countries Analyzed in Table 4.7*

Brazil
Cambodia
Ecuador
Egypt
Guatemala
Indonesia
Kenya
Lithuania
Moldova
Mongolia
Morocco
Nicaragua
Oman
Philippines
Poland
Senegal
Serbia
South Africa
Sri Lanka
Syria
Uzbekistan

TABLE A4.9 *Summary Statistics, Table 4.7*

Variable	Observations	Mean	Standard Deviation	Minimum	Maximum
Arrears	6102	0.173	0.378	0	1
FDI National Diversity	6102	2.651	1.236	1.002	4.594
Foreign	6102	0.128	0.334	0	1
FDI National Diversity*Foreign	6102	0.308	0.891	0	4.594
Manufacturing	6102	0.845	0.362	0	1
Agroindustry	6102	0.095	0.293	0	1
Construction	6102	0.028	0.165	0	1
Services	6102	0.032	0.177	0	1
Exporter	6102	0.264	0.441	0	1
Africa	6102	0.114	0.318	0	1
Latin America	6102	0.171	0.377	0	1
Asia	6102	0.339	0.473	0	1
Emerging Europe	6102	0.071	0.257	0	1
Middle East/North Africa	6102	0.305	0.460	0	1

TABLE A4.10 *Home Countries Analyzed in Table 4.8*

Australia	Estonia	Japan	Slovakia
Austria*	Finland*	Korea	Slovenia
Belgium*	France*	Luxembourg*	Sweden*
Switzerland*	Greece*	Netherlands*	Turkey*
Czech Republic	Hungary	Norway*	UK*
Germany*	Ireland	New Zealand	USA*
Denmark*	Iceland	Poland	
Spain*	Italy*	Portugal	

* = Countries with firms filing public IAs. Additional countries with public IA filings in the data set are Canada and Chile.

TABLE A4.11 *Summary Statistics, Table 4.8*

Variable	Observations	Mean	Standard Deviation	Minimum	Maximum
Directed dyad FDI flows (logged, adjusted)	15860	11.959	0.005	11.589	12.071
IA (last year)	15860	0.007	0.085	0	1
Other IA (last year)	15860	0.182	0.386	0	1
IA (last two years)	15507	0.013	0.114	0	1
Other IA (last two years)	15507	0.294	0.456	0	1
IA (last three years)	15443	0.017	0.131	0	1
Other IA (last three years)	15443	0.353	0.478	0	1
Host FDI stock (logged)	12249	18.233	0.011	17.354	18.433
Dyadic BIT in force	15860	0.397	0.489	0	1
FDI national diversity	15544	2.973	1.711	1	9.876
Dyadic trade (logged)	15860	4.621	2.636	0	12.881
Host political constraints	15860	0.302	0.208	0	.73
Contract risks (ICRG)	15860	−8.407	2.135	−12	0
Host GDP per capita (logged)	15860	7.621	1.301	4.415	10.484
Host GDP growth	15860	5.490	4.410	−31.3	46.5
Host Capital Account Openness	15860	0.398	1.533	−1.844	2.478
Home GDP per capita (logged)	15860	9.749	0.682	8.267	10.940
Home GDP growth	15860	3.150	2.518	−5.697	10.579

5

Foreign Firms and Their Diplomats in Ukraine

At first glance, Ukraine is the kind of country with little choice but to adhere to the contracts it forms with foreign firms. For sure, protest and sometime violence has rocked Ukraine in the 2000s and 2010s. But the government has considerable incentives to keep those actions separate, to the extent possible, from the treatment of foreign firms. Endowment-based explanations for a government's propensity to break contracts would predict breach in resource-rich Venezuela or a country with a large market like China. Ukraine shares neither of these traits. Rather, Ukraine competes for global capital against many possible destinations, making it the kind of country for which the need for contract sanctity has gone without question. Moreover, multilateral institutions have scrutinized Ukraine and its market economy for progress in economic and political transition since its independence in 1991, making international pressure to comply with property rights protections all the stronger. As a regular recipient of International Monetary Fund (IMF) loans, Ukraine has agreed to limit its policy freedom in order to maintain the sanctity of its sovereign bondholders' contracts. One might reasonably expect that a government under the scrutiny of both global market actors and the IMF would want to uphold its commitments to other sources of capital – including commitments made to foreign direct investors. Indeed, Ukraine has taken steps to establish credible commitments to foreign firms by signing sixty-eight bilateral investment treaties (BITs), fifty-five of which are in force as of 2013.[1] These BITs codify the security of foreign firms' property and their recourse to international law.

Nevertheless, the Ukrainian government sometimes engages in public contract disputes with foreign firms, and it sometimes breaks those contracts. Even the 2005 Orange Revolution government, heartily celebrated by Western commentators for its stance in favor of economic openness, broke contracts. Ukraine increased its commitment to contract sanctity after the Orange government's collapse and through the early 2010s, despite the turbulence of subsequent Ukrainian politics.

As Ukraine's fortunes have waxed and waned in its history as an independent country, so too has Ukraine's FDI national diversity varied as different nationalities of foreign firms have entered and exited. Ukraine is therefore an important setting in which to trace the effects of changes in the diversity of investor nationalities on the incidence of government breach of contract. Ukraine's FDI national diversity breaks down into two periods: high and increasing in the late 1990s through the early 2000s, and lower and relatively stable after about 2004 through the early 2010s. In this chapter, I connect the first period to multiple broken contracts with US and other investors. In the second period, the Ukrainian government repaired a long outstanding breach with a US investor, refrained from breach with a Norwegian investor, and canceled a threatened breach with Russian investors.

---

[1] UNCTAD, as of 1 June 2013.

Finally, the chapter takes advantage of Ukraine as a setting in which to explore additional questions raised by the nationality shield theory. I demonstrate that foreign firms' national resources are integral to breach deterrence even when there is a common threat of breach. Additionally, firms with claims on more than one home country take advantage of their multiple national resources – in particular, their diplomats.

UKRAINE'S FDI NATIONAL DIVERSITY

Figure 5.1 plots a measure of Ukraine's FDI national diversity alongside FDI national diversity in Russia, which serves as a reference point. This measure, the variable used in quantitative analyses in Chapter 4, grows rapidly from the 1990s through the early 2000s and then slowly declines after about 2004. These trends contrast with neighboring Russia, reinforcing the notion that FDI national diversity varies from country to country. Change over time in OECD-origin FDI national diversity in Ukraine sets up a difficult test for the nationality shield theory. Though OECD-origin firms are the ones most often thought of as stateless actors, the evidence presented in this chapter must demonstrate that even these firms' nationalities matter for contract sanctity. In a period of rapidly

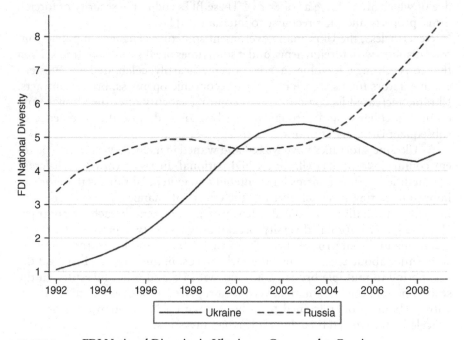

FIGURE 5.1 **FDI National Diversity in Ukraine as Compared to Russia**
Lowess-smoothed OECD-origin FDI stock national diversity measures (see Chapter 4 for calculation details).

increasing FDI national diversity, the Ukrainian government should be likely to break contracts instead of avoiding breach or settling with foreign firms: the country is gaining access to new sources of FDI that are relatively indifferent to any other nationality's contract breach. With the change in the FDI national diversity trend, Ukraine's propensity to break contracts should drop in the mid-2000s. One way to observe this is to see contract disputes avoided or settled rather than mired in conflict. In short, while the diversity of investors present in Ukraine rose, peaked, and lowered, foreign firms' abilities to deter contract breach are expected to move in the opposite direction. Indeed, reflecting on Ukraine's trajectory, the well-positioned local head of a foreign private equity firm summed it up in 2011: "the biggest disputes in Ukraine happened before and through 2004."[2]

Sources of Variation in FDI National Diversity

In the first period of Ukraine's history as an independent country, the unexpected break-up of the Soviet Union left governments scrambling to gain a foothold in it and other newly sovereign countries. As one means to this end, governments promoted their nationals' investments in Ukraine as well as the broader region. For example, the US government supported investment through programs at the Department of Defense, the Nuclear Regulatory Commission, the Department of Agriculture, the Ex-Im Bank, the US Agency for International Development, the Department of Commerce's Business Information Service for the Newly Independent States (BISNIS), and more.[3] European investors also benefitted from a wide array of national programs and European-Union-wide efforts. Additionally, a new class of Western entrepreneurs became "cowboys," running small- and medium-sized enterprises in what came to be called "the Wild East." Foreign firms invested in Ukraine's traditional strengths in agriculture and heavy industry as well as in manufacturing, finance, and retail.[4]

US firms accounted for the largest proportion of Ukraine's FDI stock throughout the 1990s, but by 2003, a variety of Western and Eastern European investor nationalities had begun to catch up (see Figure 5.2). Ukraine benefitted from the economic success of transition countries in Central Europe, many of which were in final preparations to join the European Union on 1 January 2004. As the reform process had begun to raise costs in those countries, and accession to the European Union would make investments in those countries fully subject to EU standards,

---

[2] Interview, foreign firm in financial services, Ukraine, 2009.
[3] See for example the "Report on the implementation of the humanitarian and technical assistance program to the New Independent States of the former Soviet Union," US Senate, 102nd Congress, 29 October 1992.
[4] WIIW Database on Foreign Direct Investment in Central, East, and Southeast Europe (2009).

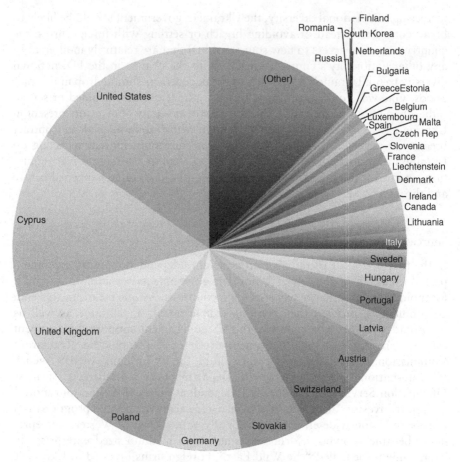

FIGURE 5.2 **FDI Nationality Distribution in Ukraine (2003)**
Source: Vienna Institute for International Economic Studies (WIIW), Database on
Foreign Direct Investment in Central, East, and Southeast Europe, 2009 Release.

Western European investors began moving further eastward in search of low
wages and low-cost inputs. Central European firms from Ukraine's neighbor
Poland as well as Slovakia, Latvia, and Hungary also joined the movement eastward. New investments flowed into industries like banking and light manufacturing, which made use of Ukraine as an export platform to the EU.[5]

Russian investors quickly entered and grew their investments in Ukraine, a
country with a long shared history with Russia and a sizeable Russian minority.[6]

---

[5] Interviews (2), foreign firms in consumer goods and finance, Ukraine, 2009.

[6] In the 2001 Ukrainian census, Ukraine's population was 17 percent Russian ethnicity and 77 percent
Ukrainian ethnicity. Russian is widely spoken; prominent politicians are sometimes poor Ukrainian
speakers.

In particular, Russians were ready participants in Ukraine's privatization processes. As was true in all post-communist countries, assets big and small in industries across the economy were privatized.[7] Privatizations begat the break-up of one-time Soviet firms into domestic Russian firms that now acted as foreign investors into privatized assets in other new countries. President Leonid Kuchma, in power in Ukraine from 1994 to 2005, presided over a government that brokered a number of notorious sales of state assets. Several of these involved Russian investors and went on to add fuel to the opposition in the Orange Revolution. Russian investors' special access to these gray sales speaks to the role of nationality in differentiating risks to contract sanctity – especially when one nationality is more likely to be entering into government contracts with lower levels of legitimacy.[8]

As Figure 5.2 demonstrates, however, it is not Russia but Cyprus that shows up as a sizeable source of Ukraine's FDI stock. In large part this can be attributed to diaspora investors from Russia who use Cyprus as a home for their firms, which accounts for Russia's otherwise small share of FDI in Ukraine. Russian individuals investing via Cypriot firms share historical and ethnic relationships with Ukraine unrelated to Cyprus. Nevertheless, Cyprus is a useful place for Russian investors to domicile their firms, because Cyprus is an EU member and it provides tax benefits. Cypriot investors share access to the Soviet-era Ukraine–Cyprus Double Taxation Treaty that is prominent enough for the Ukrainian Rada to regularly debate withdrawing from it. What is more, Cypriot nationality has benefits for Russian firms' contract sanctity. In particular, the Ukraine–Cyprus BIT has been the basis for several public international investment arbitrations (IAs) brought by Cypriot firms against Ukraine. For its part, the Ukrainian government understands that Cyprus is an attractive country from which to do business with Ukraine. Some ethnic Ukrainians also use Cypriot firms to invest back into Ukraine in a process known as "round-tripping." Suffice it to say here that Russian as well as Ukrainian individuals who domicile firms in Cyprus share risks to contract sanctity as a result of this choice, and these firms have taken advantage of Cypriot legal resources to fight breach. Even if the extent of these shared risks and resources is not as great as if firms had originated in the country of their CEO's birth, Cypriot firms' presence in Ukraine generates diversity in FDI just as any traditional national group would. By 2003, Cypriot investors were the second largest group in Ukraine after US investors. The peculiarities of applying the nationality shield theory to Cypriot investors are discussed below.

---

[7] This universality of privatization meant that firms of many nationalities bought into privatized assets. See Chapter 8 for a discussion of privatization as a source of potential variation to contract risks in its own right.

[8] Corruption has been a problem in privatization processes throughout the post-communist region. For an excellent treatment of the issue, see Schwartz (2006).

In short, a variety of OECD and some regional investors were responsible for Ukraine's increasing FDI national diversity through the early 2000s. In an interview, one Ukrainian politician summarized the growing diversity of investor nationalities in this period by pointing to South Korean firms' investment into auto parts manufacturing in the late 1990s. This event captured his feeling that Ukraine was truly integrating with the wider world economy, despite its status as a laggard in political and economic transition.[9]

Ukraine's FDI nationalities became less diverse beginning with a huge foreign investment into Ukraine: the October 2005 sale of Ukraine's major steel mill, Kryvorizhstal, to Mittal Steel for US$4.8 billion.[10] This FDI infusion, which took place under the democratizing Orange Revolution government, sparked the interest of other major Western European multinationals. Together with Russian investors, firms from a variety of Western European countries accounted for the subsequent FDI boom in consumer products, agriculture, and banking.[11] Ukraine's top ten FDI nationalities came to represent well over 75 percent of Ukraine's FDI stock by 2008 (compare Figures 5.2 and 5.3). This concentration decreased FDI national diversity even as Ukraine's FDI stock grew rapidly. US-origin investment now accounted for a relatively small proportion of Ukraine's FDI, thanks in part to a broken contract that is estimated to have cost Ukraine up to US$1 billion in US investment from 1998 to 2008.[12]

Figure 5.4 presents the average distribution of FDI stock by industry from 2000 to 2008.[13] We can be confident that the foreign firms at play in the Ukrainian economy were investing in quite a variety of industries, including finance, various forms of manufacturing, construction, and other uncategorized industries. Importantly, FDI is not accumulating predominately in those industries identified with the "obsolescing bargain," in which we would expect foreign firm leverage to be particularly constrained.[14] Indeed, manufacturing industries (with the exception of heavy industry in metals manufacturing) are thought to be some of the most mobile investments in the global economy. Furthermore, as summarized in Case Studies: Methodology, respondents informing each of the cases in this chapter come from a variety of industries, including industries involved in and not involved in prominent contract disputes and breach.

[9] Interview, Member of Rada, Ukraine, 2009.
[10] This sale as well as the role the complex national identity of Mittal Steel (soon ArcelorMittal) has played in its own contract disputes will be discussed in a subsequent section.
[11] WIIW Database on Foreign Direct Investment in Central, East, and Southeast Europe (2009).
[12] Davis, Jim, "Ukraine's Outstanding OPIC Debt: A barrier to foreign investment," *Business Ukraine Magazine*, 11 February 2008. Reprinted by the US–Ukraine Business Council.
[13] Unfortunately, data on distribution by home country and industry is unavailable.
[14] Vernon 1971.

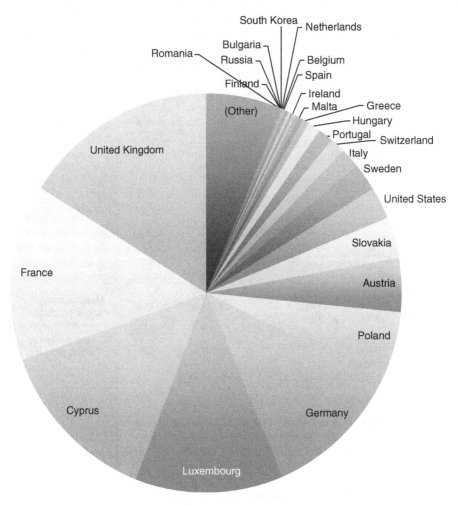

FIGURE 5.3 **FDI Nationality Distribution in Ukraine (2008)**

US$4.8 billion in FDI invested by ArcelorMittal is attributed to the four countries on which the subsidiary in Ukraine has claims: Germany, France, United Kingdom, and Luxembourg. See text for discussion.

Source: Vienna Institute for International Economic Studies (WIIW), Database on Foreign Direct Investment in Central, East, and Southeast Europe, 2009 Release.

FOREIGN FIRM PROTEST AND DIPLOMATIC ADVOCACY

By protesting to both home and host governments, foreign firms can make the consequences of government breach of contract more visible and immediately threatening to a host government's interests in maintaining capital access.[15]

---

[15] Hirschman 1970.

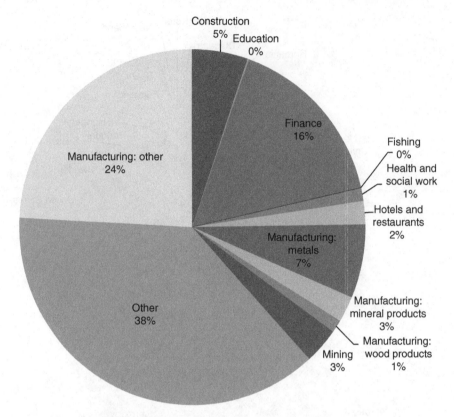

FIGURE 5.4 **FDI Stock in Ukraine by Industry (Average, 2000–2008)**
Source: Vienna Institute for International Economic Studies (WIIW), Database on Foreign Direct Investment in Central, East, and Southeast Europe, 2009 Release.

Co-national firms are aided in overcoming collective action problems and coming together to exercise protest, thanks to ties they share to institutions in both the home and host country. For example, foreign firms of the same nationality can coordinate their appeals to their home government through nationality-tied investor associations, which are often able to gain privileged access to host-government decision-makers. Host governments benefit from and often welcome the development of easy channels for communication with foreign firms. Moreover, diplomatic advocacy by the home country can tie the incidence of a breach to other issues in the bilateral relationship, adding foreign policy costs to the costs of capital loss, should the host government choose to breach. Protest can occur alongside or in lieu of intra-firm changes in investment strategies in response to breach, along the lines of the analyses in Chapter 4.

However, the likelihood that collective lobbying or diplomatic pressure will be successful in deterring breach depends in part on the broader set of foreign capital that can directly substitute or indirectly compensate for capital lost due to deteriorating relations with the targeted national group. In other words, when a country is host to a greater diversity of national investor groups, co-national actors have less leverage over the host government's capital access. This lowers the likelihood that co-national investors' own efforts, or efforts by diplomats on their behalf, will deter breach. As a result, co-national firms and home-country diplomats are expected to cut back their efforts when FDI national diversity is high. Scarce resources may be better spent on dealing with the fallout of breach. This implies that we should observe ineffective or limited lobbying and diplomatic efforts on behalf of contract sanctity in Ukraine from the late 1990s through 2004. In the following years, in contrast, diplomatic and lobbying activity should be strong and consequential. Regardless, these efforts should be consistently bilateral – and not multilateral – throughout both periods.

The following sections trace out prominent contract disputes, the presence or absence of protest by investors and diplomats, and ultimate breach or deterrence under conditions of both increasing and lower FDI national diversity in Ukraine. See Table 5.1 for summary findings.

AMERICANS AND AMMUNITION

US collective action failed to stop the Ukrainian government from breaking twelve firms' contracts from 1997 to 1999. The government subsequently violated its treaty commitment to the US Overseas Private Investment Corporation (OPIC), a US government agency that offers financing, investment funds, and political risk insurance for US investors in emerging economies. OPIC's investments are conditional on the host government's agreement to reimburse OPIC for political risk insurance claim pay-outs. The Ukrainian government failed for ten years to reimburse OPIC for a US$17.7 million claim. As a result, Ukraine is estimated to have lost up to US$1 billion in US investments that OPIC would have made, facilitated, or otherwise inspired.[16] The twelve contract breaches in the late 1990s and the non-payment to OPIC stand in contrast to conventional expectations that a government like Ukraine's is constrained to uphold its contracts with foreign firms in an era of economic globalization. Why these breaches occurred and why it took so long to resolve OPIC's breach have been considered puzzles even by the actors involved – especially as OPIC was consistently eager to resolve its dispute and re-enter Ukraine.

Unfortunately for US firms, other national groups of investors were uninterested in supporting US efforts concerning these breaches. US diplomatic pressure and co-national lobbying were ineffective for years. However, US firms and diplomats successfully came together on OPIC's behalf in the second half of the 2000s, in an environment in which Ukraine's FDI national diversity had

---

[16] Davis, Jim, "Ukraine's Outstanding OPIC Debt: A barrier to foreign investment," *Business Ukraine Magazine*, 11 February 2008. Reprinted by the US–Ukraine Business Council.

TABLE 5.1 *Summary, Major Contract Disputes in Ukraine*

FDI National Diversity	Year	Case	Nationality	Diplomacy	Co-national lobbying	Outcome	As predicted?
High	1997–1999	Twelve firms	US	Weak	Weak	Breach	Yes
	2004	OPIC	US	None	None	Breach	Yes
	Early 2005	Kryvorizhstal	Cypriot	None	None	Breach	Yes
Declining	2005	Reprivatization	(All)	Strong	Strong	Deterrence	Yes
	2005	Reprivatization	Russian	Strong	Strong	Breach/Settled	No/Yes
Low	2005–2009	OPIC	US	Strong	Strong	Settled	Yes
	2005–2009	Telenor	Norwegian	Strong	Strong	Deterrence	Yes
	2007–2009	ArcelorMittal: VAT	Multiple	Strong	Strong	Breach/Settled	No/Yes
	2006–2010	ArcelorMittal: Regulatory	Multiple	Strong	None	Deterrence	Yes

fallen and then plateaued. The Ukrainian government proved willing to follow through with restitution to OPIC after a ten-year delay.

American Bluffs

In 1997, the US government had major foreign policy interests in securing nuclear materials in Ukraine, establishing Ukraine's relationship with NATO, and gaining a foothold in Ukraine in part because of Ukraine's position vis-à-vis Russia. Despite these pressing "high politics" bilateral issues, the US Congress tied the distribution of foreign aid to Ukraine directly to the outcome of the government's contract disputes with twelve private US investors – an action unprecedented in Ukraine or elsewhere in the post-communist region. Congress threatened to withhold up to 50 percent of discretionary aid promised to Ukraine, amounting to about US$80 million, if the Ukrainian government did not ensure that "United States investors who have been subjected to . . . inappropriate, corrupt activities carried out by officials or representatives of the Ukrainian government are provided with full restitution or compensation for their losses."[17] The legislation referred to the list of twelve firms assembled by the US Embassy in Ukraine, which included major US multinationals like Cargill as well as smaller investors. Conditional US aid was clearly distinguished from unconditional aid intended to reinforce Ukraine's nuclear security, promote democracy, or restructure markets. Nevertheless, the US Secretary of State was to report to Congress on whether sufficient progress had been made to merit aid distribution, and the US Embassy in Ukraine was to confirm restitution in a series of regular follow-up meetings with the Ukrainian government.[18]

With the approval of the State Department, Congress distributed Ukraine's aid in full in 1998 – despite the protests of US firms and investor associations in Ukraine. From the point of view of US firms, the Kuchma government had taken no action on these twelve firms' broken contracts and had not assuaged US concerns about their broader contract sanctity. Congress followed up with a similar threat to withhold aid from Ukraine in legislation in 1998: the United States would not distribute the aid allocated to Ukraine in the 1999 budget if Ukraine did not make "continued progress on resolution of complaints by American investors."[19] The Kuchma government called the US bluff and again did nothing. This time, US firms in Ukraine accused the US ambassador to Ukraine of "fudging the numbers" to overstate progress toward resolution, and Ukraine received its aid in full.[20] The mandated meetings between the

---

[17] Congressional Record – House. Page H3698. Sec. 1717. Sense of Congress Concerning Assistance for Ukraine. Subsection (5). Amendment offered by Mr. Fox of Pennsylvania. June 11, 1997.
[18] Interviews (3), Washington, D.C., 2012.
[19] Congressional Record – Senate. S9999. Assistance for the New Independent States of the Former Soviet Union. September 8, 1998.
[20] "Pifer fudges the numbers," *Kyiv Post*, 25 February 1999.

US Embassy and the Ukrainian government to follow up on restitution never occurred.[21] In 1999, an US official lamented the "international brouhaha" over the broken contracts.[22] Why did diplomatic efforts crumble and fail to push the Kuchma government to restore US firms' contracts?

The diversity of foreign investor nationalities in Ukraine had increased in the years leading up to 1997, and 1997 to 1999 brought significant new entry of OECD-origin investors into the country (see again Figure 5.1). Ukraine, which has been a transition laggard compared to its western neighbors, was just becoming an attractive investment destination with healthier macroeconomic fundamentals including economic growth and better control over inflation. US investors were early entrants into Ukraine, but large Western European countries grew their investments quickly. Western European FDI gained a good reputation in Ukraine for promoting local development and economic growth. Economic integration with Western Europe also supported Ukraine's hopes to "return to Europe" now that its Soviet identity was gone.[23] Against this backdrop, the potential loss of US$80 million in US aid and the further exit and deterrence of US-origin FDI posed less of a threat to Ukraine's capital access and international standing than it might have otherwise.

European-origin investors and their home governments had strong incentives to stay removed from US disputes. Far from facing risks to contract sanctity in Ukraine, Western European firms received privileges. In its efforts to become "European," Ukraine was particularly keen to build strong relationships with Western European home countries. This speaks to geopolitics as a source of variation in US versus other firms' contract sanctity. Indeed, US investors were frustrated by what they saw as discrimination. In testimony before Congress in 2000, the head of an US investor organization in Ukraine expressed his low expectations for collaboration between European and US investors:

It is common practice for these [post-communist] governments to be told by the Europeans, in some cases rather bluntly and in others rather delicately, that you had better remember which side your bread is buttered on when it comes to letting these contracts. Certainly I have run into this in the Ukraine, where Ukraine, which aspires to be an EU member, has been told in various ways in various cases that . . . contracts better go to German or French companies, not American companies.[24]

This well-placed US executive saw that, far from worrying that the political problems of US firms were harbingers of their own future, European-origin firms benefitted from their own convivial government relations. There was fierce competition for investment between US and German and French firms.

---

[21] Interview, Washington, D.C., 2012.
[22] "US Presses Investor Disputes," *Kyiv Post*, 11 February 1999.
[23] Wilson 2005.
[24] Congressional Record – Senate. "Treatment of US Business in Eastern and Central Europe," Hearing before the Subcommittee on European Affairs of the Committee on Foreign Relations. 106th Congress, Second session, 28 June 2000.

European firms had little incentive to risk their privileges by getting involved in US firms' disputes. Indeed, at this time Western European firms likely faced less vulnerability when it came to contract sanctity.[25]

Investors from transition countries were also relatively indifferent to Americans' contract sanctity, as US disputes were not relevant enough to their own contract risks to merit coordination with US efforts.[26] The context in which transition country firms' contracts were formed resulted in different risks to contract sanctity. The Soviet economy had been characterized by soft budget constraints, meaning that bureaucrats' commitments to cut off funding to loss-making enterprises were not credible.[27] With the fall of the Soviet Union, some of the debts incurred thanks to soft budget constraints were now spread between different countries' state-owned enterprises. As privatization proceeded, both private and state actors became involved in negotiating inter-enterprise foreign debt settlements. In Ukraine, this meant that newly minted foreign investors from Russia and other countries in the region had to work out legacy debts together with their newly minted home governments and the newly sovereign Ukraine. Regional firms and governments were willing to write off the Ukrainian government's non-payment of an outstanding debt for a write-off of their firms' legacy debts. For them, this was a mutually intelligible and legitimate transaction.[28] Further, regional firms making greenfield investments in Ukraine shared a common Soviet legacy that allowed contracts to be tacit and flexible when compared with US investors' more arms-length, formal agreements. Without the historical interdependencies or flexible contracting that shaped regional investors' relations with the Ukrainian government, a US firm was constrained to see government non-payment as a breach of contract.

Moreover, firms from post-communist countries have been exposed to different contract risks as each of their newly separate governments worked out bilateral relations with Ukraine. These bilateral contract risks have been mediated by shared and sometimes conflicting cultural histories. Ukraine's bilateral relations in the region have also been shaped by the geographical distribution of assets like oil and gas pipelines that, with the fall of the Soviet Union, became sources of conflicts with Russia, Belarus, and other previous Soviet trading partners now separated by rigid national borders. With different kinds of contracts, different means of resolving disputes, and different political considerations, actors from regional countries did not support US efforts. Nor, we will see, did the United States support regional firms that did in fact face broken contracts.

For their part, US firms pressed the US Embassy for support in restoring contract sanctity. Two US investor associations, the American Chamber of

---

[25] Cases in which Western European firms' contract sanctity varies are discussed in subsequent sections and in Chapter 6.

[26] Interviews (3), Russian finance and manufacturing firms, Ukraine, 2009 and 2011.

[27] For an excellent treatment of this problem, see Kornai (1992).

[28] For helpful models of how transition countries resolved these problems, see Roland (2004).

Commerce (ACC) and the US-Ukraine Business Council (USUBC), lobbied Ukrainian officials as well as US officials on behalf of their memberships. In 1997, a US Congressman said that he knew that "25 percent of all ... the Embassy [in Ukraine] does is expedite American business problems."[29] Both the ACC and the USUBC strongly objected to the full distribution of aid after the 1997 threat. Local actors saw the repetition of the same ultimatum in 1998 as an empty threat.[30] Nevertheless, the ACC withdrew its objection to the full distribution of aid this second time around. The ACC's leadership had changed from 1998 to 1999, and its new managing director took the stance that, "in the long term, [the distribution of aid] will result in a more favorable investment environment."[31] The ACC offered no more public statements on the twelve US firms' contract disputes. Since 1999, in fact, the ACC has changed its policy and refuses to get involved in contract disputes between particular firms and the Ukrainian government, wanting instead to be a broad-based lobbying organization focused on investment policy.[32] Efforts to restore US firms' contract sanctity died out.

In 1999, the Ukrainian prime minister publicly placed fault for the firms' broken contracts on the side of naïve Americans who had gotten involved with "God knows whom."[33] In a strange twist, Ukraine's gray economy became useful political cover for the government's inaction in repairing broken contracts. Notably, this framing went unchallenged by Americans. At least one of the twelve firms went on to sue Ukraine under the US–Ukraine BIT; another decided to pursue its case in Ukrainian courts; a third made repeated, unsuccessful attempts to regain the US State Department's interest; and a fourth became the ten-year breach of contract with OPIC.

OPIC's Broken Contract

Alliant Kyiv, formed in 1992, was a joint venture to recycle 220,000 tons of government-owned ammunition. The Ukrainian government owned 41 percent of the firm; its main contribution was to deliver the ammunition and grant Alliant Kyiv the rights to sell recycled materials on world markets. The US multinational Alliant Techsystems owned a 39 percent stake and, by 1998, had invested US\$22 million and trained local personnel to use a safer recycling

---

[29] Congressional Record – House, H3674, Comment by Mr. Hastings of Florida. June 11, 1997. He went on to say, "We cannot have people, either in tourism or in business, all over the world and not have our facilities to help them."

[30] Interviews (4), US investor associations, Ukraine and Washington, D.C., 2011. For the terms of the 1998 ultimatum, see Congressional Record – Senate. S9999. Assistance for the New Independent States of the Former Soviet Union (b). September 8, 1998.

[31] "Pifer Fudges the Numbers," *Kyiv Post*, 25 February 1999.

[32] Interview, American Chamber of Commerce, Ukraine, 2009.

[33] "US Presses Investor Disputes," *Kyiv Post*, 11 February 1999.

process than the Soviet standard.[34] Alliant Techsystems bought political and expropriation risk insurance from OPIC to protect its investment. The joint venture became quite successful, making millions selling recovered gunpowder, industrial explosives, and, most importantly, scrap brass.

In the first ten months of 1998, Alliant Kyiv exported 1,640 tons of brass for US$2.13 million.[35] This was less than two-thirds of the volume of brass the Ukrainian Defense Ministry was obligated to deliver to the joint venture. Local observers speculate that the unexpected profits to be made in recycled materials tempted the Defense Ministry to process the materials itself, using the more dangerous but cheaper Soviet method. There were reports that the Kuchma administration opposed the Defense Ministry's decision to break the contract, but Kuchma, likely wary of internal divisions in advance of the 1999 presidential elections, did not publicly address the Defense Ministry's disobedience.[36] Alliant Techsystems, the US Embassy, OPIC, the Defense Ministry, and the Kuchma administration negotiated, but to no avail. In a colorful retelling, one US advocate recalled the Deputy Minister of Defense saying, "OPIC shafted us once – they'll shaft us again."[37] In 1999, Alliant Techsystems ended its investment in Ukraine and received US$17.7 million in compensation from its political and expropriation risk insurer, OPIC.

Unlike private market insurance providers, OPIC's participation in an emerging economy is contingent on the host government's agreement to reimburse it for any political risk insurance claim it pays out. Those involved with Alliant Kyiv's case at OPIC thought the reimbursement would not be a problem: US$17.7 million was a relatively small sum, OPIC had already facilitated over US$200 million in investments in Ukraine and stood ready to do more, and its threat of exit was credible.[38] OPIC was also willing to negotiate over the terms of repayment and the public reasons for which that payment was made, as OPIC did not require Ukraine to admit guilt in the matter.[39] But Ukraine did not pay, and OPIC exited in 1999. In 2000, US investors gave Congressional testimony on their treatment in Ukraine, but OPIC's broken contract was not mentioned.[40] After the previous failure of diplomatic

---

[34] A British firm (Rapierbase) and a Ukrainian firm (EKOP) each owned 10 percent; they acted as "liaisons" for either side. "Rift threatens to blow up ammunitions joint venture," *Kyiv Post*, 30 October 1998.

[35] "US Presses Investor Disputes," *Kyiv Post*, 11 February 1999.

[36] Ibid.

[37] Interview, Washington, D.C., 2012.

[38] Interview, OPIC, Cambridge, MA, 2009.

[39] From OPIC's point of view, claims and reimbursements are intended to be "no fault." The payment means only that the host government participated in such a way that the firm lost money. Interviews (2), Washington, D.C., 2012.

[40] Congressional Record – Senate. "Treatment of US Business in Eastern and Central Europe," Hearing before the Subcommittee on European Affairs of the Committee on Foreign Relations, 106th Congress, Second session. 28 June 2000.

advocacy, OPIC's broken contract received little attention from the US government or other US investors.

OPIC continued to negotiate with the Ukrainian government, reaching a provisional settlement in 2004. The settlement turned out to be cheap talk. The Kuchma government agreed that OPIC would reopen operations in March 2004, conditional on the government repaying its debt by January 2005. But the Kuchma regime would be replaced in January 2005, either by Kuchma's preferred successor, Viktor Yanukovych, or the Orange presidential candidate, Viktor Yushchenko. The Orange Revolution, from November 2004 to January 2005, overthrew the Kuchma regime and replaced it with the pro-reform, pro-Western, democratic Orange coalition. This marked a major moment of turmoil in Ukraine's domestic priorities, bureaucracy, and legal institutions.[41] Fulfilling a settlement with OPIC may have understandably fallen by the wayside, and an understanding OPIC official recognized that "reinstatement is not a priority during elections."[42] However, the Orange government never took action on the settlement, and OPIC again exited in late 2005.

The Orange government's public rationale for not providing restitution to OPIC was analogous to that offered by the Kuchma government in a 1998 letter: "payment of compensation to OPIC on an expropriation lawsuit in Ukraine may negatively affect foreign firms' opinion about the investment climate in Ukraine."[43] Put differently, the government thought that inaction over OPIC had limited repercussions, so long as expropriation was only OPIC's and other Americans' interpretation of events surrounding Alliant Kyiv. US-origin FDI might be deterred, but the Ukrainian government did not expect other foreign firms to receive an equivalent negative signal.

Collective Action and Restitution

In October 2005, Mittal Steel invested US$4.8 billion in Ukraine.[44] This investment, combined with new Western European investments in a variety of industries, left FDI less equally distributed across national groups, which reduced the effective number of national groups on which the Ukrainian government could rely for current and future FDI (see again Figure 5.3). OPIC's long absence meant that fewer small and medium-sized US enterprises had been investing in Ukraine; by 2008, US-origin FDI had fallen to seventh place among OECD countries. Although US investors held a smaller share of the government's access to FDI, they now operated in an environment in which breach with any one national group carried higher costs for the Ukrainian government's future access

---

[41] Beissinger 2013.

[42] Interview, OPIC, Cambridge, MA, 2009.

[43] "Rift threatens to blow up ammunitions joint venture," *Kyiv Post*, 30 October 1998.

[44] See subsequent sections for a discussion of this sale and Mittal Steel's role in shaping Ukraine's FDI national diversity.

to capital. These circumstances enabled US firms to come together to lobby the US government to take up OPIC's cause and to put direct pressure on the Ukrainian government to provide restitution and facilitate OPIC's re-entry.

The US–Ukraine Business Council (USUBC) became the vehicle through which US firms lobbied the US and Ukrainian governments. Founded in 1995, the USUBC was first intended to be a close-knit club of large US firms investing in Ukraine, though the original members were mostly clients of the president's public relations agency.[45] The USUBC flexed its lobbying muscles during the failed 1997 to 1999 efforts on behalf of the twelve US firms with broken contracts, but it was mainly a networking and social forum at that stage. After the lobbying failure in 1999, dues-paying members in the USUBC fell from twenty-two to eight. In 2007, Sigma Bleyzer, a large private equity investor in Ukraine and elsewhere in the post-communist region, started rebuilding the USUBC as an association capable of promoting American business interests in Ukraine. With Sigma Bleyzer's financial and organizational support, the USUBC grew to 150 members by 2011, including small and large US multinationals from a wide variety of industries.[46] The USUBC membership also grew to include US firms that were interested in but had not yet entered the Ukrainian market, giving the USUBC the ability to represent deterred US investors as it lobbied the Ukrainian government. New USUBC members understand that they join an American-centric association that takes positions on particular firms' conflicts with the government, and members sometimes contribute extra funds in support of particular campaigns.[47]

The USUBC was made more important because the other American investor association in Ukraine no longer identified itself with American investors. The American Chamber of Commerce in Ukraine had rebranded itself as "the Chamber" (hereafter Chamber/ACC), becoming a broad-based group with members from a variety of national origins. The Chamber/ACC now focused its lobbying efforts on the Ukrainian government and did not actively seek US government support. It advocated on issues around which the foreign business community was in relative consensus, which excludes particular instances of government breach of contract. The Chamber/ACC leadership perceived that lobbying on behalf of particular firms of any nationality would threaten the credibility it has built with the Ukrainian government as "the voice of foreign business in Ukraine."[48] With this change to the Chamber/ACC, the USUBC was

---

[45] Interview, USUBC, Ukraine, 2009.
[46] Microsoft was eager to join as the USUBC's 100th member. The Ukrainian president attended a gala event celebrating its membership. Interview, USUBC, Ukraine, 2009.
[47] As one example of its US focus, the USUBC conducts all of its business in English so as to avoid the complications translation can cause. The USUBC does not talk to the Ukrainian media for this reason. Its meetings are always off the record. Interviews (3), USUBC, Washington, D.C. and Ukraine, 2009 and 2012.
[48] Interview, American Chamber of Commerce, Ukraine, 2009.

left as the only investor association positioned to aggregate US interests around contract breach.

The USUBC took up OPIC as a cause in 2005. Some USUBC members expected to benefit directly from renewed access to OPIC financing or subsidized insurance.[49] But many of the USUBC's members had little to directly gain from OPIC's reinstatement. The USUBC's largest members, including firms like Procter and Gamble, IBM, KPMG, and Halliburton, have other, cheaper sources of internal or external financing for projects compared to what OPIC can provide. Large firms are also often priced out of political risk insurance markets, or they use mechanisms like diversification and currency hedging to take account of politically derived risks.[50] Executives at such firms claim to have participated in the USUBC efforts in hopes of renewing Ukrainian commitments to US investors.[51] On the diplomatic side, the US ambassador to Ukraine attributed his strong and vocal support for OPIC to USUBC efforts.[52] The Ukrainian vice prime minister, who ultimately shepherded OPIC reinstatement through his government, threw his support behind OPIC after a USUBC meeting, in which the US ambassador as well as firms like Microsoft, Baker & McKenzie, Cargill, and DHL took part.[53] Unlike the 1997 to 1999 efforts that quickly fizzled, the USUBC brought US firms, diplomats, and key Ukrainian politicians on board for a long campaign. The USUBC's leadership and representatives of its member firms became regular interlocutors with the US ambassador and the Ukrainian president and Council of Ministers, discussing OPIC with them in at least forty meetings from 2005 to 2009.[54]

Working together, US actors made the issue of an old broken contract salient to a Ukrainian government that was responsible for neither the original 1998 breach nor the breach of the provisional settlement in 2005. US actors' main task

---

[49] In his advocacy efforts, USUBC President Morgan Williams repeatedly cited OPIC's estimation that they had US$500 million of investment committed to enter Ukraine upon reopening. USUBC workshops on OPIC financing held in early 2010 attracted 260 representatives from US firms. As reported by the USUBC.

[50] The Ukrainian country leader at a major oil firm, who requested a copy of my interview questions in advance, was puzzled by the mention of political risk insurance. Before the interview, he asked around the office and called headquarters to see if the firm used it. He reported that he could only find one instance: an export credit agency might have supported the firm's investment in a several billion dollar pipeline in China. Interview, foreign firm in oil and gas, Ukraine.

[51] Interviews (3), US firms, Washington, D.C. and Ukraine, 2009 and 2011.

[52] The ambassador was disappointed that OPIC was not fully reinstated before his term ended in mid-2009. Interview, USUBC, Washington, D.C., 2012.

[53] Firms with investment interests in the United States can also join the USUBC; these members, too, stand behind campaigns on behalf of particular US firms. Interviews (3), Washington, D.C. and Ukraine, 2009 and 2011. "Hryhoriy Nemyrya met with American investors," Press office of Vice Prime Minister of Ukraine, 31 January 2008. Reprinted by USUBC.

[54] Compiled from USUBC records. In 2008, USUBC President Williams stated that the OPIC dispute was under discussion in every meeting he had attended, in Washington or Kyiv, in recent years. Morgan Williams, "OPIC programs closed for Ukraine," US-Ukrainian Business Council News Release, 13 February 2008.

was to assuage the Ukrainian government's concerns that OPIC restitution would have a negative effect on non-US foreign investment. The two governments signed a Memorandum of Understanding in 2008 addressing this point, resolving that the breach "should not be considered as constituting any admission on behalf of the Ukrainian side of any commitment, debt, complaint, or other claim of any company."[55] In 2009, US Vice President Biden lauded this progress during a visit to Ukraine, saying that bringing OPIC back would "make it easier for American companies to reinvest in Ukraine, and invest in the first place."[56] Two days before the final Council of Minister's meeting to approve the restitution settlement in 2009, OPIC's champion in the Ukrainian government took the unprecedented step of inviting the USUBC president to help draft the final resolution in order to avoid more bureaucratic hold-ups. Once signed, OPIC immediately restored operations.[57]

OPIC's reinstatement took place thanks to the growth of the USUBC and its sustained efforts to organize US lobbying and diplomatic efforts. Interestingly, OPIC played only a small role in the multi-year campaign for its own reinstatement.[58] It was the USUBC that pulled in the support of US diplomats and key Ukrainian officials, taking advantage of its membership's interest in what OPIC's re-entry meant for the treatment of US investors more broadly. The late 2000s brought an environment in which fewer other national groups were available to substitute for foregone US-origin FDI – despite the fact that Ukraine hosted FDI at unprecedentedly high levels (even as the worldwide financial crisis began). Faced with concurrent strong US diplomatic and investor pressure for restitution, the Ukrainian government restored contract sanctity for US firms.

Considering Alternative Explanations

When pushed for an explanation, US actors attribute the decade-long OPIC breach to inter-agency confusion within the Ukrainian government and its bureaucracy.[59] When the Ukrainian government violates a contract with a foreign firm, that firm interacts with low-level bureaucrats in the customs, tax, or other relevant administration, perhaps writing letters to gain a meeting with higher-level Ministry officials. Disputes remain housed within particular

---

[55] "Bogdan Danylyshyn and William Taylor sign Memorandum," Ukrainian Ministry of Economy, Minister's Press office, 11 November 2008.

[56] Statement by Vice President Biden after meeting with President Viktor Yushchenko of Ukraine. The White House, Office of the Vice President, 21 July 2009.

[57] Consistent with OPIC's position all along, the settlement did not require a direct payment of US$17.7 million. The agreed-upon US$5 million payment was off-budget, to be paid in two payments per year over ten years. The funds were to come from a commercial group recycling leftover ammunition from Alliant Kyiv. This settlement further demonstrates OPIC's willingness to compromise in order to re-enter Ukraine.

[58] Interviews (4), OPIC and USUBC, Washington, D.C., 2009 and 2012.

[59] Interview, OPIC, Cambridge, MA, 2009.

administrations, as there is no state structure with the overall mandate to interact with foreign firms.[60] Lawsuits are handled within the Ministry of Justice; only if a legal dispute becomes an IA does the Ministry of Justice call a meeting with the cabinet of ministers, prime minister, and president.[61] Foreign firms in Ukraine are conscious of these institutional disconnects between government lawyers, low-level bureaucrats, and politicians at the highest levels. This is one reason that the USUBC's ability to cultivate relationships with top Ukrainian politicians was important to OPIC's resolution. By aggregating US firms' protests, the USUBC gained the clout to bypass the bureaucratic apparatus and access politicians who can be difficult for even the most prominent of foreign firms to reach.

Yet bureaucratic confusion is an implausible explanation for the progression of US efforts. If it was only red tape that kept the Ukrainian government from realizing its genuine interest in resolving US disputes, it is unlikely that US actors would have given up their advocacy so quickly in the late 1990s and for so many years. Ukraine's successive presidents and prime ministers were in fact aware of the OPIC issue and gave lip service to its importance over the breach's ten-year duration. Rather than attributing inaction to the issue being lost in Ukraine's bureaucracy, the explanation offered here takes seriously the Ukrainian government's worries that restitution would be consummate to signaling to all foreign investors the state's willingness to expropriate. It also takes seriously the variation in US diplomats' and firms' willingness to support the cause. As by 2009 the complexity of Ukraine's bureaucratic institutions dealing with foreign investors had not changed, renewed US interest in the cause more plausibly contributed to Ukraine's actions.

Industry-based collective action played no role in bringing about OPIC's restitution. We might expect that the political risk insurance and project finance industry in Ukraine would be interested in fighting the OPIC breach, for fear of the precedent it would set for their own interactions with the government. In Ukraine, members of this industry include OPIC-like agencies from other home countries as well as public, multilateral organizations including the Multilateral Investment Guarantee Agency (MIGA), the International Finance Corporation (IFC), and the European Bank for Reconstruction and Development (EBRD). However, public funding does not keep these organizations from considering themselves OPIC's competitors. Rather than signaling shared risks, OPIC's contract breach opened up a new set of potential US clients seeking political risk insurance and financing that now did not have the option of using an

---

[60] At least four official agencies tasked with interacting with foreign firms have existed in Ukraine. Individuals in the foreign investment community, as well as at multilateral organizations, view these agencies as irrelevant. Interviews (2), including current Ukrainian agency tasked with foreign investor relations, Ukraine, 2009.

[61] Interviews (2), foreign and domestic law firms representing both the Ukrainian government and foreign firms in international litigation, Ukraine, 2009 and 2011.

US institution.[62] Respondents at various organizations acknowledged the competitive advantage they gained from what they framed as OPIC's "mistake": "OPIC really shouldn't have financed a business on a military base."[63] Given that other players gained competitive advantages as a result of OPIC's absence, and they did not see themselves engaging in analogous contracts, industry-based support for OPIC did not substitute for nor complement US actors' efforts.

NORWEGIANS, RUSSIANS, AND CELL PHONES

From 2005 to 2009, the state-owned Norwegian telecommunications firm Telenor was embroiled in a commercial dispute that spilled over into its relations with the Ukrainian government. The government faced significant pressure to breach its commitments to Telenor, not only from domestic sources but also from Russian business and political actors aiming to gain by Telenor's downfall. But with fewer other national investor groups to draw on in this period, the Ukrainian government was sensitive to retaining Norwegian investment. In fact, preserving Norwegian investment in Ukraine was necessary to keep the mobile telecommunications industry from being wholly Russian-owned, an outcome opposed by virtually all political players in Ukraine.

The nationality shield theory predicts that co-national action among Norwegians in Ukraine should have been strong in this environment of low FDI diversity. Other private Norwegian firms should have acted as though their contract sanctity were tied up with Telenor's. What is more, as a state-owned firm, Telenor likely had ready access to diplomatic resources. Indeed, while the Ukrainian government at times wavered in its treatment of Telenor, it ultimately did not break its commitment to the firm's fundamental ability to operate and own property in the country. The preservation of Telenor's contract in Ukraine stands in clear contrast to Telenor's experience in Russia, where the Russian government expropriated Telenor in the context of high FDI national diversity. In that country, Norwegian lobbying and diplomatic pressures were weak. This difference between the Ukrainian and Russian experiences corresponds to the idea that actors have less incentive to fight contract breach when FDI national diversity is high and the likelihood of successful deterrence is low – even if the state owns the firm in question.

Telenor was the majority owner of Kyivstar, Ukraine's leading mobile service provider, and it invested US$1.3 billion in Ukraine from 1997 to 2010. Telenor's conflicts grew out of its contentious relationship with Alfa Group, a Russian oligarch-owned conglomerate. By 2005, Telenor and Alfa Group's partnerships were complex: Telenor was the majority owner of Kyivstar (57 percent) and Alfa

---

[62] It is hard to draw conclusions about the effects OPIC's absence might have had on pricing in the industry, as the terms of deals tend to be entirely project-based. Interview, European Bank for Reconstruction and Development, Ukraine, 2009.

[63] Interview, international organization, Ukraine, 2009.

Group was the minority owner (44 percent); in Russia, their positions were switched as Alfa Group was the majority owner of VimpelCom (44 percent) and Telenor was the minority owner (30 percent).[64] The core of the commercial dispute between Telenor and Alfa Group was over the interpretation of the shareholders' agreements in each of these ventures. The Kyivstar agreement prevented either party from taking more than a 5 percent stake in a competing mobile provider, and the VimpelCom agreement required the board to approve any acquisition. The crux of the matter was that Russia's Alfa Group, both directly and via VimpelCom, invested significantly in two Kyivstar competitors without Telenor's approval.[65]

The Conflict in Russia

The VimpelCom conflict was specific to Russia, where Alfa Group is the domestic firm and Telenor is the foreign firm. Looking back at Figure 5.1, we see that Russia's FDI national diversity in the late 2000s has been higher than Ukraine's. As a large economy with a significant endowment of natural resources, Russia possesses the structural features expected to give its government leverage over foreign firms at the time of investment and after contracts have been struck.[66] High levels of FDI national diversity are consistent with this expectation of power on the side of the Russian government. Throughout the 2000s, Russia's political actors proved very willing to engage in high-profile conflicts with foreign firms, and there is strong evidence that the legal system was manipulated to the detriment of foreign firms' property rights.

The Norwegian government had previously intervened in Russia on Telenor's behalf in 2000 and 2004, first to deter the Russian Communications Ministry from taking back allocated frequencies, and second to lower Telenor's suddenly high tax burden.[67] In the second half of the 2000s, however, Telenor lost several legal cases that were brought by shadowy shareholders and heard in obscure Siberian towns in what were seen by international observers as politically driven rulings. Once these decisions began coming down against Telenor, Norway's government stepped back. In 2006, the Norwegian Trade and Industry Minister

---

[64] For the ease of the reader, I use the parent firm, Alfa Group, to stand in for the various wholly owned subsidiaries that were involved in transactions with and litigation against Telenor. These include Storm LLC, Altimo, Eco Telecom, Alfa Telecom, and Alpren.

[65] VimpelCom's board of directors had three members that are independent, three appointed by Telenor, and three appointed by Alfa Group. According to the shareholders' agreement, purchasing shares in other companies required an 80 percent majority of shareholder votes. Without Telenor's votes, VimpelCom did not have sufficient approval for its actions. "Russia's VimpelCom signs option to buy Ukraine's WellCom," Prime-Tass English language business newswire, 18 March 2005.

[66] E.g., Vernon 1971.

[67] "Norwegian Telenor offered ultimatum to VimpelCom," *Russian Business Monitor*, 1 April 2005. (Original source: *Vedomosti*, 30 March 2005.)

said his government would not interfere and that "there should be no concern that the conflict between Telenor and Alfa would scare away Norwegian investment in Russia."[68] With this statement, the Norwegian government explicitly attempted to downplay the bilateral implications of Russian actions against Telenor.

Similarly questionable legal procedures had resulted in broken contracts in Russia before, but foreign firms of other national origins with analogous experiences did not come to Telenor's aid. The British oil and gas firm BP had faced questionable court decisions that resulted in the effective expropriation of its stake in the joint venture TNK-BP, but BP made no public comment on Telenor's situation.[69] Neither did the Swedish-Finnish telecommunications firm TeliaSonera, which too had faced a shareholder dispute involving Alfa Group.[70] Why did these firms keep quiet? I contend that whatever solidarity they might have felt with Telenor was outweighed by these firms' sense that their contract sanctity was not tied up with the outcome of Telenor's contract dispute. Perhaps Telenor's problems helped them avoid further conflicts with the Russian government or gained them competitive advantages. Regardless, firms across different nationalities – even those having faced the same problems – remained publicly indifferent.

In an environment in which entry and reinvestment by a variety of national groups was the norm, and in which the Telenor dispute gained no supporters even from other firms facing similar problems, the Norwegian government explicitly stepped back from using its nationals' FDI in Russia as leverage in the Telenor conflict. The Russian government had little incentive to change its stance toward Telenor's operations and followed through with expropriation. By 2010, Telenor's accrued fines totaled US$1.7 billion. The Russian government froze Telenor's assets, effectively halting its ability to operate in Russia.

"The War against Telenor in Ukraine"

Telenor and Alfa Group's conflict in Ukraine began in earnest in 2005. Against Telenor's wishes, the two firms' Russian joint venture purchased a direct competitor to Kyivstar, their Ukrainian joint venture. Having benefitted from the Russian government's breach of contract with Telenor in Russia, Alfa Group continued "the war against Telenor in Ukraine," in the words of a major Russian newspaper.[71] Alfa Group's first Ukrainian lawsuit challenged the legality of Kyivstar's shareholders' agreement, though the agreement had

---

[68] "Norway, Russia don't plan to interfere in Telenor, Alfa Conflict," *Ukraine Business Daily*, 16 March 2006.

[69] Gustafson 2012.

[70] TeliaSonera had a 44 percent stake in a Russian mobile firm (Megafon) and had been involved in its own shareholder dispute with Alfa Group, owner of a 25 percent stake.

[71] "Alfa Group continues the war against Telenor in Ukraine," *Russian Business Monitor*, 22 April 2005. (Original source: *Vedomosti*, 20 April 2005.)

been negotiated just one year prior. A Ukrainian court found in favor of Telenor and upheld the shareholders' agreement, and the Ukrainian government publicly supported the verdict.[72] In this case, the Ukrainian legal system and government maintained commitments to contract sanctity. This outcome is especially important, because the government's actions aligned with the international norm of government non-interference in private, voluntary agreements, and the government also followed the Commercial Code of Ukraine's explicit prohibition of "unlawful intrusion by governmental authorities and their officers in economic relations."

However, Alfa Group shortly began winning court cases in Ukraine, restricting the authority of Kyivstar's board of directors (August 2005), banning a board of directors meeting (December 2005), and requiring that Telenor and Alfa Group should have equal representation on the board despite Telenor's owning 13 percent more shares (January 2006). The Ukrainian Supreme Economic Court upheld this last ruling (February 2006).[73] In 2007, a court ruling forbade Ernst & Young from auditing Kyivstar without board approval, which was impossible to get as Alfa Group had been boycotting Kyivstar's board meetings for nearly two years. Not only the verdicts in these cases but also their existence were contrary to the shareholders' agreement, which stated that all conflicts would be resolved in international courts and would not be prosecuted under Ukrainian law. By hearing these cases, the judicial system was complicit in a violation of the shareholders' agreement. When an international judge was finally able to rule on a case brought by Telenor, he called Alfa Group's Ukrainian lawsuits "collusive and vexatious litigation" and wrote that Ukrainian legal opinions "appear to be nothing more than a sham."[74] The Ukrainian courts did not respond immediately or in full to this or subsequent international rulings requiring them to stop hearing cases brought by Alfa Group. However, Ukrainian courts did begin to find in Telenor's favor, and Alfa Group dropped a number of lawsuits in late 2007.[75]

In the dispute, the Ukrainian government occupied an awkward space between censuring the judiciary for eating away at Telenor's property rights and distancing itself from the conflict. In 2006, three members of Parliament from eastern Ukraine, a region with considerable Russian sympathies, argued that three appeals court judges had "deliberately pass[ed] an illegal sentence

---

[72] Ukraine had only vague laws on joint-stock companies at this time. The clearest law was that shareholders' meetings require the presence of owners of at least 60 percent of the firm's shares. Interview, think tank, Washington, D.C., 2012.

[73] "Prosecutor General's Office opens criminal case," *Ukraine Business Weekly*, 10 October 2006.

[74] "US Federal Court grants Telenor motion, holds Altimo in contempt, imposes fines and orders Altimo to sell shares," *Marketwire*, 20 November 2008.

[75] While the international ruling likely influenced the Ukrainian government's behavior, it did not stop all judicial mistreatment of Telenor: one Ukrainian court ruled that the New York arbitration was unenforceable in Ukraine, despite Ukraine's membership in the international convention on the enforcement of foreign arbitral rulings (October 2007).

or ruling" in favor of Telenor.[76] The result was a prosecution of the three judges – and not of Telenor. What is more, the case was shortly abandoned. Even Ukrainian government actors from the region with the greatest potential biases against Telenor did not pursue state action against Telenor itself, instead using domestic targets to score political points. At the other extreme, those government officials sympathetic to Telenor began to speak out on the firm's behalf. For example, the vice prime minister referred to Telenor when he said, "the situation in Ukraine has reached absurdity when any district court can determine the fate of a serious strategic enterprise."[77]

Ultimately, the Ukrainian government refrained from taking actions tantamount to expropriating Telenor. In contrast to the situation in Russia, the Ukrainian government never froze Telenor's assets, and the government made some efforts to rectify injustices dealt Telenor through the judicial system. In fact, despite the intense years of conflict in 2006 and 2007, Telenor's profits from Kyivstar in 2007 were US$316 million, a year-on-year increase in profitability of 54 percent.[78] The underlying conflict ended when Telenor and Alfa Group came to an understanding in 2009 and merged their Russian and Ukrainian ventures.[79]

Norwegian Collective Efforts

Like the US investors advocating on OPIC's behalf around the same time, Norwegians were neither the largest nor the most prominent national investor group in Ukraine. But, if Telenor had exited the Ukrainian market, two powerful Russian firms – Alfa Group and MTS – would have controlled Ukraine's telecommunications industry. Even Russian-sympathetic politicians in Ukraine oppose deals that would cause Russian ownership of an entire industry. Low FDI national diversity, within the broader economy and certainly within the industry, set the stage for effective Norwegian activism on Telenor's behalf.

Norwegian actors in Ukraine were for many years committed to making their presence known as a national group. In 2004, before Telenor's conflict with Alfa Group had gotten underway in Ukraine, but when spillover from the Russian conflict seemed likely, Telenor's top executives from Norway met with then-President Kuchma, who "marked how important it is for Ukraine to optimize bilateral relations with Norway."[80] The Norwegian ambassador and the Norwegian minister of trade and industry met with Ukrainian officials to

---

[76] "Prosecutor General's Office opens criminal case," *Ukraine Business Weekly*, 10 October 2006.
[77] "Telenor supports anti-raiding commission of Ukrainian government," *The Ukrainian Times*, 14 March 2007.
[78] "Ukraine: Telenor profit exceeds US$316mn," *Emersk Ukraine News* (via Sostav.ua), 25 July 2008.
[79] The Ukrainian Anti-Monopoly Commission reviewed and approved the merger after responding to an appeal from another mobile operator in Ukraine.
[80] "Kuchma orders to open Ukrainian embassy in Norway in near future," *Ukraine Business Report*, 30 January 2004.

discuss, among other subjects, "prospects for Kyivstar's development."[81] A variety of private Norwegian investors were present at these meetings, including a producer of farm equipment, a fish exporter, and a ship-building firm, all of which had made major investments in Ukraine but none of which were involved in Telenor or Kyivstar directly.[82] As in the case of US multinationals acting on behalf of OPIC, being Norwegian suggested enough similarities for these firms to offer a common front to the Ukrainian government. Kuchma subsequently opened a Ukrainian embassy in Norway.

As the Telenor dispute progressed, Ukraine's esteem for Norwegian investors was challenged. In 2007, signs appeared on Kyiv streets and outside Telenor's offices that read "Norwegians! Respect Ukrainian Laws!!" and "Norwegians, go home!"[83] An Alfa Group document soon emerged, entitled "Logical Rationale for the Information Campaign under the Kyivstar Contract," that read in part: "in order to break the existing stereotype whereby Western business and, in particular, Norwegian business always plays fair, an information wave of negative publicity should be started."[84] An accompanying spreadsheet suggested that Alfa Group's Ukrainian subsidiary should spend US$75,000 buying Ukrainian press coverage against Norwegians in just two months of 2007.[85] Consistent with the nationality shield theory, these attacks were not framed against Telenor in particular but against Norwegians as a national group. Even if Norwegians had not previously thought of themselves as a cohesive group, their detractors were willing to spend money characterizing them in such a way. Alfa Group's efforts aimed to isolate Norwegians from other nationalities so as to differentiate the legitimacy and importance of their contracts from those of others. In other words, Alfa Group thought that the nationality of capital could matter to the public and, in turn, to political perceptions of FDI. Also consistent with the nationality shield theory, interview respondents at firms from other home countries saw no reason to publicly coalesce with Telenor or Norwegians during these anti-Norwegian campaigns, though many were personally outraged by the sentiment.[86]

As Alfa Group's negative campaign made Norwegians' implicitly shared risks explicit, Norwegian firms and diplomats redoubled their efforts to shield Telenor's and their own contract sanctity. Building on their strong bilateral relations from before Telenor's conflict, Norwegian actors used both sticks and carrots with the Ukrainian government. With the Norwegian government

[81] Ibid.

[82] "Norway to boost investments in Ukraine," *Ukraine Business Weekly*, 29 March 2004.

[83] "How the Kremlin thawed a telecoms freeze in Siberia," *The Evening Standard (London)*, 17 November 2008, 29.

[84] Kramer, Andrew, "Russian Company accused of buying press coverage," *New York Times*, 14 March 2007. It has not been uncommon for firms to buy press coverage in other countries of the former Soviet Union.

[85] Ibid.

[86] Interviews (4), US, French, British, and Swedish firms, Ukraine, 2009 and 2011.

as a co-author, Telenor publicly petitioned the Ukrainian government to investigate the "objectivity, impartiality, and independence of judges" regarding their "interference with good corporate governance and business morals."[87] At the same time, Norwegian interests formed the Norwegian Chamber of Commerce, highlighting that Ukraine's market "could be very promising not only in the area of communications."[88] These examples of co-national lobbying and diplomacy are the tip of the iceberg of efforts that occurred regularly behind closed doors from 2005 to 2009.[89]

Low FDI national diversity gave the Ukrainian government incentives to keep Telenor invested in the country, and Norwegian actors made it clear that Norwegian investment and Norway's good relations with Ukraine were at stake if the Ukrainian government took adverse action against Telenor. In the context of these pressures counteracting Alfa Group's influence, the Ukrainian government ultimately refrained from contract breach.

Considering Alternative Explanations

Telenor's Ukrainian conflict ended during the worldwide financial crisis, when FDI into emerging economies was on the wane. With fewer alternate options for FDI going forward, the Ukrainian government was surely interested in retaining investors. Thus, the financial crisis may have exacerbated the constraints under which the Ukrainian government acted. Nevertheless, the history of the dispute demonstrates that breach was possible – some judges along the way certainly flirted with breach. And nationality played a central role in the dispute's framing and in protests by and on behalf of Telenor. Thus, while the amount of FDI in Ukraine likely played a role in the dispute's resolution, the evidence strongly suggests that nationality did as well.

Another alternative explanation for Telenor's intact contract is that it received support from other European countries' diplomats or firms, since it is an investor from Europe, albeit not the European Union. Over the 2000s, the European Business Association (EBA) had grown to represent the interests of investors into Ukraine originating from across Europe. Telenor is a member of the EBA and its top executives in Ukraine have served on its board. In interviews, executives at two prominent European firms said that the EBA is willing to advocate on behalf of individual firms, mentioning Telenor as one example. Were this true, it would tend to undercut the argument that co-national collective action and not multinational collective action was an important determinant of the outcome of Telenor's contract dispute.

[87] "Telenor asks authorities to investigate outcome of 11 rulings of Ukrainian courts," *The Ukrainian Times*, 14 February 2007.
[88] "Norwegian-Ukrainian Chamber of Commerce established," *Comtex News Network, Hugin AS*, 21 November 2008.
[89] Interviews (2), government officials, Ukraine, 2009.

In fact, top administrators at the EBA were clear in interviews that the EBA does not advocate on behalf of particular firms, and it did not advocate on Telenor's behalf.[90] These administrators carried out the work of the EBA, by writing letters to officials, maintaining government contacts, facilitating meetings, and providing the EBA's public face in Ukrainian and expatriate media. That EBA staff did not see the EBA as a forum for particular firms to resolve their grievances with the government reveals a disparity between certain investors' beliefs about the EBA's activities and what the association actually does. It is possible that individual executives advocated on Telenor's behalf thanks to government connections facilitated by the EBA, but this advocacy would have been isolated and undercut by the EBA's deliberate inaction on behalf of Telenor.

For example, in 2008 the EBA set up a number of working groups on corporate raidership, the crux of the problem facing Telenor.[91] The EBA president, however, specified to the Norwegian press that EBA efforts against raidership were not on Telenor's behalf.[92] The equally multinational Chamber/ACC worked together with the EBA to lobby the Ukrainian Rada for legislation codifying shareholder rights and closing loopholes that had facilitated raidership. Both organizations consider the legislation's adoption a great success story.[93] Nevertheless, the head of Telenor's operations in Ukraine stated plainly that this legislation "does not directly influence [their] conflict."[94]

Telenor's experiences provide a good illustration of the comparative advantages of multinational investor associations as opposed to nationality-based associations. Investors from a variety of home countries share interests in certain kinds of business-friendly policy and can come together to lobby around issues like broad-based legislation. But multinational investor associations shy away from individual firms' contract disputes. The political, strategic, and diplomatic background to a national group's contract sanctity emphasizes bilateral ties and downplays the relevance of a particular breach to multilateral actors. Because member firms of different nationalities do not share the same determinants of contract sanctity, they do not share a general interest in expending resources on each other's contract disputes. In an interview at a Ukrainian subsidiary from a small Western European home country, the CEO lamented that there was no European Union-tied lobbying group, let alone an EU "embassy," that would represent firms from small countries in their contract disputes.[95]

[90] Interviews (3), EBA, Ukraine, 2011.

[91] From many observers' point of view, Alfa Group's actions toward Telenor amounted to raidership: Alfa Group sought to change the balance of power in its partnerships with Telenor, with the ultimate intention of pushing Telenor to sell out so that Alfa Group could merge the Russian and Ukrainian operations.

[92] "Ukraine: Telenor accuses Altimo of raid attempt," *Esmerk Norway News*, 10 April 2008.

[93] Interviews (4), American Chamber of Commerce and EBA, Ukraine, 2009 and 2011.

[94] "New law on joint-stock companies not to settle conflict," *Ukraine Business Weekly*, 13 October 2008.

[95] Interview, manufacturing firm, Ukraine, 2009.

One interpretation of the outcome of Telenor's conflict could be that the Ukrainian government did breach a foreign firm's contract: that of Russia's Alfa Group. From the point of view of Alfa Group, and other Russian actors that likely advocated on its behalf behind closed doors, the Ukrainian government's refusal to support its claims outright could be a violation of at least informal government commitments to the firm. The wholly different desires of Norwegian and Russian firms in this case support the point that all foreign firms cannot be considered as a single entity: interpretations of government actions can vary by investor national origins, just as contract risks vary by national origin. Because international courts validated Telenor's claims, the choice to relate the case from Telenor's point of view aligns with the most objective understanding of the Ukrainian government's actions. That the Ukrainian government showed restraint toward Telenor's contract goes to show that a firm from a major investor home country like Russia may not have sufficient leverage to negate a small national investor group's contract sanctity.

A COMMON THREAT BUT CO-NATIONAL ACTION

The nationality shield theory proposes that national origin is a key determinant of resources to fight government breach of contract. In a situation where threats to contract sanctity extend across national groups, the theory implies that national groups facing common threats still defend themselves behind their own shields. Even in situations where cross-national efforts might logically be thought to be helpful to firms, co-national action should dominate, because co-national resources are best suited to advocate for contract sanctity. A common threat to contract sanctity presented itself in Ukraine in 2005, when the Orange government threatened to nationalize and reprivatize assets across the economy. Nevertheless, it was nationality-tied resources that provided a ready source of powerful home-country support and lobbying efforts for foreign firms to successfully deter breach in Ukraine.

In January 2005, the Orange Revolution produced a coalition government with Viktor Yushchenko as president and Julia Tymoshenko as prime minister. In February, Tymoshenko created headlines when she announced that the government had a list of "3,000 cases of illegal privatizations" that it would nationalize and reprivatize. Tymoshenko proclaimed, "We will return to the state that which was illegally taken from it."[96] The Finance Minister tried to clarify this statement, saying that the list of 3,000 privatizations "may increase, but this does not mean a declaration of war against all private owners."[97]

---

[96] "Daily Alert – PM sparks unease over sell-off review," *Emerging Markets Daily News*, 17 February 2005.

[97] "Ukrainian finance minister plays down mass reprivatization fears," *BBC Monitoring Ukraine and Baltics*, 18 February 2005. Taken from a televised interview on Ukrainian ICTV television. Reported by *Interfax Ukraine*.

A week later, however, Members of the Rada proposed legislation to legalize nationalization that meets "the social needs of the state and municipalities," omitting consideration of Ukraine's international legal obligations to foreign investors such as those incurred through Ukraine's BITs.[98]

A local observer's summary of the reprivatization threat was apt: "Tymoshenko is still behaving like a revolutionary and is playing the populist card."[99] Reprivatization was popular indeed. A 2005 poll found that 71 percent of Ukrainians supported Tymoshenko's plan to revise privatization results, with 81 percent in support in the populous and cosmopolitan Kyiv and Central Ukraine.[100] This sentiment was largely a reaction to the Kuchma government's notorious sales of state assets at fire sale prices to political insiders, leading a member of the Rada to lament, "[sixty percent] of Ukrainian industry has been sold for 2 billion hrivnyas [US$3.7 million]! What bureaucrats call privatization has in fact turned out to have been a brutal robbery of state property."[101] Indeed, backlash against legacies of corrupt, insider, and otherwise non-transparent privatizations are common across post-communist countries: in a 2006 regional survey, over 80 percent of 27,000 respondents from twenty-seven transition countries wanted their governments to demand additional payments from private owners ex post, resell property for higher prices in new tenders, or return property to state ownership.[102] Unskilled workers and individuals in post-communist democracies have been more supportive of reprivatization, which played to the populist base Tymoshenko developed during the Orange Revolution.[103] Tymoshenko found a moment in which she predicted she had the permissive space to act on incentives to breach – though, in fact, she was later proven wrong.

President Yushchenko protested that Tymoshenko's plan sounded like "a full revision of privatization processes in Ukraine," but reprivatization's popularity and Ukraine's need for cash to fund its budget kept him from wholly opposing it.[104] In the weeks that followed the original announcement, Yushchenko assured reporters that the "exhaustive list" of privatizations to be reviewed would be not zero but forty, then "several dozen," then "about twenty" privatizations.[105] Nonetheless, the government never made clear the criteria that

---

[98] "Nationalization legislation proposed," *Interfax Ukraine*, 25 February 2005.
[99] "Ukraine's Yushchenko slaps down PM on privatization threat," *Agence France Presse*, 18 February 2005.
[100] Poll in Ukraine, by the Kyiv International Institute of Sociology. "Poll: 71.3% of Ukrainians back privatization," *Interfax News Service*, 14 May 2005.
[101] "Robbery of state property," *Interfax Ukraine*, 24 April 2003.
[102] Denisova et al. 2009, 2012; Wellhausen 2010.
[103] Wellhausen 2010. Workers in foreign firms have more to lose from privatization revision and are more likely to oppose it.
[104] "Yushchenko, Tymoshenko united on reprivatization," *Interfax Ukraine*, 22 February 2005.
[105] "Ukraine to draft 'exhaustive list' of companies for reprivatization," *BBC Monitoring Ukraine and Baltics*, 15 February 2005. "Yushchenko, Tymoshenko united on reprivatization," *Interfax Ukraine*, 22 February 2005. "Ukraine to review privatization of 20 major firms this year: deputy

would put a privatized asset on the list of firms to be reviewed, nor did it make the list public.

With no clarity as to what it meant for a privatization to be illegal, or how follow-on owners would be held accountable for owning property that was once distributed illegally, foreign firms across the economy felt threats to their contract sanctity. Much FDI entered Ukraine via privatization tenders. When it did not, FDI can often be traced back to privatized assets through a trail of mergers and acquisitions made over many years. Tymoshenko's threats in 2005 implicated privatizations made as long ago as 1992. "Horrified investors" worried that that broad reprivatization would "send a very bad message that the old government giveth and the new government taketh."[106] With "the property rights of thousands of enterprises in limbo," the mechanism of FDI exit and diversion operated in many national groups of investors.[107] Aggregate FDI was 14 percent lower in the first six months of the Orange government than it had been under the Kuchma regime a year earlier.[108] Thus, when the threat to contract sanctity was perceived as universal, conventional wisdom about FDI exit held true: foreign firms across the whole economy re-evaluated their strategies and decreased or diverted planned investments. This imposed heavy costs on Ukraine's Orange government, which needed tax revenue and economic growth to keep the country afloat and fulfill the coalition's development promises.

Although risks to contract sanctity were common across nationalities, investors and their representatives framed their frustrations in national terms and protested using national resources. For example, in June 2005, Yushchenko reassured Czech investors at a special forum on reprivatization attended by the Czech President Vaclav Klaus. Ukrainian television aired a program on German investors' fears of reprivatization and then one on British investors' fears.[109] The

PM," *Agence France Presse*, 26 February 2005. Yushchenko also clearly alluded to the Yukos takeover in Russia, saying that Ukraine would review privatizations "in a very different way." "Ukraine's Yushchenko slaps down PM on privatization threat," *Agence France Presse*, 18 February 2005.

[106] Chazan, Guy, "Kiev's Orange Revolution is soiled – Ukrainian cronyism scandal, symbolized by steel plant, divides new government," *Wall Street Journal Europe*, 12 September 2005. "Q&A with pro-Ukraine investment banker Michael Bleyzer," *Kyiv Post*, 27 January 2005. Bleyzer explained what he would do regarding reprivatizations: "I would take one or two showcases and review them, trying to be fair and objective. In some cases, getting additional compensation would be sufficient if there is enough assurance that that would have been the market price had the tender been run transparently; in other cases it is possible that re-tendering them would be the option. However, this is a less attractive option, as it will send a very bad message that the old government giveth and the new government taketh. So I would certainly be very careful not to do a lot of those things."

[107] Aslund, Anders, "Betraying a Revolution," *The Washington Post*, 18 May 2005.

[108] "Post-revolution Ukraine still awaits business Shangri-la," *Agence France Presse*, 16 November 2005.

[109] "German investor in Ukrainian titanium plant fears reprivatization," *BBC Monitoring Ukraine and Baltics*, 24 July 2005.

German and British ambassadors gave independent public statements demanding protection for their nationals' property; it is reasonable to assume that similar pressure from other ambassadors occurred behind the scenes. In July, a US assistant secretary of state testified on the threat of reprivatization before the US House of Representatives Committee on International Relations. The assistant secretary later visited Ukraine and participated in a specially organized group of US firms and diplomats that lobbied the Ukrainian government over threats of breach.[110] The USUBC took a strong stand against reprivatization and participated in behind-the-scenes negotiations.[111] British, French, German, and Israeli national investor associations came to imitate the USUBC in the mid-to-late 2000s, lobbying the Ukrainian government on their investors' behalf. National rather than multilateral advocates organized and pressured the Ukrainian government to commit to the sanctity of privatization contracts.

One set of co-nationals did interpret reprivatization as a more particular threat directed at their national group. Russian firms account for significant amounts of FDI into large, privatized Ukrainian assets, several of which were sold early in Ukraine's transition under non-transparent circumstances. Russian firms organized along national lines, framed reprivatization as an issue of discrimination against Russian investments, and drew on Russian political and diplomatic support to advocate for their property rights. The Russian Duma opened an investigation into the implications of Ukrainian reprivatization for Russian investors the day after Tymoshenko threatened to reprivatize 3,000 firms. Duma members claimed that the privatization review was motivated by anti-Russian sentiment and argued that Russia should take steps to defend its interests.[112] In lobbying Russian politicians for support, Russian firms framed reprivatization as "very harmful to the interests of Russia."[113] Russian President Vladimir Putin and Russian firms representing a variety of industries soon met with President Yushchenko, who promised that "nothing will happen to the lawfully acquired assets of Russian oligarchs."[114] Given the uncertainty over what it meant for a privatization to be lawful, this promise likely did little to assuage Russian concerns.

A reprivatization list was leaked in May 2005, four months after Tymoshenko's original announcement. This confirmed Russian fears, as four Russian-owned firms, in petrochemicals, steel, mining, and aluminum, were the only foreign firms among the twenty-nine privatized firms listed.[115] In the first

---

[110] Interviews (2), Washington, D.C., 2011.

[111] Interview, USUBC, Washington, D.C., 2011.

[112] "Russia moves to safeguard interests from Ukraine 'de-privatization'," *Agence France Presse*, 18 February 2005.

[113] "LukOil, TNK-BP, Tatneft, Alliance Group asking Russian Prime Minister Fradkov to protect their interests in Ukraine," *Ukrainian News*, 19 April 2005.

[114] "The fate of Russian investments in Ukraine," *Moskovskii Komsomolets*, No. 55, 16 March 2005. "Russian companies in Ukraine are kept on a short leash," *Vedomosti*, 28 April 2005.

[115] Wilson 2005: 166.

major repossession of privatized property, a Ukrainian court ordered the renationalization of a Russian-owned aluminum plant. The head of a powerful
Russian association put this action in bilateral terms: "this reprivatization is
clearly anti-Russian … We do not hear anything about European or American
assets."[116] Rather than using the worries of investors of other nationalities as a
means to support the Russian cause to ensure contract sanctity, key Russian
actors framed reprivatization in terms of bilateral animosity between the
Western-oriented Orange government and Russia.

The difference between Russian and other investors' perceived contract sanctity became clear with the nationalization and reprivatization of Ukraine's
largest steel mill, Kryvorizhstal.[117] In 2004, Kuchma's government sold the
steel mill for US$800 million to prominent Ukrainian oligarchs who invested
via Cypriot firms. This price was about half of the high bid of US$1.5 billion put
forth by Mittal Steel.[118] The Orange government repossessed the mill without
compensation in 2005, fulfilling a promise that had been part of both
Yushchenko's and Tymoshenko's election campaigns. Yushchenko, for example, had argued that Kryvorizhstal "was not privatization, but the humiliation of
honest business; it humiliated the government."[119] The steel mill was resold in
October 2005 in a transparent auction, televised with much fanfare.[120] Mittal
Steel offered the unexpectedly high winning bid of US$4.8 billion.[121]

Russian investors protested Kryvorizhstal's reprivatization, worrying that it
would lead to more actions against similar, large-scale Russian investments that
often involved oligarchs and Russian–Cypriot firms. Yanukovych, the leader of
the Russian-sympathetic Party of the Regions, argued that the Kryvorizhstal's
reprivatization had a "negative effect on the image of Ukraine," and that "any
step under this very unpopular word reprivatization will definitely affect the

---

[116] "Russian companies in Ukraine are kept on a short leash," *Vedomosti*, 28 April 2005.
[117] The mill's name was changed shortly thereafter to Kryvyi Rih, but it will be referred to as
Kryvorizhstal for the ease of the reader.
[118] States regularly reserve the right to discriminate against foreign investment at the border. While
rejecting Mittal Steel's bid perhaps walks the line of breaching commitments to fair treatment to
foreign firms, it falls outside of the question considered here – breach of contracts and commitments made to existing foreign firms.
[119] "Yushchenko: Reprivatization policy would have discredited new government," *Associated
Press Newswires*, 6 October 2005. In a televised presidential debate, Yushchenko said, "When
we are divided, the authorities can steal Kryvorizhstal in one night, and we'll have to listen for
twelve months to the fairy-tales of this government." "Ukrainian presidential candidates clash in
TV debate," *BBC Summary of World Broadcasts*, 15 November 2004. Source: *UT1* (television
station). See also Aslund, Anders, "Betraying a Revolution," *The Washington Post*, 18 May
2005. "Yushchenko: Reprivatization policy would have discredited new government,"
Associated Press Newswires, 6 October 2005.
[120] "The Great Giveaway Revisited," *Kyiv Post*, 25 September 2008.
[121] The Ukrainian government had hoped to sell Kryvorizhstal for US$2 billion at best; its windfall
price gave the government new budgetary breathing room. Wilson 2005.

image of Ukraine and push away investors."[122] In contrast, non-Russian executives in Ukraine saw Kryvorizhstal's reprivatization as a signal of a new
commitment to transparency and anti-corruption. The publisher of the
English-language newspaper of record in Ukraine gave voice to the distinction
non-Russian investors made between Kryvorizhstal and the broader reprivatization threat, writing,

> Kryvorizhstal became a symbol of the corruption of Ukraine's old regime ... Yushchenko
> and other speakers made the lucrative steel mill a talking point of the Orange Revolution,
> promising to right the injustice ... After all the controversy over reprivatization this year,
> the government showed that it has the right values – transparency, honesty, and private
> enterprise – and that it knows how to do things correctly. Congratulations to Mittal and
> to the government.[123]

Reflecting on the reprivatization some years later, foreign executives in Ukraine
cited the US$4.8 billion price as an important beacon for major multinational
entrants from Western European countries, which contributed to Ukraine's FDI
boom. In the next years, for example, the Austrian bank Raiffeisen International
invested US$1 billion and the French bank BNP Paribas invested $360 million.[124] With Mittal Steel's entry and such large, associated investments concentrated in the hands of major Western European multinationals, Ukraine's
FDI national diversity dropped precipitously and remained low relative to the
previous trend (see again Figure 5.1).[125]

The decrease in FDI national diversity helped to create an environment
beneficial to all national groups threatened by broad reprivatization threats,
including Russian investors. Now that Kryvorizhstal had been rectified,
President Yushchenko faced mounting pressure from international actors to
stop the reprivatization campaign. Additionally, with new capital to rely on to
contribute to the government budget and the Ukrainian economy, Yushchenko's
motives in supporting limited reprivatization were satisfied. New, major foreign
firms were taking a chance on the Ukrainian government's commitment to
contract sanctity, and Yushchenko delivered accordingly.[126]

One month after Kryvorizhstal, Prime Minister Tymoshenko took steps to
nationalize and reprivatize another huge plant in the eastern city of Nikopol. But
Tymoshenko was accused of merely transferring the plant from one clan to
another without raising more revenue for the state or making the allocation of

---

[122] "Yanukovych cautions cabinet against reprivatization as it confuses investors," *Ukrainian News*, 24 December 2007.

[123] Sunden, Jed, "Welcome to Ukraine, Mittal Steel," *Kyiv Post*, 26 October 2005.

[124] "2008 Investment Climate Statement – Ukraine," US Department of State.

[125] Mittal Steel made its investment through a German subsidiary, growing the German share of FDI considerably (see subsequent sections for a consideration of Mittal's multiple nationality claims).

[126] Yushchenko was known to have a deep commitment to global markets, which he demonstrated while Chairman of the National Bank of Ukraine from 1993 to 1999.

property rights any more fair.[127] Yushchenko declared that "high officials had begun to direct events in favor of corporate interests" and that "everybody should get lost," dismissing his cabinet, removing Tymoshenko from office, and ending the Orange coalition government.[128] Yushchenko then canceled all reviews of privatization deals. If the leaked list was correct, three Russian firms with questionable assets directly benefitted from the abandonment of reprivatization. Even though Russians as a national group had been relatively unsuccessful in their own advocacy, Russian firms nevertheless gained contract sanctity within an environment of low FDI national diversity.

CO-NATIONALITY AMONG "TAX HAVEN" FIRMS

Kryvorizhstal was, indeed, a foreign-invested enterprise expropriated without compensation. Nine major shareholders within the purpose-built Ukrainian Investment and Metallurgical Union (IMU) bought the plant. While firm ownership in the region can be notoriously difficult to trace, several of these shareholders were incorporated in Cyprus.[129] Nevertheless, the consortium had close ties to the Kuchma administration, and ultimate control sat with two prominent Ukrainian oligarchs: Viktor Pinchuk, Kuchma's son-in-law, and Rinat Akhmetov, a Kuchma ally.

Kryvorizhstal's ownership exemplified a particular kind of offshore incorporation, known as "round-tripping," that occurs in a number of emerging economies. Round-tripping occurs when nationals invest capital in firms incorporated abroad and then reinvest in their countries of national origin. Round-tripped investors can withdraw funds just as any foreign investor would do, giving them a fundamental source of leverage over host governments interested in access to mobile capital. The threat of withdrawing their own capital did Kryvorizhstal's owners little good, however, as the threat to their contract sanctity was nationalization.

[127] Viktor Pinchuk, previous Kryvorizhstal owner and son-in-law to former president Kuchma, said Tymoshenko's actions were "show business, seizing property from the wealthy, and in particular me." At this time, Tymoshenko also began reprivatizing a chemical-fertilizer plant owned in part by a Western firm, Worldwide Chemical LLC. This fell by the wayside after Tymoshenko was removed as prime minister. Bellaby, Mara D, "Ukrainian tycoon hopes sacking of government will end all attempts to seize his businesses," *Associated Press Newswires*, 14 September 2005.

[128] Chazan, Guy, "Kiev's Orange Revolution is soiled – Ukrainian cronyism scandal, symbolized by steel plant, divides new government," *Wall Street Journal Europe*, 12 September 2005. Bellaby, Mara D, "Ukrainian tycoon hopes sacking of government will end all attempts to seize his businesses," *Associated Press Newswires*, 14 September 2005.

[129] The nine shareholders were: the Interpipe Corporation and the Nyzhnedniprovsky pipe plant, both controlled by Viktor Pinchuk; two coking and chemical plants (Avdiyivka and Markokhim) owned by System Capital Management, which was controlled by Rinat Akhmetov; the Ukrainian-Cypriot company Bipe Co. Ltd; two banks (Dnipro Bank and Ukrinvest Bank, a part-owner of UkrSibBank); the insurance firm Aura; and the metallurgical combine Azovstal. Pinchuk and Akhmetov are popularly understood to have been Kryvorizhstal's owners. "Cabinet starts to re-privatize Kryvorizhstal," *Business Report Ukraine*, 7 February 2005.

Firms incorporated in Cyprus but with Ukrainian capital have a sort of hybrid nationality, with ethnic ties to the host country and legal ties to Cyprus. The theoretical expectation is that such firms have access to a set of resources similar to other Cypriot-Ukrainian hybrids, related to Cypriot firms, but different from other nationalities of firms. In particular, Cypriot-Ukrainian firms should be keenly interested in each other's contract sanctity as, indeed, they share a unique combination of foreign and domestic determinants of contract risks. In terms of home country resources, incorporating in Cyprus gives firms access to the Cyprus–Ukraine BIT that round-tripped Ukrainian firms have used to publicly sue Ukraine several times.[130] But diplomats from tax havens like Cyprus have proven unwilling to take public stands on behalf of their "adopted nationals." As with traditional foreign investors, the expectation is that the Cypriot-Ukrainian firm behind Kryvorizhstal was unsuccessful in arranging any sort of cross-national action on its behalf.

There was outcry in the Ukrainian oligarch community over the government's reprivatization plans, as typified by their support for the status quo during the Orange Revolution. As these oligarchs are the actors responsible for many Ukrainian-Cypriot firms, we can presume that this group of investors felt a shared sense of risks to contract sanctity. But no international diplomats came to the owners' aid, nor did foreign investors of other national origins support the Cypriot-Ukrainian owners' protests. This lack of support from other foreign investors came as a surprise to Kryvorizhstal's Cypriot-Ukrainian owners, as made clear in an interview with its most prominent oligarch owner:

(INTERVIEWER): ... [Kryvorizhstal] will be sold in two weeks' time. And your predictions that no one will take part in the privatization are not coming true.
(PINCHUK): Let's look at what will happen on 24 October. It seems to me that the closer it gets to the tender, the more serious investors will start to ponder the situation. ...
There have been a whole number of violations around the reprivatization of the combine.
(INTERVIEWER): There is something you're not saying – what might prevent the repeat sale of Kryvorizhstal?

[130] The case that first allowed round-tripped firms to access BITs was in fact brought against Ukraine: a Lithuanian-incorporated firm, owned by Ukrainian nationals, was allowed to sue the Ukrainian government under the Lithuania-Ukraine BIT in 2004. The *Tokios* case came about when a Lithuanian-incorporated printing firm, owned by a Ukrainian political refugee, had its Ukrainian accounts frozen and its offices subject to repeated police and tax enforcement raids. This occurred under the Kuchma regime, after the firm printed a book about then-opposition leader Tymoshenko just prior to the 2002 parliamentary elections. Tokios took the case to international arbitration at ICSID, where the arbiters allowed jurisdiction under the Lithuania–Ukraine BIT, writing, "the ICSID Convention contains no inchoate requirement that the investment at issue in a dispute have an international character in which the origin of the capital is decisive." *Tokios Tokeles v. Ukraine (ICSID ARB/02/18)*, Decision on Jurisdiction, April 29, 2004, Paragraph 82. This right has been challenged in at least one case, as reported in the article: "In unpublished ruling, arbitrators find that Swiss company's ties to Switzerland are too tenuous to deserve protections of investment treaty; one-off cross-border purchase of receivables in Slovak Republic is not a protected investment," *Investment Arbitration Reporter*, 14 April 2011.

(PINCHUK): The investors must stop and think. Our lawyers have sent the investors a letter describing the situation.

(INTERVIEWER): To all potential investors – Arcelor, Mittal?

(PINCHUK): Yes, all of them! We have set out the current position. The case is at the Supreme Council. Say you want to buy a flat but you are told that this flat is the subject of a court case. Will you risk buying it? I don't think so.[131]

Despite Pinchuk's and other owners' efforts in both the media and legal forums, traditional foreign firms saw Kryvorizhstal as tied up with another set of contract risks. Mittal Steel, Arcelor, and other major steel firms vied for the asset freely and without hesitation. Certainly, the risks faced by this hybrid nationality differed from those of traditional foreign firms. For Kryvorizhstal's Cypriot-Ukrainian owners, the exit and protest threats their foreignness offered were insufficient to deter their own breach.

TRUE MULTINATIONALS

Beyond cases of incorporation in tax havens, some multinationals do have origins in two or more home countries. The steel giant ArcelorMittal and its subsidiary in Ukraine provide a good example of this. Mittal Steel, a British firm, bought Kryvorizhstal for US$4.8 billion. That investment was made through a major German subsidiary. Later, Mittal Steel merged with Arcelor, a French firm with strong ties to the French state. By 2011, considerable investment in their Ukrainian subsidiary also came from Luxembourg. Thus, ArcelorMittal's operations in Ukraine have ties to and potential claims on multiple national groups of investors and multiple home governments: France, the United Kingdom, Germany, and Luxembourg.[132] What does this complicated nationality mean for ArcelorMittal's ability to ensure its contract sanctity in Ukraine?

On one hand, a firm like ArcelorMittal with multiple home countries is open to more sources of risks to contract sanctity than a traditional, one-home foreign firm, because it is sensitive to contract risks emanating from more than one bilateral relationship. This broader exposure to contract risks can alienate some of the firm's (various) co-nationals, making them unwilling to participate in collective lobbying efforts if the multiple-home firm's dispute is seen as too far removed from their experience. On the other hand, diplomats from the different home countries retain incentives to support a multiple-home firm, since the presence of multiple homes does not change a diplomat's interest in the fortunes of a firm that provides employment, taxes, and revenues in its country. However,

---

[131] "Ukrainian top businessmen call for end to reprivatization," *BBC Monitoring Ukraine and Baltics.* Source: *Ukrayinska Pravda,* 18 October 2005.

[132] Not to mention that Lakshmi Mittal, the owner of Mittal Steel and then CEO of ArcelorMittal, is of Indian heritage, and Mittal Steel was originally an Indian firm. A prominent Ukrainian journalist attributes some of Mittal's problems, including violence at the Kryvorizhstal mill, to "xenophobia against Indians." Interview, think tank, Ukraine, 2009.

if other home country governments will also advocate on the multiple-home firm's behalf, diplomats do have an incentive to free ride on others' efforts.

ArcelorMittal has proven able to counteract diplomats' incentives to free ride and received consistent diplomatic support, while various co-national firms proved willing to get involved in advocacy efforts around one contract dispute but distanced themselves from another. The difference came down to a dispute with which other firms could identify and a dispute that was wholly tied up in characteristics of the steel industry and the particular privatized asset. Thus, this case provides evidence that other forms of firm differentiation – here, along the lines of industry and asset history – can interfere with firms' willingness to lobby on behalf of a co-national. Nevertheless, the consistency of diplomatic efforts goes to show that home country resources are still consequential for firms' contract sanctity even in the absence of co-national firm lobbying.[133]

Diplomacy and Lobbying by Co-national Firms

Foreign firms have been frustrated by the non-payment of value-added tax (VAT) refunds in Ukraine since the late 1990s, but the government's need for cash during the global financial crisis brought VAT arrears to new heights. In a VAT system, a government refunds VAT to exporters. In many countries, these refunds are simply a matter of accounting, and exporters do not actually advance money in the process. In Ukraine, however, money does change hands, and the government has repeatedly reneged on repayments. ArcelorMittal became, as its Ukrainian director put it, "the outright champion" of VAT arrears.[134] ArcelorMittal did not get VAT refunded from late 2009 to 2010, and it was also asked to pay its income taxes months in advance, leaving it a creditor to the Ukrainian government for US$500 million by mid-2010. Adding insult to injury was the fact that ArcelorMittal's domestic competitors received regular VAT refunds. ArcelorMittal called attention to this discrepancy in the business press: "We are witnessing the unfair treatment of international investors."[135]

The government's VAT arrears to ArcelorMittal accounted for 30 percent of the US$1.2 billion in outstanding VAT owed to its exporters by August 2010.[136] The total debt owed by the state to foreign firms, in VAT and advance taxes, was put at over US$3 billion.[137] Unsurprisingly, other foreign firms to whom VAT was owed advocated for themselves, just as ArcelorMittal did. The nationality shield theory, however, generates predictions about what firms without broken contracts

---

[133] Industry and asset history as forms of firm differentiation will be discussed further in Chapters 6 and 8.

[134] Stack, Graham, "Value-added tax system provides case study in corruption, favors," *Kyiv Post*, 3 June 2010.

[135] Ibid. Some of these competitors have round-tripped foreign capital.

[136] "State Tax Administration: Value-added tax bonds worth Hr 16 billion ready," *Interfax Ukraine*, 6 August 2010.

[137] "German investor sues Yanukovych," *Kyiv Post*, 15 July 2010.

do in response to another's contract breach. How did other foreign firms – without their own massive VAT arrears – react to this widespread breach?

In fact, a number of non-exporting foreign firms saw ArcelorMittal's VAT problems as a harbinger of threats to their financial relationship with the Ukrainian government. This common concern allowed ArcelorMittal to assemble effectively multilateral action thanks to its broad European identity. ArcelorMittal used the European Business Association (EBA) as a lobbying group on its behalf. Though the EBA generally rejects campaigns on behalf of a particular firm, ArcelorMittal's situation touched enough constituencies to overcome the EBA's reluctance.[138] ArcelorMittal also got multilateral players in Ukraine – including the European Bank for Reconstruction and Development, the World Bank, and the IMF – to lobby on its behalf; these organizations will advocate on behalf of contract disputes when pressed by members from several of their national constituencies.[139] As a result, Ukraine's 2009 IMF package included an uncharacteristically specific stipulation about VAT repayment, and, in 2010, the Ukrainian government acknowledged that non-refund of VAT "negatively impact[ed] Ukraine's difficult talks with the IMF."[140]

Home governments' pressure, however, may have made the difference in pushing the Ukrainian government to settle with ArcelorMittal. The British Embassy was a strong advocate.[141] The German embassy was also quite vocal in public and behind closed doors, providing evidence that ArcelorMittal's use of a German subsidiary did indeed carry with it access to resources reserved for German firms.[142] French President Nicolas Sarkozy intervened directly during President Yanukovych's state visit to France in 2010.[143] Shortly after that visit, the Ukrainian government offered and ArcelorMittal accepted US$215 million of discounted VAT treasury bonds.[144] It took until 2011 for

---

[138] The content of the issue, too, might drive the probability of cross-national action. VAT non-payment got relatively close to what is often an investor association's wheelhouse – advocacy around corporate tax rates. When policy rather than particular breaches are concerned, multilateral action is more likely.

[139] Interviews (2), international organizations, Ukraine, 2009. For a deeper treatment of the role of international organizations in contract disputes, see Chapters 6 and 8.

[140] Stack, Graham, "Value-added tax system provides case study in corruption, favors," *Kyiv Post*, 3 June 2010.

[141] Interviews (2), British firms, Ukraine, 2009.

[142] Stack, Graham, "Value-added tax system provides case study in corruption, favors," *Kyiv Post*, 3 June 2010.

[143] Following the French intervention, ArcelorMittal CEO Lakshmi Mittal came to Ukraine and held a three-hour meeting with Yanukovych. Lavrov, Vlad, "ArcelorMittal becomes target after complaining about taxes," *Kyiv Post*, 25 February 2011.

[144] "State Tax Administration: Value-added tax bonds worth Hr 16 billion ready," *Kyiv Post*, 6 August 2010. ArcelorMittal was willing to accept the losses the bonds entailed: "Understanding the challenging situation the Ukrainian government is facing with VAT refunds, we have accepted that issuing the VAT T-bonds was a controversial but necessary compromise decision." "ArcelorMittal Kryviy Rih reports receiving VAT bonds worth Hr 1.7 billion from the state," *Kyiv Post*, 8 September 2010.

the VAT issue to be wholly settled, which ArcelorMittal confirmed only after the Ukrainian premier met with the head of the Parliament of Luxembourg.[145] Another of ArcelorMittal's home countries joined its many co-national firms and home-country diplomats of different nationalities in successfully advocating on the firm's behalf. This support suggests that firms would do well to acquire all the nationalities they can in order to amass resources to deter breach (Chapter 8).

Diplomacy Only

ArcelorMittal became the owner of Ukraine's largest steel mill. The Ukrainian government has an ongoing interest in ArcelorMittal's operations, as the firm employs over 50,000 people, it operates an asset with a social history that gives the firm a prominent place in Ukrainian politics, and it is the biggest economic player in one of Ukraine's less-developed regions. With disproportionate attention from the government, in a strategic industry, and with an immobile asset, conventional wisdom suggests that ArcelorMittal would likely face breach of contract (Chapter 2). Indeed, ArcelorMittal has faced threats to its contract sanctity in addition to the VAT arrears. In ArcelorMittal's more industry-specific contract disputes, other firms sharing ArcelorMittal's nationalities were unwilling to participate in collective action, as their sense of shared contract risks was weak. But ArcelorMittal's experience demonstrates that firms in vulnerable industries need not forego diplomatic support – even diplomatic support coming from a variety of home countries, none of which has total claim on the firm and each of which could free ride on the others.[146]

From 2007 to 2009, the Ukrainian government threatened to renationalize Kryvorizhstal a second time. The threats were couched in a series of regulatory rationales contesting ArcelorMittal's follow-through on clauses concerning local development that were written into the reprivatization agreement. At their core, however, these threats were a product of party politics. The head of the State Property Fund (SPF), the department responsible for Kryvorizhstal's sale to ArcelorMittal, was also the head of the Socialist Party. While the Socialist Party had been part of the Orange coalition in 2005, it afterward aligned with the Eastern-looking Party of the Regions, the party that lost out in the Orange Revolution and was unsupportive of Kryvorizhstal's reprivatization.[147] Under Socialist Party leadership, the SPF repeatedly threatened to renationalize

---

[145] "Government: VAT reimbursement to ArcelorMittal Kryviy Rih settled," *Interfax Ukraine*, 3 March 2011.

[146] Given ArcelorMittal's high sunk costs, protest is a considerably more viable means to impose costs on the host government than its own exit or incremental drawdown.

[147] In 2008, even the chair of the trade union committee of ArcelorMittal Kryviy Rih said that the investment should not be turned into "a pedestal for politicians ... Somebody's fingerprints are seen in the situation." *Interfax Ukraine Business Weekly*, 22 July 2008.

Kryvorizhstal, alleging that ArcelorMittal had failed to fulfill contractual clauses to maintain salary levels and upgrade environmental and social services. Tymoshenko, now in the opposition, called the SPF's threats against ArcelorMittal "groundless and provocative" and led attempts to fire the SPF's head.[148] In 2009, the Rada did remove the leader of the SPF and replaced her with a politician loyal to Tymoshenko. The new SPF head confirmed that ArcelorMittal had fulfilled all investment obligations.[149] Respondents with close ties to top Ukrainian politicians were confident that behind-the-scenes diplomatic pressure on ArcelorMittal's behalf contributed to Tymoshenko's efforts to replace the head of the SPF.[150]

Nevertheless, the Ukrainian government, now led by the Party of the Regions, opened criminal cases against ArcelorMittal in 2010, accusing the firm of smuggling high-grade coal under low-grade customs codes. For ArcelorMittal to have done this would be logistically difficult, given the highly standardized (and physically enormous) coal shipments to its mill and the fact that the regional coalmines only provide certain qualities of coal.[151] This left local observers certain that domestic interests, still desirous of renationalization, lay behind the cases.[152]

The firms that had lobbied on ArcelorMittal's behalf when it came to VAT arrears distanced themselves from these other, acrimonious disputes. National investor associations did not speak out on ArcelorMittal's behalf, nor did the EBA. In general, foreign executives were privately sympathetic to ArcelorMittal, though one prominent executive chastised ArcelorMittal for being "very arrogant" in its dealing with the government.[153] Yet top executives at firms in a variety of industries and of a variety of nationalities universally balked at the idea of getting publicly involved in these disputes.[154] While VAT arrears suggested shared risks to tax contracts, an issue relevant to all industries, these later disputes were viewed as industry-specific. In short, commonalities created by co-nationality were not enough to spur collective action among firms that perceived these risks to contract sanctity as particular to ArcelorMittal's unique situation.

---

[148] Ibid.
[149] "Business Briefs," *Kyiv Post*, 11 March 2009.
[150] Interviews (2), Ukraine, 2009. Confidentiality requested.
[151] Interviews (4), foreign and domestic law firms, Ukraine.
[152] For its part, ArcelorMittal released this statement: "ArcelorMittal Kryviy Rih is supplying coal to Ukraine via big international trade on a long-term contract. We have already made supplies according to this contract this year, previous supplies were cleared by the Customs service without any remarks. We have not changed supplier or coal grade since then. We strongly reject any accusations and have already communicated all proofs of this to the customs." "Customs service opens smuggling case against ArcelorMittal Kryviy Rih," *Kyiv Post*, 15 September 2010. "Is Ukraine's Biggest Foreign Investor Now Safe?" *Kyiv Post*, 13 October 2010.
[153] Interview, US firm, Ukraine, 2009.
[154] There is no evidence of industry-based public support in local or expatriate-marketed media.

Yet even when industry considerations made co-national firms appear pub-licly indifferent, home country diplomats still came to the vulnerable investor's aid. In particular, diplomats from Luxembourg and France publicly demanded that Ukraine withdraw the cases. These demands seem to have had a direct effect on Ukraine's behavior. In a press conference after meeting with French President Sarkozy, Yanukovych said that the newly raised question of the state's nation-alizing Kryvorizhstal "will most likely not reach court." The Ukrainian govern-ment soon dropped the criminal cases.[155]

Does ArcelorMittal present a case not of a multinational firm but, rather, of a truly European Union-origin firm? I contend that, no, diplomatic efforts on ArcelorMittal's behalf again came through national channels. The French pres-ident exerted leverage in one behind-closed-doors meeting, while the British, Germans, and Luxembourgians acted independently as well. Those involved in and closely observing the dispute in Ukraine noted – and sometimes lamented – the absence of EU efforts on the firm's behalf, as well as the absence of EU institutions in Ukraine to act on any firm's behalf.[156]

FIRMS AND THEIR DIPLOMATS

How do foreign firms protect themselves when host governments threaten to break contracts? Investor experiences in Ukraine show that support from home-country diplomats as well as coordinated lobbying among co-national firms have been important deterrents of breach of contract and means of achieving restitution. Moreover, co-national protest has been useful even when risks to contract sanctity are not clearly divided by nationality or when other characteristics, like industry or asset history, differentiate the contract risks facing co-national firms. The experiences of foreign firms in Ukraine over the last years suggest strongly that investors can and do turn to protest to preserve contract sanctity, and these resources are filtered by nationality.

However, the success and failure of foreign-firm protest depends not only on the advocacy itself but also on the FDI environment in which co-national actors undertake their campaigns. The entry and exit of national groups of foreign firms in Ukraine has changed the extent to which any one national group's protest presages costs sufficiently high to deter government breach of contract. With more investor nationalities at play through the late 1990s and early 2000s, the Ukrainian government had more room to undercut one group's contract sanctity without damaging its relations with other national groups.

---

[155] "Is Ukraine's Biggest Foreign Investor Now Safe?" *Kyiv Post*, 13 October 2010.
[156] Interviews (4), European Union-origin manufacturing firms (2); European Union-origin natural resources firm; European Union-origin legal firm, Ukraine, 2009 and 2011.

When fewer nationalities came to dominate the FDI environment in Ukraine after 2005, breach of contract proved a greater threat to the government's current and future access to FDI, enabling foreign firms to be more successful in deterring breach.[157] The ebb and flow of global capital has created contract risks for foreign firms in Ukraine while changing the government's ability to act in ways contrary to foreign firms' preferences and property.

---

[157] The worldwide financial crisis that hit Ukraine at the end of the decade likely made these dynamics even more salient, although Ukraine hosted levels of FDI unprecedented in its history.

6

Moldovan Deterrence Versus Romanian Gold

Moldova and Romania are two emerging economies at very different levels of development and subject to different institutional constraints: Moldova, the poorest country in Europe, has strong informal ties to Russia, while Romania is a member of the European Union. Although conventional wisdom would posit that Moldova in the 2000s was a more difficult environment for foreign investors, variation in FDI national diversity helps to explain limited expropriation in Moldova as opposed to the surprising presence of acrimonious expropriation in Romania. Since independence, the Moldovan economy has had consistently low FDI national diversity despite increasing FDI stock. In these conditions, foreign firms have on the whole acted successfully to deter expropriation, though corruption remains a problem for both domestic and foreign firms. In contrast, FDI national diversity in Romania grew quickly, providing the Romanian government more space to trade off foreign firms' contract sanctity in favor of electoral and other domestic gains. This difference in breach of contract is despite the fact that the countries' dependence on FDI has been comparable:

Moldova averaged 7.4 percent and Romania 6.3 percent FDI inflows per GDP over the period 2000 to 2008.

In this chapter, I first describe FDI national diversity in Moldova and Romania. I then compare foreign firms' contract sanctity in the two countries, drawing on some fifty interviews with the local heads of multinational subsidiaries in Moldova and Romania as well as with local representatives of international organizations and domestic government officials. Further evidence comes from interviews with international legal professionals and executives at multinational headquarters in Germany and the United States. In Moldova's environment of low FDI national diversity, robust co-national groups have successfully helped to defuse investor-government conflicts and maintain investors' ability to operate in the country. This is especially true when compared to the poor treatment prominent domestic investors have faced. In contrast, high FDI national diversity in Romania helps to explain weak to non-existent co-national associations and the presence of repeated, public, high-profile instances of government breach of contract. Moreover, the cases presented here demonstrate that foreign firm contract sanctity is not necessarily compatible with international mandates, nor is it necessarily impossible in a country known for corruption and weak rule of law. In fact, breach of contract in Romania has garnered international support, as some of Romania's contracts have conflicted with its commitments to multilateral institutions, including the European Union.

FDI NATIONAL DIVERSITY IN MOLDOVA AND ROMANIA

Moldova

Moldova was one of the most "Sovietized of the Soviet republics," populated by the Moldovan people who, thanks to Soviet nationality engineering, were made distinct from Romanians and the Romanian state of which they had historically been a part.[1] An independent country since 1991, Moldova at first had a relatively competitive political scene, but not because of a vibrant civil society or democratic leadership. Rather, incumbents in Moldova were unable to concentrate political control through force or via elections, resulting in "pluralism by default."[2] In the 2000s, Moldovan elites were better able to consolidate power: the Communist Party won 70 percent of seats in Parliament in 2001, and President Vladimir Voronin came to power alongside a healthy Communist Party majority that remained through 2009. In that year, an inspired opposition stood together in protests that made international news, but signs of a stable democratic turn-around in Moldovan politics only began to appear in 2012.[3]

---

[1]   King 2000. There is little public support for reunification with Romania.
[2]   Way 2005: 232.
[3]   The Parliament could not agree on a president, so interim presidents served for three years. Finally, a president was elected (with one vote to spare) in March 2012.

Throughout Moldova's short history, corruption and insider dealing have marked the political scene.[4] Part of the problem is the stagnant conflict with Transnistria (Pridnestrovie), a breakaway region that engaged in a military conflict with Moldova in 1992 and has since been home to Russian troops and a murky gray economy.

Moldova as a whole has considerable economic woes. Economic growth has been positive since 2000, reaching 7.8 percent in 2008 before turning negative in 2009 during the global recession. But the country has been the poorest in Europe. In the late 2000s, its GDP per capita was on par with Senegal and Cote d'Ivoire. A landlocked country without significant natural resources, Moldova depends heavily on agriculture, though it hopes to upgrade its Soviet-era industrial infrastructure. In the second half of the 2000s, the country averaged over US$250 million in official development assistance and aid, which is more than it receives in FDI.[5]

Nevertheless, FDI has flowed into Moldova since its independence, with gradual growth in annual inflows until 2004 and then quick growth from 2004 to 2008 (see Figure 6.1). FDI inflows plummeted in 2009, more attributable to the global financial crisis and changes in investors' home countries than any particular change in Moldova's (or any other emerging economy's) situation. Yet inflows were already rebounding in 2010. Annual FDI in fixed capital has grown over 14 times from 2000 to 2010.[6] External sources of finance have been key to modernization in Moldova's agricultural sector as well as efforts to upgrade infrastructure and some of Moldova's manufacturing capacity. All told, FDI inflows have been an important part of Moldova's economy, accounting for well over 10 percent of GDP during a peak in 2006 to 2008 (Figure 6.1). Importantly, these levels are not so different from its neighbor Romania: both countries had similar exposure to foreign firms as a percentage of GDP.

FDI in Moldova is thinner than in neighboring Romania or Ukraine, as foreign buyers tend to be interested in only the top three or so firms in any given industry.[7] Nevertheless, new buyers have entered. For instance, in 2003 the Turkish Efes Beverage Company bought a major brewery in a public tender set up by an US private equity firm, Horizon Capital. Horizon Capital also facilitated the 2009 sale of a major Soviet-era state bank, Moldova's Agroimbank, to a Slovenian investor via the Moldovan stock market. Local observers attribute the quick growth of FDI inflows in the mid-2000s to bets on Romania and Bulgaria's accession to the European Union (EU) in 2007. With

---

[4] In 2011, Transparency International ranked Moldova 105 of 178 countries.
[5] World Bank World Development Indicators (WDI).
[6] National Bureau of Statistics of the Republic of Moldova, Fixed capital investments tables, Accessed March 2012.
[7] Interview, foreign firm in financial services, Moldova, 2009.

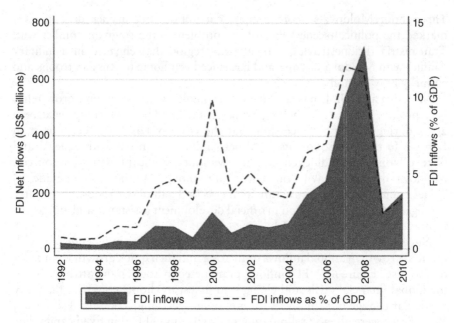

FIGURE 6.1 **FDI Inflows and FDI as a Percent of GDP in Moldova (1992–2010)**
Source: World Bank World Development Indicators.

Romania's membership, Moldova now sits on the EU's border and hosts investors seeking an export platform into the EU. Its cheap labor becomes more attractive, too, as wages rise in the new EU countries.

The Moldovan Investment and Export Promotion Agency (MIEPO) printed on the front page of a 2009 "Why Invest in Moldova?" leaflet that "companies from 86 countries have invested in Moldova."[8] I have found no evidence that this is true. Instead, despite growth in FDI, Moldova has seen minimal diversification in the home countries of foreign firms, and it has minimal exposure to OECD investors compared to Romania and other countries in the region. Through the 1990s, Moldova's major foreign investor was the country that was previously a domestic investor: Russia. With the breakup of the Soviet Union, the Moldovan state took ownership over assets within its borders, but Russian actors were quick to reassemble industrial relationships broken by the new international boundaries. For example, Moldovan wine was renowned in the Soviet Union, and Russian capital helped to reorganize the wine industry and grow wine exports to former Soviet states. By 2003, Russian FDI into Moldova accounted for 5.3 percent of total outward FDI sent by Russian firms

[8] Moldova Investment and Export Promotion Organization (MIEPO), Foreign Investment Guide, *Why Invest in Moldova?* April 2009.

into the world.[9] In 2009, Russian FDI stock in Moldova reached US$124.8 million. Another US$220.9 million in FDI stock originated in Cyprus, a location in which many ethnic Russian (and other post-Soviet) investors domicile their firms.[10] Russian FDI also effectively sustains the economy in the breakaway Moldovan region of Transnistria, though measuring investment and ownership there is difficult thanks to the region's belligerent relationship with Moldova proper.

Romania has been Moldova's other major source of foreign capital. Romania's economy returned to pre-transition levels only around 2000. In the following years, Moldova became a significant destination for what Romanian outward FDI there is. In 2005, Romania invested US$19 million in Moldova, accounting for 10 percent of Romania's outward FDI. By 2007, outflows to Moldova were US$51 million, representing some 6 percent of Romanian outward FDI.[11] In 2010, over 475 firms with Romanian capital were operating in Moldova, with the largest investors spread across industries including automotive parts, banking, oil and gas, telecommunications, retail, and manufacturing.[12]

In 1996, the OECD started reporting data on OECD investment into Moldova. France was the first to register FDI into Moldova, and French investors continue to be a visible force in the country. In the end of the 2000s, for example, the French mobile phone operator Orange was the largest in Moldova, though it had few operations elsewhere in post-Soviet Europe. The Moldovan language, which is essentially the same as Romanian, is a Romance language; this link helps to facilitate not only French but also a large amount of Italian interest in the country.[13] Post-communist OECD countries, particularly Hungary and Slovenia, are also responsible for investment in Moldova. Entry by a few other nationalities of OECD investors have led to a slight rise in OECD-origin FDI national diversity over the 2000s, and local government and business actors agreed that the prominence of FDI originating from Russia and Romania is declining. However, Moldova's FDI national diversity is still far below that of its neighbor Romania, as depicted in Figure 6.2.

Given this background, the nationality shield theory predicts that in Moldova, government breach of contract should be less of an issue and any threats of breach more easily deterred. If one surmises that a resource-poor, less developed country, with a weak democracy and endemic corruption, is likely to have a high incidence of government breach of contract, then Moldova is a strongly counterintuitive case.[14] In fact, co-national investor groups and their

[9] MIEPO, Foreign Investment Guide, *Foreign Direct Investment*, April 2009.
[10] Moldovan National Bureau of Statistics, June 2010.
[11] WIIW Database on Foreign Direct Investment in Central, East, and Southeast Europe, 2009.
[12] "Romania Started to Withdraw Its Capital from Moldova in 2009," *RIA Oreanda-News*, 21 April 2010.
[13] Interviews (4), MIEPO and Italian-Moldova Chamber of Commerce, Moldova, 2009.
[14] Cai and Treisman 2005.

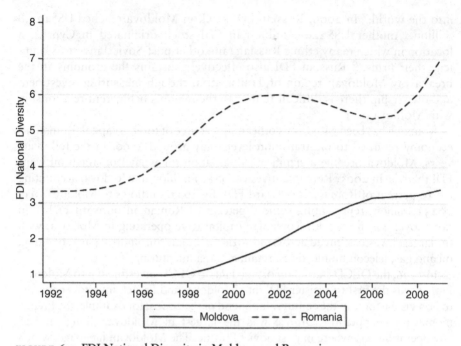

FIGURE 6.2 **FDI National Diversity in Moldova and Romania**
Lowess-smoothed OECD-origin FDI stock national diversity measures (see Chapter 4 for calculation details).

diplomatic supporters are powerful in Moldova, and evidence suggests that the government's reliance on few sources of capital gives it pause in breaking contracts with foreign firms.

Romania

The dictator Nicholae Ceausescu and his wife were executed on Romanian television on December 25, 1989. With that violent act, the communist regime ended and Romania began its transition to democracy and a market economy. Ceausescu dedicated huge portions of Romania's GDP to repaying the country's foreign debt, which, while impoverishing the country, left it nearly debt free in 1990. Nevertheless, Romania had a particularly difficult transition period in the 1990s and only returned to 1989 GDP levels in 2000. Since then, the economy has grown and structural reform progressed enough so that, while Romania missed out on the first expansion of the European Union in 2004, it and its neighbor Bulgaria became members in 2007. Romania has oil and gas reserves in the Black Sea, but on the whole it remains an agriculturally intensive economy with growth in manufacturing exports.

The first FDI to enter democratic Romania came from Germany, Italy, and France. New entrants from these countries followed a pattern: large firms invested, like France's Renault, and their home country banks came next, like France's Societe Generale.[15] More and more OECD-origin investors added to the mix as the decade progressed and Romania privatized more and more large assets to foreign interests. Neighboring Hungary and Poland were both transition success stories, as signaled by their entry to the European Union in the first wave of "post-communist" expansion in 2004. Their nationals had already begun to invest in Romania in the years leading up to EU entry. Sitting just outside the expanded EU, Romania hosted FDI that used it as an export platform to the EU. Foreign firms also sought the cheaper labor and inputs that were then outside of EU borders. By 2005, more FDI began to flow into new, greenfield investments than into privatizations of state-owned property.[16] For example, multinational corporations like Siemens and Hewlett-Packard built much lauded and locally well-respected plants in the country.

Romania is not considered a transition success on par with its Central European neighbors. Judicial corruption and corruption in the health sector remain problems in Romania, for example. In part due to corruption, the European Union stalled Romania's (and Bulgaria's) entry to the EU until January 2007. Nevertheless, the reforms Romania undertook in its efforts to join the EU made it an attractive destination for investment. FDI inflows were high even as accession was delayed and continued at high levels in 2008 before dropping off with the world financial crisis in 2009 (see Figure 6.3). FDI national diversity in Romania remained stable at a high level in the 2000s as foreign firms from a great variety of OECD countries invested and reinvested.[17] The Romanian government has recognized this national diversity. For example, Romania's investment promotion agency chose to highlight thirty-three successful large projects completed in the period from 2004 to 2010 in which investments reached EUR450 million (US$573 million). These projects come from thirteen different home countries: France, Spain, Austria, Italy, Germany, Japan, the United States, Portugal, Greece, China, Tunisia, Sweden, and Belgium.[18]

Compared to Moldova, Romania is a wealthy country, with a GDP per capita of US$12,300 in 2011 as compared to Moldova's US$3,400.[19] Romania also has deep institutional ties to OECD countries, unlike Moldova. These factors might suggest that Romania would be less likely to break contracts with foreign firms. Nevertheless, the nationality shield theory predicts that in a country with high and growing FDI national diversity, co-national coordination is weak and

---

[15] Interviews (3), foreign firms in financial and business services, Romania, 2009.
[16] Interview, Romanian government official, Romania, 2009.
[17] FDI national diversity dropped off in 2009, thanks to the exogenous shock of the worldwide financial crisis.
[18] Romania Trade & Invest, Accessed March 2012.
[19] World Bank WDI.

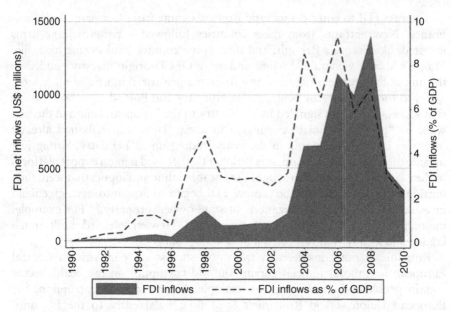

FIGURE 6.3 **FDI Inflows and FDI as a Percent of GDP in Romania (1990–2010)**
Source: World Bank World Development Indicators.

the government is increasingly prone to break contracts with foreign firms. In
fact, evidence suggests that the nationality diversity of firms in Romania undermines solidarity among co-national firms as well as undermining incentives for
diplomatic efforts on behalf of broken contracts. In this environment, Romania
has broken more contracts than Moldova.

It is worth noting that governments in both countries have made statements to
specifically reassure foreign firms that their rights are secure. In Moldova,
MIEPO publishes literature that assures readers,

The Constitution of the country guarantees the inviolability of both foreign and domestic
investors by incorporating principles protecting the supremacy of international law, the
market economy, private property, provisions against unjust expropriation, provisions
against confiscation of property, and separation of power among government branches.[20]

In Romania, the focus on contract sanctity is less direct but still written between
the lines. Romania's investment promotion agency prominently advertises the
country's BITs and healthy diplomatic relations, and, in their 2012 promotional
materials, the Prime Minister wrote:

---

[20] MIEPO, Foreign Investment Guide, *Why Invest in Moldova?* April 2009.

TABLE 6.1 *Summary, Major Contract Disputes in Moldova and Romania*

FDI National Diversity	Year	Case	Nationality	Outcome	As predicted?
Low, Moldova	2000–2002	Unistar Ventures / Air Moldova	German	Breach	No^
	2007	Union Fenosa	Spanish	Settled	Yes
	2008–2009	SunCommunications	US	Settled	Yes
	2008–2011	Ascom (Anatol Stati)	(Domestic)	Breach	.
High, Romania	2003–2011	Bechtel	US	Breach	Yes
	2005–2007	OMV / Petrom	Austrian	Breach	Yes
	2007–2014	Rosia Montana Gold Corporation	Canadian**	Breach	Yes
	2009–2011	Sterling Resources	Canadian	Breach/ Settled	Yes/No

* One owner held a US passport.
** US capital added several years into the dispute.
^ Additional factor: Corruption.

I personally want to assure you that you will find here the necessary ingredients for a successful business: an effective and efficient legislative framework, stability, predictability, and resourcefulness ... Take advantage of this European opportunity.[21]

Despite Romania's emphasis on the dependability of being "European," the following cases go to show that Moldova's lower FDI national diversity has coexisted with a stronger government commitment to foreign firm contracts than in Romania. See Table 6.1 for a summary of disputes discussed in the chapter.

FDI by Industry in Moldova and Romania

One recurring alternative hypothesis with which this book contends is that what looks like co-nationality is in fact evidence of co-industry among investors. In Chapter 4, we saw that the predicted effects of FDI national diversity remain when controlling for industry, and Chapter 5 demonstrated co-national action across industry lines. Here, one may worry that there is not sufficient diversity across nationality and industry in Romania and Moldova so that the presence or absence of co-national collective action would be confounded by industry. In fact, FDI flowing into Romania is very diversified across sectors. Using data from 1999 to 2006, Figure 6.4 shows that significant proportions of FDI have gone into services, industry, trade, and transport, as well as construction. Further, the

[21] "Romania: A European Opportunity for your Investment Projects," Brochure from Romania Trade & Invest, 2012.

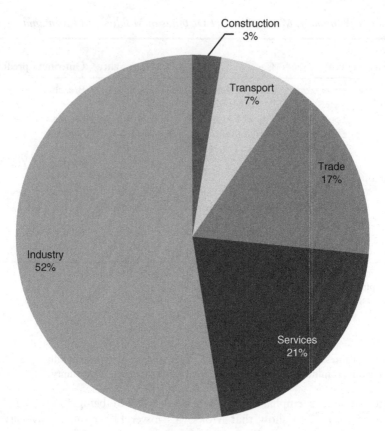

FIGURE 6.4 **FDI Stock in Romania by Industry (Average 1999–2006)**
Source: Vienna Institute for International Economic Studies (WIIW), Database on Foreign Direct Investment in Central, East, and Southeast Europe, 2009 Release.

following cases demonstrate how, in prominent cases of contract disputes in Romania, a multitude of investor nationalities have tended to operate in that same industry.

Demonstrating diversity by nationality and industry in Moldova is trickier, due to less depth in its statistical collection and its overall FDI stock. Nevertheless, Table 6.2 provides confidence in nationality diversity by sector in 1999. This table reports the nationality of Moldova's top foreign affiliates coming from large multinational corporations, categorized as industrial, terti-ary, or finance and insurance investors.[22] Not only is there a diversity of nationalities represented in each aggregated sector, but several nationalities had major foreign affiliates in a variety of industry categories. Using data from

---

[22] Note that the definition of "large" is not clear.

TABLE 6.2 *Moldova: Largest Multinational Affiliates by Nationality and Industry (1999)*

Sector	Nationality	No. of firms	Industry detail
Industrial (top 18)	United States	12	Beverages, food, chemicals, mineral products, petroleum, machinery
	Germany	1	Textiles
	France	1	Mineral products
	Switzerland	1	Paper products
	Italy	3	Fishing, beverages, leather
Tertiary (top 17)	United States	5	Trade, business services, other services
	Germany	2	Transportation, trade
	Spain	1	Electricity
	Italy	4	Construction, other services, hotel
	Turkey	1	Telecommunications
	Denmark	1	Telecommunications
	Russia	1	Gas
	Israel	1	Other services
	France/Romania	1	Telecommunications
Finance (top 5)	Australia	1	Insurance
	Romania	2	Banking
	Romania/ Turkey	1	Banking
	Greece	1	Banking

Note: The population of multinationals from which these firms are pulled is not well defined.
Sources: UNCTAD WID Country Profile: Republic of Moldova. 1999. Gathered from US Department of Commerce Business Information Services for the Newly Independent States; *Europa World Yearbook* 2000.

2008, Table 6.3 demonstrates that FDI accounted for highly significant portions of capital deployed in a number of major industries. These include specialized manufacturing industries as well as trade facilitation, finance, and real estate. In the context of low FDI national diversity, Tables 6.2 and 6.3 give us some confidence that a small number of nationalities have nevertheless been investing across a broad number of industries. This helps to rule out the worry that co-national collective action is in fact capturing co-industrial action.

Sanctity in Moldova

The first thing one is reminded of when speaking to foreign executives, local government officials, or representatives from multilateral institutions in Moldova is that "this is a small country." Some emphasize the upside that Moldova's small size helps foreign firms keep tabs on the Moldovan government. Moldova's small, albeit increasing, population of foreign investors

TABLE 6.3 *Moldova: Foreign Capital's Share by Industry (2008)*

Industry	Foreign Capital Share in Sector (Pct)
Manufacturing: other transportation equipment	93.4
Manufacturing: apparel, dressing and dying of fur	66.8
Manufacturing: coke, refined petroleum products, nuclear fuel	66.1
Manufacturing: paper and paperboard	61.4
Sales, maintenance and repair of motor vehicles; retail sale of fuel	53.4
Production and distribution of electricity	51.2
Manufacturing: non-metallic mineral products	44.9
Hotels and restaurants	35.7
Wholesale trade and commission trade	34.0
Manufacturing: leather, shoes	31.5
Financial activities	31.1
Manufacturing: food	30.1
Chemical industry	28.5
Manufacturing and distribution: gas fuel	28.3
Real estate	27.5
Manufacturing: rubber and plastic	28.2
Manufacturing: beverages	27.4
Manufacturing: dairy products	26.9
Machinery rental	24.6
Manufacturing: machinery and equipment	21.7
Processing and preserving of fish products	21.3

Foreign capital accounts for between 18.6% (Recreational activities) and 0.6% (Animal farming) of an additional twenty-seven industries.
Sources: Prohnitchi, V., A. Popa, and A. Lupusor, "Impact of Foreign Direct Investments on the Moldovan Economy." *Expert Group Centru Analitic Independent.* Chisinau, 2010. Funded by UNDP Moldova.

is close knit; networking and gossip help information spread quickly. The number of investor nationalities represented in Moldova is comparatively low. If there were a set of foreign investors in the world that could form a unified bloc, able to collectively advocate for their contract sanctity across nationalities, the set in Moldova would be a good candidate. However, consistent with the nationality shield theory, cross-national advocacy on issues of contract breach is largely absent in Moldova. Instead, nationality-based foreign investor groups are strong and relevant in Moldova, and action by these groups and their diplomats has done the work of staying the government's hand when it comes to breach of contract.

From the government's point of view, to antagonize and lose any one of these groups of co-national investors would be costly to Moldova's economy. As a result, we see fewer instances of conflicts between foreign investors and the government in the first place – especially when compared to the kinds of breach of contract that domestic firms in Moldova have faced.[23] However, low FDI national diversity is not a panacea for all problematic investor–government interactions, particularly where corruption is concerned.

Strong Co-national Action

As the director of a Western multinational with a significant presence in Moldova put it, foreign firms in the country "have grown to understand the benefit of joining interests for causes."[24] But joining interests has occurred on a decidedly national basis: Turkish firms join with Turkish, Russian with Russian, American with American, Italian with Italian.

Turkish investors into Moldova are both welcomed and resented. The Gagauz are an ethnically Turkish minority of less than 200,000 people living in an autonomous region in Moldova.[25] The linguistic and cultural affinities that Turkish investors enjoy in Gagauzia contrast with the racism and occasional violence Turkish people face elsewhere in Moldova. One of the most prominent Turkish executives in Moldova described how Turkish investors use informal ties to each other to mutually navigate both the preferences and animosity associated with their ethnicity. In his opinion, the official Turkish investor association, registered as required with the Moldovan government, could be important but currently puts their ethnicity too much in the foreground, to the detriment of the contract sanctity of the national group.[26] He and other executives, Turkish and otherwise, emphasize Turkish investors' ability to work informally with government officials thanks to the weak legal constraints Turkey puts on Turkish firms' activities abroad. For example, one Turkish executive willingly admitted to doing "gray things" to earn Moldovan government officials' trust and support. In contrast to Western executives who shared horror stories in which bribery turned into extortion, this executive characterized his firm's "gray" actions as a long-term risk management strategy.[27] Whether or not all Turkish firms indeed engage in bribery, executives of other nationalities readily associated bribery with Turkish investors in Moldova. That other foreign firms share this perception of Turkish investors underscores the

---

[23] A few contract disputes as well as one full-fledged broken contract with a German firm help to assuage the worry that Moldova generally respects contracts simply as a result of its low absolute levels of FDI or its poverty.

[24] Interview, foreign firm in financial services, Moldova, 2009.

[25] In investment promotion materials in 2008, the Gagauz government advertised that 104 of 6,700 enterprises in the region were recipients of FDI. It highlighted foreign investors from Turkey, with a Turkish-Moldovan textile joint venture serving as the flagship investment in the region. Munteanu, Igor, "Gagauzia: opportunities for investment," *Institute for Development and Social Initiatives*, 2008, 22, 26. Other investors are from Russia, Belarus, and Italy, somewhat similar to the nationality profile in the rest of Moldova.

[26] Interview, Turkish firm, Moldova, 2009.

[27] Ibid.

point that firms of other nationalities see little reason to support Turkish firms should those Turkish firms have conflicts with the government. Nor are Turkish executives interested in supporting firms of other nationalities: despite their conflicted reputation in Moldova, as of 2014 Turkish investors have not been involved in breach of contract that made Moldovan headlines or international legal circles. Threatening that record by becoming involved in other nationalities' disputes is not in these firms' best interests.

Foreign executives of various nationalities concur that Russian capital in Moldova is "different." Put nicely, one executive said that Russian capital "doesn't require due diligence and transparency in the same way [as Western capital]."[28] In both Moldova and elsewhere in Eastern Europe, Russian investors have been associated with rapaciousness in the decades following the fall of the Soviet Union; for example, Russian investors are thought to be more likely to strip assets rather than invest in and rebuild them.[29] At the end of the 2000s, analysts observed that Russian firms were becoming more conventionally oriented toward building robust businesses and making long-term investments. Nevertheless, Russian firms investing in Eastern Europe maintain a reputation for a high tolerance for risk and for making business decisions other nationalities might not undertake. Firms of other nationalities, local governments, and Russian investors themselves understand this reputation.

In interviews, executives sometimes identified Russian investment in Moldova as occupying a half-foreign/half-domestic category. Unlike in other post-Soviet states, Russian remains a commonly spoken and non-stigmatized language in Moldova, native to 16 percent of the population and the second language of over 90 percent. Russians are the most visible investor group in Moldova, a country in which 9 percent of the population is ethnic Russian (and another 11 percent is Ukrainian).[30] Both Russian executives and executives of other nationalities observe that informal ties between Moldovan officials and Russian firms matter more to their contract sanctity than any organized investor association. For example, Russian investors do have an officially registered investor association, but it is largely dormant – and the son of the long-time Moldovan President Oleg Voronin (2001–2009) became the association's head in 2010.[31] Russian investors benefit from behind-the-scenes access to political leaders as well as advocacy on their behalf from Russian government officials.

As of 2014, Russian peacekeeping troops remain in Transnistria, the breakaway Moldovan region that has been in a stalemated conflict with Moldova since 1992. Determining the ownership of firms in Transnistria is notoriously difficult, and reliable economic and business data is scarce to non-existent.

---

[28] Interview, foreign firm in financial services, Moldova, 2009.
[29] Interviews (2), international organizations, Moldova and Romania, 2009.
[30] According to the 2004 Moldovan Census.
[31] "Oleg Voronin to head Moldovan office of Moscow Entrepreneur Association," *Moldova Azi*, 12 August 2010.

Nevertheless, the common understanding is that formal and informal Russian FDI as well as direct subsidies from the Russian government allow the local economy to function. Non-Russian foreign investors tend to stay away from Transnistria.[32] Both there and in Moldova as a whole, Russian investors face risks and/or privileges common to themselves but separate from investors of other nationalities. The prospect of politically supporting Russian firms invested in Transnistria was anathema to interview respondents of other nationalities.

Other national groups of investors in Moldova share relationships with the Moldovan people and government that reinforce co-nationality and undermine cross-national ties. Romanian firms draw on their government's intimate relations with Moldova when it comes to protecting Romanian-owned property. The prominent Italian Chamber of Commerce in Moldova points out that Italy has been a migration destination for Moldovan immigrants when explaining the prominence of Italian investment in the country; the chamber presumes that those cultural connections assist Italian business efforts.[33] Moldovan diasporans investing from Israel share an ethnic and cultural identity that differentiates their interaction with the Moldovan government from that of other nationalities. In short, even in the small country of Moldova, foreign firms have cultural, geo-political, economic, ethnic, and institutional incentives to identify with the contract risks of co-nationals while maintaining distance from the problems of firms of other nationalities. But with a small number of national groups accounting for the vast majority of FDI into Moldova, the Moldovan government has a small number of outside options on which to depend should it break contracts with – and lose capital from and good relations with – any one national group.

Industry-based organizations are weak among foreign firms in Moldova. Because FDI in Moldova is thin, only a small number of foreign firms participate in any given industry and usually represent the biggest and most successful firms in that industry. While thin FDI provides the small numbers that might facilitate co-industrial collective action, it means that foreign firms are each other's main competitors; it appears that competition has outweighed any benefits of organization along industry cleavages. Domestic firms in a given industry try to compete with foreign firms while they also look to them for funding.[34] The upshot is that domestic firms stay out of foreign firms' disputes with the government. In the alcohol and winemaking industries, for example, domestic firms seek capital from Russian investors but avoid entangling themselves in the longstanding Russian-Moldovan conflicts that get played out in this industry: Russia has on several occasions implemented Moldova-specific health and safety regulations and tariffs.[35] In Moldova, when disputes arise, neither general

---

[32] E.g., Interviews (2), development banks, Moldova, 2009.
[33] Interviews (2), Italian firms, Moldova, 2009.
[34] Interviews (6), Moldovan firms, Moldova, 2009.
[35] Interviews (2), international organization representative and Moldovan firm in alcohol industry, Moldova, 2009.

protest by foreign firms nor actions taken by industrial groups have been key to keeping contract sanctity intact. Rather, co-nationals' actions have been a visible and powerful means to deter breach.

Americans and Wireless Frequencies

The American Chamber of Commerce in Moldova (AmCham) was founded by an entrepreneurial group of US executives in 2006, and it grew to over seventy members by 2012. Moldova's AmCham focuses on US firms' interests in Moldova, with a clear mission "to promote American trade and investment in Moldova" and an aggressive tagline: "fighting for your business." One fight occurred in 2008, when the Moldovan government threatened to revoke and re-auction after fifteen years what was a twenty-five-year license that allowed a US-owned cable and telecommunications firm, SunCommunications, to use certain wireless frequencies. Moldovan President Voronin and members of his family had extensive investments in the Moldovan telecommunications sector, and firms in the sector – both domestic and foreign – have expressed frustration with anti-competitive behavior.[36] According to SunCommunications' 2008 press release, new technologies

make the wireless frequencies extremely valuable. The Ministry of Informational Development announced their intention to take back these frequencies from SunCommunications in order to auction them to new investors in 2009 ... We believe that the decision ... was done incorrectly and that the laws of the Republic of Moldova and international treaties signed by Moldova protect ... SunCommunications' investors who have built this business.[37]

Regardless of the relatively clear-cut nature of the unlawful threat to foreign-owned property, non-US foreign firms kept their distance from the dispute. Foreign firms in industries likewise tied up with the Voronin family – including hotels and construction, not to mention other telecommunications firms – also stayed away.[38]

Instead, SunCommunications looked to US institutions to put pressure on the government. The AmCham fought for the firm, carrying with it the support of the tightly knit group of US investors in the country.[39] The firm threatened to exercise the US–Moldova Bilateral Investment Treaty (BIT), as referenced in the excerpt from their press release quoted above. SunCommunications also strategically

---

[36] The threat against SunCommunications' property likely emerged from both issues of fairness and the possibility of potential insider benefits from a new auction.

[37] SunCommunications, "The disconnection of the MMDS service," Accessed March 2012.

[38] Interviews (2), US firms, Moldova, 2009.

[39] The CEO of SunCommunications happened to be the AmCham president, but lobbying decisions are made by a steering committee and require the approval of the membership. There are hints that US diplomats were also involved in the dispute, though this remains confidential.

used its nationality in its struggle. In the words of a US executive at a different firm in Moldova, "An American investor is well protected by American shareholders; citing them is a good tool."[40] The exact outcome of the lobbying effort and negotiations with the Moldovan government remains confidential. But SunCommunications continues to operate in Moldova as of 2014, has acquired new licenses, and has expanded its business since 2008. US nationality brought with it legal and collective resources that proved sufficient to keep SunCommunications operating, deterring outright government breach of contract.

US investors enjoy particular benefits in Moldova that help them sustain contract sanctity in ways inaccessible to firms of other nationalities. The US Foreign Corrupt Practices Act of 1977 (FCPA) provides credibility to the claim that US firms cannot pay bribes, something executives (US and otherwise) with experience in many countries readily acknowledge. Thanks to the FCPA, US investors can avoid going down the rabbit hole through which a small bribe can give rise to bigger conflicts with government officials.[41] Interestingly, local heads of subsidiaries of major multinationals said in 2009 and 2011 that there is no equivalently strong anti-corruption legislation restricting the action of firms from major Continental European countries. In the words of one observer in Moldova, with the FCPA "Americans get off the hook, but not French and Germans."[42] In fact, thanks to action by the OECD in 1997, anti-bribery legislation in Europe has largely converged on standards equivalent to the US FCPA; however, as Kaczmarek and Newman point out, enforcement by European countries has been weaker than US enforcement.[43] Interviewees did point to the fact that British firms now contend with the UK Bribery Act of 2010, which goes further than the FCPA: it prevents British firms from paying government officials in order to expedite bureaucratic processes. Some see this extra restriction as hampering British firms' competitiveness in locations with poorly functioning bureaucracies. Regardless, the impact of national legislation on firms' latitude regarding payments to local governments, and variation in the enforcement of that national legislation, further underscores differences in contract sanctity of Continental European, British, and US firms.

The US State Department's Trafficking in Persons (TIP) Report is another tool that US firms recognize as important to their contract sanctity in Moldova. The annual TIP Report provides a credible threat of US government action that diplomats believe pushes Moldovan officials to respect US interests.[44] As part of the Trafficking Victims Protection Act of 2000, the US government may withhold non-humanitarian, non-trade-related foreign assistance from

---

[40] Interview, US firm, Moldova, 2009.
[41] "Corruption in Moldova is dysfunctional – can't bribe the right people, and the right people can't do what you want them to do," Interview, foreign firm in financial services, Moldova, 2009.
[42] Interview, international organization, Moldova, 2009.
[43] Kaczmarek and Newman 2011.
[44] Interviews (2), US government officials, Moldova, 2009.

governments that are categorized as not making "significant efforts" to combat trafficking. The United States may also oppose such assistance from the IMF or the World Bank. Moldova, which is a source, waypoint, and destination for much human trafficking in the region, has been on watch for a demotion to not making "significant efforts" since the legislation's inception. Local US actors see positive spillovers from Moldovan relations with US officials over trafficking to Moldovan relations with US-origin FDI, and they point to specific conversations in which Moldovan officials link the two issues.[45] In short, institutions like the FCPA and the TIP Report shape the contract risks and resources to fight breach that US investors – and not investors of other nationalities – face in Moldova.

Spaniards and Electricity

While the Moldovan government has occasionally threatened the property of foreign firms, disputes have on the whole been worked out such that even the firm directly involved – such as the US firm SunCommunications – remains and grows its investments in the country. Another foreign firm in Moldova, the Spanish gas and electricity multinational Union Fenosa, has faced a set of disputes with the Moldovan government that made front-page news. Union Fenosa both won and lost in local court cases, but, in the end, the firm found a solution suitable enough to expand its Moldovan investments in the following years.

Throughout the first decades of economic transition in Central and Eastern Europe, foreign energy firms like Union Fenosa have had to deal with a legacy of subsidized domestic pricing combined with monopoly pricing from Russian-origin gas and oil that accounts for the vast majority of supplies. Foreign energy executives recognize that the tension between domestic demands and energy firms' viability sometimes injects expectations of flexibility into contractual arrangements.[46] This bind has led to conflicts over foreign energy firms' contracts throughout the region, including in Moldova.[47] Union Fenosa bought three of Moldova's five distribution companies for US$25.2 million in 2000 and first turned a profit in 2006.[48] The firm's contract was then challenged when the energy regulator lowered the allowable profit margin in 2007.[49] Unfortunately for Union Fenosa, Spanish investors are not a visible, powerful group in Moldova. Nevertheless, the exit of a flagship Spanish firm like Union Fenosa

---

[45] Ibid.

[46] Interviews (2), energy firms, Cambridge, MA and Romania, 2009 and 2010.

[47] In Slovakia, for example, the government threatened in 2006 to expropriate Italy's Enel and in 2008 to expropriate the German firm E.ON should those firms increase energy prices to Slovakian households. These actions were electoral posturing rather than credible threats; no nationalizations were undertaken.

[48] "Union Fenosa Moldova Turns to $8.0 mln Net Profit in 2006," *SeeNews – South East Europe Newswire*, 6 March 2007.

[49] The margin was lowered from 23 percent to 13 percent. "Union Fenosa Moldova to Cut Investments by 30 Percent in 2008," *SeeNews*, 7 October 2007.

would do considerable harm to Moldova's prospects for attracting other Spanish investors. In fact, breach with Union Fenosa would throw the country's electricity distribution system into turmoil, and, in all likelihood, lead Moldova to rely on large energy firms from Germany or Austria that had already invested in neighboring countries.[50] With Spanish investment out of the picture, these new firms could leverage their privileged position against a desperate Moldovan government, extracting terms that Moldova would likely find worse than those with Union Fenosa. The prospect of shutting off doors to channels of investment is a deterrent for governments interested in capital access, and those shut doors mean more in a country with low FDI national diversity.

The outcome of negotiations between Union Fenosa and the Moldovan government over possible changes to contractual terms, and the involvement of the Spanish government in those negotiations, remains confidential. Nevertheless, Union Fenosa's continued presence and growth in Moldova as of 2014 demonstrates that the Moldovan government stepped back from breach enough to leave the firm's ability to operate in Moldova unchallenged. Executives at non-Spanish firms sometimes had personal sympathies for their colleagues at Union Fenosa, but their firms had no incentive to offer public support and risk that the government would make them targets. Rather, Union Fenosa benefitted from constraints on the Moldovan government even though it had few of its own in-country allies.

A Rich Moldovan

The absence of ultimate breach of contract in SunCommunications' and Union Fenosa's disputes, and the dearth of other, public disputes with foreign firms, is most obvious when foreign firms' complaints are contrasted with those of domestic Moldovan firms. In 2009, for example, the government confiscated a conference center owned by the leader of an opposition party after a court found that there were irregularities in its 1999 privatization; the owner was not invited to the final phase of the trial. The owner of a meat-processing business was thrown into prison for securities law violations, although securities law in Moldova was "non-existent."[51] Some domestic firms facing government breach of contract have found ways to get their disputes heard in public international investment arbitrations (IAs): Transnistrian and Moldovan residents sometimes hold Russian passports, so they can sometimes gain access to resources reserved for foreign firms. But executives at Russian multinationals as well as executives

---

[50] This demonstrates a necessary caveat to the literature on the obsolescing bargain, which predicts that immobile assets – like an electricity distribution network – are relatively easily expropriated. In fact, it is not clear that Moldova had the domestic capacity to take over Union Fenosa's operations. This suggests one explanation for why the Moldovan government chose to threaten only creeping expropriation regarding Union Fenosa's profit margins.

[51] "World News: Moldova rulers turn up heat on business," *Financial Times*, 29 May 2009.

at other "true" foreign firms see such IAs as evidence not of anti-foreign or anti-Russian actions, but as a sort of anomaly. Even when domestic firms do exit Moldova, these firms' actions are not costly in terms of lost access to bigger pools of foreign capital or strained diplomatic ties. Foreign firms' contract sanctity is distinct from that of domestic firms.

A dramatic instance of government breach of contract with a domestic investor was the government's treatment of Moldovan billionaire Anatol Stati. Stati managed a multinational corporation based in Moldova, the oil services company Ascom. Ascom's primary investments have been oil firms in Kazakhstan, Sudan, the Virgin Islands, and Iraq. In 2002, President Voronin annulled an agreement between the Moldovan government and Ascom that, by all respects, seems to have been in Moldova's interests: Moldova would have bought Kazakh gas from Ascom for 30 percent of the price of Russian (Gazprom) gas. Stati claims that the annulment led Moldova to overpay for gas to the tune of US$1.66 billion.[52] Politically, Stati clashed with then-President Voronin and Voronin's allies in the Communist Party, and, in all likelihood, the repeated breach of contract with Ascom over the years has been a form of political confrontation.

In 2008, Stati's son Gabriel was put on trial in Moldova for "hooliganism," and Gabriel spent considerable time in jail. Ascom withdrew its basic staff from Moldova in response.[53] Two months later, President Voronin sent a letter to President Nursultan Nazarbayev of Kazakhstan, a country in which Ascom had significant investments. In the letter, which was later leaked to the Moldovan opposition, Voronin urges Nazarbayev to pay "serious attention" to Stati and accuses Stati of using income earned in Kazakstan to conduct "blood-tainted business" in Sudan, causing "severe damage" to Moldova's reputation. Voronin also alleges that Stati "runs and finances propagandistic campaigns and in non-transparent ways funds political parties oppositional to the current government."[54] After this letter, Ascom in Kazakhstan faced frequent inspections and criminal and civil cases. Kazakhstan went on to cancel licenses for two of Stati's production subsidiaries, alleging "breach of subsoil use contracts," which Ascom saw as the culmination of a "campaign of harassment."[55] Ascom had invested over US$990 million in Kazakhstan since 1999; by 2010, the firm's assets were wholly confiscated.[56] Incidentally, during this period Kazakhstan

---

[52] "Moldovan billionaire sues ex-president, demands compensation," *BBC Monitoring Ukraine and Baltics*, 15 July 2010., "Anatol Stati seeks US$1.5bn damages from Vladimir Voronin," *Moldova Azi*, 16 July 2010.

[53] "Oil company withdraws staff from Moldova citing pressure as reason," *BBC Monitoring Ukraine and Baltics*, 26 August 2008.

[54] "World News: Moldova rulers turn up heat on business," *Financial Times*, 29 May 2009.

[55] "Kazakhs take back licenses from trio," *Upstream*, 6 August 2010. "Ascom urges international leaders to address Kazakhstan's 'Resource Nationalism' as 40 Heads of State Gather in Astana for the OSCE Summit," *PR Newswire Europe TWOTEN*, 23 November 2010.

[56] In 2010, Anatol Stati sued now ex-president Voronin, demanding he personally pay US$1.55 billion compensation for the confiscation of Ascom's assets in Kazakhstan. "Moldovan

had received significant new FDI in oil and gas as well as other industries from British, Russian, Chinese, and other investors.

On 7 April 2009, protesters across Moldova called for a repeat of what they saw as flawed parliamentary elections of the day before.[57] Thousands of people participated in demonstrations and riots in an unprecedented show of support for political change in Moldova. Over the next several days, the presidential residence and the Parliament of Moldova were badly damaged. Gabriel Stati was arrested again, accused of being the mastermind behind the demonstrations and having prepared a coup d'etat. In response, Ascom moved all of its operations out of Moldova, and the elder Stati pulled out of other personal investments; the loss of capital is estimated at US$2.3 billion.[58] But, there appeared to be no broader threat of other investors withdrawing their capital as a result of Stati's actions. In Moldova, Stati is an anomaly: few to no other multinational corporations of Moldovan origin exist. Further, despite the billions of dollars involved, foreign executives interviewed at the height of the conflict in 2009 set the Stati breaches aside as irrelevant to their own operations.[59] This was a domestic conflict, which generated threats to domestic property rights but not to foreign-owned property. Voronin and the Moldovan government could take action against Stati without the fear that interference with a domestic firm would cause foreign capital to withdraw.

Germans and Airlines

There is one major exception to the trend of foreign firms' contract sanctity in Moldova. In 2002, the Moldovan government broke its shareholders' agreement with its German partner when it unlawfully replaced the head of the privatized national airline Air Moldova.[60] The Moldovan courts ruled that Air Moldova's founding documents were null and void, agreeing that the state has the right to act as it did because the company is "state property."[61] Moldova wholly renationalized the airline, forcing the German firm out.[62] Consistent with

billionaire sues ex-president, demands compensation," *BBC Monitoring Ukraine and Baltics*, 15 July 2010.

[57] OSCE observers judged the elections as "generally free and fair."

[58] "Moldovan tycoon suspends operations in home country following riots," *BBC Monitoring Ukraine and Baltics*, 11 April 2009. "Stati accused of organizing Chisinau riots, coup attempt," *ITAR-TASS World Service*, 17 April 2009. Interview, foreign firm in business services, Moldova, 2009.

[59] Interviews (4), US, British, Romanian, French firms, Moldova, 2009.

[60] The German firm Unistar Ventures bought 49 percent of shares when Air Moldova was privatized in 2000. The agreement stipulated that 75 percent of the shareholders must agree in order to replace the head of the firm.

[61] "Moldovan court rules in favour of state agency in airline dispute," *BBC Monitoring Former Soviet Union – Political*, 6 August 2002.

[62] In 2008, the European Court of Human Rights awarded the German firm EUR6.7 million (US$9.4 million) in compensation. *Unistar Ventures GmbH v. Moldova, Application No. 19245/03, European Court of Human Rights.*

expectations, Moldova subsequently lost access to German capital. Dresdner Bank pulled out millions from a planned aircraft purchase and cut off promised loans to Moldovan firms in natural resources and other industries.[63] By way of comparison, German firms invested six times as much as Italian firms in 2003, but German and Italian firms' shares of FDI were equal in 2008. As a capital-poor country, Moldova suffered from these losses.

The best explanation for the renationalization of Air Moldova, and the government's willingness to incur the costs of breach, is corruption.[64] The staff of the aviation administration had been accused of corruption before, during, and after the Air Moldova sale.[65] Most notoriously, the man who took over for the German-approved director of Air Moldova was arrested in 2005, and he and several other top-level employees were charged with "large-scale embezzlement under a well-established criminal scheme."[66] It appears that corruption led to a clear breach of contract and the nationality-specific penalties such a breach predicts. But as of 2014, the corruption foreign firms have faced in Moldova has otherwise stopped short of this kind of outright expropriation.

Corruption, Not Broken Contracts

Foreign firms do not have an easy time of it in Moldova. Sometimes tax inspectors come too often; sometimes, in times of budgetary hardship, the government asks for taxes to be paid in advance. In 2004, the president's office called the directors of Moldova's fifty largest multinationals to an appointment, at which each director was presented with the amount his or her firm was to donate to a campaign to renovate two monasteries.[67] By 2008, one-half of one of the monasteries had been renovated. But many foreign executives say, "Well, we're not in the West," seeing these incidents as obstacles but not broken contracts.[68] The broader "business climate" in Moldova certainly gives foreign firms pause before opening operations in the country. The business climate is the kind of issue around which foreign firms in Moldova can sometimes coalesce. In

[63] Interviews (3), think tank, Moldova, 2009. "German bank threatens to stop investing in Moldova over airline row," *BBC Monitoring Former Soviet Union – Political*, 21 June 2002. "Moldovan government replaces airline director in defiance of German investors," *BBC Monitoring Former Soviet Union – Political*, 24 June 2002.

[64] Interviews (3), think tank, Moldova, 2009.

[65] In 1999 the director was accused of taking a cut on sales to a Russian firm, illegitimately selling the state-owned travel agency, and founding a competing airline to seize profitable routes from Air Moldova. "Moldovan civil aviation chief denies corruption charges," *BBC Monitoring Former Soviet Union – Political*, 11 December 1999. An audit of the Administration in 2002 revealed that much touted airliners from Brazil had been purchased at inflated prices. "Moldovan civil aviation chief sacked over airline row," *BBC Monitoring Former Soviet Union – Political*, 14 August 2002.

[66] "Former Moldovan state airline officials arrested," *BBC Monitoring Ukraine and Baltics*, 21 March 2005.

[67] The "requests" for donations stopped prior to the 2005 presidential election.

[68] Interviews (2), foreign firms in business and financial services, Moldova, 2009.

2009, for example, interviewees suggested that there was growing interest among foreign firms of different national groups to get together and pen white papers on corruption and the like. But foreign firms in Moldova, while not without problematic relations with the Moldovan government, have been largely free of experiencing particularistic government breach of contract.

Contract sanctity has been largely maintained in Moldova, despite the fact that foreign firms do not come together across national lines on specific property rights issues. Even in a country with relatively few foreign firms and relatively few nationalities represented, where cross-national collective action problems would be theoretically easier to overcome, co-national foreign firms continue to respond to co-national threats of breach. With few sources of foreign capital on which to depend, the Moldovan government has largely looked to domestic and not to foreign firms to score political points by breaking contracts.

BREACH IN ROMANIA

Since 1990, FDI national diversity in Romania has grown to a high level, considerably higher than Moldova's (see again Figure 6.2). In the late 2000s, Romania consistently hosted one of the most diverse groups of OECD investors among emerging economies, even after the general withdrawal of capital during the world financial crisis. In this diverse environment, the expectation is that co-national investor lobbying should be slower to form and diplomats should be slower to come to firms' aid, as protest is less likely to have a positive effect on contract sanctity. With so many alternate sources of foreign capital on which to rely, the Romanian government is expected to have permissive space to break contracts publicly and with prominent foreign firms.

These predictions are put to a difficult test in Romania. During the 1990s and 2000s the country took pains to institute a market economy and reform political life in order to join the European Union. The country missed out on the first expansion but did enter in 2007. Politically and economically linked to the Western European home countries of some of its largest foreign investors, and trying to prove itself as a serious and equal member of the EU, Romania has strong incentives to treat Western European firms well. On the face of it, breach of contract with a European firm would seem a costly choice indeed. And, it is a reasonable hypothesis that such a move would lead US and other nationalities of firms to reconsider their investments in Romania as well. Yet I find compelling evidence that firms have nationality-tied (and not EU-tied) conceptions of contract risk. At the same time, firms understand that their nationality is just one of many, and lobbying and diplomatic efforts on behalf of particular firms' contracts are checked. In fact, EU institutions have supported breach of contract in Romania as well as in other accession countries. Romania's deeper commitments to international institutions have sometimes reinforced the government's choice to breach contracts with foreign firms.

Weak Co-national Action

In contrast to strong nationality-tied investor associations in Moldova, nationality-tied associations in Romania tend to focus on networking and have few to no lobbying activities. This is consistent with the prediction that weak leverage in a nationally diverse FDI environment discourages co-national collective action. The American Chamber of Commerce in Romania (AmCham), for example, has a policy of not advocating for particular firms. In one anecdote, when an executive from one of their newest members brought up a particular conflict with the government, the AmCham leadership "shut her up."[69] The AmCham is worried that lobbying on a particular US firm's behalf would compromise its access to the authorities altogether.[70] Large US multinationals are members of the AmCham, but so too are enterprises originating in Romania that have interests in the United States. One foreign executive, commenting on the AmCham, assesses that the organization has a "brand," but it has basically become a "Romanian association of Romanians wanting to be Americans."[71] US members have not seen it worthwhile to change the organization's focus. The AmCham provides information to the US Embassy and claims to use it as "our loudspeaker," but executives interviewed at US firms provided few examples of active support from embassy officials. Other foreign investor associations in Romania are similarly arranged around nationality. Yet the British Chamber of Commerce is seen as mainly a social club, and the British are known to "hang out" alone. Executives of other nationalities also agree that Austrians, French, and Germans all keep to themselves.[72] None of these groups have active investor associations with strong lobbying agendas.

Russian investors in Romania epitomize the idea that national groups face different risks and thus different determinants of contract sanctity. Foreign executives of various nationalities (including Russian) agree that Russian investors are frowned upon. One foreign executive notes that the Romanian government has an "obsession with not letting Russians in. If there's a choice, they choose Western."[73] Anecdotal evidence suggests that Romanian officials have the ability to exercise their anti-Russian preference even before investment takes place.[74] Compared to Romania's eastern neighbors, very few privatization

---

[69] Interview, AmCham member, Romania, 2009. Another executive said, "We don't need AmCham lobbying." Interview, US firm, Romania, 2009.

[70] Interview, AmCham member, Romania, 2009.

[71] Interview, foreign law firm, Romania, 2009.

[72] Ibid.

[73] Interview, French firm, Romania, 2009. This executive went on to say that he thinks Russians resort to making "undercover" investments in various industries in Romania, where their identity is masked via intermediaries of other nationalities.

[74] Of course, the absence of what would otherwise be Russian investment is difficult to demonstrate, as it is the "dog that didn't bark." Nevertheless, deterring Russian investment in particular is something unavailable to a country like Moldova with so few other nationalities of investors ready to replicate the depth and breadth of their Russian-origin FDI.

tenders go to Russian buyers. Commenting on discussions over a new nuclear power plant, a foreign executive in an unrelated industry observed that Russians wanted to build it but that the government "won't ever give it to them," as the government would naturally prefer the French bidders.[75] The nationally diverse FDI in and interested in Romania suggests that the government has space to selectively deter Russian firms before contracts are formed. Russian political actors have been weak in Romania, especially as compared to Russian pressure on the Moldovan government. While Russian investors share particular risks to contract sanctity – and the formation of contracts in the first place – co-national action is nowhere near its levels in Moldova.

Do multilateral groups fill the void left by weak national coalitions? The Canadian Business Association (CBA) is an organization hoping to provide members with services beyond networking. Despite its name, the CBA is deliberately opening up to not just Canadians but to a nationally diverse membership. Such cross-national groups can be useful in pressing host governments on issues of general interest to foreign firms, like tax law or corruption. However, these groups do not advocate on behalf of particular firms facing breach of contract, lest they alienate parts of their membership. For example, in the case of one very public, acrimonious government breach of contract with a Canadian firm, the CBA's stance is that it "understands both positions." The association has taken no overt action on the firm's behalf, although the firm is a CBA member.[76]

Besides the CBA, a multilateral Romanian Foreign Investor Council (FIC) has been active since the early 1990s. US executives usually run the FIC, although large firms of various nationalities subscribe to it. The local head of a large foreign bank calls the FIC "quite influential," but he describes that influence in terms of broad-based policy reform and not particular breaches of contract.[77] Similarly, EU-tied associations also focus on broad business climate issues. Prominent foreign executives from firms with EU home countries understand this: in interviews, several lamented that EU associations suffer because they are reluctant to get involved in particular disputes. In short, as predicted by the nationality shield theory, government breach of contract with a particular firm does not draw the interest of associations that represent foreign firms across national origins.

Industry associations are not a substitute for lobbying around contract breach, either. The Romanian pharmaceutical industry association includes foreign firms, but foreign members see it as ineffective: "just complaining, not engaging."[78] Foreign-owned banks have been very isolated in Romania and have not been participants in Romanian banking associations. The local head of a prominent Western bank regretted the absence of bank associations and

---

[75] Interview, foreign firm in business services, Romania, 2009.
[76] Interviews (2), Canadian firms, Romania, 2009.
[77] Interview, French firm, Romania, 2009.
[78] Interview, foreign law firm, Romania, 2009.

attributed this to diversity among foreign firms' home-country banking cultures.[79] There is a foreign investor "club" for firms interested in infrastructure, but it is "only to find clients" and not a source of lobbying power.[80] Foreign firms in oil and gas and natural resources described occasional collaborations in the 1990s, but these have since fallen apart. In particular, co-industrial support has been absent in the several government breaches of contract with resource investors in the 2000s (discussed in subsequent sections). In the words of a local manager of a foreign firm, associating with professional groups can be "a form of survival, but they are not a proper lobby."[81] Put differently, industry associations may provide information important to firm competitiveness but do not provide support in times of conflict with the government.

The Romanian government uses public institutions to interact with foreign firms, but these institutions do not mediate complaints over contract breach. Many foreign executives interviewed shared the sentiment that "the government is only interested until firms invest here. After that, they don't care."[82] Officials at Romania's investment promotion agency, Romania Trade & Invest (RTI), dispute this view. RTI prides itself on the "after-market services" it provides to ensure the success of new foreign investments once they have been made. After-market services include such actions as simply keeping in touch with foreign firms, to supporting them in interacting with local bureaucracy, to aiding foreign executives in navigating local school systems for their children. Such services are currently seen as the "gold standard" in investment promotion, because they are key to ensuring that current foreign investors decide to reinvest in the future.[83] However, RTI does not support firms should they find themselves in conflict with the government (nor does the "gold standard" in investment promotion suggest such an after-market service). Both RTI officials and foreign executives are clear on this point. Romania does have a culture in which local directors of foreign firms can sometimes meet with officials as high up as the prime minister, but respondents that had been to such meetings agreed that they were not in themselves effective in resolving particular disputes.

Canadians and Gold

The Romanian government has broken contracts, in a high-profile way, even after joining the EU in 2007. With high FDI national diversity, the nationality shield theory's expectation is that the Romanian government has gained the

---

[79] Interview, French firm, Romania, 2009.
[80] Interview, US firm, Romania, 2009.
[81] Interview, British firm, Romania, 2009.
[82] For its part, the Romanian public does seem to care before investment. For example, there were popular celebrations when Nokia moved some operations from Germany to Transylvania. In contrast, there was a public scandal when Mercedes decided to build a plant in Hungary instead of Romania. Interviews (2), foreign firm in business services and local news media, Romania, 2009.
[83] Wellhausen 2013, Guimón 2009.

room to take such actions with relatively few penalties in terms of the loss of capital, co-national firm protest, or damaged diplomatic standing. These expectations hold true in the prominent breach of contract with a Canadian firm that inflamed public debate from the mid-2000s and still brought protesters to the street in 2013.

The Romanian state extracted gold from the Rosia Montana region in the northwest of the country for fifty years, until 2006. This is considered perhaps the richest mining region in Europe, with gold mining traceable back to ancient Rome. In 1998, the Canadian firm Rosia Montana Gold Corporation (RMGC) received permission to exploit the mines.[84] After making some US$380 million in initial investments, RMGC applied in 2006 for the state to carry out the inspections necessary for RMGC to receive environmental permits. In 2007, Romanian investigators stopped their inspections soon after the conservative-leaning coalition government disbanded. Rather than find that environmental damage would be too high to allow the mine to operate, or find that the mine can operate, or declare what RMGC needed to do to get environmental approval, the process simply stopped. The Romanian government's decision to unilaterally and without reason stop and not restart the evaluation constituted a broken commitment to RMGC. At stake was a planned US$4 billion investment to be made over sixteen years, which would employ up to 3,000 workers in a region with 80 percent unemployment. In January 2012, some Rosia Montana locals marched in the streets with signs like, "We Live on Gold, We Die of Hunger."[85] The project's fate remained in limbo until finally, on 11 November 2013, a parliamentary commission voted down a draft bill that would have allowed the project to go forward. From RMGC's point of view, this action effectively solidified the contract breach. In 2014 Gabriel Resources took steps to sue Romania for up to US$4 billion for what it labeled multiple breaches of investment treaties.[86]

However, Romanian and international actors have applauded the Romanian government for suspending operations at Rosia Montana. Local and international environmental non-governmental organizations (NGOs) worry about the protection of groundwater in an important Danube watershed area. RMGC's plans were to use cyanide at the mine, a common agent in the process of extracting gold from ore, and the firm would maintain cyanide tailings ponds in its process of wastewater management. Central Europe is particularly sensitive to cyanide mining since a tailings pond collapsed in Baia Mare, Romania in 2000; its contaminated water ultimately spilled into the Danube in Hungary. In response to this disaster, the EU issued a Mining Waste Directive in 2006 that requires mines to reduce cyanide parts per million (ppm) from a maximum of

---

[84] RMGC is a subsidiary of Gabriel Resources.

[85] "Canadian-Romanian goldmine draws protests," *Agence France-Presse*, 28 January 2012.

[86] Reguly, Eric, "Gabriel may seek billions in arbitration over stalled Romanian mine," *The Globe and Mail*, 30 April 2014.

50 ppm down to 10 ppm by 2018. According to RMGC, wastewater from the Rosia Montana mine would have had a concentration of 5 to 7 ppm. However, neighboring Hungary has banned the use of cyanide mining altogether. On top of environmental concerns, NGOs were worried about the impact the mine would have on Roman archeological findings in the area.

Local and international NGOs wanted the limbo status of the mine resolved in favor of complete suspension of operations. Like those in favor of the mine, protesters on this side of the issue marched in the streets. In January 2012, for example, hundreds turned out in Bucharest with signs like "Yes to Culture, No to Cyanide."[87] In the face of such public outcry on both sides of the issue, the Romanian government faced incentives to remain indecisive for years.

RMGC fought to reinstate its property rights: it held many public debates in Romania as well as Hungary; its leaders met several times over the years with Romanian presidents and prime ministers; it had public information campaigns on television and in print; it engaged in corporate social responsibility activities; and so on.[88] But co-nationals have not stood with it in its conflict with the government. Executives at Canadian firms are well aware of the conflict and pay close attention, but they recognize that Rosia Montana is a "hot potato."[89] Rather than jointly fight a losing battle, Canadian firms choose to manage their own risk of breach of contract by downplaying RMGC's national ties and differentiating themselves from RMGC.[90] The Canadian Embassy has helped in RMGC's educational initiatives, but the Embassy has spoken out on behalf of Canadian investment only – and not RMGC in particular.[91] RMGC acquired US investors and became Canadian-American in the late 2000s, but US firms have kept their distance and the US Embassy has not been helpful in RMGC's fight.[92]

Behind closed doors, few executives at top multinationals in Romania have been personally sympathetic to RMGC's plight. One agrees that, "in the long term, RMGC will hurt the environment." Another accuses the firm of "dirty tricks," citing evidence that RMGC "turns off locals' power and services" in order to make them move off their land around the mine site.[93] Certainly, the fact that it involves a contentious environmental issue compounds foreign firms' reluctance to go to bat for Rosia Montana.

Other mining and natural resource firms have left RMGC to fight for its property rights alone. Though one might expect investors facing similar types of disputes to coalesce, there is little evidence of that occurring in this case. Another Canadian firm, Sterling Resources, faced a broken contract from 2009 to 2011,

---

[87] Ibid.
[88] Interviews (3), Canadian firms, Romania, 2009.
[89] Ibid.
[90] Interview, Canadian firm, Romania, 2009.
[91] Ibid.
[92] Ibid.
[93] Interviews (2), foreign firms in business services, Romania, 2009.

during which time a law prevented it from developing Black Sea oil blocks that it had purchased from the government. Sterling Resources voiced its frustration, claiming there were "deliberate and discriminatory actions" against its operations including "media attacks and various actions to block the progress of the company's activities."[94] RMGC, too, complained of government misinformation about its operations. Yet Sterling Resources did not publicly stand together with its co-national – which is also a fellow firm in natural resources. For its own dispute, Sterling Resources took quick advantage of the threat of international arbitration under the Canada–Romania BIT, which corresponded with the Romanian government's decision to settle the dispute. It took until 2014 for RMGC to make serious threats of international arbitration.

Perhaps multilateral actors came to support RMGC? Certainly, institutions like the European Union must balance environmental concerns alongside the interests of capital-exporting countries and emerging economies, now that both number among their membership. From one point of view, pushing an EU member to follow through on its self-defined bureaucratic procedures regarding environmental licensing is consistent with such a balanced approach. RMGC thought as much, as it repeatedly appealed to various bodies in the European Union. But the EU largely withheld judgment, and its most decisive action has been against RMGC's interests. In a 2010 non-binding resolution, the EU called "on the Commission and the Member States not to support, either directly or indirectly, any mining projects in the EU that involve cyanide technology."[95] As far as other organizations go, the UN Development Program has no official position on the matter, despite having been pressed for one by advocates for both sides of the issue.[96] Development banks remain uninvolved.[97] And international environmental NGOs have come out strongly against RMGC, with foreigners funding and marching alongside Romanian protesters.

Thus, RMGC found itself isolated, without either a co-national or a multilateral community to call on in its fight against a long-time broken contract in an EU member state. This lack of co-national action fits with the theoretical expectation that, in an environment in which breach is more likely, co-national actors are less willing to expend scarce political capital on what is likely to be

---

[94] "Sterling buoyed by permit change," *Platts Energy in East Europe*, 21 October 2011. The local press reported suspicions that some parts of the coalition government were trying to force Sterling Resources out in favor of the state-owned company Romgaz. Consistent with these suspicions, Prime Minister Boc accused the previous prime minister, who had made the deal, of "undermining the national economy by sealing the agreement with Sterling," saying that he broke the law and planned "a business to favor certain interest groups." The former PM accused Boc of slander; Boc won the subsequent court case. "PM Boc wins lawsuit with former PM Tariceanu over Sterling business," *Rompres*, 19 October 2011.

[95] "European Parliament resolution of 5 May 2010 on a general ban on the use of cyanide mining technologies in the European Union."

[96] Interview, United Nations agency, Romania, 2009.

[97] Interview, international organization, Romania, 2009.

a losing fight. The Romanian government in fact found domestic as well as international approval (or at least indifference), despite acting against a foreign firm's property.

Americans and Transylvanian Highways

The US engineering and construction firm Bechtel Group faced trouble from the beginning over its contract to build a Transylvanian highway.[98] The Romanian government forced renegotiation of the contract several times after it was originally signed in 2003. In 2011, Romania officially broke the contract and Bechtel agreed to give up its right to compensation. US actors spoke publicly only a handful of times about Bechtel, and, in the end, the US ambassador to Romania acted as mediator in making the Romanian breach permanent.[99] German, Austrian, and other nationalities of investors were clamoring to build Romania's much-needed roads. And the European Union was satisfied with the breach of a contract it refused to support from the beginning.[100] In an environment with high FDI national diversity, the Romanian government broke a written contract that one official had lamented was "virtually unbreakable" – without obvious costly actions from US interests and without EU penalties.[101]

In 2003, the Social Democratic government under Adrian Nastase awarded Bechtel a EUR2.2 billion (US$2.5 billion) contract to build a 500-kilometer highway through Transylvania, a large region in the northwest of Romania. The contract was awarded without a public tender process, despite Romanian legislation requiring it. A "furious" European Union had just funded a road running almost parallel for EUR500 million (US$566 million).[102] As a result, the EU did not allow Romania to use any of its EUR4.6 billion (US$5.2 billion) in EU infrastructure funds to pay for the project, setting the stage for years of struggle as Romania tried to pay for the Bechtel project out of its own budget.[103] The pricey Bechtel contract figured prominently in Romania's 2004 elections, which the Nastase government lost. The new Traian Basescu government forced renegotiations in 2005, and Bechtel agreed to a price decrease of EUR126 million (US$157 million).

---

[98] Technically, Bechtel was in Romania on a services concession, which does not always qualify as FDI in a statistical sense. However, as a foreign firm operating in a host country, with the potential to send signals on contract sanctity to other foreign firms, the case is relevant to theory testing.

[99] "President Basescu: Bechtel contract unfortunate, both parties acted incorrectly," *Rompres*, 19 September 2011.

[100] "US ambassador says expropriations, poor financing hinder construction of Romania's Transylvania highway," *Mediafax News Brief Service*, 24 October 2010. "Special Report: Romania's Roads to Nowhere," *Reuters News*, 26 May 2011.

[101] "Special Report: Romania's Roads to Nowhere," *Reuters News*, 26 May 2011.

[102] John W. Miller, "Focus: EU Eyes Public Contracts as Romania's Roads Boom," *Dow Jones Capital Markets Report*, 26 June 2006. "Special Report: Romania's Roads to Nowhere," *Reuters News*, 26 May 2011.

[103] Ibid.

The Nastase-signed contract was originally confidential, but over the years the Basescu government chose to make parts public. Originally, Bechtel was to get an interest-free loan of EUR250 million (US$282 million) on top of monthly payments for its work. Bechtel was in charge of controlling costs and deciding the highway's route, and there were no provisions for an audit until 2012. Most importantly, it was virtually impossible under Romanian law for the government to pursue compensation if Bechtel failed to meet its obligations. Bechtel, on the other hand, secured access to international investment arbitration as well as a provision that banned Romania from continuing construction works on the highway for two years should Romania choose to terminate the contract.[104] These provisions led to considerable consternation among Basescu government officials who felt they had been cheated in a raw deal made by the Nastase government.

Like many large-scale construction projects, the Transylvanian highway quickly overran costs. In 2008, the Romanian press reported that total costs would more than triple to EUR7 or 8 billion (US$10 or 11 billion).[105] Romania threatened to cancel the contract, forcing another renegotiation. This time, Bechtel agreed to forego its interest-free loan and to receive 50 percent of its payment in Euros and 50 percent in Romanian Leu.[106] Still, Romanian ministers made new threats to terminate the contract after the renegotiation.[107] Romania stopped prioritizing payments, and its debts to Bechtel fluctuated between EUR100 and EUR215 million (US$141 and 302 million). The Transportation Minister suggested that rather than expect government payment, "Bechtel should take out a loan" to fund its work.[108] By 2011, the highway was only 10 percent complete, and the estimated price per kilometer had gone from EUR5.4 million to EUR16 million (US$7.2 to 21 million).[109]

The Bechtel contract and controversy made front-page news for years, and foreign firms of all nationalities steered clear. The already weak US lobbying capacity in Romania did little, publicly or privately, on Bechtel's behalf – but in interviews, executives lamented the damage done to what they see as US investors' shared reputation in Romania.[110] The prime minister declared early in the

---

[104] "Potential termination of Bechtel contract entails huge costs for Romania – Ex Transport Minister," *Mediafax News Brief Service*, 27 March 2009.

[105] "US Bechtel company, constructor of Romania's ..." *Rompres*, 16 July 2008. Scandals also arose when Bechtel hired hundreds fewer Romanian workers than expected and paid Turkish workers higher wages than locals. "US Bechtel company, the developer of the ..." *Rompres*, 28 March 2007. "The American company Bechtel has so far employed ..." *Rompres*, 9 August 2007.

[106] "Romania, US Bechtel agree to give up highway advance payment in '09," *Mediafax News Brief Service*, 22 January 2009.

[107] "Potential termination of Bechtel contract entails huge costs for Romania – Ex Transport Minister," *Mediafax News Brief Service*, 27 March 2009.

[108] "Special Report: Romania's Roads to Nowhere," *Reuters News*, 26 May 2011.

[109] "Romania's overdue debts to Bechtel run to 111 mln euros, 1 km costs 16 mln euros," *Rompres*, 30 May 2011.

[110] Interviews (3), US actors, Romania, 2009.

conflict that Romania would not agree to special treatment for Bechtel, "even if they are an American company."[111] At first, the US ambassador kept a positive public attitude about Bechtel. He focused on prospects for other US firms in the country and remained "confident that the Romanian government and Bechtel will find a way."[112] In 2011, the new US ambassador changed tactics when he told top Romanian officials that the broken contract "is also about a big Turkish company, it is not only about Romania and an American company."[113] By emphasizing the Turkish subcontractor Enka's participation in the project, the US ambassador tried to unite foreign firms' experiences across national lines. This attempt to link Turkish and US investors' experiences is telling of the weak leverage US interests alone had over the Romanian government's actions. Predictably, according to the nationality shield theory, the effort to amass a cross-national coalition failed. Enka never took a public stand together with Bechtel; Enka's opinions on the affair did not make it into the Romanian news; and neither the Turkish ambassador nor other Turkish actors took a public position on the Bechtel dispute.

In the end, Romania canceled the contract. Over the process of several renegotiations, Bechtel had given up EUR126 million, a EUR250 million interest-free loan, and, according to insiders, other still-confidential "hidden costs" to the Romanian government.[114] In late 2011, Bechtel agreed to forego its contract altogether for the six unfinished sections of highway and Romania paid no penalties. Moreover, Bechtel gave up its recourse to international investment arbitration.[115]

Far from condemning this outcome, the US ambassador "praised the breakthrough." President Basescu said the outcome was possible "thanks to the support of the US Embassy."[116] Effectively, Bechtel – and what US support system they had – cut their losses. Investors of other nationalities (including Turkish) remained aloof, as did other US actors in Romania. In this situation, much worked against Bechtel: the original contract was a symbol of a political rival; Romania had more investors to rely on than just the US contingent; and US actors recognized their weakness and were absent from Bechtel's fight. Why expend political capital on restoring contract sanctity through public, collective

[111] "Bechtel holds Romania's Transylvania highway back, Not Funding – Romanian PM," *Mediafax News Service*, 21 October 2008.

[112] "US ambassador says expropriations, poor financing hinder construction of Romania's Transylvania highway," *Mediafax News Brief Service*, 24 October 2010.

[113] "US Ambassador Gitenstein says confident Bechtel contract arrears issue to be resolved," *Rompres*, 2 June 2011.

[114] "Special Report: Romania's Roads to Nowhere," *Reuters News*, 26 May 2011.

[115] Romania agreed to pay its debt of EUR90 million (US$120 million) to Bechtel before auctioning off tenders for the other six sections. "Romania re-negotiates contract with US company Bechtel for highway," *Associated Press Newswires*, 4 August 2011.

[116] "Romania to make outstanding payments worth 90 mln euros to Bechtel in two tranches," *Rompres*, 4 August 2011.

action when those efforts are likely to fail? Better to take other steps, like distancing one's firm from Bechtel, to account for increased contract risks.

In the words of one Romanian senator, Romania's breach aligned with "the dignity of a European country" – a fascinating statement when one considers the conventional wisdom that a European country would be on the side of investors.[117] For its part, the European Union praised Romania's new public tenders for highway construction, as breach entirely aligned with the EU's desires.

In fact, post-communist member states' contracts with foreign firms have conflicted with European Union mandates on several occasions. For example, several public IAs brought against Hungary and Romania deal with subsidies offered to foreign firms as part of investment promotion efforts. Hungary and Romania later canceled those subsidies after investors had entered. Both governments have argued that they did so because they believed the subsidies were incompatible with EU rules on state aid.[118] From the governments' point of view, breach earned them approval from the EU. From the foreign firms' points of view, however, the implementation of EU law via government breach of contract was unfair and spurred international legal action.[119]

Austrians and US$20 Oil

In the vein of the Bechtel scandal, the Romanian government was close to nationalizing the Austrian oil and gas firm OMV. But, after political alliances reconfigured, the government did not nationalize but still forced a costly renegotiation of OMV's contract that was linked to a substantial decrease in its share price. In 2004, Romania's Natase government negotiated the privatization of a 51 percent stake in the Romanian state oil company Petrom to OMV for US$1.8 billion. The Natase government was the one that subsequent politicians lambasted for making a raw deal with the Bechtel contract; the OMV privatization faced similar ire. The US$1.8 billion privatization price was based on long-term world oil price estimates of US$20–30 per barrel. As the oil price – and OMV's profits – went up, the subsequent Basescu government and Romanian citizens felt cheated, with one politician calling the

---

[117] "Agreement with Bechtel must be urgently annulled (Conservative Senator)," *Rompres*, 13 July 2011.

[118] For more on conflicts between EU state aid policies and international law, see: Bermann, George, "Navigating EU Law and the Law of International Arbitration," *Arbitration International* 28(3), 2012. See also *The EU Approach to International Investment Policy after the Lisbon Treaty*, October 2010. Cases include *Micula v. Romania (ICSID ARB/05/20)*, *Electrabel S.A. v. Hungary (ICSID ARB/07/19)*, *AES Sumnit Generation Ltd and AES-Tisza Eromu Kft v. Hungary (ICSID ARB/07/22)*, *EDF International S.A. v. Hungary (UNCITRAL)*. "Micula brothers obtain first victory by a private investor against the Romanian state," *Rompres*, 3 October 2008.

[119] Woelker, Ulrich, "The EU as a Player in the BIT Arena" (Presentation at *50 Years of Bilateral Investment Treaties Conference 2009*, Frankfurt, Germany, December 2009).

privatization an "amazing theft."[120] Nevertheless, the privatization contract
was strict: the Romanian state could not increase royalties, add taxes on
production, or change the contract's foundational assumption of low oil
prices. OMV was also free to eliminate 50 percent of the firm's 50,000
Romanian jobs by 2009, and the state took over liability for environmental
damage caused by the firm before OMV took ownership.[121] When the terms of
OMV's investment were made public in 2006, unrest over the deal skyrock-
eted. To throw salt in the wound, the EU accession process required domestic
Romanian energy prices to converge with EU levels, which would be a significant added burden on Romanian households. For its part, OMV argued that
the firm's viability depended on European-level pricing.

As with the Bechtel contract, the OMV contract put Natase's now-opposition
Social Democratic Party (PSD) on the defensive and Basescu's government on the
offensive.[122] In 2006, two Natase-tied Romanian officials were arrested on
suspicion of treason for passing information on Petrom to OMV during the
privatization negotiations. Employees of Credit Suisse First Boston, which had
brokered the deal, were arrested as part of an "organized crime ring."[123]
President Basescu used popular animosity toward Russia to good effect, claiming erroneously that Russia's Gazprom "massively" bought up OMV shares and
that it "may be the real decision maker" behind the Austrian firm.[124]

Against PSD politicians' protests, Basescu called for the review of the contract, and the relevant ministry drew up an "Emergency Ordinance" to increase
taxes and royalties on oil production.[125] In 2007, the Romanian Senate
approved a bill cancelling the privatization and sent it to the lower house, the
Chamber of Deputies, where it died.[126] The former economic minister responsible for Petrom's privatization was a member of the Chamber of Deputies when
the bill came through, and he and the PSD were particularly sensitive to the
broader implications of the bill and an "Emergency Ordinance." By enabling
serious breach with OMV, the bill would also enable the government to break

---

[120] "Official: Romania's Petrom Sale, Relinquishing Oil Reserves – "Amazing Theft," *Mediafax
News Brief Service*, 18 August 2006. "Romanian president seen under public pressure to review
energy privatization," *BBC Monitoring European*, 17 November 2006. Such a deal is not
unheard of in the post-Soviet region, either: Kazakhstan is rumored to have entered contracts
pricing oil at US$5 per barrel. Interviews (2), think tanks, Azerbaijan, 2013.

[121] "Romanian scandals to delay further sales," *Platts Energy in East Europe*, 8 December 2006.

[122] "OMV views Pres' Petrom sale criticism as politics," *Dow Jones International News*,
19 September 2005. "Romanian opposition party defends Petrom privatization contract,"
BBC Monitoring European, 20 September 2005.

[123] "Romanian scandals to delay further sales," *Platts Energy in East Europe*, 8 December 2006.

[124] Ibid.

[125] "Romania's ANRM To Propose Higher Royalties On Oil Prod," *Mediafax News Brief Service*,
21 September 2007. "Romania Oil Tax, Royalty Hikes Will Not Change Contracts – Econ
Min," *Mediafax News Brief Service*, 2 October 2007.

[126] "Romanian Senate initiates cancellation of oil firm Petrom's privatization by Austria's OMV,"
Hungary Business Newswire, 5 December 2007.

contracts with British, American, Canadian, and Romanian firms.[127] Even a country with high FDI national diversity is expected to step back from breach when its actions would threaten many of its sources of capital, out of fear that its actions would trigger costly responses from many co-national groups.

While it avoided nationalization, however, the PSD was unable to avert the "creeping" expropriation of OMV. In 2007, OMV agreed to contribute to a social fund to subsidize individual consumer prices. This was despite the fact that OMV's stock lost 4.7 percent in a matter of days when the OMV CEO first discussed such a "solidarity fund" with President Basescu a year earlier.[128]

The Austrian ambassador to Romania supported OMV and publicly pointed out that 4,500 Austrian companies had invested EUR12 billion (US$16 billion) in Romania, in banking, real estate, insurance, construction materials, IT, and oil and gas.[129] An appeal like this, emphasizing Austrian contributions to the Romanian economy, is consistent with the nationality shield theory. But Austrian firms themselves kept a low public profile – with a low likelihood of success in an environment saturated with nationalities of investors, better to hold back than to protest. There was no apparent public support from actors of other nationalities, nor from the EU. Bechtel and its US supporters and RMGC and its Canadian supporters did not publicly link their situations to that of OMV. Rather, OMV's fate was largely determined by rival Romanian political coalitions.

Foreigners and Privatization

Privatization contracts in Romania have been particularly vulnerable to breach. Such contracts in Central and Eastern Europe often come with provisions about preserving the "scope of investment" to prevent asset stripping, limiting layoffs, and restructuring in order to ensure the new owners' commitments to reinvestment. Romanian privatizations have taken place throughout the 1990s and 2000s, but without consistent institutions to monitor compliance over the long term, some owners did take actions akin to asset stripping despite contractual provisions. This has given rise to gray situations in which private owners claim that their actions were justified on a competitiveness basis and that without flexibility in the interpretation of scope clauses, their investments would fail. The

---

[127] "MP says deputies to reject bill on annulling Petrom sale," *Mediafax News Brief Service*, 7 December 2007. "Producers oppose royalty hike," *Platts Energy in East Europe*, 9 November 2007.

[128] "Romania's President met with CEO Of Austrian oil co OMV," *Mediafax News Brief Service*, 20 November 2006. "Romanian govt drops examination of energy privatizations," *Dow Jones Commodities Service*, 16 January 2007.

[129] "OMV expects Romania to honor Petrom contract, not raise fees," *Dow Jones International News*, 25 October 2007. "Austria becoming big investor in Romania," *Austria Today*, 31 October 2007.

Romanian government, in contrast, argues that violations of scope clauses lend legal justification to renationalizing and reprivatizing property.

Of 352 privatizations made by the Romanian government to foreign investors, eighteen had been revoked and renationalized by 2009.[130] Is this number of broken contracts large or small? In fact, foreign investors tend to buy into some of the largest privatized assets, so renationalizations of foreign-owned assets have had a large and visible impact in the country. Unprompted, executives at foreign firms of different nationalities brought up the revocation of privatization contracts in Romania as a "big issue."[131] Yet, like other broken contracts, by all accounts the costs around renationalization have been a co-national affair. For example, in 2011 Turkish investors sued Romanian's privatization agency over renationalization of their property. Yet top executives at firms of a variety of other nationalities, in a variety of industries characterized by privatized assets, had taken no action costly to the Romanian government in response to this conflict.

DETERRENCE VERSUS BREACH

Romania is not the place one would expect contract breach, and Moldova is not the place for contract sanctity. As a European Union member state, and a wealthier country, with an economy more integrated into international financial markets, Romania has reasons to welcome and respect the contracts of foreign firms. But, the EU sometimes approves of breach, and Romania's economic characteristics have not offset the contrary effect of the presence of high FDI national diversity. Romania has alternative sources of capital on which to rely when it breaches with any one group. Accordingly, any one group of co-national firms has fewer incentives to organize lobbying campaigns, and diplomats have fewer incentives to put bilateral relations on the line over battles unlikely to be won. As a result, Romania has broken contracts even as it has moved closer to the transition success stories of Central Europe.

Moldova, on the other hand, is poor. With legacy ties to its Soviet past, a relatively weak democracy, and endemic corruption, one might expect breach of contract to be widespread. In fact, domestic firms find their contracts broken considerably more often than foreign firms. While a few foreign firms have gotten embroiled in disputes with the Moldovan government, and foreign firms in general struggle with navigating corruption in the country, breach of contract that devalues or precludes the operation of a foreign firm has been rare. Moldova has fewer outside options for capital should it choose to breach. And, when disputes arise, low FDI national diversity facilitates effective protest,

---

[130] By 2009, Romania had privatized 11,261 firms to domestic investors, and 1,144 privatizations, or 10 percent, had been revoked and renationalized. Data from interview, business services firm, Romania, 2009.

[131] Interviews (3), foreign firms in business services and foreign law firm, Romania, 2009.

though this protest still takes place along national lines even in such a small country. Foreign firms and diplomats exert pressure on behalf of their co-nationals but retain distance from other firms' disputes. Breach is contained thanks to co-national, and not cross-national, threats of FDI diversion and collective action by firms and their diplomats.

7

Investor-Government Relations in History

For a market economy to work, private property rights must be secured such that voluntary transactions can take place. The state has been the actor tasked with maintaining this security. The state fails at its task when it does not adequately restrain itself from infringing on private property rights. Carving out state property and private property, and respecting the difference, is part and parcel of what we know as state respect for the rule of law. Rule of law does not require the state to give up the ability to act counter to private property: every state reserves the right to interfere with private property in some instances, for example, when invoking eminent domain. Rather, the state must exercise its sovereignty within the constraints of predetermined rules. This compact over property protections is at the core of the social contract between citizens and their state.

Foreign firms entering a host economy are not part of the social contract between citizens and the state. Put differently, the state is not obliged to protect foreigners' property rights in order to continue to legitimately exist. Foreign firms thus lack the direct connection that citizens and domestic firms have between their property and the legitimacy of the government. Nevertheless, when host states allow foreign firms to do business within their territory, they make an analogous commitment to refrain from unlawful interference with those foreign firms' property. This commitment is not the intimate social contract between a sovereign and its own citizenry. Rather, this commitment is contractual in the arms-length, impersonal, and contingent sense of the word. Why does the state make such commitments? So long as the host government sees advantages to hosting foreign capital, the property rights contract with foreign firms has teeth.

Despite the built-in threat of FDI diversion in the face of contract breach, foreign firms have long been wary of sovereign governments' respect of their property rights – and rightfully so. The empirical record shows that foreign firms' economic carrots and sticks sometimes fail to deter breach. Accordingly, governments in capital-sending countries have made sundry efforts to legally bind host governments to respect contracts. On the whole, efforts made through multilateral institutions have failed. In their place, home-country governments have chosen to sign predominately bilateral treaties that provide international legal recourse to their firms.[1] By the 1990s, three trends converged: host countries have become more reliant on long-term, foreign-owned investment, host governments signed bilateral treaties protecting foreign firms' property rights, and foreign firms from a multitude of home countries have begun providing capital. The growing national diversity of FDI around the world suggests that more and more groups of co-national firms are evaluating threats to their contract sanctity and responding accordingly.

In this chapter, I review developments in investor-state relations over the last centuries and, in particular, I focus on the series of failed multilateral legal efforts to codify foreign firms' rights. These failures capture the fundamental conflict between sovereignty and property that foreign firms have butted up against again and again. Nevertheless, even as multilateral efforts failed, FDI began to come from an increasing variety of sending countries. With foreign firms calling more and more countries home, the stage was set for the nationality shield theory and the negative effects that FDI national diversity can have on the security of foreign firms' property.

BREACH BEFORE 1990

While this book has focused on investor-state disputes since 1990, the history of foreign firms' relations with host governments is long and fraught. For as long as firms have done business overseas, they have had to interact with sovereign governments on unequal footing. Host governments have taken advantage of their sovereignty in times of war when seizing the local assets of investors coming from enemy states. In fact, one reason the British did not support the Confederacy in the American Civil War (1861–1865) was for fear of the sanctity of British investments in the North.[2] Even setting aside the extenuating circumstances of war, instances of government breach of contract have occurred and continue to occur. In the twentieth century, what many see as the heyday of nationalization and expropriation took place in the 1960s and 1970s. Later, some equated the dying out of mass nationalization with the end of expropriation,[3] but creeping expropriation and other forms of government breach of contract continue as more and more states are publicly sued over such issues. While earlier nationalizations often occurred when governments rejected the idea of FDI, today's breaches of contract take place in countries that actively expend resources on attracting FDI.

[1] Jandhyala et al. 2011.
[2] Jones 1992.
[3] E.g., Minor 1994.

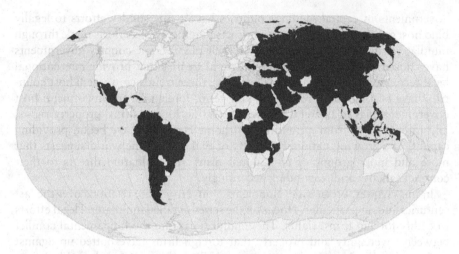

FIGURE 7.1 **Emerging Economies that Nationalized Foreign Property (1917–1985)**
Note: Figure excludes OECD countries that nationalized property with due notice and compensation.
Sources: Hajzler 2012; Kobrin 1980, 1984; Minor 1994. Author's records.

Figure 7.1 reports emerging economies that nationalized assets in the period from 1917 to 1985. The first major nationalizations of the twentieth century came in the Russian Revolution of 1917. Soviet nationalization stood out for its completeness and the total absence of compensation to foreign firms. Assets nationalized from US investors were valued at the time at US$175 million.[4] An analogous total nationalization came after the 1959 communist revolution in Cuba. A contemporary observer valued the assets of the 137 US firms this affected at US$1.4 billion.[5] In both the Soviet Union and Cuba, the basic compact between foreign firms and the host government ceased to exist: the host government no longer desired foreign investment and thus had no reason to maintain its credible commitment to foreign firms' property rights. In these cases, communist ideology had it that property rights belonged to the nation, and not to foreign interests; mass expropriation followed.

In the interwar period, non-communist regimes were more selective in breaking contracts. The difference was that governments desired long-term foreign investment in general, even if foreign ownership in certain circumstances was revoked. For example, under Mustafa Atatürk's presidency, Turkey at first expressly committed to foreign investment as a means of development. However, after nearly a decade in power, President Atatürk authorized in 1932–1933 the takeover of key parts of Turkey's infrastructure, namely foreign-owned public utilities, coalmines, and railroads. Turkey unilaterally decided to

[4] Root 1968.
[5] Ibid.

force changes to ownership, although Turkey paid compensation for these assets that seems to have satisfied foreign firms.[6] In Bolivia in 1937, the country's "shaky new military government ... anxious to win public support" became the first to nationalize an oil firm in Latin America, after accusing the United States' Standard Oil of tax fraud.[7] In Mexico in 1938, the government took over US-owned ranches as well as some US oil interests, valued together at the time at US$120 million.[8] In this case, the US ranchers' claims were settled in the 1940s, though not before Nelson Rockefeller and guests at his party "lustily sang a Mexican song hailing the expropriation of foreign oil properties."[9] The limited Turkish, Bolivian, and Mexican breaches are different from the comprehensive Soviet and Cuban actions, especially as they were conducted in ways that did not challenge the concept of foreign investment wholesale.

Nationalization in the 1960s and 1970s was both broad and deep in many host countries. Kennedy defines "mass expropriators" as governments that nationalized foreign firms in all of banking, natural resources, services, and manufacturing.[10] In the period 1960 to 1985, twenty-eight political regimes in the developing world fit that description (see Table 7.1). These governments are mostly in sub-Saharan Africa and North Africa and the Middle East, although the Chilean Allende regime's expropriation of US copper interests, among other takings, was particularly infamous in the United States.[11] The regimes in Table 7.1 account for 63 percent of expropriatory government actions in the period.[12]

The broad and varied instances of breach under these regimes demonstrate the many political and economic roles government breach of contract has served. Jodice carried out the first multivariate regression analysis of nationalization events, using data from 1968 to 1976, and he found that poorer and more war-torn countries were more likely to nationalize.[13] At the same time, a rise in economic nationalism and an ideology of state intervention in the economy shaped domestic narratives around expropriation.[14] Governments choosing nationalization saw foreign investment as "a symbol of Western industrialization and Western colonialism" to be rejected.[15] In these countries, the basic belief that foreign investment is an important part of domestic economic development was weak. Expropriation became a means to reject

---

[6] Berrios et al. 2011.

[7] Yergin 2008: 257.

[8] Root 1968.

[9] Rockefeller served "only milk and Coca-Cola" at the party. Rivas 2002: 55.

[10] Kennedy 1992.

[11] Ingram 1974, Moran 1974.

[12] That is, 374 expropriatory acts out of 598. An act is counted as the nationalization of at least one firm in a country-year. Kennedy 1992.

[13] Jodice 1980.

[14] Lipson 1985: 146.

[15] Kobrin 1984: 339–340. Quoted in Kennedy 1992: 74.

TABLE 7.1 *Regimes that Nationalized Property in Banking, Natural Resources, Services, and Manufacturing (1960–1985)*

Years	Country	Head of Government	Acts	No. of firms
1965–1978	Algeria	Boumedienne	33	107
1975–1978	Angola	Neto	15	128
1974	Benin	Kerekou	4	10
1962–1983	Burma	Ne Win	10	24
1970–1973	Chile	Allende	30	46
1970–1977	Congo	Ngouabi	10	31
1969–1978	Democratic Yemen	Robaje	5	30
1956–1967	Egypt	Nassere	7	70
1975–1978	Ethiopia	Mengistu	26	105
1959–1979	Guinea	Toure	7	9
1967–1975	India	I. Gandhi	6	48
1957–1965	Indonesia	Sukarno	15	24
1979–1980	Iran (Islamic Republic of)	Khomeini	17	58
1968–1977	Iraq	al-Bakr/Hussain	7	8
1972–1977	Jamaica	Manley	7	12
1969–1974	Libyan Arab Jamahiriya	Qadaffi	11	33
1975–1978	Madagascar	Ratsiraka	12	50
1965–1975	Morocco	Hassan	13	30
1975–1980	Mozambique	Machel	18	43
1967–1974	Nigeria	Gowon	7	35
1968–1975	Peru	Velasco	28	47
1970	Somalia	Barre	5	10
1971–1976	Sri Lanka	Bandaranaike	6	254
1970–1978	Sudan	Nimeiri	13	25
1969–1981	Trinidad and Tobago	Williams	9	10
1970	Uganda	Obote	5	9
1963–1978	Tanzania	Nyerere	28	127
1964–1980	Zambia	Kaunda	20	21
		Total	374	1404

Sources: Kennedy 1992; Kobrin 1980, 1984.

"the general context as well as the specific enterprise."[16] Nevertheless, unlike the Soviet Union or Cuba, regimes' nationalist or ideological rejection of the presence of FDI was not absolute.

Expropriations in Africa from 1960 to 1977 are representative of the scope of government breach of contract in this era. African regimes expropriated large extractive enterprises owned by multinational corporations; local subsidiaries of multinationals, predominately in banking and insurance; and small and medium enterprises owned by resident aliens from former colonial powers as well as

[16] Kennedy 1992.

migrant populations.[17] A number of African regimes, like the formerly French colony Algeria and the formerly British colony Tanzania, were avowedly socialist and undertook expropriations across the economy (see again Table 7.1). Revolution in the wake of colonialism provided a ready foundation for mass expropriation of foreign-owned assets.[18] Yet even these countries did not wholly reject the idea that foreign investment is useful to domestic development. Algeria and Tanzania, for example, continued to work to attract FDI in "approved" projects.[19] In efforts to walk the line between domestic incentives to expropriate and the desire for foreign capital, African countries began to exploit more options along the continuum from contract sanctity to nationalization. Instead of only changing ownership from foreign to domestic, governments forced renegotiation of concession agreements, requisitioned foreign profits, and used "indigenization" policies to limit foreign participation in some sectors, forcing foreign investors to partially divest.[20]

International oil and gas firms have often made headlines in their struggles over property rights abroad. Scholars count between 99 and 120 government breaches of contract in the oil and gas sector from 1960 to 2008, including nationalizations, the forced sale of foreign assets, and forced contract renegotiations.[21] However, the broader phenomenon of government breach of contract was not (and is not) limited to this sector. While oil and gas expropriations accounted for 19 percent of 508 expropriations from 1960 to 1976, manufacturing accounted for 27 percent of expropriations. Indeed, relative to the size of these industries' share of total FDI stock, oil and gas and manufacturing were less likely to be expropriated than other industries in this period.[22]

Figure 7.2 uses two different measures to summarize how many countries broke contracts with foreign firms annually since 1960. The first measure is nationalization, which peaked in the 1970s as up to thirty countries nationalized at least one foreign-owned firm per year. For the period 1956 to 1972, emerging-economy governments seized foreign-owned assets worth US$10 billion, amounting to nearly 25 percent of the total stock of FDI in the world at the end of 1972.[23] Again, it was not the same cohort of countries nationalizing property each year. For the period 1960 to 1976, Jodice counts seventy-six different states expropriating 1,535 firms that came from twenty-two different home countries.[24] The second measure in Figure 7.2 is a count of states sued by

---

[17] Akinsanya 1981.
[18] A similar revolutionary dynamic lay behind Iran's mass expropriations in 1979.
[19] Akinsanya 1981: 778.
[20] Akinsanya 1981.
[21] Data from Kobrin 1980, 1984; Hajzler 2012; Guriev et al. 2011.
[22] Jodice 1980, 182. Banking and insurance as well as mining and smelting each accounted for over 10 percent of recorded events.
[23] Williams 1975. Jodice calculated that approximately 12 percent of FDI flows in 1967 were nationalized in the following nine years. Jodice 1980: 185.
[24] Jodice 1980.

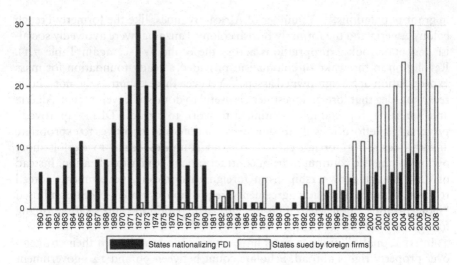

FIGURE 7.2. **Annual Count of Emerging Economies Breaking Contracts with Foreign Firms (1960–2008)**
Sources: Hajzler 2012; Kobrin 1980, 1984; Minor 1994. United Nations Conference on Trade and Development (UNCTAD) Database of Treaty-based Investor-State Dispute Settlement Cases. International Arrangements Section, Division on Investment, Technology, and Enterprise Development. Author's records.

foreign investors in public, international lawsuits known as international investment arbitrations (IAs). While IAs were relatively uncommon early in this period, they would grow to prominence in the 1990s and 2000s as more and more investors gained the ability to sue states for a variety of kinds of breach of contract (Chapter 2). Ironically, the rise in the legalization of investor-state disputes corresponded with a series of failures by multilateral institutions to codify multilateral law on the issue. The targeting of foreign firms during the first half of the twentieth century and certainly the 1960s and 1970s fueled a series of attempts by both capital-exporting and capital-importing countries to deal with breach, though the first set of countries favored stopping breach wholesale and the second did not.

LEGAL ATTEMPTS TO FORESTALL BREACH

Conflicts in international law at the end of the nineteenth century already illuminated the tensions between foreign-firm property rights and host-government sovereignty. In the first globalization (1870–1914), customary international law held sway over the status of foreign investments.[25]

---

[25] Feis 1964.

International norms required states to make prompt, full compensation, in convertible currency, for takeovers of foreign property. Such takeovers were to be limited to "exceptional public purposes."[26] In the 1890s Carlos Calvo, an Argentinian jurist, developed a clear challenge to customary law. Calvo argued that foreigners should be treated like local citizens and participate in local commerce on an equal basis with local citizens. The implications were that previous international norms were moot, and no state should use diplomats or any form of pressure to enforce its citizens' private property claims in a foreign country.[27]

The conflict between customary law and the "Calvo Clause" famously came to a head when Mexico used the Clause to defend its 1938 expropriation of US-owned property. US Secretary of State Cordell Hull responded to Mexico's actions in a note to the Mexican minister of foreign affairs, which re-articulated the terms of customary law in what has come to be known as the "Hull Doctrine": "no government is entitled to expropriate private property, for whatever purpose, without provision for prompt, adequate, and effective payment therefore."[28] The United States also rejected the idea that home governments should be banned from coming to the aid of their citizens' investments abroad. These positions resurfaced with the US Congress's passage of the Hickenlooper Amendment in 1962, which required the president to cut off assistance to countries that expropriate US firms without prompt, adequate, and effective compensation. Ironically, US firms came to reject this formal linkage between foreign policy and expropriation as so antagonistic as to be counterproductive in efforts to reach settlements. While the United States considered using the Amendment in various Latin American cases in the 1960s, it was only applied in Ceylon (Sri Lanka) in 1963.[29] Nevertheless, the Calvo Clause, the "Hull Doctrine," and the Hickenlooper Amendment illustrate the ongoing conflict between capital-sending and capital-receiving countries' positions on government breach of contract.

What are the obligations of host governments to foreign firms? Traditional capital-receiving countries have long pushed back with the reverse of this question: what are the obligations of foreign firms to the countries in which they invest? Since 1907, international organizations have come together at least twenty times to specify what exactly is lawful treatment of foreign firms. See

---

[26] Lipson 1985: 73.
[27] Lipson 1985: 282, note 51; 80. Ginsburg (2005) argues that the Calvo Clause allowed recourse to home-country resources once local remedies are exhausted.
[28] Schachter 1984.
[29] Around the same time, two other amendments formally linked foreign policy to expropriation. The Sugar Act Amendment, passed in 1971, gave the president authority to reduce or eliminate a country's sugar quota when there was evidence of discrimination against a US firm. In 1972, the Gonzalez Amendment required US representatives to the International Development Bank and the World Bank to vote against loans to nations that expropriated US property without adequate compensation. See Lipson 1985.

Appendix Table A7.1 for a detailed summary of the negotiations discussed here as well as additional major efforts.

Early efforts to write obligations into international law failed. By the 1960s and 1970s, the United Nations Conference on Trade and Development (UNCTAD), the OECD, and the International Labor Organization were able to adopt only voluntary standards for both host governments and multinational firms. These include recommendations that firms follow local laws, refrain from collusion, offer good working conditions, and disclose operational data to host governments. However, observers sympathetic to both sides see these voluntary standards as having little real effect on foreign-firm behavior. At the same time, a series of UN General Assembly resolutions reserved to host governments special rights over natural resources and over the treatment of foreign firms in related industries. In one of these resolutions, the General Assembly declared that nationalization is "an expression of the full permanent sovereignty of the State."[30] Pushed through by developing country UN members, these resolutions did not identify any consensus among capital exporters and capital importers. UNCTAD attempted in 1977 to negotiate an International Code of Conduct on the Transfer of Technology, which recognized a sovereign right of states to facilitate and regulate the transfer of technology from foreign firms to domestic actors. Capital-exporting countries balked at the legally binding code and negotiations were abandoned in 1985. Like the efforts that had preceded them, negotiations to encode UN resolutions or other pacts into international law failed.

One attempt: UN Code of Conduct on Transnational Corporations

A special UN Commission on Transnational Corporations, formed by the UN Economic and Social Council, attempted in 1977 to negotiate a legally binding code of conduct on transnational corporations. The steep rise in expropriation events in the 1970s spurred this particular multilateral effort (see again Figure 7.2). As they were among the main capital-exporting countries at the time, the United States, UK, Germany, and Japan were made permanent members of the Commission. The other forty-four Commission members were distributed over world regions. Negotiations on the code remained active until 1983 but never reached a consensus; a 1992 intergovernmental group finally discarded the code and recommended other strategies to strengthen investor–host country relationships.

The draft code provides a good example of the struggle between capital-exporting and capital-importing governments to codify both the right to private property and the maintenance of sovereignty. As might be expected, the Commission suffered from conflicting purposes from the beginning. Officially,

---

[30] UN General Assembly, "Declaration and Action Programme on the Establishment of a New International Economic Order," 6 May 1974.

the Commission's highest priority was to set a code to include standards for the treatment of multinational corporations. These standards were to codify host-government rights and responsibilities with regard to nationalization and compensation, dispute settlement procedures, fair and equitable treatment, and transparency and jurisdiction issues.[31] However, capital importers saw the Commission as providing a forum where, first and foremost, action could be taken to strengthen a host country's power over multinational corporations. Put differently, capital importers expected the Commission to address what *dependencia* theorists see as the fundamentally asymmetric ability of multinational corporations to constrain host governments' freedom of action.

In the draft Code, Paragraph 10 in particular faced strong opposition from capital-exporting countries. It makes steep demands of foreign firms:

> 10. Contracts between Governments and transnational corporations should be negotiated and implemented in good faith. In such contracts, especially long-term ones, review or renegotiation clauses should normally be included. In the absence of such clauses and where there has been a fundamental change of the circumstances on which the contract or agreement was based, transnational corporations, acting in good faith, shall/should co-operate with Governments for the review or renegotiation of such contract or agreement.[32]

Such language in the draft Code instructs multinational corporations to allow governments to renege on and renegotiate contracts when there has been an undefined "fundamental change of circumstances." Requiring firms to recognize a government's ad hoc right to renegotiate inserts unmistakable uncertainty into foreign-firm property rights. Indeed, forced contract renegotiation is a relatively common form of creeping expropriation. From a foreign firm's point of view, one can see why legalizing fungible contracts as provided for in this paragraph would be anathema.

The draft Code required other commitments from multinational corporations to which capital-exporting countries would not agree.[33] The Code read that multinational firms "should carry on their activities in conformity with the development policies ... set out by the Governments of the countries in which they operate."[34] Behind this provision is the presumption that host governments' development policies can discriminate against FDI in general or certain foreign firms in particular. This is, however, in conflict with the idea championed by capital-sending governments that foreign firms have a right to most-favored-nation treatment (MFN) as well as treatment consistent with that of national firms. Arguably, the host-government autonomy suggested in the code would also conflict with historical customary international law,

---

[31] Correa and Kumar 2004: 32–33.
[32] As quoted in Correa and Kumar (2004).
[33] Text from the draft as of summer 1986. Correa and Kumar 2004.
[34] Ibid. Paragraph 9.

which presumes a very narrow scope for legitimate government interference with foreign-owned property.

While the 1977 draft was abandoned, its content reappears in host governments' justifications for breach of contract. For example, the draft stated that firms should honor government requests to stop or limit repatriation of funds "with a view to contributing to the alleviation of pressing problems of balance of payments and finance of such [capital-importing] countries."[35] The notion that foreign firms' property rights are contingent upon whether the host economy is in economic crisis has carried over into contemporary host government–foreign firm relations, though it remains a sticking point. For example, the Argentinian government has argued that it had the right to break contracts with foreign firms during a stated public economic emergency, its 2001–2002 devaluation and default. Host governments have also claimed that their adverse actions toward foreign firms rightfully privilege domestic over foreign firms, facilitate the growth of foreign exchange, or allow the host society to more equitably share in the rents when commodity prices spike (Chapter 2). One may likely have normative opinions on these or other justifications for breach of contract (or, perhaps, their veracity). Regardless, governments in capital-exporting countries have proved unwilling to enter into a multilateral legal regime that they see as trading off increased risks to their firms' contract sanctity. Nor have emerging-economy governments agreed to comprehensive international law on foreign investment.

Limited Multilateral Success

While multilateral international law on FDI remained muddy, the World Bank did take steps to establish a set of rules and a venue in which conflicts between foreign firms and host governments could be heard. The World Bank's impetus to do this came in response to two episodes: the World Bank chose to intercede as arbiter in a dispute between the city of Tokyo and French bondholders over a loan repayment in 1964, and it again played arbiter when Egypt nationalized the British Suez Canal Company in 1966.[36] Rather than continue to play an ad hoc role, the World Bank established the International Center for the Settlement of Investment Disputes (ICSID), the first public, international IA tribunal dedicated to investor–state disputes.[37] At ICSID, private foreign firms

---

[35] Ibid. Paragraph 27.

[36] Ibid.: 374.

[37] Other forums in which investor–state disputes are heard include the Permanent Court of Arbitration, the Arbitration Institute of the Stockholm Chamber of Commerce, the International Chamber of Commerce, and the London Court of International Arbitration. IA also takes place on an ad hoc basis using rules issued by the United Nations Commission on International Trade Law (UNCITRAL) in 1976 and updated in 2010. In contrast to arbitration at ICSID, parties generally have the option of keeping litigation at these other courts and under UNCITRAL rules confidential.

can bring cases against sovereign governments.[38] As ICSID is a World Bank institution, the World Bank could in theory apply pressure on host governments if they delay compliance with the outcome of an IA, though a prominent legal scholar writes, "One has the impression that this benefit of ICSID arbitration is regularly recited but rarely tested."[39] ICSID heard very few cases from its inception through the 1980s. It was the rise of a new set of Bilateral Investment Treaties (BITs) that facilitated the influx of cases since the 1990s (Chapter 2).

The World Trade Organization (WTO) provides foreign direct investors multilateral protection of their property rights only at the fringes. The General Agreement on Trade in Services (GATS), negotiated from 1986 to 1993, precludes WTO members from using investment measures that affect trade in services.[40] The Agreement on Trade-Related Investment Measures (TRIMS), negotiated from 1986 to 1995, limits investment measures related to trade in goods. Aside from these limitations, however, the WTO allows member governments to set policies specific to (i.e., discriminating against) foreign firms.[41] Moreover, disputes arising under GATS and TRIMS are, like all disputes in the WTO, resolved only at the inter-state level. This means that firms with a grievance must lobby their home governments to file a case with the WTO. Even if the home government agrees to file a case on its firm's behalf, the host government need not change its policy toward that particular, damaged firm. This is because WTO remedies do not require the host country to reverse its actions but operate by allowing the home government to retaliate via trade measures. Suffice it to say, foreign firms have not found direct or speedy reprieve for broken contracts under limited WTO protections.[42] From the point of view of the multinational corporation, therefore, protections under GATS and TRIMS do not incontrovertibly deter breach of contract by WTO member governments.

The OECD began negotiations on a Multilateral Agreement on Investment (MAI) in 1995. OECD countries intended the MAI to be a legally binding treaty to ensure foreign firms have both most-favored-nation treatment and national treatment (that is, treatment equivalent to that of domestic firms) both pre- and

---

[38] Before ICSID, the Permanent Court of International Justice under the League of Nations, the International Court of Justice, the Iran–US Claims Tribunal, courts applying European and American conventions on human rights, and ad hoc tribunals had heard a handful of cases having to do with cases of indirect expropriation. Most of these cases were, however, brought by states against states. Hoffmann 2008, Reinisch 2008.

[39] Bishop 2009: 23. Data on compliance with ICSID awards is not wholly public – firms may be reluctant to reveal payment delays to shareholders – but the general sense in the legal community is that countries have been relatively compliant. The major exception is Argentina, which took some years to settle (rather than pay full awards) with litigants (Chapter 1).

[40] "Investment measures" are government policies toward FDI or multinational corporations.

[41] Developing countries that are WTO members have five- or seven-year windows to delay the elimination of TRIMS.

[42] See, for example, Chaudoin 2015, Davis 2012.

post-investment.[43] Emerging economies balked at this, as did anti-globalization activists in France, the United States, and other OECD countries.[44] In fact, the MAI would have created a "rich-rich treaty" – and developed states realized they did not want their investors suing each other.[45] Negotiations quickly fizzled and were abandoned in 1998.

Recognizing the limited nature of its protections for firms engaged in direct investment, the WTO opened a Working Group on Trade and Investment in 1996. The Working Group intends to explore a Possible Multilateral Framework on Investment in the style of the failed OECD MAI, but it has no negotiating authority. What is more, further exploration of the issue was planned for the WTO trade negotiation round after the Doha Development Round. Progress has thus been delayed as the Doha Round, which commenced in 2001, remains stalled in 2014.

Over more than 100 years of negotiation efforts, only a handful of piecemeal multilateral efforts have generated protections for foreign investment. The Energy Charter Treaty has since 1994 provided a legal basis for IAs in the energy industry. Hicks and Johnson count forty-seven International Investment Preferential Trade Agreements (IIPTAs) from 1992 to 2007, including NAFTA and CAFTA-DR.[46] Through the end of 2011, UNCTAD counted 318 non-BIT instruments that included investment protections, as compared to 2,731 BITs. Bilateral protections have carried the day, although these efforts have not codified obligations of foreign firms to host governments.

The trend of devolving investment protection efforts to the bilateral level corresponds with the rise over the last decades of more and more bilateral investment relationships. With more sending countries investing in more host countries, the stage has been set for the nationality shield theory's predictions that bilateral relations do much to shape the kinds of investment protections a particular foreign firm enjoys.

SOURCES OF NATIONAL DIVERSITY

Whereas once foreign firms came from the United States, the United Kingdom, and a handful of other Western European countries, these countries' dominant roles as FDI senders is declining. New nationalities of firms are becoming major players in global capital flows.

---

[43] The vast majority of BITs provide protection for foreign investment only post-establishment, though home countries like the United States and Japan have pushed for pre-establishment protections in model BITs.

[44] For an analysis of French protest, see Ancelovici 2002.

[45] The United States and Canada found this out the hard way under NAFTA Chapter 11, which facilitates lawsuits by firms of one NAFTA country against governments of another NAFTA country.

[46] Hicks and Johnson 2012. For the relationship between trade agreements and FDI, see Manger (2009) and Büthe and Milner (2008, 2014).

The growth of multinational corporations in more and more home countries is not surprising. As Dunning laid out in his "eclectic paradigm," firms choose to become multinational as a result of ownership, internalization, and locational factors.[47] Ownership factors include the firm's management style, advantages the firm might derive as a result of its particular home country, and the firm's historical legacy. Traditional home countries have robust support structures for internationally minded firms, but there is no reason that such characteristics cannot develop in other countries, too. Internalization factors are those aspects of a firm that lead it to keep investments in-house (internal) as opposed to participating in the global economy through external contracting or strict trade relationships. New trade theory posits that the most efficient firms become the most active abroad. One could imagine firms becoming efficient and finding internalization advantageous regardless of national origin. In fact, the relatively weaker intellectual property protections in emerging economies might make multinational corporations from those countries particularly likely to internalize rather than risk licensing relationships.[48] As with ownership factors, there is no reason to believe that internalization factors are limited to firms coming from traditional capital-exporting advanced industrialized countries.

Locational factors, the third set of factors that leads firms to become multinationals, account for the distribution of foreign direct investors' current and potential investments across different host countries. Those investors willing to invest in emerging economies are willing to trade off more locational risk in exchange for potentially higher rewards. In the distribution of all possible foreign investors, from risk-seeking to risk-averse, it is improbable that all risk-seeking firms originate in advanced industrialized countries like the United States and the United Kingdom. In fact, investors from emerging economies might have particular advantages when investing in emerging economies. Multinational corporations from non-traditional sending countries may have products better targeted to markets in emerging economies, be better able to navigate red tape and bureaucratic holdups common in them, or be more geographically proximate to them. These characteristics would suggest that non-traditional foreign firms would be more likely to invest in emerging economies than would their traditional counterparts.[49] The takeaway is that there is nothing intrinsic about firms outside of the United States and Western Europe that prevents them from being foreign investors themselves, and foreign investors into emerging economies in particular. Indeed, the increasing national diversity of foreign investors over the twentieth century corresponds with the growth and internationalization of trade and finance more generally.

[47] Dunning 1980.
[48] Wells 1983.
[49] Ibid.

Trends in FDI Nationalities

Increasing diversity among sending-country nationalities has occurred alongside FDI growth since the twentieth century. For example, US firms increased their manufacturing activities abroad over the twentieth century, especially in the 1960s, but so too did British and other Western European firms. Japanese firms grew from effectively no foreign manufacturing activity in the early 1900s, to substantial activity in the 1960s. Today, Japanese manufacturers are major foreign investors, especially in Asian countries.[50]

Emerging economies, too, have been home to multinational corporations. By the late 1970s, 963 emerging economy parent firms had established subsidiaries and branches in at least 125 countries.[51] Table 7.2 summarizes the outward foreign investment position of fourteen emerging economies in the late 1970s. Hong Kong, Singapore, and the Philippines were the largest capital exporters of this group, although several Latin American countries also had positive outflows of FDI to a number of foreign subsidiaries.

US multinational corporations dominated FDI into Latin America before the 1950s. From the mid-1950s on, however, non-US firms grew to account

TABLE 7.2 *Outward FDI from Selected Emerging Economies (late 1970s^)*

Country	Outward FDI US$ millions	No. subsidiaries	Subsidiaries in manufacturing (Pct)
Hong Kong	976	325	62%
Singapore	370	89	64%
Philippines	276	66	39%
India	88	215	78%
Korea	71	155	16%
Venezuela	64	18	50%
Brazil	41	147	17%
Argentina	38	146	52%
Colombia	35	37	49%
Mexico	23	62	35%
Ecuador	19	2	0%
Chile	14	11	64%
Peru	4	37	49%

^ Data from one year between 1975–1978, as available.
Sources: Wells 1983, Table 1.2. By permission of The MIT Press. Data collected by Harvard Business School, various sources.

[50] Tsurumi 1976: 2 (Table 1–1).
[51] Wells 1983: 2.

for one-third of all new foreign capital. In the 1970s, FDI diversified further, thanks in particular to investments from West German, Japanese, Swiss, Canadian, British, and French firms.[52] For example, using methodology employed in Chapter 4 of this book, a weighted measure of the effective number of foreign investor nationalities present in Brazil grew from 3.9 in 1969, to 6.4 in 1974 and 7.2 in 1982, meaning that FDI national diversity in Brazil increased considerably.[53] While foreign capital had previously originated in a small number of home countries, by the early 1980s more and more nationalities of foreign firms were present across Latin America.

Figure 7.3 summarizes recent trends in the national origins of FDI. In 1980, US firms accounted for the biggest share of outward FDI in the world, but their share has steadily declined in the last decades. The shares of outward FDI

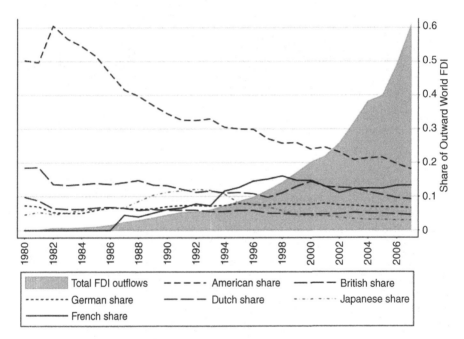

FIGURE 7.3 **Total World FDI Outflows and Traditionally Large FDI Home Countries' Shares (1980–2007)**
Note: The countries identified here accounted for 55 percent of world FDI outflows in 2007, down from 80 percent in 1987.
Source: International Monetary Fund, International Investment Position, Global Historical Statistics.

---

[52] Wells 1983, Lipson 1985.
[53] Data from Lipson 1985: 106. See Chapter 4 for calculation details.

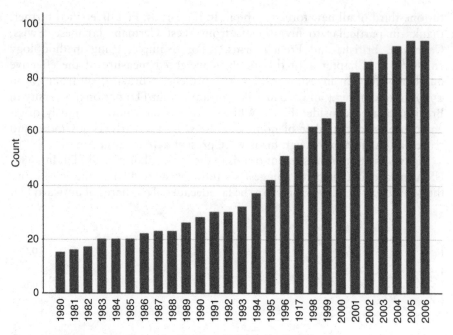

FIGURE 7.4 **Countries Reporting Outward FDI to the IMF (1980–2006)**
Source: International Monetary Fund, Balance of Payment Statistics.

flows from Japan as well as from major European capital exporters, including Germany, France, the Netherlands, and the United Kingdom, have remained relatively stable. Instead, other home countries have contributed to the quick rise in world FDI. Figure 7.4 summarizes data from the International Monetary Fund (IMF), which reported outward FDI data from fifteen capital exporters in 1980. By 2006, some ninety-four countries registered positive outward FDI. Firms from OECD capital-exporting countries are still the bulk of those making contracts with host governments.[54] Nevertheless, increasing investor national diversity is the norm, from home countries both within and outside of the OECD.

Table 7.3 summarizes the increasing diversity of multinational corporations' nationalities in one sector, banking, over just the short period of the 1990s and 2000s. Traditional OECD countries continue to account for the lion's share of multinational banks. But the number of multinational banks coming from other home countries in Asia, Europe, Latin America, the Middle East, and Africa doubled from 1995 to 2009. This expansion holds true even when

[54] OECD-origin FDI forms the basis of quantitative analyses in Chapter 4.

TABLE 7.3 *Count, Multinational Banks by Home Region*^

	Region	1995	2000	2005	2009
OECD:	Western Europe	389	539	625	686
	United States and Canada	123	162	153	159
	Japan, Australia, and New Zealand	38	37	35	39
Other:	East Asia and Pacific	39	57	58	71
	Eastern Europe and Central Asia	25	55	69	85
	Latin America and Caribbean	64	76	65	62
	Middle East and North Africa	38	53	64	89
	South Asia	12	13	15	17
	Sub-Saharan Africa	29	37	57	81
	Total	757	1029	1141	1289

^ Eight offshore host countries are excluded: Antigua and Barbuda, Bahrain, Barbados, Cyprus, Mauritius, Panama, Seychelles, Singapore.
Source: Claessens and van Horen 2011: 23 (Table 2).

excluding banks from eight countries that often serve as offshore or "tax haven" home countries for foreign firms.

National Diversity and Tax Havens

Tax havens emerged in the 1920s, although the 1970s to the 1990s were the "golden years" of growth in the number of jurisdictions and the amount of capital they touch.[55] The definition of a tax haven is, however, hotly contested. Major international organizations have used at least eleven different sets of criteria to identify ninety-one jurisdictions as tax havens. Only seven jurisdictions fit all of these eleven sets of criteria: the Bahamas, Bermuda, the Cayman Islands, Guernsey, Jersey, Malta, and Panama.[56]

FDI statistics for a tax haven might capture FDI that "passes through": the tax haven is neither the origin nor the end destination of the FDI. Consider Chinese government statistics on the top ten sources of FDI in 2007. Of them, the British Virgin Islands, the Cayman Islands, Samoa, and Mauritius are small countries or jurisdictions often understood to be tax havens.[57]

---

[55] Palan et al. 2010: 108. See Chapter 3 for further consideration of tax havens and the nationality shield theory.
[56] Ibid.: 45. Palan et al. (2010) ultimately define a tax haven as "a jurisdiction that deliberately creates legislation to ease transactions undertaken by people who are not resident in their domains, with a purpose of avoiding taxation and/or regulations, which they facilitate by providing a legally backed veil of secrecy to obscure the beneficiaries of those transactions."
[57] Other sources are Hong Kong, Singapore, South Korea, Japan, the United States, and Taiwan. MOFCOM, quoted in Palan et al. 2010: 54 (Table 2.2).

Certainly, we do not think of massive Samoan firms accounting for the rapid growth of FDI in China. Chinese statistics also point to another pass-through phenomenon – that of "round-tripping," in which investors from the host country channel capital through a second country and reinvest in the host country. Aside from offering tax benefits, round-tripping gives otherwise domestic investors access to foreign jurisdictions and the exit options that foreign incorporation offers. Chinese capital is famously round-tripped through Hong Kong, Singapore, and Taiwan, also among the top ten sources of FDI in 2007.

Table 7.4 shows stocks of FDI out of and into the twenty-seven countries of the European Union, from 2004 to 2008. FDI between the EU and

TABLE 7.4 *EU-27 Outward and Inward Investment Stocks^ (2004–2008)*

FDI Stock Sent from EU-27 Destination	Pct	FDI Stock Coming into EU-27 Origin	Pct
United States	28%	United States	38%
Offshore financial centers	21%	Offshore financial centers	23%
Switzerland	10%	Switzerland	10%
Canada	5%	Gulf states^^	7%
African, Caribbean and Pacific countries	5%	Japan	4%
Russian Federation	4%	Brazil	4%
Turkey	3%	Canada	4%
Singapore	2%	African, Caribbean and Pacific countries	3%
Brazil	2%	Australia	2%
Japan	2%	Singapore	2%
Hong Kong	2%	Russian Federation	2%
Gulf states^^	2%	Norway	2%
China (excl. Hong Kong)	2%	Hong Kong	1%
Australia	2%	Iceland	1%
Mexico	2%	India	1%
Norway	2%	Mexico	<1%
South Africa	2%	Uruguay	<1%
Egypt	1%	South Africa	<1%
Ukraine	1%	Egypt	<1%
India	1%	China (excl. Hong Kong)	<1%

^ Table reports shares of EU-27 country investment in FDI stocks in and out of the EU-27, as marked.
^^ Gulf states: United Arab Emirates, Bahrain, Iraq, Kuwait, Oman, Qatar, Saudi Arabia, Yemen
Sources: "The EU Approach to International Investment Policy after the Lisbon Treaty," 2010. *Directorate-General for External Policies: Policy Department,* European Parliament, 22.

advanced industrialized countries accounts for a large share of total FDI stocks in both directions. Table 7.4 also shows that FDI from the EU flows into a great variety of other destinations, and that a variety of countries account for FDI into the EU. Significant amounts of FDI stock come from countries in the Middle East, Brazil, Singapore, Russia, and even Uruguay. This cross-section of FDI stocks gives another impression of the trend toward more diversity among sending (and receiving) countries.

However, offshore financial centers (OFCs) account for above 20 percent of outward stock and inward stock to the EU-27. OFCs are a category of jurisdictions relatively indistinguishable from tax havens. The IMF defines them as centers where "the bulk of financial sector transactions on both sides of the balance sheet are with individuals or companies that are not residents of OFCs."[58] OFCs need not share the secrecy provisions and effective absence of tax usually integral to definitions of tax havens.[59] This makes it perhaps politically easier to label the City of London and US International Banking Facilities (IBFs) as OFCs – which the IMF does.[60]

Tax haven FDI goes to show the variety of nationalities involved in global investment transactions today. In fact, what appear as single nationality sources in aggregated statistics may in fact be masking underlying nationality diversity. The efforts in this chapter to describe growing national diversity in home countries thus underestimate the true state of affairs. Far from being irrelevant to the broader story of nationality diversity told in this book, money that flows through tax havens is influenced by the political economic characteristics of those jurisdictions.

CONTINUING TENSIONS, GROWING DIVERSITY

With foreign investors from more home countries bringing more cultures, histories, languages, and business practices into emerging economies, host governments have to take more bilateral relationships into account when interacting with foreign firms. The clash between host-government sovereignty and foreign-firm property rights plays out across more and more home–host country pairings. In this context, host governments continue to sometimes break contracts in a variety of ways, with investors of a variety of nationalities.

---

[58] Ibid.: 29 (Box 1.2).
[59] The IMF writes that the definition of OFCs "more popularly" includes "low or zero taxation; moderate or light financial regulation; banking secrecy and anonymity," IMF 2000: 29.
[60] Ibid.: 38–39.

APPENDIX

TABLE A7.1 *Summary, Attempted Multilateral Agreements on the Treatment and Regulation of FDI (1907–2010)*

Agreement	Organization	Initiated	Contents	Status
The Porter Doctrine	Hague Peace Conference (44 countries)	1907	Creditors agreed not to collect contract debts by force if debtor states would accept binding arbitration.	Latin American states entered major reservations; ratified only by Mexico.
International Conference on Treatment of Foreigners	League of Nations	1929	Attempt to codify international property law confirming "national treatment" for foreign investment, or equality between foreign and domestic investments. European powers wanted clear statement that compensation must be according to international minimum standards.	Defeated by a coalition of Latin American, Eastern European, and ex-colonial states.
Conference for the Codification of International Law	The Hague	1930	Negotiations over imposing responsibility for protecting foreign investment. No discussion of areas in which host government could still assert sovereignty.	Proposed convention vetoed by India, Latin American and East European states.
Codification of Calvo Clause	Seventh Inter-American Conference	1933	Attempt to codify proposition that foreigners conducting local commerce, just as domestic citizens, must forgo the right of appealing to their home governments for support.	Latin American states agreed. Rejected by the United States, which specifically reserved its rights to the contrary under international law.

Charter	International Trade Organization	1945–1948	1946 draft charter referenced the rights of investors and obligations of host states but did not address investment security. In 1947–1948, the US delegation proposed inclusion of requirement for "prompt, adequate, and effective compensation."	Negotiations failed. Opposition to US amendments from Latin America, India, and Australia delegations. Proponents of foreign investment withdrew support because of strong emphasis on sovereign rights.
General Assembly Resolutions on Permanent Sovereignty over Natural Resources	United Nations	1952 – 1966	Introduced by Uruguay and Bolivia. Endorsed the right of all states to nationalize and freely exploit natural resources. Word "nationalization" dropped from final version. 1952 version includes non-binding recommendation that member states "have due regard, consistent with their sovereignty, to the need for maintaining the flow of capital in conditions of security."	Non-binding resolutions with no international legal standing. 1962 resolution diluted compensation standards from "just compensation" to "appropriate" payments. 1966 resolution deleted all references to international law.
Convention on Settlement of Investment Disputes between States and Nationals of Other States	World Bank	1965	Intended to facilitate the flow of investment from industrialized to developing countries by providing IA facilities, through the International Center for the Settlement of Investment Disputes (ICSID).	Came into force in 1966.

(continued)

TABLE A7.1 (*continued*)

Agreement	Organization	Initiated	Contents	Status
Convention on the Protection of Foreign Property	OECD	1962–1967	Intended to define and protect against expropriation and confirm fair and equitable treatment (although not most-favored-nation treatment) for foreign firms.	Greece, Portugal, and Turkey objected. Failed. But, it has become a substantive model for BITs.
Set of Multilaterally Agreed Equitable Principles and Rules for Control of Restrictive Business Practices (RBPs)	UN Conference on Trade and Development (UNCTAD)	1968	Recommended norms stating that enterprises should follow host-country RBP laws; provide information on business practices to host governments; and refrain from collusion, predatory pricing, etc.	Non-binding with no legal standing. Adopted unanimously in 1980. Considered ineffective by UNCTAD review groups.
General Assembly Resolution 3041/XXVII	United Nations	1972	Resolution that nationalization is "the expression of sovereign power . . . in virtue of which it is for each state to fix the amount of compensation and the procedure for these measures." Disputes were to fall "within the sole jurisdiction" of the nation's courts.	Non-binding resolution with no international legal standing.
Charter of Economic Rights and Duties of States	United Nations	1974	Outlined rights of developing countries and duties of	Non-binding resolution with no international legal standing.

			multinational firms and home countries. Endorsed restrictions on foreign capital in developing countries, including the exclusive use of municipal courts to settle disputes.	120 in favor; 10 abstained; 6 against (US, UK, West Germany, Denmark, Belgium, and Luxembourg).
Guidelines on International Investment and Multinational Enterprises	OECD	1976	Voluntary recommended norms of behavior for foreign firms and host governments, including provisions on information disclosure, environment, combating bribery, tax policy, employment and industrial relations, etc.	Adopted in 1976, revised in 1991 and 2000. No legal standing.
Tripartite Declaration of Principles on Multinational Enterprises and Social Policy	International Labor Organization (ILO)	1977	Voluntary recommended norms regarding employment, training, working conditions, and industrial relations for foreign firms and host governments.	Approved in 1977 by ILO Governing Body, amended in 2000. No legal standing.
UN Code of Conduct on Transnational Corporations	UN Economic and Social Council	1977	Established standards for the conduct of foreign firms and their treatment by host governments, covering national treatment, transparency, nationalization and compensation, etc.	Negotiations abandoned in 1992. Recommended seeking alternative methods to manage investor–host country relations.

(continued)

Agreement	Organization	Initiated	Contents	Status
International Code of Conduct on Transfer of Technology	UN Conference on Trade and Development (UNCTAD)	1977	Intended to facilitate and increase technology transfer by prohibiting restrictive business practices and recognizing a sovereign right of states to facilitate and regulate technology transfer.	Negotiations abandoned in 1985. Developed countries opposed legally binding code.
Convention Establishing the Multilateral Investment Guarantee Agency (MIGA)	World Bank	1985	Provides political risk insurance. Also provides advisory services on the legal framework for FDI in member host countries.	Adopted in 1985. MIGA established in 1988 at the World Bank.
Agreement on Trade-Related Investment Measures (TRIMs)	WTO	1986	Applies only to investment measures related to trade in goods. Member countries maintain rights to regulate FDI, except with regard to trade-related performance requirements such as local content or trade balancing requirements. Developing countries required to eliminate TRIMs within five or seven years.	Adopted in 1995.
General Agreement on Trade in Services (GATS)	WTO	1986	Applies to investment measures affecting trade in services.	Adopted in 1993.

Energy Charter Treaty	The Hague	1991	Treaty confirms national sovereignty over energy resources and protects foreign firms against discriminatory treatment and breach of contract.	Legally binding instrument with 51 signatories in 2011 (Russia withdrew in 2009).
Multilateral Agreement on Investment (MAI)	OECD	1995	Legally binding treaty to ensure protection and legal rights for foreign firms. Was to ensure national treatment and most-favored-nation status to foreign firms in both pre- and post-investment phases.	Negotiations abandoned in 1998.
Multilateral Framework on Investment	WTO	1996	EU and Canada pushed for a Possible Multilateral Framework on Investment (PMFI) with the OECD MAI as a model.	Working Group on Trade and Investment studied the issue without a negotiating mandate.

Source: Lipson 1985, Correa and Kumar 2003, Dolzer and Stevens 1995, original documents.

8

When National Diversity Erodes Property Rights

Usually arguments about nationality and economic globalization refer to the country that hosts FDI and the role its national borders do or do not play in a world of mobile capital. Kobrin writes that the world is reaching a point where "degree becomes kind, where the erosion of autonomy and control over an economy and economic actors renders the presumptive right of states as the supreme authority within their borders relatively meaningless."[1] Such a lament that multinational corporations can penetrate state authority and bully emerging economies into submission resounds in the literature. For those convinced of the presumptive power of global commerce over national sovereignty, however, this book suggests a more complex picture. When foreign firms' power resources are very dispersed, host governments can go so far as to infringe aggressively on foreign firms' property rights – bullying multinational corporations right back, one might say.

Put differently, today's emerging economies can sometimes find themselves with "room to move" on their commitments to foreign firms' contracts.[2] What does this "room to move" mean in practice? Host governments can, under certain predictable conditions, take actions adverse to foreign firms that raise revenues; address issues with certain sectors or assets; achieve foreign policy goals; prioritize domestic interests; commit corrupt acts; or simply get the government out of a contract that has turned sour. Such actions carry external costs, particularly in terms of lost capital access and diplomatic tensions with the home country whose nationals' assets are at stake. But when the host government has permissive space to act, those external costs are not so high as to deter the government from breaking contracts. Host governments can accomplish goals – the variety of which has only been hinted at in this book – without wholly foregoing economic integration.

---

[1] Kobrin 2001: 191.
[2] Mosley 2000, 2005.

Do host governments realize this? Countries around the world keep statistics on the nationalities of foreign firms entering their economy. In Ukraine, Moldova, and Romania, government officials responsible for investor relations can recite the top nationalities of investors by rote. Officials talk about strategies to attract FDI from certain nationalities and, sometimes, to avoid or downplay FDI from others. Nationality remains a salient category; it follows that the variety of nationalities in a host country is salient and recognized by government officials, too.

One personal experience offers some evidence that officials recognize nationality shields as well as the shields' diminished strength when nationally diverse FDI is available. In 2009 I interviewed a prominent member of the Ukrainian Rada who had served as an ambassador and was deeply involved in the high priority area of Ukrainian-European Union relations. He said to me that the entry of South Korean FDI into Ukraine in the early 2000s meant that Ukraine had really made it in the world. But, as I reminded him, Ukraine quickly canceled the low-tax zones from which the South Korean firms benefitted. This breach addressed what was becoming a pressing domestic problem: by many accounts, the low-tax zones had become hotbeds in which domestic firms engaged in corrupt activities. Nevertheless, the action caused massive South Korean exit and deterrence. In response to this line of questioning, the MP did a quick about-face. He began regaling me with stories about the many other nationalities of investors that had grown their investments and entered Ukraine, despite this "issue with the Koreans." The MP clearly understood that deterring South Korean investment was a cost, but not one that shut down FDI access wholesale. In short, his thinking when it came to FDI revolved around nationality. For him, the strategy around FDI, foreign firms' interactions with the government, and a sense of Ukraine's integration into the world was a product of the national distributions of investors.

BREACH FOR THE BETTER?

What does a host government's sometime ability to break contracts mean for development outcomes? It is important to note that the nationality shield theory has little to say about when breach might be "for the better." There is no reason to expect the normative status of breach to be correlated with the diversity of foreign firm nationalities in a host country. Nonetheless, the question remains: can breach ever contribute to good governance or economic growth?

On one hand, a government's commitment to its own contracts, both domestic and foreign, is a key element of rule of law and therefore of good governance. By acting within the rules of the society it governs, rather than above those rules, governments can provide domestic and foreign investors with confidence that the government will in the future keep its hands off investments made today – an important input to economic development. From a foreign firm's point of view, contract sanctity, rule of law, good governance, and investment certainly go hand in hand.

Yet from a host government's or a host polity's point of view, foreign firms' contract sanctity need not equate to normatively positive outcomes. The record suggests that a government's choice to break contracts with foreign firms has sometimes reinforced democratic accountability. Chapter 5 examined Ukraine's broken contracts with Russian and Cypriot investors, contracts which many in Ukrainian domestic society saw as relics of a different era in which "Wild East" capitalists ran roughshod over the state. Breaking those contracts – negotiated under non-transparent conditions, selling a desperate government's assets at rock-bottom prices – may have been better for the Ukrainian political economy than honoring them would have been. In Chapter 6, we saw that Romania broke its obligations to a Canadian gold mining firm by unlawfully suspending the environmental permit review process. Mining and the environment are especially salient to the Romanian public after mining-related ecological disasters in the region. Unsurprisingly, many Romanian citizens held the view that a previous Romanian administration made a mistake in allowing the investment to go forward, and the new government rightfully reasserted the country's principled belief in environmental sanctity. International NGOs have supported Romania's actions, and the EU unofficially backed it as well. Indeed, one could argue that breach in this case is a means by which Romania is "racing to the top" in its de facto if not de jure environmental standards.[3] These examples provide just a small insight into the narratives host governments and host polities construct around foreign firms' contracts – narratives which often make claims about fairness, justice, environment, and security that host-country actors may see as normative justification for breach.

Governments, however, always have the incentive to tell a good story, and there is no reason to presume that host governments will consistently "breach for the better." Autonomy indicates freedom, and free choice can result in bad outcomes. Political factions can wield contract breach as a tool for personal gain, leaving social effects of secondary interest at best. Breach motivated by corruption, for example, is unlikely on its face to generate positive outcomes. And even in moments of investor diversity, breach of contract with foreign firms does have direct costs in the form of the loss of co-national capital as well as potential diplomatic penalties. Even if a broken contract brings about a short-term benefit, incurring these costs might do more damage to economic and political development in the long run. For example, the 2012 US retaliation against Argentina's breach of contract with two US firms was costly: Argentina's exporters, who avoided US$17.3 million in US duties in 2011, faced new, high US tariffs.[4] Whether violating US firms' contract sanctity was worth it in the long run, or whether it justified incurring this penalty on exporters, is an open question.

---

[3] Vogel 1997.
[4] Palmer, Doug, "Obama says to suspend trade benefits for Argentina," *Reuters*, 26 March 2012.

Rodrik coined the term the "globalization paradox," arguing that countries cannot simultaneously pursue "democracy, national determination, and economic globalization."[5] Certainly, this book does not find that these three notions can coexist in all times and all places. When FDI national diversity is low, Rodrik's paradox holds: governments face constraints on their ability to simultaneously access capital and prioritize domestic goals like democracy and national determination. However, in those moments when FDI national diversity is high, host governments can almost have it all. Host governments can exercise autonomy, respond to democratic pressures, and violate norms of economic globalization with some investors while retaining access to others. Once a host government chooses to breach, it loses access to a slice of foreign capital, but it does not forego economic integration wholesale. Slightly limited economic globalization, national determination, and democracy can coexist. What is more, these moments are not one-shot games – they occur and reoccur in countries around the world as foreign firms enter and exit host economies, as FDI widens and deepens.

CYCLES OF SANCTITY AND BREACH

Host governments must, of course, make sufficient commitments to foreign firms' contracts to attract a diversity of investor nationalities in the first place. Some scholars argue that governments make these commitments once contracts and treaties are formal and legalized; others argue that a government's interest in its own reputation with states or investors drives compliance.[6] The approach here suggests that potential host governments take actions to commit to foreign firms' property rights, but they do so not to ensure one universal reputation. Rather, governments pursue many good reputations with different national groups.

When a government first opens its country to FDI, it takes actions that tie its hands with respect to many nationalities of investors. Governments sign instruments like multiple BITs. They exercise restraint when a conflict arises and the incentives to breach are tempting. And they take actions that suggest wider commitments to contract sanctity, like codifying and strengthening domestic tax and corporate law. In these moments, host governments do give up some autonomy in the quest for FDI. When foreign firms find the government sufficiently credible, they begin to invest. As those early investors' contracts remain intact, more and more firms from more diverse origins choose to enter or reinvest. Investor diversity may come about thanks to government strategy or simply organically, as firms with interests in investing in a host country are in all likelihood distributed across many home countries.

---

[5] Rodrik 2011.
[6] Goldsmith and Posner 2005, Simmons 2000, Mosley and Singer 2008; Chayes and Chayes 1993.

At some point, these dynamics imply that the host government will face a highly nationally diverse set of foreign firms. It is then that the host government discovers a new realm of possibilities with respect to investors: it can reconsider its existing commitments to foreign investors' property rights and face less overwhelming penalties for doing so. Once a host government breaks contracts, however, it starts to face costs. Firms of the targeted nationality are likely to withdraw or divert capital, and relations with that home government may sour. Certainly, the host government has incentives to frame breach as a one-time occurrence. This credibility decreases, however, as a government breaks more contracts and faces growing costs from more national groups.[7] As the number and concentration of firm nationalities decreases, the power of national groups of foreign firms to maintain their contract sanctity increases. Co-national firms become more willing to coalesce to protect their shared contract sanctity when the likelihood of success is higher. Similarly, home country diplomats are more likely to act to ensure their nationals' contract sanctity by linking contract sanctity to other bilateral issues, pressuring host-country officials directly, or otherwise expending political capital. When FDI national diversity decreases in a host country, co-national actors have interests in reinforcing their nationality shield.

As the field of nationalities shrinks, and each remaining nationality's shield is strengthened, the host government will at some point lose the permissive space to break contracts. Now the choice to break a contract would generate high external costs, with the loss of yet another nationality's capital and the loss of good relations with yet another home government. The importance of obligations to foreign actors now overwhelms the variety of domestic incentives to breach. Whether or not breach can be for the better, the window to exercise breach is smaller. All else equal, the host government must reform its behavior in order to access a greater diversity of FDI, regaining foreign firms' trust by (re)making credible commitments to contract sanctity with each of many nationalities.[8] If successful in doing so, more and more firms from a diversity of home countries will again invest. And so a host government is likely to face cycles of investor diversity and permissive space to breach. When that permissive space re-emerges, a host government can again weigh the priorities of its domestic political economy against foreign contracts – and those domestic priorities can win.[9]

---

[7] The rate of breach may vary in interesting ways across countries and regimes. This is a fruitful area for future research.

[8] All else is not equal if extenuating circumstances in the market make foreign firms more risk-seeking. In that case, firms' propensity to invest in countries with governments that are engaging in contract breach may increase. For example, the combination of an increase in commodity prices and the presence of natural resource endowments may allow some well-endowed countries to access more replacement capital.

[9] These dynamics clearly lend themselves to empirical testing, a fruitful area for future research as time passes and more data becomes available.

OVERCOMING NATIONAL DIFFERENCES?

Given the impact that FDI national diversity has on contract sanctity, how can savvy investors use this information to maintain their contract sanctity? Individual firms may be able to reinforce their contract sanctity by increasing the national diversity of the capital they command. Firms with claims on more home countries expose themselves to more risk factors. But, they also have access to more pools of co-national firms and more home governments that can come to their aid in contract disputes. Put differently, foreign firms can benefit from becoming "true" multinationals, through mergers and acquisitions or by investing in a third country via a subsidiary in a second country. With ownership from France, the United Kingdom, and Luxembourg, and investing via its subsidiary in Germany, ArcelorMittal in Ukraine has been able to amass broad diplomatic support on its behalf (Chapter 5). Conditions of true multinationality may also emerge when firms from different home countries engage in consortia or joint ventures abroad. European and US firms have co-invested in the Chinese nuclear, solar, and wind industries, for example.[10] The nationality shield theory predicts that a host government has more pools of FDI at risk were it to violate these contracts, because such consortia involve more than one collective good of contract sanctity. All else equal, investors with access to more home governments likely have more resources on which to draw relative to single-nationality foreign firms.

Do European Union member state firms gain "true" multinationality as a matter of course? Certainly, the European Union is an important force shaping the activities of a set of capital-sending countries and their firms abroad. The Lisbon Treaty, which entered into force in 2009, extends exclusive EU competence to FDI. As such, the EU has plans to unify legal protections for its member states' foreign firms. This EU competence is complicated by the fact that EU members participate in some 1,500 BITs. Even if the EU concluded its own international investment agreements to replace these treaties, firms can retain rights under a BIT for decades even after its signatories withdraw. Nonetheless, if or when the European Union is able to unify legal rights for EU-origin firms investing abroad, EU-origin nationalities of investors would have shared treaty rights and procedural resources.

However, a stronger EU legal role in dispute settlement does not clearly affect other elements that generate shared contract sanctity among co-nationals. Factors like bilateral histories with the host country and networks of business practices among co-national firms would still differentiate EU-origin firms' contract sanctity along national lines. Without greater political integration, it is unclear that an EU institutional identification would trump home countries' interests in their own firms. Home governments would still have a disproportionate interest in promoting their firms – their "national champions" – and

---

[10] Nahm and Steinfeld 2014a, 2014b.

diplomats would remain disinterested in fighting contract breaches faced by firms of other nationalities. We saw in Chapter 6 that the European Union was a player in several prominent contract breaches in Romania – but repeatedly on the side of breach. Even several years after the Lisbon Treaty, the EU takes few public actions on behalf of member state firms' broken contracts. In 2012 it stood aside, issuing only vague statements while the Spanish government dealt with Argentinian expropriation (Chapter 1). In short, even with greater legal integration, EU member states are likely to continue to constitute different home countries for the purposes of the nationality shield theory. While networks of states stand behind much new research in international political economy, bilateral relations condition both contract disputes and their resolution. Access to a network like the EU is unlikely to be a substitute for access to particular home governments.

LIMITS OF INTERNATIONAL ORGANIZATIONS

Indeed, international organizations like the European Union have not done heavy lifting in the nationality shield theory. The main exception is the World Bank's International Center for the Settlement of Investment Disputes (ICSID), which has done much to publicize ongoing investor–host government disputes. However, ICSID is a tribunal and not an institution tasked with deterring breach per se. As far as multilateral efforts around contract sanctity, the world's governments have failed many times to set up an organization governing FDI (Chapter 7). In Chapter 5, we saw that when the US political risk insurer OPIC faced contract breach, analogous agencies from multilateral banks acted as competitors, leaving OPIC to its own battle. The absence of international organization support around breach raises the question: might there be circumstances in which international organizations can play a role in enforcing contracts and coordinating investor and diplomatic action, outside the bounds of nationality?

Regional development banks like the European Bank for Reconstruction and Development, the Asian Development Bank, the Inter-American Development Bank, and the African Development Bank often provide financing to foreign firms and sometimes obtain equity in foreign-owned projects. The World Bank also provides financing and support through the International Finance Corporation and the Multilateral Investment Guarantee Agency. As investors themselves, development banks have an interest in the sanctity of the contracts they enter into with host governments. Like any investor, they devote time and resources to fighting their own contract disputes with the government. The costs of losing access to development bank capital, which is often broadly deployed in an emerging economy, might carry more weight with the host government than the costs of breaking contracts with wholly privately owned foreign firms. Development banks also have the ability to tie their foreign aid activities to the status of their investments' contracts. These factors likely help individual bank-backed development projects maintain their own contract sanctity.

However, the presence of multilateral financing in an economy alone is unlikely to blur national differences in contract sanctity. For an international organization to take a stand on a dispute that involves its capital is easy. But for an organization to take a stand on a dispute that does not involve its capital, a sufficient plurality of members would have to agree.[11] Members – often share-holders – are national governments. National governments that have more power over the organization's activities are the ones that may be able to use it as a piece of their nationality shield.[12] The United States tried to do this in 1972, when Congress passed the Gonzalez Amendment that required US representatives at the World Bank and the International Development Bank to vote against loans to nations that expropriated US property without adequate compensation.[13] But, consistent with the nationality shield theory, no other government required its representatives to vote against loans following the expropriation of US property, and the Amendment did not dictate US representatives' voting if other nationalities' property was expropriated. International organizations might appear to assist national groups, but these are ultimately coalitions of home countries that may not have incentives to fight for other members' property rights.

OTHER COSTS TO BREACH

Are there other costs to breach that might explain the waning and waxing of governments' permissive space to breach? It is possible that another axis of differentiation among foreign firms, in addition to nationality, might also affect the incidence of breach. To the extent that alternative sources of costs to breach can be ruled out as causal factors in generating permissive space, the nationality shield theory is reinforced.

Much previous scholarship has differentiated investors by industrial sector, predicting that firms with immobile assets face a higher likelihood of contract breach. It is possible that firms take co-industrials' contract sanctity into account in their investment decisions, but it is ex ante unclear whether that means firms would decrease or increase investments. Co-industrial firms may be good at cooperating (or colluding) around general policy issues, but when the dispute at

---

[11] Even that may not be sufficient. In Chapter 5 we saw that the European Bank for Reconstruction and Development has an explicit policy of staying out of disputes that do not involve its investments.

[12] Kilby (2011) finds that the Asian Development Bank's actions follow US and Japanese interests. Copelovitch (2010a, 2010b) argues that a core group of five countries needs to agree for the IMF to take action, whereas Stone (2011) argues that the United States effectively directs IMF activity.

[13] The Gonzalez Amendment came on top of the Hickenlooper Amendment of 1962 that required the president to cut off assistance to countries that expropriated US property without compensation. Chapter 7.

stake is a broken contract, competitive incentives to benefit from co-industrials' misfortune appear to outweigh cooperative impulses. As far as coordinated protest, in the course of researching this book I found little evidence of collective action within an industry on behalf of any given firm's broken contract. Firms across immobile industries, like oil and gas, mining, and infrastructure, have sometimes attempted but ultimately failed to organize collective efforts. Indeed, co-industrial firms lack the sorts of resources for protest – especially diplomats – that firms of the same nationality can use to bolster contract sanctity.

Asset history could be another characteristic that differentiates firms' responses to a given government breach of contract. While some foreign investors build greenfield, or from-scratch, facilities in host countries, others merge with or acquire existing domestic firms or buy previously state-owned property. Investors into privatized assets have a written contract with the host government and an implicit obligation to the host government and domestic polity that is similar to each other and different from other foreign firms.[14] Public and political feeling about the prior exploitation of assets and prior owners may reasonably affect such investors' contract sanctity. If another investor's asset is not in the public eye and has no history of controversy – or no history at all – then that investor may not see significant shared risks in a privatization-related breach. Breach of a privatization contract could thus elicit FDI diversion from the subset of investors interested in privatized assets but apparent indifference from others. Yet, as with industry, a common asset history does not in itself provide firms with resources to exercise collective protest. Nonetheless, in the context of continuing privatization processes in emerging economies worldwide, exploring the implications of asset history for investor–host government disputes is all the more important.[15]

What if firms respond differently to different kinds of government breach of contract? As we have seen, modern international investment law has made a variety of types of creeping expropriation increasingly visible. Targeted firms might use different collective action strategies to respond to instances of forced renegotiations of contracts, for example, as opposed to nationalization. Additionally, firms and diplomats might respond differently to particular subject areas of breach, like the breach of defense contracts or the revocation of environmental licenses.[16] There is certainly variation in the particular strategies firms and their governments use to fight the variety of contract breaches discussed in this book. Nevertheless, the evidence strongly supports the finding that firms and diplomats are more likely to come together to fight

---

[14] For analysis of the attention domestic citizens and businesspeople pay to privatization, see Wellhausen (2010), Denisova et al. (2009, 2012), and Frye (2006).

[15] Time controls in country-level statistical analyses help to account for waves of privatization in emerging economies. Privatization-based coalitions were considered and rejected as alternative explanations for cases in Chapters 5 and 6.

[16] Compare OPIC's case in Chapter 5 to RMGC's case in Chapter 6.

breach – of whatever kind, in whatever way – when the FDI environment suggests they might be successful.

In a 1985 study, Lipson anticipates the idea that variation among firms matters and suggests that, in addition to industry or asset history, the methods of financing an investment and a firm's place in a country's national development program may systematically affect its government relations.[17] This book considers these factors but posits that both are linked to national origins. Firms of a given nationality have the propensity to use the same kind of financial intermediaries, thanks to business traditions and the kinds of equity and debt institutions available in the home country. Additionally, host governments and societies tend to have the same kinds of expectations of co-national firms. As discussed in Chapter 5, even Norwegian investors in Ukraine gained a nationality-specific reputation. According to the nationality shield theory, nationality is a sort of focal point that collects many similarities among firms that are relevant to contract sanctity. Importantly, nationality also provides many resources to fight breach in a way that firm characteristics like industry or asset history, or the circumstances of a particular breach, do not.

One may also think of domestic audience costs as potential costs to breach. If actors within host governments can split over the decision to breach, so too can constituencies in the domestic polity. For example, there may be domestic penalties when the national government mistreats foreign firms in a federalist system, where investment promotion efforts in subunits may not match central government motives.[18] However, the theory here is that emerging-economy governments, for a variety of reasons, do not face a level of audience costs that regularly deter breach.[19] One task of the case studies in Chapters 5 and 6 is to demonstrate that domestic audience costs have not played an obviously constraining role when it comes to breach of contract, whether in middle-income and weakly democratic Ukraine, less-developed Moldova, or the EU member state Romania.

Finally, leaders in emerging economies are pushed to take into account different time horizons.[20] On one hand, breach has long-term costs, in terms of loss of capital access and diplomatic strain. On the other hand, breach can achieve short- and medium-term goals, like raising revenue, addressing asset- and industry-specific goals, garnering votes, or enacting foreign policy. Systematic

---

[17] Lipson 1985: 190.

[18] Jensen 2006.

[19] However, the notion of domestic audience costs is perhaps one way to account for the dearth of contract breach in advanced industrialized countries. The United States and Canada have been sued by each other's firms under NAFTA provisions, and European countries have on occasion faced public IAs. These anomalies aside, expectations of government breach of contract in such locations are comparatively low. Breach would conflict with the idea of robust rule of law, both in commercial transactions and with regard to the government, which characterizes advanced industrial countries.

[20] Blake 2013.

variation in time horizons may account for variation in governments' willingness to breach in some ways, like nationalization, rather than others, like forced contract renegotiation.[21] Yet many types of regimes, with many types of leaders, have broken contracts in the vast majority of emerging economies at one point or another since 1990. The form and function of breach varies in interesting ways only hinted at here, but the space to breach is the necessary condition for governments to act on any of its multitude of incentives.

THE PERSONAL AND THE CORPORATE

Foreign executives are sometimes openly supportive of the government's rationale for breaking the contract of another foreign firm. Executives note the naiveté of another firm's expectations around its government relations, or they accuse another firm of involvement in illegitimate dealings. Others, in contrast, are adamantly in favor of foreign firms' rights. These gritty executives are intensely sympathetic to the plight of their colleagues and friends, whether co-national or otherwise, and they express sarcasm and anger toward the host government on others' behalf. In interviews in Ukraine, Moldova, and Romania, as well as in the United States, Germany, Azerbaijan, and Russia, individuals' emotions and perceptions of others' broken contracts vary – even among individuals working at co-national firms.

Irrespective of where their personal sympathies lie, however, executives make clear distinctions between their individual emotions and whether and how their multinational corporation chooses to respond to a breach. It is costly to a firm to take actions that punish the host government. Drawing down investments following another's broken contract or taking a public stand against the host government has consequences for a firm's bottom line, not to mention the firm's own relations with the host government. Beyond bringing government attention a firm's way, advocating for another firm might cause a firm to lose customers in the host country or threaten relationships with local suppliers if, for example, the government's actions have popular support. For an individual in a confidential interview to express a personal opinion, the stakes are low. For a firm to involve itself in another's fight, the stakes must be high enough to risk negative reprisals.

Home governments face an analogous calculus as to whether or how to get involved in a dispute facing one of their firms. Such involvement can bring negative attention to the bilateral diplomatic relationship and to that home country's investors more broadly. Home governments must weigh their potential success in strengthening their nationals' property rights abroad, and any direct benefits that solving a particular dispute might generate, against the costs of spending limited political capital on this aspect of the bilateral relationship.

---

[21] For a foray into this topic, see Jensen and Johnston (2011).

But co-national actors share a collective good in the protection of their property rights and the sanctity of contracts with the host government, and this collective good stands behind co-national action around instances of contract breach. Firms and their home governments have incentives to advocate for a co-national because benefits accrue not only to the firm with property at stake but to all members of the group. Common determinants of risk – like home-host government relations, historical animosities, similar contracting styles, and more – make improved contract sanctity with one firm a boon to co-national firms. As shown in Chapters 5 and 6, co-national firms and their home governments have indeed come together to fight for their collective contract sanctity, though they are more likely to fight when FDI national diversity is low and the likelihood of deterring breach is high. Even if a co-national firm is unwilling to engage in collective action over a given breach, we saw in Chapter 4 that investor decision-making tracks nationality. Firms of the same nationality are significantly more likely to draw down or divert FDI following evidence of co-national breach than are firms of other nationalities.

In interviews, senior executives as well as diplomats refer to their and other firms' national origins over and over. When speaking to relations between foreign firms and government officials, nationality-tied considerations consistently trumped considerations about industry, for example. One executive in Ukraine, reflecting on a co-national firm's dispute, declared, "There but for the grace of God go we."[22] Her firm produced for Ukrainian consumption, but she referred to a co-national firm that produced for export in a different industry. Despite their differences, the executive's understanding was that their common origins transmitted shared risks. In Moldova, a prominent executive explained, "American investors have grown to understand the benefit of banding together."[23] As the nationality shield theory predicts, firms in Moldova have found their strongest allies among their co-nationals – American with American. The diverse investor environment in Romania, in contrast, is not conducive to co-national cooperation. It is not that foreign executives there lack the underlying emotions about breach shared by their counterparts abroad. As one French executive in Romania put it, "Maybe I'm personally sympathetic" regarding a Canadian firm's dispute with the Romanian government. "But," he went on, "I would never say that on the record, and the firm has no opinion."[24] Without a collective good of contract sanctity at stake, his firm remains publicly indifferent to a government violation of another foreign firm's property rights. National boundaries differentiate risks of government breach of contract, and differential risks means differential willingness to respond to breach in ways costly to the host government.

---

[22] Interview, Western firm in manufacturing, Ukraine, 2009.
[23] Interview, US firm in business services, Moldova, 2009.
[24] Interview, French firm, Romania, 2009.

THE SHIELD OF NATIONALITY

Many see multinational corporations as "meta-national" – stateless firms unencumbered by their home-country nationalities. But the nationality shield theory takes seriously the bilateral relationship that is embedded in each investment transaction. Much of a multinational corporation's power to enforce its contracts with a host government derives from its nationality. I find that nationality provides an immediate, easily accessible, relevant source of information in the political economy of FDI. Shared nationality provides a focal point for signals about contract sanctity, which I have shown to be relevant both to intra-firm decision-making and to the willingness and ability of co-national actors to advocate on behalf of their collective contract sanctity. Far from fading from relevance in a world of economic globalization, foreign firms' nationalities continue to generate information on breach, incentivize coordinated action among co-national firms, and provide nationality-specific institutions and diplomatic resources with which to fight threats to contract sanctity. Multinational corporations can sanction host governments that threaten contract sanctity not because of the "multi," but because of the "national." Firms are not engaging in "transnational" actions by the definition Keohane and Nye employ. Rather, governments and government institutions act as mediators in interactions between firms and host governments over contract sanctity.[25] The circumstances described here fit better with Krasner's worldview in which national actors retain the traditional trappings of sovereignty even in a globalized era.[26] Growing interdependence does not negate domestic control over a country's political economy. In fact, interdependence itself can enhance a government's ability to choose to act contrary to global norms around property rights protections.

With common risks and resources to fight threats, co-national actors can be formidable and can successfully deter breach. But when many nationalities of investors provide capital for host governments, each nationality's shield against breach is weakened. Hosting a greater diversity of FDI nationalities gives a government more options to substitute for FDI diversion and diplomatic penalties from any particular national group. The implication is powerful: foreign firms' behavior does not consistently do the work of increasing government respect for rule of law with regard to foreign firms themselves. Moreover, the vulnerability of a foreign firm's contract depends on the set of foreign firms present in the host country – a value difficult to estimate in real time.

The record of variation in contract sanctity shows that host governments do not choose to maximize capital access at all times. Host governments in less-developed, low-income, and middle-income countries continue to flex national

---

[25] Keohane and Nye (1971) do point out that transnational organizations tend to be "linked primarily to one particular national society" (336).

[26] Krasner 1999, 2009.

power over foreign firms by breaking contracts. By hosting nationally diverse FDI, economically integrated host governments gain the permissive space to break contracts to their advantage. And what an advantage it is. When host governments breach contracts with certain foreign firms and are met with apparent indifference by others, it follows that investor diversity can be a liability to investors while providing an opening for governments to prioritize other goals over the property and preferences of foreign capital.

Case Studies: Methodology

The case studies in Chapters 5 and 6 draw on foreign firms' relations with host governments in Ukraine, Moldova, and Romania. Here, I explain the choice of these countries as settings from which to draw cases of contract sanctity and breach. I then explain the methodology behind interviews conducted with executives and officials. Keeping confidentiality in mind, I provide as much information as possible on interview subjects.[1]

Ukraine, Moldova, and Romania are sufficiently similar emerging economies to make them useful settings from which to draw cases that test the nationality shield theory. Choosing three countries that are similar with respect to geography, history, and culture helps to establish a baseline set of potential foreign investors into the area, as these are standard, positively signed determinants of FDI.[2] These contiguous countries are located in Southeastern and Eastern Europe. All three countries share a communist history and a short lifespan as market economies, with Moldova and Ukraine sharing short lifespans as sovereign nations. Both Ukraine and Moldova were constituent parts of the Soviet Union until their independence in 1991 and 1992, respectively. Romania was under the control of a brutal dictator, Nicolae Ceauşescu, until he was executed on Christmas Day, 1989. Romanian is spoken in both Romania and Moldova (where Soviet nationality policy renamed it "Moldovan"). Russian is spoken – and faces significantly less stigma than elsewhere in Central and Eastern Europe – in both Moldova and Ukraine. Importantly, all three countries have relatively consistent average levels of dependence on foreign capital, as measured by FDI per GDP. This makes the capital constraints each country faces more

---

[1] See Mosley, ed. 2013 for an excellent overview of approaches to interviewing as a form of data collection.

[2] Were I to compare the experiences of foreign firms in countries in various locations around the world, I would introduce considerable variation in the prospective investor pool and complicate comparisons of trends in FDI deterrence and exit.

TABLE M.1 *Key Characteristics of Ukraine, Moldova, and Romania (Average 2000–2008)*

	FDI National Diversity	FDI Stock per GDP	GDP (US$)	Population	GDP per capita (US$)	Natural Resources per Total Exports
Ukraine	4.2	4.88%	86 billion	47 million	1,835	14.99%
Moldova	2.1	7.42%	3.1 billion	3.6 million	872	4.27%
Romania	5.6	6.28%	94 billion	22 million	4,670	12.86%

Sources: World Bank World Development Indicators, OECD, Author's calculations.

comparable. Table M.1 summarizes this and other key features of the economies of the three countries under consideration.

These three countries share characteristics that make them unlikely locations for government breach of contract, according to conventional explanations. First, none of these three countries has a large internal market by international standards, especially in comparison with emerging economies like China and India. Thus, foreign firms are unlikely to be so market-seeking as to be unwilling to withdraw capital should risks arise. Ukraine is a highly populous country, but it has a low GDP per capita. Even if one were to consider Ukraine a country with a particularly attractive market, Chapter 5 demonstrates variation in contract sanctity in Ukraine over time, holding its market's attractiveness relatively constant. Second, these countries are not classified as rich in natural resources, especially when compared to their eastern neighbor, Russia. Resource-seeking firms often have no choice but to invest in certain resource-rich geographies, giving the government an inherently strong bargaining position. I deliberately choose countries in which the government does not have such an asymmetric bargaining position. However, to the extent that Ukraine and Romania do have natural resource endowments, I demonstrate how FDI national diversity explains both the presence and absence of breach with respect to those endowments.

Third, Ukraine, Moldova, and Romania are all countries in transition. The transition label means that these countries have moved over the last decades from command economies to market economies based on private property rights. The European Bank of Reconstruction of Development (EBRD) is a dedicated international institution that tracks the progress that post-communist countries make on reform efforts. The European Union, too, pays close attention to government behavior in its post-communist neighbors. Under such scrutiny, one might think that widespread, negative publicity would emerge should a transition government deviate from contract sanctity. If any countries in the world were to suffer from a general loss of capital following breach of contract (instead of nationality-specific losses), it would be post-communist countries in which government actions are under a particular microscope.

Fourth, in contrast to their Central European neighbors, all three countries have taken a relatively long time to transition to democracy. As of 2008, however, Ukraine received a score of 7, Moldova 8, and Romania 9 on the Polity IV scale measuring democracy, with 10 being fully democratic and scores at 7 or above usually coded as democracies. Looking at breach in relatively democratic countries helps to move beyond expectations that only autocrats engage in expropriation. Nevertheless, one could argue that as young or relatively weak democracies, these countries do not yet have a culture of contract sanctity. In other countries – particularly advanced industrial countries – such a culture may be doing some of the work of enforcing government contracts with foreign firms.[3] If so, these three countries would in fact be likely to break contracts, so variation is again a puzzle. However, the norm of rule of law has been developing in the region, and democracy-promotion activities by domestic NGOs suggest that local actors not only understand rule of law but are expending resources to grow it abroad.[4] These developments counter the argument that governments in these countries are most likely to break contracts.

Ukraine, Moldova, and Romania display considerable variation on the explanatory variable of interest: FDI national diversity. Ukraine's diversity was low in the early 1990s, increasing to the mid-2000s, and then sharply dropping in the late 2000s. Moldova's FDI national diversity, while rising somewhat over the years, has remained low, especially compared to that in Romania. Romania's FDI national diversity began low but quickly rose to make the country one of the most diverse in the world. These trends allow for tests that leverage over-time variation in Ukraine and cross-country variation between Romania and Moldova.

Other forms of variation across the countries help to account for alternative explanations for breach. First, one may expect membership in international organizations to push governments to respect contracts. The countries vary on this point: as of 2007, Romania is a member of the European Union, Ukraine has European aspirations, although it has been given few actual signals that it would ever join the EU, and Moldova remains tied to Russia and arguably to now-defunct Soviet

---

[3] A basic scope condition of the nationality shield theory is that governments in emerging economies are the ones most likely to act on space to breach when it is available to them. I thus do not study cases from an advanced industrial country. Among advanced industrial countries, the United States and Canada have had the most experience with public breach of contract under the terms of NAFTA. Nevertheless, as the theory would predict, the fallout from US and Canadian cases has been mainly along bilateral lines and not, for example, affecting relations with Mexico. Future research may indeed look into breach in advanced countries. In 2012, Chinese investors filed a notable case against Belgium, seeking compensation for Belgium's nationalization of Chinese investments in the firm Fortis during the financial crisis.

[4] Gans-Morse 2012, Petrova and Tarrow 2007.

institutions. Second, one may expect a higher incidence of breach to occur in poorer countries, although both relatively wealthy and poor emerging economies have broken contracts (Chapter 2). Variation in GDP and GDP per capita help to account for this hypothesis: Romania is the wealthiest of the three, with Ukraine below, while Moldova is the poorest country in Europe (see again Table M.1).

INTERVIEW STRATEGY

From 2009 to 2013, I conducted 161 interviews in Ukraine, Moldova, and Romania as well as the United States, Germany, Azerbaijan, and Russia. The majority of interviews were conducted in English, with some conducted in Russian in Ukraine, Moldova, and Azerbaijan. Table M.2 provides a summary of interview respondents. Respondents included local heads of firms and foreign investor associations from 17 different home countries. I spoke to partners at seven law firms (some of which are multinational corporations themselves) who had represented the host government and/or foreign firms in international legal proceedings. Some respondents had unsuccessfully attempted to organize class action lawsuits against these host governments. Respondents also included government officials responsible for relations with foreign firms, former diplomats, elected politicians, and officials from finance ministries. Respondents at think tanks provided third-party insights into the conduct and progress of particular contract disputes. I also interviewed representatives from organizations interested in foreign investment and the rule of law, including the IMF, the European Bank for Reconstruction and Development (EBRD), the World Bank's International Center for the Settlement of Investment Disputes (ICSID), and the Organization for Security and Cooperation in Europe (OSCE). I interviewed several local firms that were in the same industry as foreign firms involved in prominent disputes. In this way, I was able to document the general absence of domestic–foreign collective action regarding foreign firms' contract disputes.

The purpose of interviews was, first, to establish investors' experiences around the maintenance of contract sanctity. Second, interview evidence allowed me to reconstruct narratives around contract breach, moments when a government maintained contract sanctity even when under pressure to do otherwise, and moments when a government chose to provide restitution. Interviews typically ran from one to three hours. All interview respondents were promised complete confidentiality, which means that identifying characteristics such as industry and nationality have sometimes been removed but not changed in resulting narratives.

In the core set of interviews with foreign firms, I spoke to the local CEO or Managing Director of typically large multinational corporations' affiliates. I chose to speak to top executives, because these are the individuals closest to investment decisions, whether those decisions are made locally or in the home country. Additionally, these executives are usually responsible for their firms'

TABLE M.2 *Interview Subjects*

Home country	Industry	Count	Home country	Field	Count
Austria	Finance	1	Argentina	Government official	1
Azerbaijan	Services	1	Azerbaijan	Government official	2
Azerbaijan	Natural resources	2	Austria	Government official	1
Canada	Investor organization	1	Czech Republic	Government official	1
			European Union	Government official	2
Canada	Legal	1	Ghana	Government official	1
Canada	Natural resources	2	Moldova	Government official	4
Denmark	Manufacturing	2	Poland	Government official	3
France	Finance	3	Romania	Government official	2
France	Manufacturing	1	Russia	Government official	1
France	Natural resources	1	Switzerland	Government official	1
Germany	Finance	2	Ukraine	Government official	4
Germany	Investor organization	2	United States	Government official	6
			Azerbaijan	Think tank	3
Germany	Manufacturing	1	Moldova	Think tank	3
Germany	Natural resources	1	Romania	Think tank	2
Germany	Services	1	Slovak Republic	Think tank	1
Israel	Investor organization	3	Venezuela	Think tank	1
			Ukraine	Think tank	5
Moldova	Investor organization	1	.	International organization	6
Moldova	Services	4			
Norway	Infrastructure	1		*Total other*	50
Romania	Services	4			
Russia	Finance	3			
Russia	Manufacturing	9			
Russia	Services	1			
Sweden	Manufacturing	1			
Turkey	Investor organization	1			
Ukraine	Finance	1			
Ukraine	Legal	4			
Ukraine	Services	2			
United Arab Emirates	Investor organization	1			
United Kingdom	Infrastructure	1			
United Kingdom	Investor organization	1			

(*continued*)

TABLE M.2 (*continued*)

Home country	Industry	Count
United Kingdom	Legal	1
United Kingdom	Manufacturing	1
United Kingdom	Natural resources	2
United Kingdom	Services	3
United States	Agriculture	2
United States	Finance	6
United States	Infrastructure	1
United States	Information technology	2
United States	Investor organization	10
United States	Legal	3
United States	Manufacturing	6
United States	Natural resources	4
United States	Services	5
(Europe)	Investor organization	5
	Total investors	111

Note: Interviews undertaken from 2009 to 2013 in Ukraine, Moldova, Romania, United States, Germany, Azerbaijan, and Russia.

overall strategy within a host country. Therefore, such executives' insights into their own and other firms' contracts are the best source of information on the possibility of changes in investment plans or participation in collective action around disputes. I targeted firms that had been directly involved in public contract disputes as well as prominent firms that did not have public records of contract disputes. I defined "prominent" as those firms that were on the board of investor associations or were often commented upon in local media. Targets were also deliberately drawn from a variety of industries. The final sample included respondents from manufacturing, banking and finance, business services, natural resources, food and agriculture, logistics, telecommunications, and trade.

Interviews were semi-structured. All respondents were asked both about their firms' relations with the government (and possible broken contracts) and about a list of other firms' contract disputes in the country in recent years. I compiled the list of contract disputes from a variety of sources, including publicly disclosed IA records; coverage of contract disputes in local media, especially local media written for an expat audience; international media coverage; testimony given to and legislation written by the US Congress; official firm and government communications; and secondary literature. In each country, all executives interviewed for this book were aware of all the contract disputes on my lists. Respondents also spoke to their interactions with home-government institutions, co-national firms, non-co-national firms, co-industrial firms, domestic firms, and investor associations (where applicable). At the close of several interviews, respondents referred me to individuals at other firms, which resulted in additional interviews at previously targeted large multinational affiliates. As multinational executives in emerging economies are often well known to each other, several references were to individuals that I had previously interviewed.

In drawing on interview evidence in Chapters 5 and 6, I take care to trace contract disputes that did not result in public IAs. While I used public IAs as a reasonable indicator of contract breach in quantitative analyses in Chapter 4, I go on to test the nationality shield theory as it relates to disputes that do not make their way to the peak of the international legal system. The same mechanisms of costly diversion or exit by co-national firms and protest exercised by and on behalf of co-national firms should be at play in these cases just as in cases that led to public IAs. I also am sure to trace contract disputes as opposed to respondents' frustrations with government in general. For example, a respondent may have faced constant visits from tax authorities that were intent on finding the smallest discrepancy in the firm's books. That situation is not the one under study here. Rather, a contract breach occurs when, for example, the government unilaterally cancels tax breaks that are part of the firm's investment contract. That said, the line between frustrating circumstances and contract breach is not always clear. In my analysis, I use respondents' own understanding to draw the line beyond which frustration becomes contract breach. I found these understandings to be essentially uniform across respondents targeted by a given government action or respondents who observed that action. Ultimately, I understand the presence of a settlement to mean that a breach was mended or avoided, depending on the case.

References

Abbott, K. W. and D. Snidal. 2003. "Hard and Soft Law in International Governance." *International Organization* 54(3): 421–56.

Acemoglu, D. and J. Robinson. 2006. *Economic Origins of Dictatorship and Democracy.* Cambridge, UK: Cambridge University Press.

Ahlquist, J. S. and A. Prakash. 2009. "FDI and the Costs of Contract Enforcement in Developing Countries." *Policy Sciences* 43(2): 1–20.

Aisbett, E. 2009. "Bilateral Investment Treaties and Foreign Direct Investment: Correlation v. Causation." In *The Effect of Treaties on Foreign Direct Investment*, editors K. Sauvant and L. Sachs, Oxford, UK: Oxford University Press, 395–437.

Akinsanya, A. 1981. "Host Governments' Responses to Foreign Economic Control: The Experiences of Selected African Countries." *The International and Comparative Law Quarterly* 30(4): 769–90.

Albertus, M. and V. Menaldo. 2012. "If You're Against Them You're With Us: The Effect of Expropriation on Autocratic Survival." *Comparative Political Studies* 45(8): 973–1003.

Alfaro, L., S. Kalemli-Ozcan, and V. Volosovych. 2008. "Why Doesn't Capital Flow from Rich to Poor Countries? An Empirical Investigation." *The Review of Economics and Statistics* 90(2): 347–68.

Allee, T. and C. Peinhardt. 2010. "Delegating Differences: Bilateral Investment Treaties and Bargaining Over Dispute Resolution Provisions." *International Studies Quarterly* 54(1): 1–26.

2011. "Contingent Credibility: The Impact of Investment Treaty Violations on Foreign Direct Investment." *International Organization* 65(3): 401–32.

Ancelovici, M. 2002. "Organizing Against Globalization: The Case of ATTAC in France." *Politics and Society* 30(3): 427–63.

Baker, J. 1999. *Foreign Direct Investment in Less Developed Countries: The Role of ICSID and MIGA.* Westport, CT: Quorum Books.

Bandelj, N. 2008. *From Communists to Foreign Capitalists: The Social Foundations of Foreign Direct Investment in Postsocialist Europe.* Princeton, NJ: Princeton University Press.

Bebchuk, L. 1984. "Litigation and Settlement under Imperfect Information." *The RAND Journal of Economics* 15(3): 404–15.

Behrman, J., J. Boddewyn, and A. Kapoor. 1975. *International Business-Government Communications: US Structures, Actors, and Issues.* Lexington, MA: Lexington Books.

Beissinger, M. 2013. "The Semblance of Democratic Revolution: Coalitions in Ukraine's Orange Revolution." *American Political Science Review* 107(3): 574–92.

Berger, S. 2000. "Globalization and Politics." *Annual Review of Political Science* 3: 43–62.

Berrios, R., A. Marak, and S. Morgenstern. 2011. "Explaining Hydrocarbon Nationalization in Latin America: Economics and Political Ideology." *Review of International Political Economy* 18(5): 1–25.

Blake, D. 2013. "Thinking Ahead: Government Time Horizons and the Legalization of International Investment Agreements." *International Organization* 67(4): 797–827.

Blomström, M. and A. Kokko. 1995. "Policies to Encourage Inflows of Technology through Foreign Multinationals." *World Development* 23(3): 459–68.

Blustein, P. 2005. *And the Money Kept Rolling In (and Out): Wall Street, the IMF, and the Bankrupting of Argentina.* New York: Public Affairs.

Biglaiser, G. and D. Lektzian. 2011. "The Effect of Sanctions on US Foreign Direct Investment." *International Organization* 65(3): 531–51.

Biglaiser, G. and K. DeRouen. 2006. "Economic Reforms and Inflows of Foreign Direct Investment in Latin America." *Latin American Research Review* 41(1): 51–75.

Büthe, T. and H. Milner. 2008. "The Politics of Foreign Direct Investment into Developing Countries: Increasing FDI through International Trade Agreements?" *American Journal of Political Science* 52(4): 741–62.

2009. "Bilateral Investment Treaties and Foreign Direct Investment: A Political Analysis." In *The Effect of Treaties on Foreign Direct Investment: Bilateral Investment Treaties, Double Taxation Treaties, and Investment Flows,* edited by K. Sauvant and L. Sachs. Oxford, UK: Oxford University Press, 171–224.

2014. "Foreign Direct Investment and Institutional Diversity in Trade Agreements: Credibility, Commitment, and Economic Flows in the Developing World, 1971–2007." *World Politics* 66(1): 88–122.

Busse, M. and C. Hefeker. 2007. "Political Risk, Institutions and Foreign Direct Investment." *European Journal of Political Economy* 23(2): 397–415.

Cai, H. and D. Treisman. 2005. "Does Competition for Capital Discipline Governments? Decentralization, Globalization, and Public Policy." *American Economic Review* 95(3): 817–30.

Calvo, G. and E. Mendoza. 2000. "Rational Contagion and the Globalization of Securities Markets." *Journal of International Economics* 51(1): 79–113.

Cardoso, F. and E. Faletto. 1979. *Dependency and Development in Latin America.* Berkeley, CA: University of California Press.

Carter, David B. and Curtis S. Signorino. 2010. "Back to the Future: Modeling Time Dependence in Binary Data." *Political Analysis* 18(3): 271–92.

Chaudoin, S. 2015. "Audience Features and the Strategic Timing of Trade Disputes." *International Organization.* Forthcoming.

Chayes, A. and A. Chayes. 1993. "On Compliance." *International Organization* 47(2): 175–205.

Cho, A. and N. Dubash. 2003. "Will Investment Rules Shrink Policy Space for Sustainable Development? Evidence from the Electricity Sector." *World Resources Institute.* Working Paper.

Coase, R. H. 1960. "The Problem of Social Cost." *Journal of Law and Economics* 3(3): 1–44.

Cole, H. and W. English. 1991. "Expropriation and Direct Investment." *Journal of International Economics* 30(2): 201–27.

Copelovitch, M. 2010a. "Master or Servant? Common Agency and the Political Economy of IMF Lending." *International Studies Quarterly* 54(1): 49–77.

2010b. *The International Monetary Fund in the Global Economy: Banks, Bonds, and Bailouts.* Cambridge, MA: Cambridge University Press.

Correa, C. and N. Kumar. 2003. *Protecting Foreign Investment: Implications of a WTO Regime and Policy Options.* London: Zed Books.

Davis, C. 2004. "International Institutions and Issue Linkage: Building Support for Agricultural Trade Liberalization." *American Political Science Review* 98(1): 153–169.

2012. *Why Adjudicate? Enforcing Trade Rules in the WTO.* Princeton, NJ: Princeton University Press.

Davis, C. and S. Meunier. 2011. "Business as Usual? Economic Responses to Political Tensions." *American Journal of Political Science* 55(3): 628–46.

De Soto, H. 2000. *The Mystery of Capital: Why Capitalism Succeeds in the West and Fails Everywhere Else.* New York: Basic Books.

DeBacker, J., B. Heim, and A. Tran. 2012. "Importing Corruption Culture from Overseas: Evidence from Corporate Tax Evasion in the United States." *NBER Working Paper* No. 17770.

Denisova, I., M. Eller, T. Frye and E. Zhuravskaya. 2009. "Who Wants to Revise Privatization? The Complementarity of Market Skills and Institutions." *American Political Science Review* 103(2): 284–304.

2012. "Everyone Hates Privatization, but Why? Survey Evidence from 28 Post-Communist Countries." *Journal of Comparative Economics* 40(1): 44–61.

Desbordes, R. 2010. "Global and Diplomatic Political Risks and Foreign Direct Investment." *Economics and Politics* 22(1): 92–125.

Desbordes, R. and J. Vauday. 2007. "The Political Influence of Foreign Firms in Developing Countries." *Economics and Politics* 19(3): 421–51.

Dolzer, R. and C. Schreuer. 2012. *Principles of International Investment Law.* Oxford, UK: Oxford University Press.

Dolzer, R. and M. Stevens. 1995. *Bilateral Investment Treaties.* The Hague: Martinus Nijhoff Publishers.

Doremus, P., W. Keller, L. Pauly, and S. Reich. 1999. *The Myth of the Global Corporation.* Princeton, NJ: Princeton University Press.

Drezner, D. 2001. "Globalization and Policy Convergence." *International Studies Review* 3(1): 53–78.

Dunning, J. 1980. "Toward an Eclectic Theory of International Production: Some Empirical Tests." *Journal of International Business Studies* 11(1): 9–31.

Duncan, R. 2006. "Price or Politics? An Investigation of the Causes of Expropriation." *The Australian Journal of Agricultural and Resource Economics* 50(1): 85–101.

Eaton, J. and M. Gersovitz. 1984. "A Theory of Expropriation and Deviations from Perfect Capital Mobility." *NBER Working Paper* No. 972.

Elkins, Z., A. Guzman, and B. Simmons. 2006. "Competing for Capital: The Diffusion of Bilateral Investment Treaties, 1960–2000." *International Organization* 60(4): 811–46.

Evans, P. 1979. *Dependent Development: The Alliance of Multinational, State, and Local Capital in Brazil.* Princeton, NJ: Princeton University Press.

1997. "The Eclipse of the State? Reflections on Stateness in an Era of Globalization." *World Politics* 50(1): 62–87.

Fails, M. 2012. "Inequality, Institutions, and the Risks to Foreign Investment." *International Studies Quarterly* 56(3): 516–29.

Farrell, D., J. Remes, and H. Schulz. 2004. "The Truth About Foreign Direct Investment in Emerging Markets." *The McKinsey Quarterly* 1: 25–35.

Fearon, J. 1997. "Signaling Foreign Policy Interests." *Journal of Conflict Resolution* 41(1): 68–90.

Feis, H. 1964. *Europe, The World's Banker, 1870–1914: An Account of European Foreign Investment and The Connection of World Finance with Diplomacy before the War*. Council on Foreign Relations, New York: A.M. Kelley.

Franck, S. 2007. "Foreign Direct Investment, Investment Treaty Arbitration, and the Rule of Law." *Global Business and Development Law Journal* 19(3): 337–531.

2009. "Development and Outcomes of Investment Treaty Arbitration." *Harvard International Law Journal* 50(2): 435–89.

Frieden, J. 1994. "International Investment and Colonial Control: A New Interpretation." *International Organization* 48(4): 559–93.

Frye, T. 2006. "Original Sin, Good Works, and Property Rights in Russia." *World Politics* 58(4): 479–504.

Fuentes, M. and D. Saravia. 2010. "Sovereign Defaulters: Do International Capital Markets Punish Them?" *Journal of Development Economics* 91(2): 336–47.

Gans-Morse, J. 2012. "Threats to Property Rights in Russia: From Private Coercion to State Aggression." *Post-Soviet Affairs* 28(3): 263–95.

Ginsburg, T. 2005. "International Substitutes for Domestic Institutions: Bilateral Investment Treaties and Governance." *International Review of Law and Economics* 25(1): 107–23.

Goldsmith, J. and E. Posner. 2005. *The Limits of International Law*. New York: Oxford University Press.

Goldstein, J., D. Rivers, and M. Tomz. 2007. "Institutions in International Relations: Understanding the Effects of the GATT and the WTO on World Trade." *International Organization* 61(1): 37–67.

Graham, B. 2014. "Diaspora-Owned Firms and Social Responsibility." *Review of International Political Economy* 21(2): 432–66.

Guimón, J. 2009. "Government Strategies to Attract R&D-intensive FDI." *The Journal of Technology Transfer* 34(4): 364–79.

Guriev, S., A. Kolotilin, and K. Sonin. 2011. "Determinants of Nationalization in the Oil Sector: A Theory and Evidence from Panel Data." *Journal of Law, Economics, and Organization* 27(2): 301–23.

Gustafson, T. 2012. *Wheel of Fortune: The Battle for Oil and Power in Russia*. Cambridge, MA: Belknap Press.

Hajzler, C. 2012. "Expropriation of Foreign Direct Investments: Sectoral Patterns From 1993 to 2006." *Review of World Economics* 148(1): 119–49.

Hallward-Driemeier, M. 2003. "Do Bilateral Investment Treaties Attract Foreign Direct Investment? Only a Bit and They Could Bite." *World Bank Policy Research Working Paper* No. 3121.

Hawkins, R., N. Mintz, and M. Provissiero. 1976. "Government Takeovers of US Foreign Affiliates." *Journal of International Business Studies* 7(1): 3–16.

Henisz, W. 2002. *Politics and International Investment: Measuring Risks and Protecting Profits*. Northampton, MA: E. Elgar.

Henisz, W. and O. Williamson. 1999. "Comparative Economic Organization – Within and Between Countries." *Business and Politics* 1(3): 261–78.

Hicks, R. and K. Johnson. 2012. "The Politics of Globalizing Production: Why We See Investment Chapters in Preferential Trade Agreements." *Manuscript.*

Hirschman, A. 1970. *Exit, Voice, and Loyalty: Responses to Decline in Firms, Organizations, and States.* Cambridge, MA: Harvard University Press.

Hirst, P. and G. Thompson. 1995. "Globalization and the Future of the Nation-state." *Economy and Society* 24(3): 408–42.

1999. *Globalization in Question.* Cambridge, MA: Polity Press.

Hoffmann, A. 2008. "Indirect Expropriation." In *Standards of Investment Protection,* edited by A. Reinisch. Oxford, UK: Oxford University Press.

Holburn, G., and B. Zelner. 2010. "Political Capabilities, Policy Risk, and International Investment Strategy: Evidence from the Global Electric Power Generation Industry." *Strategic Management Journal* 31(12): 1290–1315.

Huang, Y. 2003. *Selling China: Foreign Direct Investment During the Reform Era.* Cambridge, MA: Cambridge University Press.

Humphreys, M. and R. Bates. 2005. "Political Institutions and Economic Policies: Lessons from Africa." *British Journal of Political Science* 35(3): 403–28.

Hymer, S. 1976. *The International Operations of National Firms: A Study of Direct Foreign Investment.* Cambridge, MA: MIT Press.

Ingram, G. 1974. *Expropriation of US Property in South America: Nationalization of Oil and Copper Companies in Peru, Bolivia, and Chile.* New York: Praeger.

Jandhyala, S., W. Henisz, and E. Mansfield. 2011. "Three Waves of BITs: The Global Diffusion of Foreign Investment Policy." *Journal of Conflict Resolution* 55(6): 1047–73.

Jakobsen, J. 2006. "Does Democracy Moderate the Obsolescing Bargain Mechanism? – An Empirical Analysis, 1983–2001." *Transnational Corporations* 15(3): 67–106.

Jakobsen, J. and I. de Soysa. 2006. "Do Foreign Investors Punish Democracy? Theory and Empirics, 1984–2001." *Kyklos* 59(3): 383–410.

Jensen, N. 2003. "Democratic Governance and Multinational Corporations: Political Regimes and Inflows of Foreign Direct Investment." *International Organization* 57(3): 587–616.

2006. *Nation-States and the Multinational Corporation.* Princeton, NJ: Princeton University Press.

2008. "Political Risk, Democratic Institutions, and Foreign Direct Investment." *Journal of Politics* 70 (4): 1040–52.

Jensen, N. and D. Young. 2008. "A Violent Future? Political Risk Insurance Markets and Violence Forecasts." *Journal of Conflict Resolution* 52(4): 527.

Jensen, N. and N. Johnston. 2011. "Political Risk, Reputation, and the Resource Curse." *Comparative Political Studies* 44(6): 662–88.

Jensen, N., G. Biglaiser, Q. Li, E. Malesky, P. Pinto, S. Pinto, J. Staats. 2012. *Politics and Foreign Direct Investment.* Ann Arbor, MI: The University of Michigan Press.

Jodice, D. 1980. "Sources of Change in Third World Regimes for Foreign Direct Investment, 1968–1976." *International Organization* 34(2): 177–206.

Johnston, N. 2013. "The Politics of Compensation for Expropriation." PhD Diss, Washington University in St. Louis.

Jones, H. 1992. *Union in Peril: The Crisis over British Intervention in the Civil War.* Chapel Hill, NC: University of North Carolina Press.

Kaczmarek, S. and A. Newman. 2011. "The Long Arm of the Law: Extraterritoriality and the National Implementation of Foreign Bribery Legislation." *International Organization* 65(4): 745–70.

Katzenstein, P. 1985. *Small States in World Markets: Industrial Policy in Europe.* New York: Cornell University Press.

Kempton, D. and R. Preez. 1997. "Namibian-De Beers State-Firm Relations: Cooperation and Conflict." *Journal of Southern African Studies* 23(4): 585–613.

Kennedy, C. 1992. "Relations Between Transnational Corporations and Governments of Host Countries: A Look to the Future." *Transnational Corporations* 1(1): 67–91.

Keohane, R. and J. Nye. 1971. "Transnational Relations and World Politics: An Introduction." *International Organization* 25(3): 329–49.

Kerner, A. 2009. "Why Should I Believe You? The Costs and Consequences of Bilateral Investment Treaties." *International Studies Quarterly* 53(1): 73–102.

Kilby, C. 2011. "Informal Influence in the Asian Development Bank." *Review of International Organizations* 6(3–4): 223–57.

King, C. 2000. *The Moldovans: Romania, Russia, and the Politics of Culture.* Stanford, CA: Hoover Institution Press.

Knutsen, C., A. Rygh and H. Hveem. 2011. "Does State Ownership Matter? Institutions' Effect on Foreign Direct Investment Revisited." *Business and Politics* 13(1): 1–33.

Kobrin, S. 1980. "Foreign Enterprise and Forced Divestment in LDCs." *International Organization* 34(1): 65–88.

1982. *Managing Political Risk Assessment: Strategic Response to Environmental Change.* Berkeley, CA: University of California Press.

1984. "Expropriation as an Attempt to Control Foreign Firms in LDCs: Trends from 1960 to 1979." *International Studies Quarterly* 28(3): 329–48.

2001. "Sovereignty@Bay: Globalization, Multinational Enterprise, and the International Political System." In *The Oxford Handbook of International Business*, edited by A. Rugman. Oxford, UK: Oxford University Press, 181–205.

Kono, D. 2006. "Optimal Obfuscation: Democracy and Trade Policy Transparency." *American Political Science Review* 100(3): 369–84.

Kornai, J. 1992. *The Socialist System: The Political Economy of Communism.* Princeton, NJ: Princeton University Press.

Kostova, T. and S. Zaheer. 1999. "Organizational Legitimacy under Conditions of Complexity: The Case of the Multinational Enterprise." *The Academy of Management Review* 24(1): 64–81.

Krasner, S. D. 1999. "Globalization and Sovereignty." In *States and Sovereignty in the Global Economy*, edited by D. Smith, D. Solinger, and S. Topik. London, UK: Routledge.

2009. *Power, the State, and Sovereignty: Essays on International Relations.* New York: Routledge.

Land, B. 2009. "Capturing a Fair Share of Fiscal Benefits in the Extractive Industry." *Transnational Corporations* 18(1): 157–77.

Lanine, G. and R. Vander Vennet. 2007. "Microeconomic Determinants of Acquisitions of Eastern European Banks by Western European Banks." *Economics of Transition* 15(2): 285–308.

Leblang, D. 2010. "Familiarity Breeds Investment: Diaspora Networks and International Investment." *American Political Science Review* 104(3): 584–600.

Li, K., D. Griffin, H. Yue, and L. Zhao. 2011. "National Culture and Capital Structure Decisions: Evidence from Foreign Joint Ventures in China." *Journal of International Business Studies* 42(4): 477–503.

Li, Q. 2009. "Democracy, Autocracy, and Expropriation of Foreign Direct Investment." *Comparative Political Studies* 42(8): 1098–1127.

Li, Q. and A. Resnick. 2003. "Reversal of Fortunes: Democratic Institutions and Foreign Direct Investment Inflows to Developing Countries." *International Organization* 57(1): 175–211.

Li, Q. and T. Vashchilko. 2010. "Dyadic Military Conflict, Security Alliances, and Bilateral FDI Flows." *Journal of International Business Studies* 41(5): 765–82.

Likosky, M. 2009. "Contracting and Regulatory Issues in the Oil and Gas and Metallic Minerals Industries." *Transnational Corporations* 18(1): 1–42.

Lipson, C. 1985. *Standing Guard: Protecting Foreign Capital in the Nineteenth and Twentieth Centuries.* Berkeley, CA: University of California Press.

Locke, R. 2012. *Promoting Labor Rights in a Global Economy.* New York: Cambridge University Press.

Loewendahl, H. 2001. "A Framework for FDI Promotion." *Transnational Corporations* 10(1): 1–171.

Lohmann, S. 1997. "Linkage Politics." *Journal of Conflict Resolution* 41(1): 38–67.

Malov, D. and P. Ucen. 2009. "Slovakia." *European Journal of Political Research* 48(7–8): 1100–105.

Makino, S. and E. Tsang. 2011. "Historical Ties and Foreign Direct Investment: An Exploratory Study." *Journal of International Business Studies* 42(4): 545–57.

Manger, M. 2009. *Investing in Protection: The Politics of Preferential Trade Agreements between North and South.* New York: Cambridge University Press.

Minor, M. 1994. "The Demise of Expropriation as an Instrument of LDC Policy, 1980–1992." *Journal of International Business Studies* 25(1): 177–88.

Mitchener, K. and M. Weidenmier. 2010. "Supersanctions and Sovereign Debt Repayment." *Journal of International Money and Finance* 29(1): 19–36.

Montt, S. 2007. "The BIT Generation's Emergence as a Collective Action Problem: Prisoner's Dilemma or Network Effects?" *The Latin American and Caribbean Journal of Legal Studies* 2(1), Art. 6.

Moran, T. 1973. "Transnational Strategies of Protection and Defense by Multinational Corporations: Spreading the Risk and Raising the Cost for Nationalization in Natural Resources." *International Organization* 27(2): 273–87.

1974. *Multinational Corporations and the Politics of Dependence: Copper in Chile.* Princeton, NJ: Princeton University Press.

Moran, T., E. Graham, and M. Blomström. 2005. *Does Foreign Direct Investment Promote Development?* Washington, DC: Peterson Institute for International Economics, Center for Global Development.

Morrow, J. 2000. "Alliances: Why Write Them Down?" *Annual Review of Political Science* 3(1):63–83.

Mosley, L. 2000. "Room to Move: International Financial Markets and National Welfare States." *International Organization* 54(4): 737–73.

2003. *Global Capital and National Governments.* New York: Cambridge University Press.

2005. "Globalisation and the State: Still Room to Move?" *New Political Economy* 10(3): 355–62.

2011. *Labor Rights and Multinational Production.* New York: Cambridge University Press.

2013. *Interview Research in Political Science,* editor. Ithaca, NY: Cornell University Press.

Mosley, L. and D. Singer. 2008. "Taking Stock Seriously: Equity Market Performance, Government Policy, and Financial Globalization." *International Studies Quarterly* 52(2): 405–25.

Mosley, L. and S. Uno. 2007. "Racing to the Bottom or Climbing to the Top? Economic Globalization and Collective Labor Rights." *Comparative Political Studies*, 40(8): 923–48.

Murphy, D. 2004. *The Structure of Regulatory Competition: Corporations and Public Policies in a Global Economy.* New York: Oxford University Press.

Nahm, J. and E. Steinfeld. 2014a. "Scale-Up Nation: China's Specialization in Innovative Manufacturing." *World Development* 54(1): 288–300.

　2014b. "The Role of Innovative Manufacturing in High-Tech Product Development: Evidence from China's Renewable Energy Sector." In *Production in the Innovation Economy*, edited by R. Locke and R. Wellhausen. Cambridge, MA: MIT Press.

Nebus, J. and C. Rufin. 2009. "Extending the Bargaining Power Model: Explaining Bargaining Outcomes among Nations, MNEs, and NGOs." *Journal of International Business Studies* 41(6): 996–1015.

Neumayer, E. and L. Spess. 2005. "Do Bilateral Investment Treaties Increase Foreign Direct Investment to Developing Countries?" *World Development* 33(10): 1567–85.

North, D. 1990. *Institutions, Institutional Change, and Economic Performance.* New York: Cambridge University Press.

Ohmae, K. 1999. *The Borderless World: Power and Strategy in the Interlinked Economy.* New York: Harper Paperbacks.

Olson, M. 1965. *The Logic of Collective Action: Public Goods and the Theory of Groups.* Cambridge, MA: Harvard University Press.

O'Neal, J. 1994. "The Affinity of Foreign Investors for Authoritarian Regimes." *Political Research Quarterly* 47(3): 565–88.

Oye, K. 1992. *Economic Discrimination and Political Exchange: World Political Economy in the 1930s and 1980s.* Princeton, NJ: Princeton University Press.

Oye, K. and R. Wellhausen. 2009. "The Intellectual Commons and Property in Synthetic Biology." In *Synthetic Biology: The Technoscience and its Societal Consequences*, edited by M. Schmidt. New York: Springer, 121–140.

Palan, R., R. Murphy, C. Chavagneux. 2010. *Tax Havens: How Globalization Really Works.* Ithaca, NY: Cornell University Press.

Pandya, Sonal. 2015. "Democratization and FDI Liberalization, 1970–2000." *International Studies Quarterly.* Forthcoming (DOI: 10.1111/isqu.12125).

Pelc, K. 2010. "Eluding Efficiency: Why Do We Not See More Efficient Breach at the WTO?" *World Trade Review* 9(4): 629–42.

Petrova, T. and S. Tarrow. 2007. "Transactional and Participatory Activism in the Emerging European Polity: The Puzzle of East-Central Europe." *Comparative Political Studies* 40(1): 74–94.

Pinto, P. 2013. *Partisan Investment in the Global Economy: Why the Left Loves Foreign Direct Investment and FDI Loves the Left.* New York: Cambridge University Press.

Pinto, P. and S. Pinto. 2008. "The Politics of Investment Partisanship and the Sectoral Allocation of Foreign Direct Investment." *Economics and Politics* 20(2): 216–54.

Post, A. 2009. "Liquid Assets and Fluid Contracts: Explaining the Uneven Effects of Water and Sanitation Privatization." PhD Diss, Harvard University.

Poulsen, L. and E. Aisbett. 2013. "When the Claim Hits: Bilateral Investment Treaties and Bounded Rational Learning." *World Politics* 65(2): 273–313.

Ramamurti, R. 2001. "The Obsolescing Bargaining Model? MNC-Host Developing Country Relations Revisited." *Journal of International Business Studies* 32(1): 23–39.

Reinhardt, E. 2000. "Aggressive Multilateralism: The Determinants of GATT/WTO Dispute Initiation, 1948–1998." *Manuscript.*

Reinisch, A. 2008. *Standards of Investment Protection*, editor. Oxford, UK: Oxford University Press.

Rivas, D. 2002. *Missionary Capitalist: Nelson Rockefeller in Venezuela.* Chapel Hill, NC: University of North Carolina Press.

Robertson, G. and E. Teitelbaum. 2011. "Foreign Direct Investment, Regime Type, and Labor Protest in Developing Countries." *American Journal of Political Science* 55(3): 665–77.

Robinson, R. 1963. *The First Turkish Republic: A Case Study in National Development.* Cambridge, MA: Harvard University Press.

Rodrik, D. 1997. *Has Globalization Gone Too Far?* Washington, D.C.: Peterson Institute of International Economics.

2011. *The Globalization Paradox: Democracy and the Future of the World Economy.* New York: WW Norton & Company.

Roland, G. 2004. *Transition and Economics: Politics, Markets, and Firms.* Cambridge, MA: MIT Press.

Root, F. 1968. "The Expropriation Experience of American Companies: What Happened to 38 Companies." *Business Horizons* 11(2): 69–74.

Rudra, N. and N. Jensen. 2011. "Globalization and the Politics of Natural Resources." *Comparative Political Studies* 44(6): 639–61.

Salacuse, J. 2010. "The Emerging Global Regime for Investment." *Harvard International Law Journal* 51(2): 427–73.

Salacuse, J. and N. Sullivan. 2005. "Do BITs Really Work?: An Evaluation Of Bilateral Investment Treaties and Their Grand Bargain." *Harvard International Law Journal* 46(1): 67–130.

Sauvant, K. 2008. *Appeals Mechanism in International Investment Disputes.* Oxford, UK: Oxford University Press.

Sauvant, K. and L. Sachs. 2009. *The Effect of Treaties on Foreign Direct Investment: Bilateral Investment Treaties, Double Taxation Treaties, and Investment Flows*, editors. New York: Oxford University Press.

Schachter, O. 1984. "Compensation for Expropriation." *The American Journal of International Law* 78(1): 121–30.

Schwartz, A. 2006. *The Politics of Greed: How Privatization Structured Politics in Central and Eastern Europe.* London: Rowman & Littlefield Publishers.

Shafer, M. 1983. "Capturing the Mineral Multinationals: Advantage or Disadvantage?" *International Organization* 37(1): 93–119.

Shleifer, A. and R. Vishny. 2002. *The Grabbing Hand: Government Pathologies and Their Cures.* Cambridge, MA: Harvard University Press.

Siegel, J., A. Licht, and S. Schwartz. 2011. "Egalitarianism and International Investment." *Journal of Financial Economics* 102(3): 621–45.

2013. "Egalitarianism, Cultural Distance, and Foreign Direct Investment: A New Approach." *Organization Science* 24(4): 1174–94.

Simmons, B. 2000. "International Law and State Behavior: Commitment and Compliance in International Monetary Affairs." *American Political Science Review* 94(4): 819–35.

Simmons, B. 2010. "Treaty Compliance and Violation." *Annual Review of Political Science* 13: 273–96.

Simmons, B. 2014. "Bargaining over BITs, Arbitrating Awards." *World Politics* 66(1): 12–46.

Singer, D. 2007. *Regulating Capital: Setting Standards for the International Financial System.* New York: Cornell University Press.

Simpson, J. and A. Wickelgren. 2007. "Naked Exclusion, Efficient Breach, and Downstream Competition." *American Economic Review* 97(4): 1305–20.

Stone, R. 2011. *Controlling Institutions: International Organizations and the Global Economy.* New York: Cambridge University Press.

Stopford, J. 1998. "Multinational Corporations." *Foreign Policy* 113(4): 12–24.

Stopford, J., S. Strange and J. Henley. 1991. *Rival States, Rival Firms: Competition for World Market Shares.* Cambridge, MA: Cambridge University Press.

Strange, S. 1996. *The Retreat of the State: The Diffusion of Power in the World Economy.* New York: Cambridge University Press.

Stremitzer, A. 2010. "Opportunistic Termination." *Journal of Law, Economics, and Organization* 28(3): 381–406.

Sutherland, P. 1979. "The World Bank Convention on the Settlement of Investment Disputes." *International and Comparative Law Quarterly* 28(3): 367–400.

Tan, D. and K. Meyer. 2011. "Country-Of-Origin and Industry FDI Agglomeration of Foreign Investors in an Emerging Economy." *Journal of International Business Studies* 42(4): 504–20.

Thomas, J. and T. Worrall. 1994. "Foreign Direct Investment and the Risk of Expropriation." *Review of Economic Studies* 61(1): 81–108.

Tobin, J. and Rose-Ackerman, S. 2004. "Foreign Direct Investment and the Business Environment in Developing Countries: The Impact of Bilateral Investment Treaties." *Yale Law & Economics Research Paper* No. 293.

Tomz, M. 2007. *Reputation and International Cooperation: Sovereign Debt Across Three Centuries.* Princeton, NJ: Princeton University Press.

Tomz, M. and M. Wright. 2010. "Sovereign Theft: Theory and Evidence about Sovereign Default and Expropriation." In *The Natural Resources Trap: Private Investment without Public Commitment,* edited by W. Hogan and F. Sturzenegger. Cambridge, MA: MIT Press.

Tsurumi, Y. 1976. *The Japanese are Coming: A Multinational Interaction of Firms and Politics.* New York: Ballinger Publishing Company.

Tudor, I. 2008. *The Fair and Equitable Treatment Standard in International Foreign Investment Law.* Oxford, UK: Oxford Monographs in International Law.

Van Harten, G. 2005. "Private Authority and Transnational Governance: The Contours of the International System of Investor Protection." *Review of International Political Economy* 12(4): 600–23.

2010. "Five Justifications for Investment Treaties: A Critical Discussion." *Trade, Law and Development* 2(1): 19–58.

Vachani, S. 1995. "Enhancing the Obsolescing Bargain Theory: A Longitudinal Study of Foreign Ownership of U.S. and European Multinationals." *Journal of International Business Studies* 26(1): 159–80.

Vandevelde, K. 1998. "The Political Economy of a Bilateral Investment Treaty." *The American Journal of International Law* 92(4): 621–41.

Veeser, C. 2002. *A World Safe for Capitalism: Dollar Diplomacy and America's Rise to Global Power*. New York: Columbia University Press.

Vernon, R. 1971. *Sovereignty at Bay*. New York: Basic Books.

Vogel, D. 1997. *Trading Up: Consumer and Environmental Regulation in a Global Economy*. Cambridge, MA: Harvard University Press.

Way, L. 2005. "Authoritarian State Building and the Sources of Regime Competitiveness in the Fourth Wave: The Cases of Belarus, Moldova, Russia, and Ukraine." *World Politics* 57(2): 231–61.

Wellhausen, R. 2010. "Who Wants to Reject or Repair Privatization? Explaining Public Support for Weakening Property Rights." Presented at the Midwest Political Science Association, Chicago, IL.

2013. "Innovation in Tow: R&D FDI and Investment Incentives." *Business and Politics* 15(4): 467–91.

2015. "Investor-State Disputes: When Can Governments Break Contracts?" *Journal of Conflict Resolution* 59(2), Forthcoming.

Wells, L. 1983. *Third World Multinationals: The Rise of Foreign Investments from Developing Countries*. Cambridge, MA: MIT Press.

2005. "Protecting Foreign Investors in the Developing World: A Shift in US Policy in the 1990s?" *In International Business and Government Relations in the 21st Century*, edited by R. Grosse. Cambridge, MA: Cambridge University Press, 421–62.

Wells, L. and R. Ahmad. 2007. *Making Foreign Investment Safe: Property Rights and National Sovereignty*. Oxford, UK: Oxford University Press.

Williams, M. 1975. "The Extent and Significance of the Nationalization of Foreign-Owned Assets in Developing Countries, 1956–1972." *Oxford Economic Papers* 27(2): 260–73.

Williamson, J. 2000. "What should the World Bank Think about the Washington Consensus?" *The World Bank Research Observer* 15(2): 251–64.

Williamson, O. 1979. "Transaction Cost Economics: The Governance of Contractual Relations." *Journal of Law and Economics* 22(3): 233–61.

Wilson, A. 2005. *Ukraine's Orange Revolution*. New Haven, CT: Yale University Press.

Wolf, M. 2004. *Why Globalization Works*. New Haven, CT: Yale University Press.

Wu, S. 2006. "Corruption and Cross-Border Investment by Multinational Firms." *Journal of Comparative Economics* 34(4): 839–56.

Yackee, J. and J. Webb. 2008. "Bilateral Investment Treaties, Credible Commitment, and the Rule of (International) Law: Do BITs Promote Foreign Direct Investment?" *Law and Society Review* 42(4): 805–32.

Yergin, D. 2008. *The Prize: The Epic Quest for Oil, Money, & Power*. New York: Simon and Schuster.

Young, S. and A. Tavares. 2004. "Multilateral Rules on FDI: Do We Need Them? Will We Get Them? A Developing Country Perspective." *Transnational Corporations* 13(1): 1–30.

QUANTITATIVE DATA SOURCES

Barbieri, K., O. Keshk, and B. Pollins. 2009. "Trading Data: Evaluating our Assumptions and Coding Rules." *Conflict Management and Peace Science* 26(5): 471–91.

Blake, D. 2013. "Thinking Ahead: Government Time Horizons and the Legalization of International Investment Agreements." *International Organization* 67(4): 797–827.

Chinn, M. and H. Ito. 2006. "What Matters for Financial Development? Capital Controls, Institutions, and Interactions." *Journal of Development Economics* 81(1): 163–92.

Claessens, S. and N. van Horen. 2012. "Foreign Banks: Trends, Impact, and Financial Stability." *IMF Working Paper* WP/12/10.

Country risks, Belgian Export Credit Agency (ONDD).

Ghosn, F., G. Palmer, and S. Bremer. 2004. "The MID3 Data Set, 1993–2001: Procedures, Coding Rules, and Description." *Conflict Management and Peace Science* 2(2): 133–54.

Henisz, W. 2002 [2010]. The Political Constraint Index (POLCON) Dataset. 2010 Release.

Honaker, J., G. King, and M. Blackwell. 2013. "Amelia II: A Program for Missing Data." In STATA 13.

International Monetary Fund:

  Balance of Payment Statistics.

  Direction of Trade Statistics.

  Inward Direct Investment Positions, 2009.

  International Investment Position, Global Historical Statistics.

  "Offshore Financial Centers." 2000. *IMF Background Paper, Monetary and Exchange Affairs*.

International Centre for the Settlement of Investment Disputes (ICSID), Cases pending and concluded. (www.icsid.worldbank.org).

International Country Risk Guide (ICRG) Risk Ratings, Political Risk Services.

Mayer, T. and S. Zignago. 2011. "Notes on CEPII's distances measures: The GeoDist database." *CEPII Working Paper* No. 2011-25.

Marshall, M., K. Jaggers, and T. Gurr. "Polity IV Project: Political Regime Characteristics and Transitions, 1800–2010." Sponsored by the Political Instability Task Force.

Nofal, B., C. Nahon, and C. Fernandez. "Inward FDI in Argentina and its policy context." *Columbia FDI Profiles* Vale Columbia Center on Sustainable International Development, 17 May 2010.

Organization for Economic Cooperation and Development (OECD), FDI positions abroad.

Prohnitchi, V., A. Popa, and A. Lupusor, "Impact of Foreign Direct Investments on the Moldovan Economy." *Expert Group Centru Analitic Independent* Chisinau: 2010. Funded by UNDP Moldova.

Reinhart, C. and K. Rogoff. 2009. *This Time is Different: Eight Centuries of Financial Folly*. Princeton, NJ: Princeton University Press.

United Nations Conference on Trade and Development (UNCTAD) Database of Treaty-based Investor-State Dispute Settlement Cases (pending and concluded). International Arrangements Section, Division on Investment, Technology, and Enterprise Development.

UNCTADstat (www.unctadstat.unctad.org).

UNCTAD World Investment Reports, various years.

Vienna Institute for International Economic Studies (WIIW), Database on Foreign Direct Investment in Central, East, and Southeast Europe, 2009 Release.

World Bank World Development Indicators.

World Bank Enterprise Surveys.

World Trade Organization, International Trade and Tariff Data.

Index

Abbott, K. W., 33–34
advanced industrial countries
  FDI flow to emerging economies by, 95–101
  national diversity in FDI, 62–75, 68f
Africa
  FDI national diversity in, 62–75, 63f
  history of expropriations in, 197–199, 198t
  regime competition and FDI in, 38–40
African Growth and Opportunity Act, 49
Agreement on Trade-Related Investment
  Measures (TRIMS), 204–206
Agroimbank, Moldovan FDI and, 158–162
Akhmetov, Rinat, 147–149
Alfa Group, 133–141
Algeria
  breach of contract with French firms in, 43–44
  history of expropriations in, 198–199, 198t
Allee, T., 96
Alliant Kyiv, breach of OPIC contract with,
  126–128
American Chamber of Commerce, 51–52
  in Moldova (AmCham), 172–174
  in Romania (AmCham), 180–182
  in Ukraine (ACC), 125–126, 128–131,
  139–141
ArcelorMittal, 52–54, 149–154, 225–226
  diplomatic advocacy and Ukrainian FDI,
  152–154
  Ukrainian non-payment of value-added tax
  and, 150–152
Argentina
  breach of contracts by, 10–12, 44–45, 57–58,
  204, 221–223

foreign firm payments withheld by, 19,
  91–94
investment arbitrations in, 31–32,
  33–34
revenue-raising expropriations in, 85–91,
  87t
arms-length contracts, ethnic and cultural ties
  and, 45
Ascom, 175–177
  Kazakhstan's nationalization of assets
  of, 1–4
Asian countries, FDI national diversity in,
  62–75, 67f
asset-specific contract breach
  by host nations, 9–10
  motivations for, 18–24
  public international investment arbitrations
  and, 85–91, 89t
Ataka (Bulgarian political party),
  21–23
Atatürk, Kemal, 16–17, 196–197
Australia, breach of contract with Philip Morris
  and, 21–23
Austria, investment in Romania, 189–191
authoritarian regimes, FDI and, 38–40

Baker & McKenzie, Ukrainian FDI and,
  128–131
Bandelj, N., 56–57
banking, multinational banks, by home region,
  211t
Basescu, Traian, 186–191
Bates, R., 38–40, 76–77

Bechtel Group
  Bolivian contract with, 21–23
  Romanian contract with, 186–189
Biden, Joseph, 128–131
bilateral agreements
  foreign firm nationality and, 42–43
  government breach of contracts and, 9–10
  issue linkage in, 48–51
Bilateral Investment Treaties (BITs). *See also*
    international investment arbitrations (IAs)
  cycles of sanctity and breach and, 223–224
  deterrence of breach and, 33–34
  dyadic FDI and, 95–101
  FDI and, 1–4
  FDI national diversity and contract risk and,
    79–80t, 81, 82t–83t, 84f
  government breach of contract and, 4–6, 14,
    27–33
  host government policies and, 36–38, 71–75
  in intermediate home countries, 52–54, 64–69
  national origins and contract sanctity and,
    40–47
  negative association with contract risk, 79–81
  round-tripped firms and, 64–69
  size of FDI nationality shares and, 102
  in Ukraine, 113
  US-Moldova treaty, 172–174
Blake, D., 81
Bolivia
  Bilateral Investment Treaties and, 33–34
  FDI in, 1–4
  history of nationalization in, 196–197, 196f
  "water war" in, 21–23
Bosnia and Herzegovina, breach of privatization
    contracts in, 21–23
"bracketing" strategies, for contract sanctity,
    48–51
Brazil
  Bilateral Investment Treaties and, 33–34
  FDI national diversity in, 62–75
  nationalization of firms in, 25–26
breach of contract. *See also* government breach
    of contract
  in Argentina, 10–12
  Bilateral Investment Treaties and, 14, 27–33
  capital flight and, 36–38
  corruption and, 23–24
  cycles of contract sanctity and, 223–224
  deterrence through BIT, 33–34
  FDI and, 9–10, 12–13
  foreign policy issues and, 20–21
  future issues in, 24

global patterns of, 38–40
government motivation for, 18–24
government procedures for, 24–27
history of, 14
international investment arbitrations and,
    85–91, 87t, 89t
nationalization as, 25
quantitative analysis of, 61–111t
sector-specific breach, 19–20
bribery, nationality and patterns of, 42
Bulgaria
  breach of privatization contracts in, 21–23
  EU membership for, 158–162
  FDI in, 1–4
bureaucratic structures, Ukrainian breach of
    contract with US and, 131–133
Burkina Faso, sector-specific breach of contract
    in, 19–20
Büthe, T., 100

CAFTA-DR, 204–206
Calvo, Carlos, 200–206
Calvo Doctrine, 200–206
  multinational corporations and, 6–8
Canada
  Bilateral Investment Treaties and, 33–34
  investment arbitrations with US, 31–32
  limits on foreign investment in, 71–75
  non-revenue investment arbitrations and,
    85–91, 89t
  Romanian breach of contract with, 9–10,
    21–23, 180–186, 221–223
Canadian Business Association (CBA), 180–182
capital access
  contract sanctity and, 36–38
  in Moldova, Russian and Romanian sources
    of, 158–162
  in Ukraine, FDI as source of, 119–121
Cargill, Ukrainian breach of contract with,
    121–133
carveouts, in Bilateral Investment Treaties, 81
case studies methodology, 235
Ceaușescu, Nicholae, 162–165, 235
Central America, FDI national diversity in,
    62–75, 64f
Central Europe
  investment arbitrations in, 31–32
  Russian investment in, 44
  Ukrainian FDI from, 114–118
Ceylon, breach of US contract with, 201
Chavez, Hugo, 23–24
Chevron, arbitration with Ecuador, 29–33

chief executive orientation, FDI national
diversity and breach risk, 78–79
Chile
history of mass expropriation in, 197–198,
198t
non-revenue investment appropriations in,
85–91, 89t
China
Argentinian investment from, 57–58
co-national firm protest in, 51–52
FDI in, 16–17
politicization of Taiwanese investment by,
43–44
targeted investment promotion in, 44–45
Civil War (US), governments' neutrality during,
198t
co-industrial firms
co-nationality precedence over, 58–59
contract sanctity and, 5n.14
costs of breach of contract for, 227
government breach of contract and, 57–58
personal *vs.* corporate rights and, 230–231
collective action
co-national firm protest as, 51–52
costs of breach of contract and, 227
Ukrainian breach of Norwegian contracts,
137–139
Ukrainian breach of US contracts, 128–131
colonial history
contract sanctity and, 43–44, 45
nationalization as response to, 197–198
commodity prices, sector-specific breach of
contract and, 19–20
co-national firms
contract sanctity and, 4–6
costs of breach of contract for, 227
cultural and political commonalities in,
40–47
cycles of sanctity and breach and, 223–224
differential FDI drawdown following breach,
dyadic tests of, 95–101
diplomacy and lobbying by, 150–152
dyadic FDI drawdown following breach and,
95–101, 99t
FDI national diversity data and, 64–69
home government diplomacy and, 48–51
impact of breach on investment decisions,
61–62
industry expectations and, 55–59
Moldovan breach and advocacy by, 169–172
Moldovan contract sanctity and, 167–169
nationality and risk of breach and, 61–62

nationality shield theory and, 12, 45–46,
58–59
protests by, 51–52
punishment in government breach of, 102
Romanian breach and weakness of, 180–182
tax havens and, 147–149
Ukrainian breach of contract with Norway,
133–141
Ukrainian contract breach and protests by,
119–121, 141–147
conflict, breach of contract linked to, 20–21
contract risk
Bilateral Investment Treaties and, 79t, 81,
82t, 84f
categories of, 27
dyadic FDIs in host country and, 95–101
FDI national diversity and, 8–9, 13, 54–55,
61–62, 71–75, 79–81, 79t
investor expectations of breach and index of,
76–77, 77f
in post-communist countries, 121–133
public international investment arbitrations
and, 85–91, 90t, 95–96
size of FDI nationality shares and probability
of, 102–110t, 105t–106t
Ukrainian nationalization and reprivatization
policies and, 141–147
contract sanctity. *See also* breach of contract
Bilateral Investment Treaties and, 28–29,
40–47
cycles of breach and, 223–224
democracy and, 38–40
diplomacy and, 48–51
ethnic, linguistic and cultural ties to foreign
investors and, 45
foreign firm diversity and, 8–9
government motives for breaching, 9–10
in Moldova, 167–169, 178–179
national diversity and, 36–60
national origin and, 4–6, 40–47
recuperation mechanisms for, 47–52
Russian FDI and, 44
in Ukraine, 111t
for Ukrainian-European contracts, 121–133
Ukrainian nationalization and reprivatization
policies and, 141–147
corporate raidership, Ukrainian breach of
Norwegian contract and, 139–141
corruption
dyadic FDI drawdown following breach and,
95–101
FDI flows and, 45

corruption (cont.)
FDI national diversity and, 79–81
government breach of contract and, 9–10, 23–24
investor expectations of breach and, 76–77, 77f
nationality and patterns of, 42
in Romania, 162–165
Costa Rica
international investment arbitration and, 49
non-revenue investment arbitration and, 85–91, 89t
costs of breach of contract, 227
creeping expropriation
FDI and, 26
public investment arbitrations and, 32–33
site-specific assets, 57
Cuba
expropriation of US property in, 49
history of nationalization in, 196f, 198t
cultural ties
foreign investment and, 56–57
government relations with foreign firms and, 45
currency devaluation
FDI national diversity and breach risk, 78–79
government breach of contracts and, 10–12
customary law, government breach of contract and, 200–206
Cyprus
government breach of contract in, 19
tax haven firms and, 147–149
Ukrainian FDI national diversity and, 114–118, 145–147, 221–223
Czech Republic
FDI in, 16–17
revenue-raising expropriations in, 85–91, 87t

Daewoo, Uzbekistan nationalization of shares in, 1–4
De Beers, 55–56
démarche, government breach of contract and, 50
democracy
breach of contract and democratic accountability, 221–223
FDI and, 8–9, 38–40
FDI enticements and, 72
transition linked to risk of breach, 111t, 235
Democratic Republic of Congo
nationalization of firms in, 25–26
sector-specific breach of contract in, 19–20

dependencia theory, government breach of contract and, 202–204
Desbordes, R., 42–43
developed countries, investment arbitration by, 31–32
developing countries. *See* emerging economies
DHL, Ukrainian breach of contract with, 128–131
diaspora investment, 56–57
in Moldova, 169–172
round-tripped firms and, 64–69
Ukrainian FDI national diversity and, 114–118
diplomacy
co-national firm lobbying and, 150–152
differential FDI drawdown following breach, dyadic tests of, 95–101
foreign firm ties to, 154–155
government breach of contract and, 48–51
"true" multinationals and tax havens and, 52–54
Ukrainian breach and advocacy by, 119–121
Ukrainian breach of contract with US and, 121–133
Ukrainian "true" multinationals and, 149–154
direct-to-international arbitration, in Bilateral Investment Treaties, 29–33
distribution of FDI stock, FDI national diversity calculations and, 62–75
diversion strategies
differential FDI drawdown following breach, dyadic tests of, 95–101
from government breach of contract, 47–52
Doha Development Round, 204–206
domestic investors, Moldovan breach of contract with, 175–177
domestic policy
contract sanctity and, 36–38, 42
cost of contract breach and, 229
government breach of contracts and, 21–23
in intermediate home countries, 52–54
multinational corporation autonomy and, 6–8
Double Taxation Treaties (DTTs), "true" multinationals and tax havens and, 52–54
Dunning, J., 207
dyadic foreign direct investment
Bilateral Investment Treaties and, 27–28, 40–47
differential drawdown as result of breach and, 61–62, 95–101, 99t

firm nationality and risk of breach and, 61–62
size of FDI nationality shares and probability
of investment arbitration filing, 77f,
102–110

East Asian countries, investment arbitrations in,
31–32
Eastern Europe
FDI in Ukraine from, 114–118
investment arbitrations in, 31–32
Russian investment in, 44, 169–172
Ukrainian FDI from, 114–118
"eclectic paradigm" of FDI, 207
economic crisis
government breach of contracts and, 10–12
Ukrainian national FDI diversity and,
139–141
economic growth
government breach of contract linked to,
221–223
limits of FDI and, 44–45
Moldovan barriers to, 158–162
Ukrainian FDI diversity linked to, 121–133
economic integration
nationality shield theory and, 14
Ukrainian FDI diversity linked to, 121–133
Ecuador
Bilateral Investment Treaties and, 33–34
Chevron arbitration with, 29–33
revenue-raising expropriations in, 85–91,
87t
sector-specific breach of contract in, 19–20
Efes Beverage Company, 158–162
Egypt
FDI national diversity in, 62–75
government breach of contract with UAE
and, 19
nationalization of firms in, 25–26
Suez Canal nationalization in, 204–206
emerging economies
Bilateral Investment Treaties and, 40–47
breach of contract with ex-colonial foreign
investors in, 43–44
co-national firm protest in, 51–52
contract sanctity and, 8–9, 36–38, 220
cost of contract breach in, 227
decline in FDI and, 47–52
erosion of property rights and national FDI
diversity in, 62–75, 66f, 67f, 74f, 220–233
FDI and, 1–4, 2n.5, 3n.9–3n.11
foreign firm protections protested by,
204–206

government arrears as form of breach in,
91–94
history of mass expropriation in, 197–198,
198t
local development linked to FDI in, 44–45
locational risk in FDI and, 207
motives for government breach of contract in,
18–24
nationalization of FDI by, 25–26, 196f, 198t
outward FDI and, 64–69, 208–211, 208t
stock positions in FDI and national diversity
in, 71–75, 73f
trends in FDI national diversity in, 71–75, 74f
US military presence and FDI in, 42–43
Energy Charter Treaty, 204–206
energy sector
FDI in Moldova in, 174–175
investment arbitrations in, 32–33
Enka, Romanian Transylvanian highway
project and, 188
espousal provisions, Bilateral Investment
Treaties, 29–33
Estonia, Ukrainian government and, 1–4
ethnic identity
government relations with foreign firms and,
43–44, 45
Moldovan contract risk and, 169–172
European Bank of Reconstruction and
Development (EBRD), 111t, 235
Ukrainian breach of contract with US and,
131–133
Ukrainian non-payment of value-added tax
and, 150–152
European Business Association (EBA)
Ukrainian contract breach with Norway and,
139–141
Ukrainian non-payment of value-added tax
and, 150–152
European emerging countries, FDI national
diversity in, 62–75, 66f
European Union (EU)
Argentinian breach of contract dispute and,
10–12, 11n.35
environmental damage in Romanian gold
extraction and, 182–186
government breach of contracts and, 21–23
Moldova FDI and, 158–162
overcoming national differences in, 225–226
reform in post-communist countries and, 235
Romanian membership in, 162–165, 179,
221–223
targeted investment promotion by, 44–45

European Union (EU) (cont.)
    Ukrainian contract breach with Norway and,
        139–141
    Ukrainian FDI national diversity and,
        114–118, 152–154
exit strategies, and government breach of
    contract, 47–52
export firms, government arrears as form of
    breach and, 91–94
expropriation
    diplomatic strategies for deterrence of, 49
    history of mass expropriation, 197–198
    insurance against, 38–40
    nationalization as, 25, 85–91, 87t
    non-revenue-raising expropriations,
        international investment arbitrations and,
        85–91, 89t
    revenue-raising expropriations, 9–10, 18–24,
        85–91, 87t
    in Russia, 133–141

fair and equitable treatment (FET) standards, in
    Bilateral Investment Treaties, 40–47
financial crisis, government breach of contract
    during, 19
firm-level tests for government breach, national
    diversity in FDI and, 91–94, 93t, 94f
foreign aid programs
    government breach of contract and, 49
    Ukrainian breach of contract with US and
        restrictions on, 121–133
Foreign Assistance Act (1962), 49
Foreign Corrupt Practices Act (FCPA) (US)
    contract sanctity and, 42
    US FDI in Moldova and, 172–174
foreign direct investment (FDI). *See also under*
    national diversity in foreign direct
    investment
    authoritarian regimes and, 38–40
    benefits of, 17
    Bilateral Investment Treaties and, 27–28
    bilateral politics and, 42–43
    case studies methodology, 111t
    case studies methodology involving, 235
    contract sanctity and diversity of, 8–9
    in emerging economies, 1–4, 2n.5,
        3n.9–3n.11
    exit and diversion strategies for breach,
        47–52
    globalization and, 1–4
    government breach of contract and, 9–10,
        12–13, 16–17, 18–24

growth statistics for, 17
history of, 16–17, 194–213
host government embrace of, 16–17
industry diversity in, 62–75, 70f
local development and, 44–45
in Moldova, 13, 158–162, 160f
motivations behind, 16–17
multinational corporation autonomy and,
    6–8
national diversity and risk of breach, 13,
    54–55, 61–62
obsolescing bargain framework in, 55–59
personal *vs.* corporate rights and, 230–231
political risk insurance industry and, 26
public investment arbitrations and, 32–33
in Romania, 13
shield of nationality and, 4–6, 12
social tensions as result of, 21–23
"true" multinationals *vs.* tax havens and,
    52–54
Ukrainian case study in, 112–155
Ukrainian nationalization and reprivatization
    policies and, 141–147
US military presence in emerging economies
    and, 42–43
foreign policy
    FDI by state-owned firms and, 43
    FDI diversity and, 13
    government breach of contracts and, 9–10,
        20–21
    Ukrainian breach of contract with US and,
        121–133
France
    Bilateral Investment Treaties in, 40–47
    ex-colonial emerging economies breach of
        contract with, 43–44
    Japanese dispute with bondholders from,
        204–206
    Moldovan FDI from, 158–162
    Romanian FDI from, 162–165
    Ukrainian non-payment of value-added tax
        and advocacy by, 150–152
Franck, S., 85
free rider incentives, "true" multinationals in
    Ukraine and, 149–154
Frieden, J., 55–59
Friendship, Commerce, and Navigation treaties,
    27–28
Frye, T., 21–23

Gagauz, in Moldova, 169–172
gaming licenses, selective enforcement of, 1–4

General Agreement on Trade in Services (GATS), 204–206
Georgia, Russian expropriation in, 20–21
Germany
  Bilateral Investment Treaty with Pakistan, 27–28
  dyadic FDI drawdown following breach in Thailand and, 101
  FDI national diversity in, 62–75, 68f
  international arbitration in, 40–47
  Moldovan FDI from, 177–178
  Romanian FDI from, 162–165
  Ukrainian non-payment of value-added tax and advocacy by, 150–152
Ghana, sector-specific breach of contract in, 19–20
globalization
  FDI and, 1–4
  national diversity in FDI and, 206–213
  nation-states and, 4–6
  paradox of, 8–9, 221–223
global South, FDI from, 44–45
Gonzalez Amendment, 226–227
government breach of contract
  benefits of, 12
  Bilateral Investment Treaties and, 27–33
  case study methodology for research on, 111t, 235
  categories of, 27
  co-national firm protest and, 51–52
  co-national firm punishment and, 102
  conditions that catalyze, 35
  costs of, 227
  cycles of contract sanctity and, 223–224
  deterrence in Moldova and Romania of, 192–193
  deterrence using BITs, 33–34
  development outcomes and, 221–223
  differential FDI drawdown, dyadic tests of, 95–101
  economic impact of, 61–62
  in emerging economies, 195–200, 196f, 200f
  FDI and, 16–17
  FDI national diversity and, 36–60, 78–81
  firm-level tests for breach, 91–94
  firm national origin and risk of, 40–47
  historical overview of, 194–213
  industry targeting and, 55–59
  investor expectations of breach, 76–77, 77f
  legal attempts to forestall breach, 200–206
  limits of international organizations, 226–227

models of FDI national diversity and, 79–81
in Moldova, 175–177
monadic testing of FDI national diversity and, 75–91
motivations for, 18–24, 44–45
national diversity and, 36–60
nationalization, historical overview of, 195–200, 198t
national origin as resource against, 47–52
personal *vs.* corporate reactions to, 230–231
public international investment arbitrations and, 85–91, 87t, 89t, 95–96
recuperation mechanisms, 47–52
in Romania, 179–192
shield of nationality and, 59–60
state-level explanations, 38–40
"true" multinationals and tax havens and, 52–54
unmet expectations as motive for, 44–45
government non-payment
  FDI national diversity and incidence of, 61–62
  firm-level tests of FDI national diversity and, 91–94, 94f
  Ukrainian breach of contract with US and, 121–133
gravity model expectations, FDI national diversity and, 62–75
gross domestic product per capita
  dyadic FDI drawdown following breach and, 95–101
  FDI national diversity and, 69–70, 71f, 235
  in Moldova, 158–162, 160f
  natural resource rents per GDP and, 78–79
  negative association with contract risk, 79–81
  in Romania, 162–165, 164f
  size of FDI nationality shares and breach risk, 102–110t

Halliburton, Ukrainian FDI and, 128–131
Helms Amendment, 49
Henisz index, FDI national diversity and breach risk, 78–79
Herfindahl-Hirschman Index (HHI), FDI national diversity, 62–75
Hickenlooper Amendment (Foreign Assistance Act), 49, 201
home countries
  control over multinationals by, 50
  diplomacy in breach of contract by, 48–51
  FDI national diversity data from, 64–69
  personal *vs.* corporate rights and, 230–231

home countries (cont.)
  share size of FDI nationality and probability
    of IA, 102–110, 110t
  "true" multinationals and tax havens, 52–54
  Ukrainian non-payment of value-added tax
    and advocacy by, 150–152
Hong Kong
  FDI national diversity in, 62–75, 67f
  outward FDI trend and, 208–211, 208t
Horizon Capital, Moldovan FDI and, 158–162
host governments
  absolute number of national groups and,
    54–55
  Bilateral Investment Treaties and, 29–34,
    40–47
  breach of contract by, 2n.7, 9–10, 15–35,
    38–40, 221–223
  co-national firms and, 4–6
  contract sanctity and, 36–38
  cycles of sanctity and breach and, 223–224
  distribution of FDI stock and, 54–55
  domestic motivations for breach of contract
    by, 21–23
  dyadic FDI and political constraints in,
    95–101
  ethnic, linguistic and cultural ties to foreign
    investors and, 45
  expropriation of assets by, 26
  FDI case studies, methodology for, 111t
  FDI contracts with, 1–4
  FDI national diversity and, 54–55, 64–69
  firm constraints on, 40–47
  foreign policy motivations for breach of
    contract and, 20–21
  industries targeted for breach by, 55–59
  industry diversity in, 69–70, 70f
  legal obligations concerning FDI of, 201–202
  liberalized capital flows and FDI national
    diversity and, 71–75
  motives for breach of contract by, 18–24
  multinational corporations and, 6n.17,
    6–8
  protests by co-national firms in, 51–52
  site-specific investments and relations with, 56
  size of FDI nationality shares in, 102–110
  sovereignty rights of, 198t, 200–206
  "true" multinationals vs. tax havens and,
    52–54
  wealthy countries' investments privileged by,
    44–45
Hull, Cordell, 201
Hull Doctrine, 201

human trafficking, contract sanctity in Moldova
    and, 173
Humphreys, M., 38–40, 76–77
Hungary
  environmental damage in Romanian gold
    extraction and, 182–186
  as transition economy, 162–165
  Ukrainian FDI from, 114–118
hybrid nationality, Ukrainian co-national tax
    haven firms and, 147–149
Hymer, Stephen, 45–46

IBM, Ukrainian FDI and, 128–131
incidence-rate ratios, international investment
    arbitrations and, 89t, 90–91
India
  Bilateral Investment Treaties and, 33–34
  FDI national diversity in, 62–75
  manufacturing immobility in, 55–56
Indonesia, breach of contract with United
    Kingdom, 20–21
industrial conflict, FDI and, 21–23
industry associations, Romanian contract risk
    and, 180–182
industry diversity
  in FDI, 62–75, 70f
  government arrears as form of breach and,
    91–94, 94f
  international investment arbitrations and,
    85–91, 89t
  in Moldova, 158–162, 165–167, 167t, 168t,
    171–172
  national diversity in FDI and, 69–70, 70f
  in Romania, 165–167, 166f
  in Ukraine, 117–118, 120f
informal contracts, ethnic and cultural ties and,
    45
Inter-American Development Bank, 49
intermediate home countries
  FDI national diversity data and, 64–69
  "true" multinationals and tax havens and,
    52–54
internalization factors, national diversity in FDI
    and, 207
International Banking Facilities (IBFs), national
    diversity in FDI and, 211–213, 212t
International Center for the Settlement of
    Investment Disputes (ICSID)
  establishment of, 204–206
  investment arbitration and, 30–31, 40–47,
    85–91
International Chamber of Commerce, 30–31

International Code of Conduct on the Transfer of Technology, 201–202
International Development Bank, 226–227
International Finance Corporation (World Bank)
  firm-level tests of government breach and, 91–94
  Ukrainian breach of contract with US and, 131–133
International Investment Agreements (IIAs), chronology of, 28f
international investment arbitrations (IAs)
  Bilateral Investment Treaties and, 29–33
  dyadic FDI drawdown following breach and, 95–101, 99t
  national diversity in FDI and likelihood of, 61–62, 85–91, 90t
  size of FDI nationality shares and probability of, 102–110t, 104t, 105f
  Ukrainian breach of contract with US and, 131–133
International Investment Preferential Trade Agreements (IIPTAs), 204–206
International Labor Organization, host government obligations and, 201–202
international law, government breach of contract prevention and, 200–206
International Monetary Fund (IMF)
  contract risk and, 79–81
  FDI defined by, 16–17
  FDI national diversity and breach risk, 78–79
  loans to Ukraine by, 113
  Ukrainian nonpayment of value added tax and, 19, 150–152
international organization, breach of contract and limits of, 226–227
inverse Herfindahl-Hirschman Index (HHI)
  FDI industry diversity, 62–75, 70f
  FDI national diversity calculations, 62–75
Investment and Metallurgical Union (IMU), 147–149
investment institutions
  interviews with, methodology concerning, 238–241
Investment Promotion Agencies (IPAs)
  FDI and, 16–17
  growth of, 72
  in Romania, 162–165, 180–182
investor expectations of breach, FDI national diversity and, 76–77, 77f
issue linkage
  contract sanctity and, 48–51
  government breach of contract and, 20–21

Italy
  Moldovan FDI from, 169–172
  Romanian FDI from, 162–165

Japan, French bondholder dispute with, 204–206
Jensen, N., 38–40
Jobbik (Hungarian political party), 21–23
Jodice, D., 197–198
Johnston, N., 38–40
judgment-proof status, investment arbitrations and, 33–34

Kaczmarek, S., 173
Kazakhstan
  Moldovan energy contract with, 175–177
  nationalization of assets in, 1–4, 25–26
  sector-specific breach of contract in, 19–20
Kennedy, C., 197–198
Kerner, A., 100
Kobrin, S., 26, 220
KPMG, Ukrainian FDI and, 128–131
Kryvorizhstal steel plant, 117–118, 145–147
  Arcelor Mittal purchase of, 149–154
  renationalization proposal for, 152–154
  Ukrainian co-national tax haven firms and, 147–149
Kuchma, Leonid, 121–133, 141–149
Kyivstar, 133–141

labor rights, multinational corporations' impact on, 6–8
Latin America
  FDI national diversity in, 62–75, 64f
  history of mass expropriation in, 197–198, 198t
  international investment arbitrations in, 31–32
  outward FDI trends and, 208–211, 208t
Latvia, Ukrainian FDI from, 114–118
Lebanon
  FDI in, 1–4
  revenue-raising expropriations in, 85–91, 87t
Lesotho, nationalization of firms in, 25–26
"liability of foreignness," contract sanctity and, 45–46
linguistic ties, government relations with foreign firms and, 45
Lipson, C., 25, 229
Lisbon Treaty, 225–226
Lithuania
  asset-specific breach of contract in, 19–20
  non-revenue investment arbitrations and, 85–91, 89t

Lloyd's of London, 26
local development, FDI and, 44–45
local market entry, FDI for, 56–57
locational factors, national diversity in FDI and, 207
Locke, R., 6–8
logit analysis
  government arrears as form of breach, firm-level testing, 91–94
  size of FDI nationality shares and, 102–110t
London Court of International Arbitration, 30–31

Mali, sector-specific breach of contract in, 19–20
manufacturing
  public investment arbitrations in, 32–33
  Ukrainian FDI in, 117–118
meta-contracts, Bilateral Investment Treaties as, 28–29
Mexico
  government breach of contract in, 9–10, 200–206
  history of nationalization in, 196–197, 196f
  NAFTA breach of contract issues and, 21–23
Microsoft, Ukrainian FDI and, 128–131
Middle East
  FDI national diversity in, 62–75, 65f
  history of mass expropriation in, 197–198, 198t
Militarized Inter-state Disputes (MIDS), 100
Milner, H., 100
Mittal Steel
  merger with Arcelor, 149–154
  Ukrainian FDI by, 117–118, 128–131, 145–147
mode of entry, deterrence of breach and, 47–52
Moldova
  breach of contract disputes in, 157–165, 165t
  case studies methodology involving, 235
  contract sanctity in, 167–169
  corruption and contract risk in, 178–179
  deterrence *vs.* breach in, 192–193
  domestic investors', breach of contract, 175–177
  FDI in, 13, 221
  FDI national diversity in, 111t, 158–162, 160f, 162f
  German FDI in, 177–178
  industry-specific FDI in, 165–167, 167t, 168t
  Spanish investment in, 174–175
  table of key characteristics of, 236t

Turkish investment in, 43–44
US FDI in, 172–174
Moldovan Investment and Export Promotion Agency (MIEPO), 158–162, 164–165
monadic testing, national diversity in FDI, 75–91
Mongolia, sector-specific breach of contract in, 19–20
Morales, Evo, 21–23
Mosley, L., 6–8
most favored nation (MFN) treatment
  Bilateral Investment Treaties and, 28–29
  multinational corporation nationality and, 6–8
  protections for, 204–206
Multilateral Agreement on Investment (MAI), 204–206
multilateral agreements
  on government breach of contract, 202–204
  limited success of, 204–206
  summary of, 214–219t
multilateral business groups
  multilateral investors associations, 131–133, 139–141
  Romanian FDI and, 180–182
Multilateral Investment Guarantee Agency (MIGA), 26, 131–133
multinational banks, by home region, 211t
multinational corporations
  global growth of, 206–213, 220
  home government control of, 50
  host governments and, 1–4, 16–17
  nationality issues with, 6–8
  overcoming national differences, 225–226
  "true" multinationals and tax havens, 52–54
  in Ukraine, 117–118, 121–133
multinational investor associations, Ukrainian contract breach with Norway, 139–141

Namibia, De Beers dispute in, 55–56
Nastase, Adrian, 186–189
  nationalization of Austrian OMV by, 189–191
national diversity in FDI. *See also* nationality
  accumulated FDI stock measurements and, 71–75, 73f
  advanced industrial countries, 62–75, 68f
  Bilateral Investment Treaties and, 81, 82t–83t, 84f
  calculation methods for, 62–75

case study methodology concerning, 235
co-national punishment and, 102
contract risk measures and, 79–81,
    79t–80t
contract sanctity and, 36–60
costliness of breach for host government and,
    54–55
cycles of sanctity and breach and, 223–224
data issues in calculation of, 64–69
diplomacy and collective action in deterrence
    of breach, 13, 47–52
dyad test, differential drawdown following
    breach, 95–101
FDI stock in emerging economies and, 62–75,
    73f
FDI stock per GDP and, 62–75, 71f
firm-level tests for breach and, 91–94, 93t
foreign firm contract enforcement and, 12
global integration and, 14
historical change in, 71–75
industry-specific analysis, 69–70, 70f
international investment arbitrations and
    contract risk, 85–91, 87t, 89t, 90t
investment risk and, 79–81
in Moldova, 111t, 158–162, 160f, 162f, 167t,
    168t
monadic tests of, 75–91
outward FDI and, 208–211, 208t,
    209f–210f, 212t
overcoming national differences and,
    225–226
property rights erosion and, 220–233
quantitative analysis of, 12–13, 61–62
risk of government breach and, 8–9
in Romania, 111t, 162–165
share size of nationality and probability of
    investment arbitration, 102–110t, 104t,
    105f, 105t–106t
shield of nationality theory and, 59–60
sources of, 206–213
tax havens and, 211–213
"true" multinationals and tax havens and,
    52–54
in Ukraine, 111t, 114–118, 133–141
Ukraine compared with Russia, 114–118,
    114f
Ukrainian contract breach with Norway and
    absence of, 133–141
variation in countries of, 13
national investor associations, Ukrainian
    nationalization and reprivatization policies
    and, 141–147

nationalist ideology, sector-specific breach of
    contract and, 19–20
nationality. *See also* co-national firms; national
    origin
bilateral politics and, 42–43
competing nationalities and contract sanctity,
    44
co-national firms and, 4–6
co-national protests and, 51–52
contract sanctity and, 36–60
FDI and, 54–55
government breach of contract and, 61–62
host government relations with foreign firms
    and, 43–44
multinational corporations and power of,
    6–8
outward FDI trend and, 208–211, 208t
share size in FDI and, 102–110t, 104t, 105f,
    105t–106t
"true" multinationals and tax havens, 52–54
Ukraine FDI distribution by, 116f, 117–118,
    119f
nationality shield theory. *See* shield of
    nationality
case studies methodology, 235
interview strategy in research on, 238–241,
    239t–240t
nationalization
in Argentina, 10–12
of FDI, 24–27
historical overview of, 195–200, 198t, 200f
Romanian nationalization of Austrian OMV,
    189–191
of site-specific investments, 55–59
state structure and probability of, 38–40
in Ukraine, 141–147
national origin
co-national action in Ukrainian contract
    breach and, 141–147
contract sanctity and, 40–47
FDI national diversity data based on, 64–69
as resource, 47–52
trends in FDI and, 208–211, 209f–210f
national security issues, government breach of
    contract and, 20–21
national treatment provisions
Bilateral Investment Treaties, 81
protections for, 204–206
nation-states, globalization and, 4–6
natural resource rents per GDP, multivariate
    regression of FDI national diversity and,
    78–79

natural resources investment
case studies methodology concerning, 111t,
235
sector-specific breach of contract and, 19–20
Nazarbayev, Nursultan, 175–177
Netherlands
Bilateral Investment Treaties in, 40–47
FDI national diversity in, 62–75, 68f
Newman, A., 173
Nicaragua, Bilateral Investment Treaties and,
33–34
non-governmental organizations
environmental damage in Romanian gold
extraction and, 182–186
FDI and, 56
non-revenue-raising expropriations,
international investment arbitrations and,
85–91, 89t
North American Free Trade Agreement
(NAFTA), 204–206
Bilateral Investment Treaties and, 33–34
government breach of contract issues in,
21–23
international investment arbitrations and,
31–32
Norway
Argentinian investments from, 57–58
Bilateral Investment Treaties in, 40–47
Lithuanian breach of contract with, 19–20
Ukrainian breach of contract with, 20–21,
133–141, 229

Obama, Barack, Argentinian breach of contract
and, 10–12
obsolescing bargain
government breach of contract and, 55–59
multivariate regression of FDI national
diversity and, 78–79
Ukrainian FDI and industry diversity and,
117–118
Occupy Wall Street, multinational corporate
autonomy protested by, 6–8
OECD Convention on Combating Bribery of
Foreign Public Officials, 42
OECD countries
dyadic FDI drawdown following breach and,
95–101
FDI national diversity calculations for, 62–75
host government obligations and, 201–202
in Moldova, 158–162
Multilateral Agreement on Investment and,
204–206

in Romania, 179–192
Romanian FDI from, 162–165
Ukrainian FDI national diversity and,
114–118, 121–133
"off-equilibrium" behavior, Bilateral
Investment Treaties and, 33–34
offshore financial centers
FDI and, 52–54
industry diversity and, 69–70, 70f
national diversity in FDI and, 211–213, 212t
Ukrainian co-national tax haven firms and,
147–149
oil and gas industry
FDI in Moldova in, 174–175
history of expropriations in, 199
investment arbitrations in, 32–33
Olympic Entertainment Group, Ukrainian
breach of contract with, 1n.4, 1–4
Oman, FDI in, 1–4
OMV, Romanian nationalization of, 189–191
O'Neal, J., 38–40
opportunity costs
of FDI, 24–25
partial breach of contract as, 79–81
Orange Revolution, 113–114
asset nationalization and reprivatization and,
141–147
Ukrainian breach of US contract and,
126–128
Ukrainian FDI national diversity and,
114–118
OTE, Armenian government and, 1–4
outward FDI
global trends in, 208–211, 208t,
209f, 210f
growth of, 64–69
tax havens and, 211–213, 212t
Overseas Private Investment Corporation
(OPIC) (US), 26
in Ukrainian breach of contract with,
121–133
ownership factors, national diversity in FDI and,
207
Oye, K., 48–51

Pakistan
Bilateral Investment Treaties and, 33–34
Bilateral Investment Treaty with Germany,
27–28
Palan, R. R., 52–54
Panama, revenue-raising expropriations in,
85–91, 87t

Pandya, S., 72
Paraguay, nationalization of firms in, 25–26
"pass-through" countries for FDI, 52–54,
    211–213
Peinhardt, C., 96
Permanent Court of Arbitration, 30–31
Petrom (Romanian state oil company),
    189–191
Philip Morris, Uruguay breach of contract with,
    21–23
Philippines, outward FDI trend and, 208–211,
    208t
Pinchuk, Viktor, 147–149
Poland
    as transition economy, 162–165
    Ukrainian FDI from, 114–118
policy uncertainty, FDI and, 38–40
political constraints
    dyadic FDIs and breach drawdown, 95–101
    FDI national diversity and breach risk,
        78–79
    Moldovan FDI national diversity and,
        158–162
    size of FDI nationality shares and probability
        of IA filing, 77f, 102–110t
    Ukrainian nationalization and reprivatization
        policies and, 141–147
political risk insurance
    breach of contract and, 26
    Ukrainian breach of contract and, 121–133
Political Risk Services International Country
    Risk Guide (ICRG)
    dyadic FDI drawdown following breach and,
        95–101
    monadic testing of FDI national diversity and,
        76–77, 77f
Polity IV democracy scale, 237
pre-establishment measures, FDI national
    diversity and, 71–75
Preferential Trade Agreements (PTAs), 27–28
    dyadic FDI drawdown following breach and,
        100
price subsidies, FDI in Moldova and, 174–175
private property rights
    contract sanctity and, 36–38
    deterrence of expropriation through
        diplomacy, 49
    FDI and, 1–4
    government breach of contract and, 20–21,
        38–40
    host government sovereignty and, 200–206
    investor-government relations and, 194–195

investor national origins and, 40–47,
    220–233
personal *vs.* corporate rights, 230–231
in Romania, 182–186
private-public contracts, nationality shield
    theory and, 59–60
privatization
    costs of breach of contract and, 227
    government breach of contract and, 21–23
    in Romania, 189–191
    Romanian FDI national diversity and, 191–192
    in Ukraine, 141–147
    Ukrainian FDI national diversity and,
        114–118, 121–133
Procter and Gamble, Ukrainian FDI and,
    128–131
project finance industry, Ukrainian breach of
    contract with US and, 131–133
protest strategies
    of co-national firms, 51–52
    for contract recuperation, 47–52
public international investment arbitrations. *See
    also* international investment arbitrations
    (IAs)
    contract risk and FDI national diversity,
        85–91, 89t, 90t
    differential FDI drawdown following breach,
        95–96, 100
    global distribution of, 31f
    government arrears as form of breach and,
        91–94
    by industry, 32t
    in Moldova, 175–177
    non-revenue-raising expropriations and,
        85–91, 89t
    revenue-raising expropriations and, 85–91, 87t
    size of FDI nationality shares and, 102–110t
    statistics on, 30f
    in Ukraine, 113–114, 117–118
public opinion, government breach of contracts
    supported by, 9–10
Putin, Vladimir, 50
    Ukrainian nationalization and reprivatization
        policies and, 141–147

recuperation mechanisms, for breach of
    contract, 47–52
regulatory taking
    breach of privatization contracts and, 21–23
    government breach of contracts and, 9–10
    non-revenue investment arbitrations and,
        85–91, 89t

Renault, 162–165
reprivatization, Ukrainian policies for, 141–147
Resnick, A., 38–40
restitution, in Ukrainian breach of US contracts, 128–131
revenue enhancement
  government breach of contract and, 9–10, 18–24
  international investments arbitrations and, 85–91, 87t
risk mitigation strategies, national diversity in FDI and, 71–75
risks to investments, investor expectations of breach and, 76–77, 77f
Rockefeller, Nelson, 196–197
Rodrick, D., 8–9, 221–223
Romania
  Austrian firm nationalized by, 189–191
  breach of Canadian contract, 9–10, 21–23, 180–186, 221–223
  breach of contract disputes in, 157–165, 165f, 221–223
  breach of privatization contracts in, 21–23
  case studies methodology involving, 235
  co-national firm strategies in, 51–52
  deterrence *vs.* breach in, 192–193
  EU membership for, 162–165, 179
  FDI in, 13, 221
  FDI national diversity in, 111t, 162–165, 235–236t
  gold extraction in, 182–186
  government breach of contracts in, 9–10, 21–23, 179–192
  industry-specific FDI in, 165–167, 166f
  Moldovan FDI from, 158–162
  personal *vs.* corporate rights in, 230–231
  table of key characteristics of, 236t
  US FDI in, 186–189
Romanian Foreign Investor Council (FIC), 180–182
Romania Trade & Invest (RTI), 180–182
Rosia Montana Gold Corporation (RMGC), 182–186
round-tripping
  FDI national diversity data on, 64–69
  tax havens and FDI national diversity and, 211–213, 212t
  Ukrainian co-national tax haven firms and, 147–149
rule of law
  emergence in transitional democracies of, 237
  FDI and, 36–38

government breach of contract and, 38–40, 221–223
investor-government relations and, 194–195
  in Moldova, 175–177
  nationality shield theory and, 14
Russia
  expropriation of Telenor in, 133–141
  FDI national diversity in, 114f, 134–135
  Georgian property expropriation by, 20–21
  government control of multinational compliance with host countries, 50
  history of nationalization in, 196f, 198t
  investment in post-communist Europe from, 44
  Moldovan FDI from, 158–162, 169–172
  Romanian FDI by, 180–182
  Ukrainian FDI from, 44–45, 114–118, 221–223
  Ukrainian nationalization and reprivatization policies and, 141–147

Sarkozy, Nicolas, 150–152
search costs, multinational corporations and, 6–8
second country subsidies, "true" multinationals and, 52–54
sector-specific breach of contract
  motivations for, 19–20
  nationality and, 58
security issues, contract sanctity linked to, 48–51
services, investment arbitrations in, 32–33
shield of nationality
  basic principles of, 12
  breach of contract disputes and, 10–12
  case study methodology for, 111t
  cycles of sanctity and breach and, 223–224
  diplomacy and, 13
  economic integration and rule of law and, 14
  FDI national diversity and, 221
  firm-level tests of government breach and, 91–94, 93t
  globalization and, 1–4, 232–233
  government breach of contract and, 59–60
  investor expectations of breach and, 76–77, 77f
  limits of international organizations and, 226–227
  Moldovan contract sanctity and, 167–169
  monadic testing of FDI national diversity and, 75–91
  national diversity of FDI and, 71–75
  overcoming national differences and, 225–226

personal *vs.* corporate rights and, 230–231
public international investment arbitrations
 and, 85–91, 89t
Romanian FDI diversity and, 162–165
"true" multinationals and tax havens and,
 53–54
Ukrainian contract breach with Norway and,
 133–141
Ukrainian non-payment of value-added tax
 and, 150–152
Sigma Bleyzer, 128–131
Simmons, B., 30
Singapore
 FDI national diversity in, 62–75, 67f
 outward FDI trend and, 208–211, 208t
site-specific investments, vulnerability to breach
 of, 55–59
Slovakia
 government breach of contract in, 21–23
 non-revenue investment arbitrations and,
 85–91, 89t
 Ukrainian FDI from, 114–118
Slovenia, Moldovan FDI from, 158–162
Snidal, D., 33–34
social networks, diaspora investment and,
 56–57
social tensions, FDI and, 21–23
Societe Generale, 162–165
soft budget constraints, Ukrainian FDI and,
 121–133
soft law, Bilateral Investment Treaties and,
 33–34
South Africa
 Bilateral Investment Treaties and, 33–34
 FDI in, 1–4
 FDI national diversity in, 62–75, 63f
 nationalization of firms in, 25–26
South Korea
 FDI in Ukraine from, 77, 117–118,
 221
 FDI national diversity in, 62–75, 67f
South-South FDI, growth of, 64–69
sovereign debt crisis, FDI national diversity and
 breach risk, 78–79
sovereignty
 FDI and, 194–195, 220
 history of firm investment and, 198t
 multinational corporation nationality and,
 6–8
 sector-specific breach of contract and, 19–20
Sovereign Wealth Funds (SWFs), 43
Soviet Union

history of nationalization in, 196f–196, 198t
 Moldova and, 158–162, 235–236t
 Ukraine FDI national diversity and breakup
 of, 114–118, 121–133, 235–236t
Spain
 Argentinian breach of contract with, 10–12,
 11n.36–12n.36, 44–45, 57–58
 Moldovan FDI by, 174–175
 non-revenue international investment
 arbitrations and, 85–91, 89t
Sri Lanka, breach of contract in, 20–21
state-owned firms
 foreign investment by, 43
 Norwegian-Ukrainian contract breach and,
 134–135
 Romanian privatization of, 189–191
 Ukrainian nationalization and reprivatization
 policies and, 141–147
State Property Fund (SPF) (Ukraine), 152–154
state structure, government breach of contract
 and, 38–40
Stati, Anatol, 175–177
Stati, Gabriel, 175–177
Sterling Resources, Romanian breach of
 contract with, 184–185
Stockholm Chamber of Commerce, 30–31
stock positions in FDI, national diversity and,
 71–75, 73f
SunCommunications, Moldovan FDI from,
 172–174

Taft, William Howard, 49
Taiwan, Chinese *vs.* US investment in, 43–44
Tanzania
 breach of contract with British firms in,
 43–44
 government breach of contracts in, 9–10
 history of expropriations in, 198–199, 198t
tax havens
 national diversity in FDI and, 211–213, 212t
 "true" multinationals and, 52–54
 Ukrainian co-national FDI and, 147–149
Telenor, Ukrainian breach of contract with,
 133–141
TeliaSonera, Russian joint venture with,
 134–135
Thailand, dyadic FDI drawdown following
 breach in, 101
third-party firms, government breach of contract
 and, 59–60
Tobit estimators, multivariate regression of FDI
 national diversity, 78–79

Togo, government breach of contract in, 19
Trafficking in Persons (TIP) Report, contract
  sanctity in Moldova and, 173
Trafficking Victims Protection Act of 2000,
  contract sanctity in Moldova and, 173
transition countries
  case studies methodology concerning, 111t, 235
  government arrears as form of breach in,
    91–94
  Romania as example of, 162–165
  Ukrainian FDI from, 121–133
transnational corporations
  terminology concerning, 6–8
  UN Code of Conduct on Transnational
    Corporations and, 202–204
Transnistria (Moldova), Russian presence in,
  170–171
Transylvania highway project, Romanian-US
  contract breach and, 186–189
"true" multinationals
  tax havens *vs.*, 52–54
  Ukrainian FDI national diversity and,
    149–154
Turkey
  FDI in, 16–17
  FDI national diversity in, 62–75
  history of nationalization in, 196–197,
    196f
  Moldovan FDI from, 43–44, 158–162,
    169–172
  Romanian Transylvanian highway project
    and, 188
Turkmenistan, FDI in, 1–4
Tymoshenko, Julia, 141–147, 152–154

Ukraine
  case studies methodology involving, 235
  casinos and gaming licenses in, 1n.4, 1–4
  European Union investment in, 44–45
  FDI in, 1–4, 112–155, 221
  FDI national diversity in, 111t, 114–118,
    114f, 119f
  foreign firm protest and diplomatic advocacy
    in, 112–155
  government breach of contract by, 20–21
  industry diversity in FDI in, 117–118, 120f
  Norwegian contract with, breach of, 133–141
  Orange Revolution in, 21–23
  personal *vs.* corporate rights in, 230–231
  public international investment arbitrations
    in, 96
  Russian contract with, breach of, 133–141

Russian FDI in, 44–45
South Korean FDI in, 77, 117–118, 221
summary of contract disputes in, 122t
table of key characteristics of, 236t
Value-added tax repayment withheld by, 19
Ukraine-Estonia Bileratal Investment Treaty, 1–4
UN Code of Conduct on Transnational
  Corporations, 202–204
UN Commission on International Trade Law
  (UNCITRAL)
  investment arbitrations and, 30–31
  public international investment arbitrations
    and, 85–91
UN High Commissioner for Refugees, FDI cases
  and, 1–4
Union Fenosa, FDI in Moldova by, 174–175
United Arab Emirates, Egyptian government
  breach of contract with, 19
United Kingdom
  Bilateral Investment Treaties in, 40–47
  ex-colonial emerging economies breach of
    contract with, 43–44
  Indonesian breach of contract with, 20–21
  Suez Canal nationalization in Egypt and,
    204–206
  Ukrainian non-payment of value-added tax
    and advocacy by, 150–152
United Kingdom Bribery Act, 42
United Nations Conference on Trade and
  Development (UNCTAD), 201–202,
  204–206
United States
  Argentinian investments by, 44–45, 57–58,
    221–223
  Bilateral Investment Treaties and, 27–28,
    33–34
  FDI national diversity in, 62–75, 68f
  international investment arbitrations with
    Canada, 31–32
  Mexican breach of contract with, 201
  Moldovan FDI from, 172–174
  Romanian breach of contract with, 180–182,
    186–189
  Ukraine FDI from, 114–118, 121–133
Uruguay, breach of contract issues in, 21–23
US-Ukraine Business Council (USUBC),
  125–126, 128–131
  Ukrainian nationalization and reprivatization
    policies and, 141–147
utilities sector, public investment arbitrations in,
  32–33
Uzbekistan, FDI in, 1–4

value-added tax (VAT) refunds, Ukrainian non-payment of, 150–152
Venezuela
Bilateral Investment Treaties and, 33–34
government breach of contract in, 23–24
international investment arbitrations in, 31–32
nationalization of firms in, 1–4, 25–26
sector-specific breach of contract in, 19–20
Vernon, R., 55–59
VimpelCom, 133–141
Voronin, Oleg, 170
Voronin, Vladimir, 158–162, 172, 175–177

Working Group on Trade and Investment (WTO), 204–206
World Bank, 26, 40–47. *See also* International Center for the Settlement of Investment Disputes (ICSID)
Enterprise Surveys by, 61–62, 91–94
foreign firm-host government conflicts and, 204–206

Gonzalez Amendment, 226–227
targeted investment promotion by, 44–45
Ukrainian non-payment of value-added tax and, 150–152
World Health Organization (WHO), Uruguay breach of contract with Philip Morris and, 21–23
World Trade Organization (WTO)
FDI protection and, 204–206
protests at, 6–8

Yanukovych, Viktor, 126–128, 150–152
Young, D., 38–40
Yukos oil firm and Lithuanian breach of contract, 20–21
Yushchenko, Viktor, 126–128, 141–147

Zaire, copper nationalization in, 55–56
Zambia, copper nationalization in, 55–56
Zimbabwe, nationalization in, 25–26

Printed in the United States
By Bookmasters